W9-CBI-004

The **Rough Guide** to

Chicago

written and researched by

Rich McHugh

with additional contributions by
Shea Dean and Max Grinnell

www.roughguides.com

Contents

Architecture colour
section following p.80

Food colour section
following p.176

Washington
Park   **University
of Chicago**
   Colour maps following
p.296

◄◄ The Cloud Gate ◄ Lake Michigan shoreline

Introduction to
Chicago

Soaring skyward from the pancake-flat prairies of the Midwestern heartland, Chicago has the feel of the last great American city. With its vibrant architecture, ethnic neighbourhoods and extremes in temperature, Chicago offers a microcosm of what is most interesting about American cities. Having come into its own during the late nineteenth century, the city remains an economic and cultural hub and still evinces its traditional blue-collar roots. Chicago has the buzz of a large metropolitan area, combined with a small-town spirit and refreshing lack of pretension. Over 44 million visitors flock here annually, seduced by its pioneering architecture, world-class museums and galleries, vibrant nightlife, Michigan Avenue shops and the bustle of the Loop.

Founded in 1833, Chicago was a raw frontier outpost on the sharp edge of civilization and wilderness. Owing to its strategic position as a **mid-continental hub**, Chicago soon became the engine of the growing nation's westward expansion, reaching its zenith during the industrial age. The grain, lumber, meatpacking, steel and railroad trades all took turns dominating the economic landscape, bringing hitherto unbridled opportunity for thousands of immigrants and fostering a can-do spirit. Capitalism ruled with a fist comprised of crisp bills, pork-belly futures and railroad stocks.

In 1871, the city emerged from the ashes of one of the worst fires in US history to redefine American **urban architecture**. Chicago became a crucible of innovation, where visionary designers, ambitious industrialists and ingenious inventors could find their greatest expression. Prototypical skyscrapers soon rose gloriously along the shores of Lake Michigan during the 1880s and 1890s. Meanwhile, Chicago's cultural importance bloomed following the creation of the University of Chicago in 1892 and the city's prestigious hosting of the World's Columbian Exhibition in 1893.

While the lurid legacy of Al Capone and his empire of organized crime is still one of the city's overarching associations, most traces of the mob-run opium dens, brothels and speakeasies that studded the city during the 1920s Prohibition era have disappeared. Cleansing the deep stains of "machine" politics has proved a more difficult undertaking, however,

Fact file

• Chicago covers approximately **228 square miles**, of which 5 percent (7300 acres) is devoted to parkland. There are 198 neighbourhoods, 26 miles of lake waterfront, 15 miles of bathing beaches, over 7300 restaurants, 200 theatres and 53 inches of annual snowfall.

• The city's **population** has been declining since 2000. The estimated figure for 2007 was 2,836,659 – down just under 1 percent from the 2000 census. Of this total 36 percent is black, 31 percent white, 28 percent Hispanic, and 5 percent Asian. The population of the greater metropolitan area is 8,711,080 (2007 estimate).

• The city boasts the world's largest public library (Harold Washington Library), biggest illuminated fountain (Buckingham Fountain), largest free public zoo (Lincoln Park Zoo), largest food festival (Taste of Chicago), largest aquarium (Shedd Aquarium), largest modern art museum (Museum of Contemporary Art) and busiest roadway (Dan Ryan Expressway).

• Chicago is the birthplace of roller skates, blood banks, malted milkshakes, the cafeteria, McDonald's, spray paint, the winding watch, the zipper, the bifocal contact lens, the railroad sleeping car, the pinball machine and the steel-frame skyscraper.

with allegations of corruption and fraud over city contracts tainting the accomplishments of City Hall to this day. Contrary to popular belief, the name "**Windy City**" does not refer to the gusts that whip up over the lake but the city's history of bellicose "windy" politicos, notorious for spinning a line.

Along with a compelling history and a panoply of attractions, Chicago is also one of America's great lifestyle cities. Visitors can cycle along the lakefront, saunter through parks, wander down hushed tree-lined streets punctuated by turreted brownstone mansions and chichi restaurants or delve into distinctive neighbourhoods. Here they will find the traditions of first-generation immigrants intermingling with the classic Americana of hot dogs, pizza and baseball – each experience contributes to the dynamism and diversity of this formidable city. Chicago is America's geographical and cultural crossroads. It's no exaggeration to say that modern blues was invented here during the first half of the twentieth century, when tens of thousands of African-Americans migrated from the South, bringing with them the music of their birthplace. With the relocation of legendary blues clubs from the South Side to the more polished north, performances have become a more diluted tourist spectacle. However, live music is something Chicago does with aplomb, spanning every conceivable genre. Alternative rock came of age here in the 1990s with the Smashing Pumpkins and today the scene is one of the healthiest in the country. In more recent years, the city's R&B profile has risen with the success of artists like Kanye West, Common, and the controversial musical stylings of R. Kelly. There is a phenomenal array of venues ranging from jazz bars to Art Deco theatres and edgy, hole-in-the-wall clubs.

▼ Buzzing Chicago bar

Immigrant Chicago

From the mid-nineteenth century, over 2.5 million **immigrants**, including Swedes, Italians, Poles, Russians, Ukrainians, Germans, Greeks, Puerto Ricans, Chinese, Japanese and Mexicans, have flocked to this pulsating industrial metropolis, enticed by Chicago's frontier spirit and endless opportunities in transportation, construction and manufacturing.

Fleeing the devastating famine that started in 1845, **Irish** immigrants came here, rising from their humble beginnings digging canals to dominate the urban linchpins of politics, police and religion – most Chicago mayors since 1933 have been of Irish origin. The mid-nineteenth century also saw the arrival of **Poles** and **Ukrainians**, who settled in Bucktown and Wicker Park, and **Swedes**, who made Andersonville and Edgewater their home. Following the 1893 World's Columbian Exposition, Chicago became a truly international city, inspiring a new wave of immigration. In the 1890s, impoverished **Italian** and **Greek** immigrants settled in the West Side, which encompasses the neighbourhood of Pilsen, currently home to one of the largest concentrations of **Mexicans** living outside of Mexico. While much of this area has suffered from Disneyfication, immigrant cultures are still preserved and nurtured through the much-vaunted Greek school system as well as the Mexican Fine Arts Center.

With its rough and tough spirit and competitive zeal, Chicago is passionate about **sport**. Baseball, basketball, football and ice hockey dominate the sporting agenda and Chicagoans are fiercely loyal to their teams; the ever-inconsistent Chicago Cubs' games remain well attended thanks largely to the atmosphere at the ivy-covered Wrigley Field, bastion of baseball traditionalism. Occasionally, as with the Michael Jordan-led Bulls of the Nineties and the 2005 White Sox, local fervour is rewarded with championships.

What to see

The compact **heart of Chicago** is the Loop; from here the city spreads to the north, south and west, bounded to the east by Lake Michigan, which provides Chicago with some of its most attractive open space and serves as a clear point of reference for getting your bearings. The Chicago River, which cuts through the heart of downtown Chicago to Lake Michigan, separates the business district from the shopping and entertainment areas of the North Side, which merit, at the very least, several days' worth of exploring. Usually bypassed, Chicago's dichotomous South Side, which includes the leafy and bookish neighbourhood of

Hyde Park and increasingly gentrified immigrant enclaves to the west, provides a rewarding and well-rounded insight into Chicago's history.

Shopping on the Magnificent Mile

The best place to start exploring Chicago is **the Loop**, the city's downtown and birthplace and home to perhaps the finest display of modern architecture in the world, from the prototype early skyscrapers of the 1880s and 1890s through the "Chicago School" period to Mies van der Rohe's Modernist masterpieces and his Postmodern successors. As well, you'll find here the quarter-mile-high Sears Tower, the Art Institute, the city's premier art museum, and Millennium Park, an urban playground of whimsical steel sculptures amidst landscaped gardens.

Chicago's most commercial area – **Near North** – is where you're likely to spend much of your time. Just north of the river and divided into the River North, N Michigan Avenue and Streeterville areas, near North is where most of the city's hotels and restaurants are concentrated and the area is full of tourists and well-to-do locals and people-watchers. The famed "Magnificent Mile" stretch of N Michigan Avenue cobbles together

N Michigan Avenue

a continuous stretch of fashionable shops, designer boutiques and department stores on the famed Magnificent Mile. East of Michigan Avenue, on Streeterville's lakefront, sitting squarely on the edge of the neighbourhood, is Chicago's most popular tourist destination, Navy Pier. Formerly a military facility and a branch of the University of Illinois, this elaborate complex is marked by the hard-to-miss giant Ferris wheel and contains chain restaurants, shops and concert venues. On the other side of Michigan Avenue, **River North** is to Chicago what SoHo is to New York, a thriving gallery district where former run-down warehouses now house a diverse array of art works and antiques, not to mention a number of the city's finest restaurants.

Further north brings you to the **Gold Coast**, where a few streets of upscale boutiques and gorgeous brownstones make for a pleasant stroll, while **Old Town** to the northwest has a slightly more casual vibe and serves as the home to the venerable Second City improvisational comedy club and a host of colourful Victorian homes. Old Town blends into **Lincoln Park**, a leafy residential area that borders the park of the same name and is home to an enclave of young professionals. The streets, lined with restored apartments and condos, also hold some of the city's best restaurants and bars, giving the neighbourhood a lively social scene.

One of the most rapidly developing neighbourhoods, **Lakeview**, still further north, draws a younger crowd than Lincoln Park with its myriad cafés, bars, restaurants and boutiques. Baseball fans will want to pay homage at the shrine of Wrigley Field, noted baseball mecca and home to the much-loved Chicago Cubs. A quintessential sporting preamble requires a hop around the bevy of raucous sports bars in the surrounding **Wrigleyville** neighbourhood. Beyond here, the last contiguous neighbourhood before

Suggested Itineraries

Chicago can be experienced in an endless number of ways – architecture tours, baseball or football games, blues clusbs and so on. The following are suggested itineraries for trips up to a week, while giving you an idea of what's possible to see in one day. They're mainly designed around the key sights and include suggestions for where to have lunch. Of course if any of the days seem too sight-oriented, don't be afraid to simply wander around, as there's something to be said for serendipitous encounters.

Two days
- Sears Tower observatory, Historic Skyscrapers Tour, Shopping along Michigan Ave. A walk through the Gold Coast and Old Town, *3rd Coast Café* (lunch), Steppenwolf Theatre, *Alinea* (dinner).
- Art Institute of Chicago, Millennium Park, *Billy Goat Tavern* (lunch), a drink at the *Signature Room* in the John Hancock Center, blues show at *Buddy Guy's Legends*.

Four days
As above plus …
- River North galleries, Prairie Avenue Historic District, Oak Street Beach, Italian beef sandwiches at *Mr Beef*, drinks at the Drake Hotel, Second City comedy show, *Frontera Grill* (dinner).
- House of Blues Gospel Brunch, Museum Campus, Lincoln Park zoo, Chicago History Museum, Wicker Park Historical District, jazz or blues show and whatever's on offer at the *Green Mill Tavern*.

Chicago's Lakefront

The third largest of the Great Lakes and the fifth largest freshwater lake in the world, **Lake Michigan** is to Chicagoans what Central Park is to New Yorkers – an oasis in which to escape the grinding congestion and frenetic pace of downtown and a place to relax, play, exercise and socialize.

Defining the iconic **cityscape** where glass-and-steel architectural marvels rise above undulating waters, the lake is gloriously fronted by manicured parks, a marina and beaches. During the summer, young and old play volleyball, bask in the sun or rollerblade, run or cycle along mile after mile of serpentine pathways, which skirt the water's edge. Some of the best places to luxuriate along the waterfront are **Grant Park**; the new, sculpture-filled **Millennium Park**; **Oak Street Beach**, a popular place to sun and be seen; **Navy Pier**, a playground of shops, amusement rides, museums and shows; and **Lincoln Park**, which boasts a zoo, a conservatory and a gorgeous stretch of lakefront path that's perfect for running, rollerblading or biking.

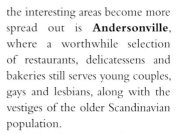

the interesting areas become more spread out is **Andersonville**, where a worthwhile selection of restaurants, delicatessens and bakeries still serves young couples, gays and lesbians, along with the vestiges of the older Scandinavian population.

North of Andersonville visitors will reach **Rogers Park**, which is home to one of the largest South Asian communities in the United States. A walk west down Devon Avenue will be enhanced by the fragrant smells wafting from nearby Indian restaurants and groceries, making it a pleasant way to spend an afternoon. The suburban **North Shore** beyond is home to scholarly Northwestern University and has a wealth of scenic beaches and parks, as well as a burgeoning art scene.

Heading south from the Loop, the **Near South** encompasses the lakefront Grant Park, with its world-class museums, the historic **Printers Row district** and **Chinatown**'s kaleidoscopic restaurants and street life. Further south, the **South Side** proper takes over, much of it a no-go zone for visitors, except for **Hyde Park** and **Kenwood**, an island of middle-class prosperity around the Gothic campus of the **University of Chicago**.

Chicago's **West Side** holds the twin culinary attractions of **Greektown** and **Little Italy**, the latter mainly a tourist hangout, and the former considerably less so. The city's large Mexican community makes its base southwest of here in **Pilsen**, known as well for its home-style eateries, Fine Arts Center, and colourful murals which adorn a number of public spaces throughout the community.

Northwest of Old Town, Chicago's blue-collar side takes over. The **Ukrainian Village**, with its wonderfully ornate churches and Eastern European roots, is worth a stop on your way to the city's most bohemian neighbourhood, **Wicker Park**, full of carefully restored Victorian homes, a flourishing alternative music scene, edgy bars and eclectic thrift stores. **Bucktown**, just north, is a more gentrified version of Wicker Park, with plenty of restaurants, bars and nightclubs to choose from, along with corresponding high rents and an increasingly homogeneous make-up.

Nine miles west of the city, the affluent and attractive suburb of **Oak Park** holds the childhood home of Ernest Hemingway and more than a dozen well-preserved examples of the influential architecture of Frank Lloyd Wright; the most interesting and groundbreaking of these are maintained as monuments and open for viewing.

When to go

Chicago's **climate** ranges from the unbearably hot and humid in midsummer to well below freezing from December through February, with spring and autumn amounting to little more than a month or two in between. The **best times to visit** are in the early summer (May–June) and early autumn (Sept & Oct), when the weather is at its most pleasant; there's usually snow from December to March, while the heat of late summer is best avoided. Whatever time of year you come, be sure to dress in layers: buildings tend to be overheated during winter and air conditioned to the extreme in summer. Also bring comfortable, sturdy shoes – you're going to be doing a lot of walking.

Chicago climate

	Jan	Feb	Mar	Apr	May	Jun	Jul	Aug	Sep	Oct	Nov	Dec
Average daily temperature (°F)												
Av. high	29	34	45	58	70	80	84	82	75	63	48	35
Av. low	13	18	28	39	48	57	63	62	64	42	31	20
Average rainfall (Inches)												
Av. rainfall	1.7	1.4	2.7	3.6	3.2	3.8	3.6	4.1	3.5	2.6	2.9	2.2

18

things not to miss

It's not possible to see everything that Chicago has to offer in one trip – and we don't suggest you try. What follows is a selective and subjective taste of the city's highlights: stunning architecture and engaging museums, wide-ranging cultural events, and memorable restaurants and bars. They're arranged in five colour-coded categories to help you find the very best things to see, do and experience. All entries have a page reference to take you straight into the Guide, where you can find out more.

01 Boat tours Page **44** • The Chicago River, which snakes through the city centre, is best experienced on a boat tour, with the Chicago Architectural Foundation's cruises being the best.

02 **Millennium Park** Page **46** • The embodiment of Chicago's visionary zeal and innovation, Millennium Park is an urban playground of whimsical steel sculptures and fountains, landscaped gardens, theatre and music venues, and an ice-skating rink in winter.

04 **Cocktails at the Signature Room** Page **190** • From high atop the John Hancock Tower, the Martinis will hit you a bit harder, but it's OK: you'll have a world-class view and the opportunity to see much of the city (and a few nearby states) from the snazzy digs here.

05 **Robie House** Page **127** • Frank Lloyd Wright's so-called "organic" reached a new and distinct level in this house that he created for a local bicycle manufacturer. After checking out the interior, you may want to wander around Hyde Park a bit.

03 **Field Museum** Page **68** • Supported by a sizeable donation offered by noted merchant Marshall Field, this museum has a collection of noteworthy taxidermy (lions, tigers and bears, oh my!), some great natural history exhibits, and the famed skeleton of noted T. Rex "Sue".

06 Maxwell Street Market

Page **118** • A long-standing West Side tradition, this open-air bazaar is a great place to meander through on a Sunday afternoon, featuring a variety of ethnic food stands, live music, antique-peddlers and sketch artists.

08 Second City comedy club

Page **91** • Located in the heart of Old Town, Second City has been a proving ground for improvisational comedy neophytes for four decades. Come for the mainstage show, and you might want to stick around for the late-night offerings.

07 Steppenwolf Theatre

Page **206** • Founded in a basement, the Steppenwolf has grown into a world-renowned theatre company, and ensemble members include John Malkovich, Laurie Metcalf and Gary Senise.

09 The Oriental Institute

Page **128** • This University of Chicago research institute uncovers it's newly excavated ancient Near and Far Eastern finds for public viewing. Lots of exotic Asian items to be admired.

11 **Deep Dish Pizza** Page **162**
• Dig in to this very hearty pie which flips the natural order of things by placing the tomato base on top of the cheese and a host of toppings.

12 **Baseball at Wrigley Field** Page **100** • The ivy-covered walls, the boisterous crowd, and free-flowing hot dogs and beer all add up to the quintessential baseball experience, no matter who wins the game.

10 **Architectural Walking Tours of the Loop** Page **44** • Given the Loop's prominent place in the development of American architecture, visitors should check out one of the architectural tours offered by either the Chicago Architecture Foundation or the Chicago Greeter Program.

13 **Oak Park** Page **149** • Take a walk through Ernest Hemingway's birthplace for a peek into one of Chicago's close-in and leafy suburbs. Along the way, make sure to stop by for a tour of the Frank Lloyd Wright Home and Studio.

14 Chicago History Museum
Page **93** • From Abraham Lincoln's deathbed to engaging exhibits that take visitors through the city's two World's Fairs, the Chicago History Museum is a solid way to learn about the past two centuries of history in the Windy City.

15 Green Mill Tavern Page
199 • Take in some stellar jazz during the wee hours of the morning at this former speakeasy and pretend you're living during the Roaring Twenties, when Al Capone might easily have been sitting next to you.

17 The lakefront path Page
10 • Jog, walk or, even better, rent a bike and explore the spectacular shores of Lake Michigan. Rent a bike from Navy Pier or North Avenue Beach and make your way north and south along the lake.

16 Tiffany Dome Page **46** • This
sparkling masterwork by Louis Tiffany is the real highlight of the Chicago Cultural Center. Your eyes will be glued to the elaborate roof of Preston Bradley Hall, particularly if you can take in a concert at the Center.

18 Art Institute of Chicago
Page **48** • With one of the largest art holdings in North America, the Art Institute of Chicago is sure to keep you occupied for hours. Be sure to visit the Impressionist wing.

Basics

Basics

Getting there

A major hub for domestic and international travel, Chicago is well served by air, rail and road networks. Flying into O'Hare International Airport is your quickest and easiest approach, given the sheer volume of domestic and international flights that route through here. One of the country's largest carriers, United Airlines, is based here, and nearly every major airline offers service to Chicago. Midway Airport, on the city's southwest side, sees a much smaller flow of mostly domestic flights, but is nonetheless a less stressful option for those already in the US.

Airfares always depend on the season, with the highest being around May to September, when the weather is best; fares drop during the low season, December to March (excluding holidays). Note also that flying on weekends ordinarily adds substantially to the cost of a round-trip fare; the price ranges quoted below assume mid-week travel.

If you want to travel during major American holiday periods (around the Fourth of July, Thanksgiving, Christmas and New Year's Day), be sure to book well ahead. While prices fluctuate wildly around these times, it's possible to find cheaper fares with some digging, though they'll require at least the standard three-week (or 28-day) advance purchase.

You can often cut costs by **booking online** or using a **specialist flight agent** – either a consolidator, who buys up blocks of tickets from the airlines and sells them at a discount, or a discount agent, who in addition to dealing with discounted flights may also offer special student and youth fares.

If you're travelling from Europe or Australasia, and the US is only one stop on a longer journey, you might want to consider buying a **Round-the-World (RTW) ticket**. Although Chicago does figure on some standard RTW itineraries, it is more likely you will have to work it into a more expensive tailor-made ticket.

Flights from the US and Canada

From most places in **North America**, flying is the fastest and easiest way to reach Chicago. The city is connected with all of the major US cities – New York, Boston, Washington DC, Atlanta and Miami in the east, and Seattle, San Francisco and Los Angeles in the west – with at least several flights a day from each. As domestic fares depend more on passenger volume than anything else, it pays to search for flights leaving from an airport with plenty of traffic to the city. Prices are notoriously volatile but you should be able to find a round-trip ticket for $200–250 from most major east coast or central cities and $250–300 from the west coast. Fares from **Canada** range from CN$250–300 from Toronto and Montreal to around CN$400 from Vancouver.

Flights from the UK and Ireland

There are several direct flights leaving daily **from London**'s Heathrow Airport to Chicago's O'Hare. British Airways offers three flights, one in the morning, the other two in the afternoon, while United has three – usually in mid-morning, around noon, and in the late afternoon. American Airlines offers direct flights from Manchester to Chicago (one daily, leaving mid-morning). All other British Midland flights first route through London Heathrow before heading to Chicago, which will add extra to the transatlantic fare.

Round-trip fares to Chicago can cost as little as £350 and as much as £650 (June–Aug and at Christmas). If a direct flight to Chicago is not a priority, your flight options increase substantially: several carriers – KLM, Alitalia and Northwest Airlines among them – fly between the London area airports and route either through a European city (Amsterdam, Milan or Paris) or a US city

(New York, Washington DC, Detroit or Atlanta) before continuing on to Chicago.

American Airlines and Aer Lingus fly direct to Chicago **from Ireland** with fares starting from around €475. Although other major carriers (such as British Airways, Continental, Delta and Northwest) do route through Ireland, they don't link directly with Chicago, so you'll be forced to deal with layovers and transfers.

Flights from Australia, New Zealand and South Africa

There are no direct scheduled flights to Chicago from Australia, New Zealand or South Africa.

Most Chicago-bound flights **from Australia** leave from Sydney or Melbourne and usually route through Tokyo, Los Angeles or Las Vegas. The major carriers – Qantas (in partnership with American Airlines) and United Airlines – offer several flights a day to the US west coast, from which onward travel to Chicago is easily arranged. Flights take about thirteen hours to the west coast, and five hours onward to Chicago.

Fares vary depending on the season (between June and Sept being the most expensive) and flight availability, with fares as low as A$1300 and as high as A$3800, though A$2450–2800 is the more usual range.

Chicago-bound flights **from New Zealand** leave Auckland, Christchurch or Wellington and route through Los Angeles, before making the onward flight to Chicago. The two major carriers, Air New Zealand and Qantas, along with their US partners, United Airlines and American Airlines, generally fly from

Six steps to a better kind of travel

At Rough Guides we are passionately committed to travel. We feel strongly that only through travelling do we truly come to understand the world we live in and the people we share it with – plus tourism has brought a great deal of benefit to developing economies around the world over the last few decades. But the extraordinary growth in tourism has also damaged some places irreparably, and of course climate change is exacerbated by most forms of transport, especially flying. This means that now more than ever it's important to travel thoughtfully and responsibly, with respect for the cultures you're visiting – not only to derive the most benefit from your trip but also in order to preserve the best bits of the planet for everyone to enjoy. At Rough Guides we feel there are six main areas in which you can make a difference:

• Consider what you're contributing to the local economy, and indeed how much the services you use do the same, whether it's through employing local workers and guides or sourcing locally grown produce and local services.

• Consider the environment on holiday as well as at home. Water is scarce in many developing destinations, and the biodiversity of local flora and fauna can be adversely affected by tourism. Patronise businesses that take account of this rather than those that trash the local environment for short-term gain.

• Give thought to how often you fly and what you can do to redress any harm that your trips create. Reduce the amount you travel by air; avoid short hops by air and more harmful night flights.

• Consider alternatives to flying, travelling instead by bus, train, boat and even by bike or on foot where possible. Take time to enjoy the journey itself as well as your final destination.

• Think about making all the trips you take "climate neutral" via a reputable carbon offset scheme. All Rough Guide flights are offset, and every year we donate money to a variety of charities devoted to combating the effects of climate change.

• Travel with a purpose, not just to tick off experiences. Consider spending longer in a place, and really getting to know it and its people – you'll find it much more rewarding than dashing from place to place.

Auckland (add about 15 percent to the fare for Christchurch and Wellington departures). In general, expect to pay NZ$2950–4200.

In terms of reaching Chicago from **South Africa**, flights leave from Cape Town or Johannesburg, with intermediary stops at London or Amsterdam. Some flights make two stops along the way, with stopovers in Detroit, Atlanta or Washington DC. The airlines running the South Africa–Chicago route include Delta, United Airlines and American Airlines. Typically you can expect to pay ZAR11775–18660 for a round-trip flight.

Trains

Travel **by train** can be a picturesque and leisurely option, though it's not generally much cheaper than air travel and can even cost more. Amtrak (☎1-800/872-7245, ⓦwww .amtrak.com) services Chicago and runs trains from most major US cities. Coming from Toronto via Amtrak, visitors will have to connect between a Canadian Via Rail service (Toronto ☎416/366-8411, rest of Canada ☎1-888/842-7245, US ☎1-800/872-7245, ⓦwww.viarail.ca) in Windsor, Ontario and an Amtrak train in Detroit.

Peak **fares** are usually in effect from June to September. Round-trip fares from New York (19hr) cost $170–220, from Boston (17hr) $190–275, San Francisco or Los Angeles (52hr) $350, Seattle (45–50hr) $350–500, Detroit (6hr) $60, Milwaukee (1hr 30min) $44, San Antonio (32hr) $245, and New Orleans (19hr) $235–335. You'll find seasonal special offers (30 percent discount on select routes during the fall and spring for example), as well as discounts of 15 percent for seniors and students, for most Amtrak rail journeys; check the company's website (look under the Hot Deals tab) or call them for details. If Chicago is part of a longer itinerary, you might consider buying one of Amtrak's **rail passes**.

Overseas visitors and US residents can buy USA Rail passes, valid for fifteen ($389), thirty ($579) or forty-five ($749) days with unlimited stopovers. Each pass allows a set number of travel "segments", and pass holders must also make sure to have a physical ticket before they board (you can't just flash the pass). The rules and regulations for the pass are a bit byzantine, but it's certainly worth looking into if you are a rail fan.

Buses

The national bus line, **Greyhound** (☎1-800-231-2222, ⓦwww.greyhound.com), runs frequent buses from major Midwestern cities (Cleveland, Indianapolis, Milwaukee or Minneapolis), usually around ten per day from each city. Beyond the Midwest, Greyhound does run a few buses daily from New York, Washington DC and Denver, plus a few that make the two-day journey from the west coast. Two smaller companies stop at Greyhound's station: Lakefront Lines (☎1-800/638-6338, ⓦwww.lakefrontlines .com) operates services between Charleston (West Virginia) and Chicago, passing through Ohio, Indiana, and Kentucky, while the Michigan-based Indian Trails (☎1-800/292-3831) runs buses between Chicago and points in Michigan.

Fares depend on the season, though on all routes you'll pay slightly more if you travel between Friday and Sunday. Standard midweek round-trip fares cost around $170–210 from different east coast cities (16–25hr), $240–250 from the west coast (46–50hr) and only $83 from a nearby Midwest city such as Cleveland (6hr). The price drops if you buy your ticket seven days in advance or take advantage of student and senior discounts or special offers (eg "two-for-one" companion fares). If Chicago is just one stop on a longer itinerary, check out the various **Discovery passes**, which include the International Ameripass, open to overseas travellers. It offers unlimited travel in the entire Greyhound network for as little as seven days ($329) up to sixty days ($750).

Airlines, agents and operators

Online booking

ⓦ www.cheapflights.com
ⓦ www.expedia.com
ⓦ www.hotwire.com
ⓦ www.lastminute.com
ⓦ www.orbitz.com
ⓦ www.priceline.com
ⓦ www.travelocity.com

Airlines

Aer Lingus US & Canada ☎ 1-800/474-7424, UK ☎ 0870/876 5000, Republic of Ireland ☎ 0818/365 000, South Africa ☎ 1-272/2168-32838, New Zealand ☎ 1649/308 3355; ✆ www.aerlingus.com.

Air Canada ☎ 1-888/247-2262, UK ☎ 0871/220 1111, Republic of Ireland ☎ 01/679 3958, Australia ☎ 1300/655 767, New Zealand ☎ 0508/747 767; ✆ www.aircanada.com.

Air France US ☎ 1-800/237-2747, Canada ☎ 1-800/667-2747, UK ☎ 0870/142 4343, Australia ☎ 1300/390 190, South Africa ☎ 0861/340 340; ✆ www.airfrance.com.

Air India US ☎ 1-800/223-7776, Canada ☎ 1-800/625-6424, UK ☎ 020/8560 9996 or 8745 1000, Australia ☎ 02/9283 4020, New Zealand ☎ 09/631 5651; ✆ www.airindia.com.

Alaska Airlines US ☎ 1-800/252-7522, ✆ www.alaskaair.com.

Alitalia US ☎ 1-800/223-5730, Canada ☎ 1-800/361-8336, UK ☎ 0870/544 8259, Republic of Ireland ☎ 01/677 5171, New Zealand ☎ 09/308 3357, South Africa ☎ 11/721 4500; ✆ www.alitalia.com.

All Nippon Airways (ANA) USA & Canada, ☎ 1-800/235-9262, UK ☎ 0870/837 8866, Republic of Ireland ☎ 1850/200 058; ✆ www.anaskyweb.com.

American Airlines ☎ 1-800/433-7300, UK ☎ 0845/7789 789, Republic of Ireland ☎ 01/602 0550, Australia ☎ 1800/673 486, New Zealand ☎ 0800/445 442; ✆ www.aa.com.

Asiana Airlines US ☎ 1-800/227-4262, UK ☎ 0207/514 0201/8, Australia ☎ 02/9767 4343, ✆ www.flyasiana.com.

British Airways US & Canada ☎ 1-800/247-9297, UK ☎ 0870/850 9850, Republic of Ireland ☎ 1890/626 747, Australia ☎ 1300/767 177, New Zealand ☎ 09/966 9777, South Africa ☎ 114/418 600; ✆ www.ba.com.

Continental Airlines US & Canada ☎ 1-800/523-3273, UK ☎ 0845/607 6760, Republic of Ireland ☎ 1890/925 252, Australia ☎ 02/9244 2242, New Zealand ☎ 09/308 3350; ✆ www.continental.com.

Delta US & Canada ☎ 1-800/221-1212, UK ☎ 0845/600 0950, Republic of Ireland ☎ 1850/882 031 or 01/407 3165, Australia ☎ 1300/302 849, New Zealand ☎ 09/977 2232; ✆ www.delta.com.

Iberia US ☎ 1-800/772-4642, UK ☎ 0870/609 0500, Republic of Ireland ☎ 0818/462 000, South Africa ☎ 011/884 5909, ✆ www.iberia.com.

JAL (Japan Air Lines) US & Canada ☎ 1-800/525-3663, UK ☎ 0845/774 7700, Republic of Ireland ☎ 01/408 3757, Australia ☎ 02/9272 1111, New Zealand ☎ 09/379 9906,

South Africa ☎11/214 2560; 🖰www.jal.com or www.japanair.com.

JetBlue US ☎1-800/538-2583, UK ☎ 001-801-365-2525, 🖰www.jetblue.com.

KLM (Royal Dutch Airlines) See Northwest/KLM.

Korean Air US & Canada ☎1-800/438-5000, UK ☎0800/413 000, Republic of Ireland ☎01/799 7990, Australia ☎02/9262 6000, New Zealand ☎09/914 2000; 🖰www.koreanair.com.

Lufthansa US ☎1-800/3995-838, Canada ☎1-800/563-5954, UK ☎0870/837 7747, Republic of Ireland ☎01/844 5544, Australia ☎1300/655 727, New Zealand ☎0800/945 220, South Africa ☎0861/842 538; 🖰www.lufthansa.com.

Northwest/KLM US ☎1-800/225-2525, UK ☎0870/507 4074, Australia ☎1300/767310; 🖰www.nwa.com.

SAS (Scandinavian Airlines) US & Canada ☎1-800/221-2350, UK ☎0870/6072 7727, Republic of Ireland ☎01/844 5440, Australia ☎1300/727 707; 🖰www.scandinavian.net.

Swiss US ☎1-877/379-7947, Canada ☎1-877/559-7947, UK ☎0845/601 0956, Republic of Ireland ☎1890/200 515, Australia ☎1300/724 666, New Zealand ☎09/977 2238, South Africa ☎0860/040 506; 🖰www.swiss.com.

Turkish Airlines US ☎1-800/874-8875, Canada ☎1-866/435-9849, UK ☎020/7766 9300, Republic of Ireland ☎1/844 7920, Australia ☎02/9299 8400; 🖰www.thy.com.

United Airlines US ☎1-800/864-8331, UK ☎0845/844 4777, Australia ☎13 17 77; 🖰www.united.com.

US Airways US & Canada ☎1-800/428-4322, UK ☎0845/600 3300, Republic of Ireland ☎1890/925 065; 🖰www.usair.com.

USA 3000 Airlines US ☎1-877/USA-3000, 🖰www.usa3000airlines.com.

Virgin Atlantic US ☎1-800/821-5438, UK ☎0870/380 2007, Australia ☎1300/727 340, South Africa ☎11/340 3400; 🖰www.virgin-atlantic.com.

Agents and operators

Flight and travel agents (UK and Ireland)

Expedia UK ☎0870/050 0808, 🖰www.expedia.co.uk. Easy-to-navigate online agent offering a diverse range of holiday packages and good deals on flights.

Flightbookers UK ☎0870/814 0000, 🖰www.ebookers.com. Low fares on an extensive selection of scheduled flights, plus Chicago accommodation packages. Recommended.

Flynow UK ☎0870/660 004, 🖰www.flynow.com. Wide range of discounted tickets.

Joe Walsh Tours Ireland ☎01/241 0800, 🖰www.joewalshtours.ie. Family run, general budget fares agent.

North South Travel UK ☎01245/608 291, 🖰www.northsouthtravel.co.uk. Discounted fares worldwide – profits are used to support projects in the developing world, especially the promotion of sustainable tourism.

Quest Travel UK ☎0870/442 3542, 🖰www.questtravel.com. Specialists in Round-the-World and Australasian discount fares.

STA Travel UK ☎0870/1600 599, 🖰www.statravel.co.uk. Worldwide specialists in low-cost flights and tours for students and under-26s, though other customers welcome.

Trailfinders UK ☎0845/058 5858, 🖰www.trailfinders.com. One of the best-informed and most efficient agents for independent travellers; Amtrak passes available.

Travel Bag UK ☎0800/082 5000, 🖰www.travelbag.co.uk.com. Specializing in Round-the-World tickets, with good deals aimed at the backpacker market.

United Vacations UK ☎0870/606 2222, 🖰www.unitedvacations.co.uk. Tailor-made package holidays, fly-drive deals, rail tours, cruises, organized sightseeing tours, and more.

Tour operators (UK and Ireland)

American Holidays UK ☎028/9023 8762, Dublin ☎01/673 3840; 🖰www.american-holidays.com. Specialists in travel to the US offering tailor-made city breaks and escorted tours.

British Airways Holidays UK ☎0845/606 0747, 🖰www.britishairways.com/travel/holidaysindex. An exhaustive range of package and tailor-made holidays around the world, with Chicago city breaks.

Kuoni Travel UK ☎01306/747 734, 🖰www.kuoni.co.uk. Build your own holiday package to Chicago; good family offers.

Thomas Cook UK ☎0870/750 5711, 🖰www.thomascook.com. Long-established one-stop 24-hour travel agency for package holidays or scheduled flights, with bureaux de change issuing Thomas Cook traveller's checks, travel insurance, and car rental. Three-night city breaks in Chicago start from £399 per person, staying in a three-star hotel.

Twohigs Ireland ☎01/648 0800, 🖰www.twohigs.com. Specialists in US travel, among other regions.

World Travel Centre Ireland ☎01/416 7007, 🖰www.worldtravel.ie. Discount flights and other travel services.

Travel and flight agents (Australia and New Zealand)

Flight Centre Australia ☎ 13 31 33 or 02/9235 3522, ⓦ www.flightcentre.com.au, New Zealand ☎ 0800/243 544, ⓦ www.flightcentre.co.nz. Specialist agent for budget flights, especially Round-the-World tickets.

STA Travel Australia ☎ 1300/733 035, ⓦ www .statravel.com.au, New Zealand ☎ 0508/782 872, ⓦ www.statravel.co.nz. Discount flights, travel passes, and other services for youth/student travelers.

Trailfinders Australia ☎ 1300/780 212, ⓦ www .trailfinders.com.au. One of the best-informed and most efficient agents for independent travellers; Amtrak passes also available.

Specialist agents

Adventure World Australia ☎ 02/8913 0755, ⓦ www.adventureworld.com.au, New Zealand ☎ 09/524 5118, ⓦ www.adventureworld.co.nz. Chicago hotel bookings, car rental, and organized tours.

Canada & America Travel Specialists Australia ☎ 02/9922 4600, ⓦ www.canada-americatravel .com.au. Flights and accommodation in North America, plus Amtrak passes and Greyhound Ameripasses.

Sydney International Travel Centre ☎ 02/9250 9320, ⓦ www.sydneytravel.com.au. US flights, accommodation, city stays, and car rental.

travel.com.au Australia ☎ 1300/130 482 or 02/9249 5444, Ⓕ 02/9262 3525. Comprehensive online travel company.

United Vacations Australia ☎ 1300/887 870, ⓦ www.unitedvacations.com.au. Features hotel deals for Chicago.

Viator Australia ☎ 02/8219 5400, ⓦ www.viator .com. Small selection of Chicago tours and discounts; also sells City Pass – admission to six top Chicago attractions for 50 percent off regular admission (from US$59 per person).

Arrival

Those travelling to Chicago by bus or train arrive just west of the Loop, within a stone's throw of public transportation and dozens of hotels. While flights touch down at O'Hare and Midway airports in the northwest and southwest corners of Chicago, respectively, efficient El trains will take you downtown within a half hour to forty five minutes. Taking a taxi from the airport won't save you much time and can be expensive, especially if you're going it alone. Alternatively, airport shuttles will cost less but tend to make multiple stops on the journey downtown.

By air

If arriving by air, you'll most likely be coming into **O'Hare International Airport** on the city's northwest side, about seventeen miles outside the city centre. There are several ways of getting into Chicago proper from here, the quickest and most reliable option being the Chicago Transit Authority (CTA) Blue Line El train, which runs 24 hours and costs $1.75 one-way. You'll reach downtown from O'Hare in 45 minutes. The station at O'Hare is underneath the main parking garage, a short walk from most of the airport's terminals. From Terminal 5, though, you'll need to take the free Airport Transit System shuttle to Terminal 3 and follow the signs marked "City Transport".

Another option is to take one of the airport shuttles, which drop you off at your requested hotel for around $27, plus tip. Shuttles pull up in front of the main entrances of each terminal every ten to fifteen minutes. Most of the shuttle companies have information desks inside by the baggage claim area. Shuttles generally run between 6am and 11.30pm. If you want to try and reserve ahead, call Airport Express (☎ 1-888/284-3827, ⓦ www.airportexpress.com) one of the better shuttle services.

Taxis are your most expensive option, and you're at the whim of Chicago traffic – a single fare could run you anywhere from $45 and up, plus tip. Even in off-peak times, however, cabs are plentiful and can be found curbside at any terminal, outside of baggage claim. Usually the ride takes twenty minutes, but with traffic you could be looking at up to an hour. If you can find someone to split the fare, then a cab could be decent value.

From **Midway Airport**, the quickest and cheapest way to reach downtown is to take the CTA Orange Line El train, which departs every five minutes (off-peak, every 15min) and makes the ten-mile trip in 25 minutes. To find the El stop, follow the signs to the parking garage – the station is directly behind the garage. If you arrive at Midway late at night or very early in the morning, bear in mind that the Orange Line stops running between 1am and 4am from Monday to Saturday, and between 1am and 7am on Sundays and holidays.

You can pick up a taxi just outside the baggage claim area. A ride into downtown will set you back about $22, taking anywhere from fifteen minutes to an hour, depending on traffic. If you're with other travellers, you might try the shared-ride service, whereby passengers can share a cab for a flat rate of $14 per person; however, be sure to let the driver know beforehand that you want to do this.

Another option is to take the Airport Express shuttle (6am–11.30pm; ☎1-888/284-3826), which leaves from just outside the main terminal. Shuttles run every fifteen minutes between Midway and downtown Chicago (for around $22), and also the northern suburbs.

For driving directions from both airports, see opposite.

Major expressways

I-55	Stevenson Expressway
I-90 East	Kennedy Expressway
I-94 North	Dan Ryan Expressway
I-290 East	Eisenhower Expressway

By train and bus

Chicago is the hub of the nationwide Amtrak rail system, and almost every cross-country route passes through Union Station (☎312/558-1075), at Canal and Adams streets, just one block west of the Loop. The closest El stop is about four blocks away at Quincy and Wells streets, while cabs are available outside the station on the upper and lower levels.

Greyhound and a couple of regional bus companies pull into the large modern terminal at 630 W Harrison St (☎312/408-5980 in Chicago, ⊛www.greyhound.com), between Des Plaines and Jefferson streets, a ten-minute walk from the Loop. The nearest El stop (Blue Line) is on Clinton Street, two blocks northeast of the terminal.

By car

When driving to Chicago you'll need to be aware of at least four major **expressways** feeding into downtown Chicago: I-90/94 from the northwest and north; I-290 from the west; I-55 from the southwest; and I-90/94 from the south.

From O'Hare International Airport (on the northwest side), take I-90 East to Ohio Street, which will take you to Michigan Avenue, just north of the Loop. From the northern suburbs, take I-94 to the same Ohio Street exit. Alternatively, take the scenic route along Lake Shore Drive (Highway 41).

Getting around

For a city as spread out as Chicago, the public transportation system is extensive and service is remarkably efficient. Most sights can be reached on the city's El train system, while buses, though slower, fill in the gaps. Other options include taking a taxi and renting a car or a bike.

The CTA

The Chicago Transit Authority's **subway and elevated train system** – better known as the "El" – runs on eight lines that cover most downtown areas and neighbourhoods, with the exception of parts of Lincoln Park toward Lake Michigan, the area east of Michigan Avenue toward Navy Pier and Hyde Park. Each colour-coded line (Blue, Brown, Green, Orange, Purple, Red, Yellow and Pink) radiates from the Loop. Trains are clean and run frequently during the day – roughly every fifteen minutes or so – though at night service on the Orange, Brown, Green, Purple, Yellow and Pink lines shuts down between 1am and 4am. The Red Line and Blue Line (between Forest Park and O'Hare), however, run 24 hours.

Fares are $2.25 a ride; you'll need to buy a **transit card** from a vending machine at El stations before you pass through the turnstiles. Cards will hold as little as $2.25 and as much as $100. Transfers (two allowed) deduct an additional 25¢ from the original fare and are valid for two hours on CTA "El" and bus routes.

Convenient **CTA Visitor Passes** allow unlimited travel for a set number of days; the one-day pass ($5.75) is good value, as are three-day ($14) and seven-day ($23) passes, which are valid for consecutive days of travel. You can buy passes at the airport on arrival, at any of the visitor information centres, as well as in Union Station and many of the currency exchange offices downtown.

The CTA also runs Chicago's **buses**, which accept Transit Cards and Visitor Passes, as well as coins and bills in exact change. Fares are the same as the El ($2.25), and for an extra 25¢ you can transfer between buses and trains within a two-hour window. Most bus lines operate daily; during rush hour and peak times, buses run every five minutes, every 8–12 minutes during off-peak hours. Service is sporadic between midnight and 4am, but the major bus lines run all night.

Useful bus routes

#6 Jackson Park Express To get from downtown to Hyde Park and the Museum of Science and Industry.

#10 Museum of Science and Industry A very effective way to get to the Museum of Science and Industry from the Loop. Pick it up on State St.

#22 Clark Runs along Dearborn and Clark sts, and is one of the best buses for getting to Lincoln Park and the North Side.

#29 State Runs between the Loop and Navy Pier, on State St, Illinois St and Grand Ave.

#36 Broadway Similar to the #22, it runs along Clark between the Loop and Lakeview, then jumps to Broadway for its long slog north.

#72 North A good way to get from Lincoln Park and Old Town to Bucktown and Wicker Park.

#146 Marine–Michigan Runs between Museum Campus, the Loop (via State St) and to Andersonville (via Lake Shore Drive).

#151 Sheridan This Loop–Lincoln Park–Lakeview route runs along Michigan Ave, Stockton Ave (good for the Lincoln Park Zoo) and Sheridan Rd.

Chicago Transit Authority

For route information and timetables, as well as disabled access, for CTA trains and buses call ☏ 12/836-7000 or log on to ⊛ www.transitchicago.com. For passes and other information call ☏ 1 888/968-7282 or visit the website.

Metra

The commuter rail network run by **Metra** (information line: ☎312/322-6777 weekdays, ☎312/836-4949 evenings and weekends, ⊛www.metrarail.com) serves Chicago's suburbs, stopping at four main stations in the city: Union Station, Ogilvie Transportation Center, LaSalle Street Station (LaSalle St and Congress Parkway), and Millennium Station (where Randolph St meets the northern tip of Grant Park). You're not likely to need Metra unless you want to visit Hyde Park (and the Museum of Science and Industry) or McCormick Place. (See individual chapters for details on getting to these locations.)

Fares start at $2.15 and go up to $8.05, depending on the distance travelled. A discount weekend pass offering unlimited travel on Metra costs $5. Tickets can be bought from agents or vending machines at stations or on the train if there's no ticket seller on duty at the station.

Taxis

Taxis are plentiful and are worth using if you're in a hurry or happen to be in areas that aren't well served by public transportation, especially late at night. If you know you'll be spending time in the more outlying areas like the South Side, it's a good idea to book a return cab in advance (see below for a list of cab companies).

Fares are $2.25 to start the meter, $1.80 for each mile thereafter and $1 charge for a second passenger, $0.50 for each additional passenger. Most fares between the Loop and locations within a few miles of there (River North, N Michigan Ave, the Gold Coast, Old Town, Museum Campus, Little Italy and Greektown) will run from $7 to $12. For points farther out (ie Andersonville and Hyde Park), expect to pay at least $17–24. Bear in mind that the tip should be 15 to 20 percent of the fare.

Taxis can be hailed on the streets, or you can use the taxi stands outside train and bus stations and hotels. For reliable taxi service, two of the better companies in the city are Yellow Cab (☎312/829-4222) or Flash Cab (☎773/561-1444).

By car

There's not much reason to **rent a car** in Chicago, unless you want to explore outposts like Oak Park or Evanston; public transportation will get you to most places fairly efficiently, while congestion and a dearth of parking spaces, especially in the Loop and the surrounding areas, can make for a harrowing experience.

If you absolutely need a car, be prepared to pay hefty overnight **parking charges** ($30+) to park your car at a garage or lot, or else pay close attention to street parking signs to avoid being ticketed, which will cost you a minimum of $50 for even a minor parking offense.

During peak hours, on-street parking can be impossible, while streets in the residential areas either have two-hour ($2) parking meters or require resident permits. In most cases, you're better off putting your car in a parking lot or garage (from $11 per hr to $17 for four hours to $25 per day). In the Loop, try the cheap underground garages on the north end of Grant Park (enter through Columbus Drive or Michigan Ave).

If your car is towed, expect to pay at least $150 to liberate it from the City of Chicago Auto Pound Headquarters (☎312/744-4444).

Car rental agencies

Ace Rent-A-Car ⊛www.acerentacar.com (online reservations only).
Alamo US ☎1-800/462-5266, ⊛www.alamo.com.
Avis US & Canada ☎1-800/331-1212, UK ☎0870/606 0100, Republic of Ireland ☎021/428 1111, Australia ☎13 63 33 or 02/9353 9000, New Zealand ☎09/526 2847 or 0800/655 111; ⊛www.avis.com.
Budget US ☎1-800/527-0700, Canada ☎1-800/268-8900, UK ☎0870/156 5656, Australia ☎1300/362 848, New Zealand ☎0800/283 438; ⊛www.budget.com.
Dollar US ☎1-800/800-3665, Canada ☎1-800/229-0984, UK ☎0808/234 7524, Republic of Ireland ☎1800/575 800; ⊛www.dollar.com.
Enterprise Rent-a-Car US ☎1-800/261-7331, ⊛www.enterprise.com.
Hertz US & Canada ☎1-800/654-3131, UK ☎020/7026 0077, Republic of Ireland ☎01/870 5777, New Zealand ☎0800/654 321; ⊛www.hertz.com.

National US ☎1-800/CAR-RENT, UK ☎0870/400 4581, Australia ☎0870/600 6666, New Zealand ☎03/366 5574; ⓦwww.nationalcar.com.
Thrifty US & Canada ☎1-800/847-4389, UK ☎01494/751 500, Republic of Ireland ☎01/844 1950, Australia ☎1300/367 227, New Zealand ☎09/256 1405, ⓦwww.thrifty.com.

Cycling

Chicago is a bike-friendly city, with miles of bike lanes, plenty of bike racks and some twenty El stations where riders can store their bikes indoors and hop on the train. Bikes are permitted on El trains, except during peak hours on weekdays (7–9am and 4–6pm). The popular lakefront path provides twenty-plus miles of uninterrupted cycling through well-tended parkland, with many sightseeing attractions, shopping districts, and other diversions close by. For more information on biking in Chicago, visit Chicagoland Bicycle Federation's website at ⓦwww.biketraffic.org or the City of Chicago's Bicycle Program at ⓦwww.chicagobikes.org.

Cyclists' protocol is taken very seriously in Chicago. When using the cycle lanes, especially along the lakefront, which can become very congested in the evenings and during the weekends in summer, always keep to the right. If you need to pass a pedestrian, rollerblader or cyclist, warn them by stating clearly "on your left" and overtaking accordingly.

Of the main **bike rental outfits**, Bike and Roll Chicago has locations at 1600 N Lakeshore Drive, on North Avenue Beach, and Millennium Park (see p.28 for details), where you can rent bikes for $8 per hour or $30 per day. The North Avenue Beach location is open from May 1 to September 31, and the Millennium Park store is open year-round (excepting weekends during the winter months).

City tours

Most **tours** of Chicago explore either architecture or the city's neighbourhoods, though any number of smaller, specialized tours do exist, from ethnic food samplings and exploring financial exchanges to haunted house tours.

River tours and lakefront cruises are often the best way to get a feel for the city's size.

There are a handful of companies that operate them, any of which will be sufficient, but the Chicago Architecture Foundation (see p.44) puts on the most detailed and comprehensive tours. For more leisurely sightseeing at slightly more expense, you might try the cruise lines that offer lunch and dinner trips up and down the lake, the latter often around sunset.

Bicycle tours

Bike and Roll Tours ☎312/729-1000 or 1-888/245-3929 (North Avenue Beach & Millennium Park), ⓦwww.bikeandroll.com. Three- to four-hour guided tours ($30) covering the lakefront, Lincoln Park, Grant Park, Chinatown and Hyde Park's Osaka Garden. Segway tours ($49) also available. Free self-guided tour maps also provided.
Bike Chicago Rentals and Tours ☎312/595-9600 (Navy Pier), ⓦwww.bikechicago.com. Tours of the lakefront and neighbourhoods (June–Aug Mon–Fri).

Bus and trolley tours

American Sightseeing Tours ☎312/251-3100 or 1-800/621-4153, ⓦwww.americansightseeing .org/chicago. Two- to five-hour tours ($25–60) ranging from bus tours of all the major neighbourhoods – the Grand Tour takes in most of the city – to river cruise and walking architectural tours to a "Roaring Twenties" dinner tour and bus tours to Oak Park; reservations required.
Chicago Trolley Company Tours ☎312/663-0260, ⓦwww.chicagotrolley.com. One-hour and forty-five minute hop-on hop-off tours (all-day pass $29, three-day pass $40.50; check online for reduced prices) on motorized board-at-will trolleys (or double-decker buses), which make thirteen stops in the downtown area, including Sears Tower, Navy Pier, Museum Campus and the Art Institute.
Gray Line Tours ☎1-800/621-4153, ⓦwww .grayline.com. One of the better bus-tour companies offering a good variety of tours, from the four-hour city-wide "Inside Chicago" tour ($40) to the seven-hour "Ship and Shore tour" ($79) taking in the entire city by bus, plus lunch and a cruise on Lake Michigan. Tours leave from the *Palmer House Hilton*, 17 E Monroe St.

Cruises and river trips

Chicago Architecture Foundation ☎312/922-3432, ⓦwww.cruisechicago.com or www .architecture.org. Intelligent, remarkably extensive list

Orientation

For the most part, Chicago is a very easy city to navigate as the urban grid is laid out, as, well, a grid. The centre of this grid is at the corner of State and Madison in the heart of the Loop. Eight blocks north of here is Chicago Avenue, which marks 800 North. Blocks tend to be marked off in increments of 100, with some provisions for diagonal streets (like Clark St and Lincoln Ave). In terms of walking around, eight city blocks in Chicago constitute about 1.6 kilometers, so it's a good way to figure out how far any given destination might take to reach.

of tours, many with an architectural bent. Highly recommended. See box on p.44 for further details.
Chicago from the Lake ☎ 312/527-2002, ⓦ www.chicagoline.com. Ninety-minute, informative architectural river cruises and historical river/lake cruises operating from May through Oct; $34. Tours leave from River East Arts Center, 465 N McClurg Court. Between March and November, tours leave almost every hour.
Odyssey Cruises ☎ 708/990-0800 or 1/888/273-2469, ⓦ www.odysseycruises.com. Pricey brunch, lunch, dinner and romantic midnight cruises ($61–153 per person) on a huge, super-sleek yacht, departing from 600 E Grand Ave at Navy Pier. Reservations are required.
Shoreline Sightseeing ☎ 312/222-9328, ⓦ www.shorelinesightseeing.com. Architecture cruises and 30min sightseeing tours ($22) leaving from Shedd Aquarium, Buckingham Fountain and Navy Pier.
Spirit of Chicago ☎ 1-866/211-3804, ⓦ www .spiritofchicago.com. Swanky harbour cruises, with bar and live music. Lunch and dinner cruises from $50 and $100; sunset cruises $61. Boats depart from 600 E Grand Ave at Navy Pier. Year-round.
Wendella Boats ☎ 312/337-1446, ⓦ www .wendellaboats.com. Well-run architecture and sightseeing cruises ($19), leaving from the pier near the Wrigley Building at 400 N Michigan Ave. Summer only.

Specialist tours and activities

Chicago Blues Tour ☎ 773/772-5506, ⓦ www .chicagobluestour.com. Twice-yearly tour ($40) of

South Side blues clubs and the Blues Heaven Foundation, formerly the home of Chess Records.
Chicago Ethnic Grocery Store Tours ☎ 773/465-8064, ⓦ ethnic-grocery-tours.com. Led by a guide with an encyclopedic knowledge of the city's ethnic food, these tours also offer the chance to sample food along the way ($75).
Loop Tour Train ☎ 1-877/244-2246. Free 40min architecture and history tours co-sponsored by the Chicago Architecture Foundation, Chicago Office of Tourism and the Chicago Transit Authority (May 4 to Sept 28). Departs from the Randolph/Wabash El station every Sat at 11am, 11.40am, 12.25pm and 1pm. Pick up tickets on the day of the tour at the Chicago Office of Tourism Visitor Information Center (see p.37).
Untouchable Tours ☎ 773/881-1195, ⓦ www .gangstertour.com. Guides dressed as gangsters lead bus tours of Prohibition-era haunts and hideouts of Chicago gangsters in Chinatown, Pilsen, Little Italy, Greektown and Lincoln Park. Tours ($27) depart from in front of Rock 'n' Roll McDonald's, at 600 N Clark St.

Walking tours

Chicago Architecture Foundation ☎ 312/922-3432, ⓦ www.cruisechicago.com or ⓦ www .architecture.org. Offers by far the largest, most extensive list of walking tours in Chicago, with well over fifty different routes and themes.
Walk Chicago Tours ☎ 708/557-5400, ⓦ www .walkchicagotours.com. Walk Chicago Tours live up to their motto of "A Story on Every Corner" by offering rather lively and informative walking tours of Pilsen, the Loop and Lincoln Park. Tours are also handicapped accessible.

The media

Chicago serves as the media centre for much of the Midwest, and it has a nation-ally respected newspaper and television network. Historically, it was one of the leaders in early days of American television and it continues to be a nerve centre of media activity. Examples of this include the Tribune Corporation and Harpo Studios, homebase for Oprah Winfrey.

Newspapers and magazines

Chicago's **main newspapers** include the *Chicago Tribune* (50¢; ⓦwww.chicago tribune.com), which covers a mix of local, national and international news in a tone that's less staid and, at times, breezier than that of its east coast counterparts. Despite the staff cuts at the *tribune* as of late, Chicago newspaper legends like Rick Kogan and John Kass remain.

The city's other major newspaper, *The Sun-Times* (50¢; ⓦwww.suntimes.com), tends to be more sensational in its coverage, focusing less on international news and more on local stories. The paper's lead film critic, Roger Ebert, is best known for his nationally aired TV show, *Siskel and Ebert*, on which he entertainingly sparred with the late *Tribune* film columnist Gene Siskel. Besides the two major newspapers, there's the *Daily Herald* (ⓦwww.dailyherald .com), Chicago's largest suburban daily paper – read mostly in the surrounding counties.

The **free weekly** *Chicago Reader* (ⓦwww .chicagoreader.com) is indispensable for current arts and entertainment listings, and often has quirky editorials on a variety of topics. Other free papers have joined the scene but none comes close to cracking the *Reader*'s hold on the city. In 2005, the popular *Time Out* weekly city guides entered the Chicago market, and it's well worth picking one of these up as well. Some of the articles and listings can be viewed for free at their website ⓦwww .timeout.com/chicago.

Most downtown **newsstands and bookstores** sell a huge variety of national and international newspapers, the best of which is probably Borders, 830 N Michigan Ave, at N Pearson St (☎312/573-0564).

After 9/11, much of the Chicago media developed a growing interest in worldwide affairs, and radio and television shows dedicated to such matters popped up like mushrooms after a hard rain.

TV and radio

You can still catch local **TV** offerings from the four major networks (NBC, ABC, Fox and CBS), as well as a respectable line-up of shows and news on the city's own two local channels – WGN and WTTW – plus the low-budget Cable CLTV (Chicagoland TV). When visiting the city, it's worth taking a look at the WTTW programmes "Check Please", where locals give honest reviews of Chicago eateries, or "Chicago Stories", which features historical vignettes about the city's past.

Local news seems to follow the usual boiler-plate formula of "if it bleeds, it leads", so if you're looking for international news (or anything else), you'd be better off sticking with the national cable channels (CNN, MSNBC or, if desperate, Fox News Channel).

Radio programming in Chicago is a bit more robust and thoughtful, with several high-profile college stations, a smattering of Spanish-language stations, and the uniformly excellent programming on Chicago Public Radio, WBEZ. Before visiting the city, you'd do well to listen to a few archived episodes of their well-produced local news show, "Eight-Forty-Eight" on their website, ⓦwww .chicagopublicradio.org.

Broadcast TV stations

Channel 2 (WBBM/CBS)
Channel 5 (WMAQ/NBC)

Live talk shows

Although Chicago, unlike New York, is not somewhere you'd choose to seek out live talk shows, a few options do exist if you want to be part of the studio audience. Oprah Winfrey, veritable queen of Chicago and national media personality, hosts **The Oprah Winfrey Show** from her West Side Harpo Studios, 1058 W Washington Ave. For more details, see p.116.

Known for his bawdy brand of entertainment, **Jerry Springer** tapes his eponymous show here in Chicago at the NBC Tower, 454 N Columbus Drive, on the second floor (☏312/321-5365). Go if you must – it's sensational American TV at its worst, or best, depending on your perspective.

Channel 7 (WLS/ABC)
Channel 9 (WGN)
Channel 11 (WTTW/Network Chicago)
Channel 32 (WFLD/Fox)
Cable CLTV/Chicagoland

Radio stations

Local AM stations

WSCR (670) Sports
WGN (720) Talk
WBBM (780) News
WLS (890) Talk and news
WMVP (1000) Sports

Local FM stations

WBEZ (91.5) Talk, music and news (including National Public Radio programming)
WXRT (93.1) Rock
WNUA (95.5) Jazz
WBBM (96.3) Pop
WLUP (97.9) Rock
WFMT (98.7) Classical
WUSN (99.5) Country
WKQX (101.1) Alternative rock
WVAZ (102.7) Old-school R&B
WKSC (103.5) Mainstream Top Forty
WGCI (107.5) Contemporary R&B and hip-hop

Travel essentials

Costs

Accommodation is likely to be your biggest single expense. The least expensive, reasonable double hotel rooms go from $95 a night, though you'll probably find some good deals on weekends and during Chicago's winter; see Chapter 000, "Accommodation", for more details. After accommodation, you could get by on $45–55 per day, which will buy you a basic diner breakfast, a fast-food lunch (pizza, burger or sandwich), and a budget sit-down dinner with beer, plus El fare. Beyond this, a little more luxury – such as fancier meals, taking taxis, going to a concert or play – will mean more like $100 a day. The sales tax in Chicago is 10.25 percent and it will be added to just about everything you buy in stores, except for certain groceries.

Crime and personal safety

For the most part, violent crime in Chicago is concentrated in a few areas, notably those of the South Side and West Side. Most tourists probably won't be wandering into these areas, therefore shouldn't expect to encounter problems beyond those they would expect in any major city.

Overall, common sense should keep you out of trouble: stick to well-lit streets at night, and avoid parks, parking lots and alleys. Always lock your car, keep an eye on the kids at all times, and know where you're going or at least give the impression that you do. Don't have expensive jewellery on view and don't openly carry nice cameras, bags, or any other items that might draw attention to you. Men should keep wallets in the front pocket, women should wear purses across the shoulder. When riding the subway at night (not advisable after midnight), have your wits about you and do not fall asleep – you'll be easy prey for any thief. Should you run into trouble and need emergency police assistance, find a phone and call ☎911 or hail a cab and ask the driver to take you to the nearest police station. For non-emergencies, call ☎312/744-4000.

If you're planning to explore Hyde Park, or others areas of the **South Side**, take special care: there are a few extremely dangerous sections sprinkled along the way to both neighbourhoods. The same can be said of the area around **Cabrini Green** just west of the Gold Coast, and larger stretches of the West Side, especially around the **United Center**. It's best not to walk in these areas or drive through here at night.

Electricity

As with most destinations in the United States, the standard voltage in Chicago is 120.

Entry requirements

Citizens of the UK, Ireland, Australia, New Zealand, South Korea, most Western European countries and some Eastern European ones (check with your nearest embassy or consulate), who plan to visit the US for less than ninety days, need only a round-trip ticket, passport, and a visa waiver form. The latter (an I-94W) is available from your travel agency, at the airline check-in desk, or on board the plane, and must be presented to immigration once you arrive. Since January 2009, all travellers planning to enter on the visa waiver program must register in advance for the also Electronic System for Travel Authorization (ESTA) at ⓦesta.cbp.dhs.gov.

All **passports** must be machine readable, and governments of countries that participate in the visa waiver program have been required to issue passports with biometric microchip identification since October 2006; consult your embassy for further information well in advance of travel, if in any doubt whether your passport will pass muster.

Canadian citizens, used to being able to make an oral declaration, have also had to provide documentation since January 2008, although an enhanced secure driver's license is still an acceptable alternative to a passport. This may change though, so again, check for updates.

Residents of countries not mentioned above will need a valid passport, as well as a non-immigrant visitor's visa, which is valid for a maximum of ninety days. Visa procedures vary by country and by your status on application, so contact the nearest US embassy or consulate for details.

The date stamped in your passport by immigration upon arrival is the latest you're legally allowed to stay. Leaving a few days later may not matter, especially if you're heading home, but more than a week or so can result in a protracted, rather unpleasant interrogation from officials, which may cause you to miss your flight. You may also be denied entry the next time you try to visit the US.

Should you need a **visa extension**, you'll have to apply through the nearest US Immigration and Naturalization Service (INS) office before your time is up. In Chicago, the office is at 101 W Congress Parkway (☎312/385-1500 or 1-800/870-3676, ⓦwww.ins.usdoj.gov). Be prepared to discuss why you're hoping to stay on – they're likely to assume you are working in the US illegally, so any evidence of your pre-existing (and abundant) funds might strengthen your case. If you can, bring an upstanding American citizen to vouch for you. You'll also have to explain why you didn't plan for the extra time initially.

Most travellers won't need to be inoculated to enter the US, unless they're en route from areas where cholera and typhoid are endemic; check with your doctor before you leave.

US embassies

Australia Moonah Place, Yarralumla, Canberra, ACT 2600 ☎02/6214 5600, ⓦcanberra.usembassy.gov
Canada 490 Sussex Drive, Ottawa, ON K1N 1GB ☎613/238-5335, ⓦottawa.usembassy.gov

Ireland 42 Elgin Rd, Ballsbridge, Dublin 4
☎01/668 8777, ◎dublin.usembassy.gov
New Zealand 29 Fitzherbert Terrace, Thorndon
☎04/462 6000, ◎newzealand.usembassy.gov
South Africa 877 Pretorius St, Arcadia 0083
☎012/431 4000, ◎southafrica.usembassy.gov
UK 24 Grosvenor Square, London W1A 1AE
☎020/7499 9000, ◎www.usembassy.org.uk

Foreign consulates in Chicago

Australia 123 N Wacker Drive, Suite 1330
☎312/419-1480, ◎www. dfat.gov.au/missions
/countries/usch.html
Canada Two Prudential Plaza, 180 N Stetson Ave,
Suite 2400 ☎312/616-1860, ◎www.chicago.gc.ca
Ireland 400 N Michigan, Suite 911 ☎312/337-
1868, ◎www.irishconsulate.org
New Zealand 8600 W Bryn Mawr Ave, Suite 500N
☎773/714-9461, ◎www.newzealandconsulate.us
South Africa 200 S Michigan Ave ☎312/939-
7929, ◎www.southafrica–newyork.net
UK Wrigley Building, 13th floor, 400 N Michigan Ave,
Suite 1300 ☎312/970-3800, ◎ukinusa.fco.gov.uk

Health

The United States is not known for its access
to free or subsidized health care, and Chicago
is certainly no exception. Emergency rooms
at local hospitals will not refuse to treat you/
your based on ability to pay, but the wait at
such facilities may be quite long, especially
during the evening and early morning hours.
It's best to travel with some type of insurance.

If you have an immediate medical
emergency you should dial ☎911 from any
phone in order to have a medical vehicle
provide assistance. For further details on
healthcare for visitors, contact the official US
government agency CDC ☎1-877/394-
8747, ◎www.cdc.gov/travel.

Major hospitals

Advocate Illinois Masonic Medical Center 836
W Wellington Ave, Lincoln Park ☎773/975-1600.
John H. Stroger Jr. Hospital of Cook County
1901 W Harrison St, Near West Side ☎312/864-
6000.
Mercy Hospital 2525 S Michigan Ave, Near South
Side ☎312/567-2000.
Northwestern Memorial Hospital 251 E Huron
St, River North ☎312/926-2000.
University of Chicago Medical Center 5841 S
Maryland Ave, Hyde Park ☎773/702-1000.

24-hour pharmacies

CVS Pharmacy 1201 N State St, Gold Coast
☎312/640-2842.
Walgreens 641 N Clark St, River North
☎312/587-1416.
Walgreens 757 N Michigan Ave, Gold Coast
☎312/664-8686.
Walgreens 2001 N Milwaukee Ave, Wicker Park
☎773/772-2370.

Insurance

Even though EU health-care privileges apply
in the US, residents of the UK would do well
to take out an **insurance policy** before
travelling to cover against theft, loss, illness
or injury. Before paying for a new policy, it's
worth checking if you are already covered –
some all-risks home-insurance policies may
cover your possessions when overseas, and
many private medical schemes include cover
when abroad. In Canada, provincial health
plans usually provide partial cover for medical
mishaps overseas, while holders of official
student/teacher/youth cards in Canada and
the US are entitled to meagre accident

Rough Guides travel insurance

Rough Guides has teamed up with Columbus Direct to offer you **travel insurance**
that can be tailored to suit your needs. Products include a low-cost **backpacker**
option for long stays; a **short break** option for city getaways; a typical **holiday
package** option; and others. There are also annual **multi-trip** policies for those who
travel regularly. Different sports and activities (trekking, skiing, etc) can be usually be
covered if required.

See our website (◎www.roughguides.com/website/shop) for eligibility and
purchasing options. Alternatively, UK residents should call ☎0870/033 9988;
Australians should call ☎1300/669 999 and New Zealanders should call ☎0800/55
9911. All other nationalities should call ☎+44 870/890 2843.

coverage and hospital in-patient benefits. Students will often find that their student health coverage extends during the vacations and for one term beyond the date of last enrolment.

After exhausting these possibilities, you might want to contact a specialist travel insurance company, or consider the travel insurance deal Rough Guides offers (see box above). A typical travel-insurance policy usually provides cover for the loss of baggage, tickets, and – up to a certain limit – cash or cheques, as well as cancellation or curtailment of your journey. Most of them exclude so-called dangerous sports unless an extra premium is paid: this can mean whitewater rafting and trekking, though probably not kayaking. Many policies can be chopped and changed to exclude coverage you don't need – for example, sickness and accident benefits can often be excluded or included at will. If you do take medical coverage, ascertain whether benefits will be paid as treatment proceeds or only after return home, and if there is a 24-hour medical emergency number. When securing baggage cover, make sure that the per-article limit – typically under £500 – will cover your most valuable possession. If you need to make a claim, you should keep receipts for medicines and medical treatment, and in the event you have anything stolen, you must obtain an official theft report from the police.

Internet

Finding an internet outlet is fairly easy in Chicago – the city has numerous **internet cafés** that charge, on average, $3–4 for half an hour's use. The hostels also have a few terminals (*Hostelling International – Chicago* has twelve), and they charge $6 per hour. Guests with their own computer can take advantage of free wi-fi. Another option is to head to the Harold Washington Library in the Loop, where you can log on for free. All of the Chicago Public Libraries offer free wi-fi, and two additional branches close by Include the Lincoln Park branch at 1150 W Fullerton Ave and the Near North branch at 310 W Division St. Increasingly, many cafés and bookstores offer up free wi-fi for those with their own

laptops. A useful website – ⓦwww.kropla .com – has information on where you can plug your laptop in when abroad.

Laundry

Laundry service is available at most large hotels, though it is a pricey affair. Both of the city's hostels have self-service laundry facilities. Central Chicago doesn't have any self-service laundromats but visitors may wish to trek over to Coachlight Laundromat at 3475 N Broadway St in Lakeview (ⓣ773/528-6799 or Sudz Laundromat at 1246 N Ashland Ave in Wicker Park (ⓣ773/252-1206).

Mail

Ordinary **mail** sent within the US costs 42¢ (at press time) for letters weighing up to an ounce, while standard postcards cost 27¢. For anywhere outside the US, airmail letters cost 94¢ up to an ounce and 72¢ for postcards and aerograms. Airmail between the US and Europe may take a week and 12–14 days to Australasia.

You can have mail sent to you c/o General Delivery (known elsewhere as **post restante**), Chicago, IL 60601. Letters will end up at the post office at 200 E Randolph St (Mon–Fri 7.30am–5.30pm), which will only hold mail for thirty days before returning it to sender – so make sure the envelope has a return address. Alternatively, most hotels will accept and hold mail for guests. Hotels also frequently sell postage for smaller items though most of them will not usually be able to help you send packages.

Maps

Our maps should be sufficient for most purposes; commercial maps and the free city plans available from tourist offices can help fill in the gaps. For a pocket-sized map, try the laminated *Streetwise Chicago* ($5.95; ⓦwww .streetwisemaps.com), which is available from most book, travel, and map stores.

The American Automobile Association (ⓣ1-800/222-4357, ⓦwww.aaa.com) provides free maps and assistance to its members, and to British members of the AA and RAC.

Money

US currency comes in $1 bills and coins, and bills of $2, $5, $10, $20, $50 and $100.

All are the same size and they have a variety of security features, including different coloured inks and a watermark. The dollar is made up of 100 cents (¢) in coins of 1 cent (usually called a penny), 5 cents (a nickel), 10 cents (a dime), and 25 cents (a quarter). $1 coins are less frequently seen.

Change – especially quarters – is needed for buses, vending machines and telephones, so always carry plenty, though automatic machines are increasingly fitted with slots for dollar bills.

In terms of the exchange rate, at the time that the information in this guide was compiled one US dollar ($) was trading at £.69 and €.74. For more up-to-date currency exchange rates, consult ⓦ www.xe.com.

Banks and ATMs

With an ATM card, you'll be able to withdraw cash just about anywhere in Chicago, though you'll be charged a fee for using a different bank's network. If you have a foreign **cash-dispensing card** linked to an international network such as Cirrus or Plus – be sure to check with your home bank before you set off – you can make withdrawals from ATMs in the US. The flat transaction fee is usually quite small – your bank will able to advise you on this. Make sure you have a personal identification number (PIN) that's designed to work overseas. You may also be able to use your debit card for purchases, as you would at home.

Most **banks** in Chicago are open Monday to Friday, from 9am to 5pm, though a limited number have Saturday hours, usually open no later than 1pm.

Travellers' cheques

Travellers' cheques in US dollars are widely accepted as cash in restaurants, stores and museums. The usual fee for travellers' cheque sales is one or two percent, though this may be waived if you buy them through a bank where you have an account. It pays to get a selection of denominations so you'll have some flexibility. Make sure to keep the purchase agreement and a record of cheque serial numbers safe and separate from the cheque themselves. In the event that cheque are lost or stolen, the issuing company will expect you to report the loss immediately to their office; most companies claim to replace lost or stolen cheque within 24 hours.

Credit and debit cards

For many services in the US, it's simply taken for granted that you'll be paying with plastic. When renting a car or checking into a hotel, you will be asked to show a **credit card** – even if you intend to settle the bill in cash. Most major credit cards issued by foreign banks are honoured in the US: locally, Visa, MasterCard, American Express and Discover are the most widely used. If you use your credit card at an ATM, remember that all cash advances are treated as loans with interest accruing daily from the date of withdrawal; there will also be a transaction fee on top of this. Not all foreign **debit cards** are valid for transactions in shops in the US.

Visa TravelMoney is a disposable prepaid debit card with a PIN that works in all ATMs that take Visa cards. When your funds are depleted, you simply throw the card away. Since you can buy up to nine cards to access the same funds – useful for couples or families traveling together – it's a good idea to buy at least one extra as a backup in case of loss or theft. You can call a 24-hour toll-free customer service number in the US (☎1-800/847-2911), or visit the Visa TravelMoney website (ⓦ usa.visa.com). The card is available in most countries from branches of Thomas Cook and Citicorp.

Wiring money

Having money wired from home is never convenient or cheap and should be considered a last resort. The quickest way to do this is to have someone take cash to the office of a money-wiring service and have it wired to the office nearest you: in the US, this process should take less than fifteen minutes. You take along ID and pick up the money in cash. Among reliable companies offering this service are **Moneygram International** (ⓦ www.moneygram.com) and, for rather higher fees, **Western Union** (ⓦ www.westernunion.com). If you have a few days' leeway, sending a postal money order through the mail is cheaper; postal orders are exchangeable at

Public holidays

The following are public holidays on which banks, post offices and many (although by no means all) shops and attractions will be closed:

Jan 1 **New Year's Day**
Third Mon in Jan **Martin Luther King, Jr.'s Birthday**
Third Mon in Feb **Presidents' Day**
Last Mon in May **Memorial Day**
July 4 **Independence Day**
First Mon in Sept **Labor Day**
Second Mon in Oct **Columbus Day**
Nov 11 **Veterans' Day**
Fourth Thurs in Nov **Thanksgiving**
Dec 25 **Christmas Day**

any post office. The equivalent for foreign travellers is the international money order but it may take up to seven days to arrive by mail. An ordinary cheque sent from overseas takes two to three weeks to clear.

Opening hours and public holidays

Office hours are generally 9am to 5pm. Stores open as early as 8am and can close as late as 11pm on weeknights; on weekends, stores may open an hour later and close an hour earlier, especially on Sundays. Most **museums** follow roughly the same hours, though a few have extended hours (5–9pm) one day during the week and one on the weekend. Public spaces – plazas, monuments, and such – are generally open 24 hours, but Chicago parks close around 11pm (or earlier, depending on the park) and reopen around 7am.

Phones

All telephone numbers within Chicago use either the ☎312 or 773 area code, which you need to dial if you are calling from within the city. If you are dialing a location outside Chicago, dial 1 before the area code and the seven-digit phone number. For detailed information about calls, area codes, and rates in the Chicago area, consult the front of the telephone directory in the *White Pages*.

In general, telephoning direct from your hotel room is considerably more expensive

than using a payphone, costing up to $1 for a local call, though some hotels offer free local calls. Don't even think of calling abroad direct from a hotel phone – you'll be charged a small fortune. Without doubt, the cheapest way of making **international calls** is to buy a pre-paid **phonecard** with a scratch-off PIN number, available from newsagents and some groceries. These come in denominations of $5 and $10 and can be used from any touchpad phone – hotels rarely charge for accessing the freephone number (but check), although using them from payphones invariably incurs an extra charge or around 50¢. Rates vary but calls to most developed countries only cost a few cents a minute. Another convenient but pricier way of phoning home from abroad is via a telephone **charge card** from your phone company back home. Using a PIN number, you can make calls from most hotel, public, and private phones that will be charged to your account: check with your service provider.

Another option is to drop into a cyber café, and take advantage of a simple computer program like Skype (⑩www.skype.com), which allows you to make calls to other users at no charge. Making calls through Skype to actual phone lines can also be done for a small fee.

Mobile phones

If you are planning to take a **mobile phone** (universally known as cell phones in America) from outside the USA, you'll need to check with your service provider whether it will work in the country. Unless you have a **tri-band** or **quad-band** phone, it is unlikely that a mobile bought for use outside the US will work there. If you do have such a phone, you'll have to contact your service provider's customer care department to ensure it is enabled for international calls. Be aware that you will incur hefty roaming charges for making calls and also be charged extra for incoming calls, as the people calling you will be paying the usual rate. If you want to retrieve messages while you're away, ask your provider for a new access code, as your home one is unlikely to work abroad. As the cost of using mobiles abroad is still fairly prohibitive, you may want to rent a phone if you're travelling to the US. For a comprehensive overview of the capabilities of various phones and a useful database of roaming charges, check out ⓦwww.mediacells.com.

Time

The city of Chicago is located in the Central Standard Time zone, which is six hours behind Greenwich Mean Time.

Tipping

Tipping is customary and expected at restaurants (usually not less than 15 percent) and bars ($1 for a round of drinks), though you needn't feel pressure to leave a large tip if service is especially poor.

Tourist information

For maps, tours and citywide information, you'll want to head for the **Chicago Office of Tourism**, which has two locations. The better and more central of these is on the first floor of the Chicago Cultural Center, 77 E Randolph St (Mon–Thurs 8am–7pm, Fri 8am–6pm, Sat 9am–6pm, Sun 10am–6pm; ☎1-877/244-2246, ⓦwww.cityofchicago.org/tourism). The second location is inside the Chicago Water Works building, 163 E Pearson St at Michigan Ave (same hours and contact details).

Before setting off for Chicago, you may want to contact one of the tourist organizations listed below for help in planning your itinerary.

Tourist offices

Chicago Convention and Tourism Bureau 2301 S Lake Shore Drive, Chicago, IL 60616 ☎1-877/244-2246; outside the US, Mexico, and Canada ☎312/567-8533-8847, ⓦwww.choosechicago.com
Illinois Bureau of Tourism 100 W Randolph St, Suite 3-4000, Chicago, IL 60601 ☎312/814-732 or 1-800/226-6632, ⓦwww.enjoyillinois.com

Travellers with disabilities

Chicago is trying to be one of the better disabled-friendly cities in the US, but it still has a long way to go. Modernization issues plague many of Chicago's older buildings; however, ramps and other forms of access are being added to museums, sites, and sports facilities, and the city's public transportation system has facilities such as station elevators and buses equipped with lifts and ramps. Check with the CTA (☎1-888/968-7282) to find out which stops are wheelchair-accessible; maps showing these stations are online at ⓦwww.transitchicago.com. For wheelchair-accessible taxis, call ☎1-800/281-4466.

For general information on accessibility, contact the Mayor's Office for People with Disabilities (☎312/744-6673), the Department of Disabilities (☎312/744-2400) or the Department of Tourism (☎1-877/244-2246 or ☎312/201-8847, TTY number for the hearing impaired is ☎1-866/710-0294). Additionally, the Easy Access Chicago organization has an excellent resource with additional information

Useful telephone numbers

For **international calls to Chicago**, dial your country's international access code + 1 for the US + 312 or 773 for Chicago.
Emergencies ☎911 for fire, police or ambulance
Directory assistance ☎411 (for numbers in Chicago); ☎1 + (area code) + 555-1212 (for numbers in other area codes)
Operator ☎0

International calls from Chicago
Australia ☎011 + 61 + phone number
Canada ☎011 + 1 + phone number
New Zealand ☎011 + 64 + phone number
Republic of Ireland ☎011 + 353 + phone number
South Africa ☎011 + 27 + phone number
UK ☎011 + 44 + phone number

for persons with disabilities visiting Chicago; ⓦ www.easyaccesschicago.org.

Websites

The following is a selective list of Chicago-related websites to help get you started.

Chicago Public Library ⓦ www.chipublib.org. A handy resource whose encyclopedic "Learn Chicago" section covers just about everything you want to know, from vital city statistics and symbols to major and minor disasters.

Chicago Reader ⓦ www.chicagoreader.com. The city's free and voluminous entertainment weekly newspaper has an excellent website with day-by-day details of what's on when and where: music, galleries, restaurants, bars, clubs, theatre and readings, as well as reviews and features.

Chicago Tribune ⓦ www.chicagotribune.com. Homepage of the city's morning newspaper, covering local news, sports and weather updates, plus arts, entertainment, restaurant and bar listings in its extensive Metromix search engine (ⓦ www.metromix.com).

City of Chicago ⓦ www.egov.cityofchicago .org. The city's official homepage, with links to major attractions, accommodations, and tours, with an events calendar and more in its "About Town" section. There is also an excellent guide to the city's historical landmarks.

Illinois Hotel and Lodging Association ⓦ www .stayillinois.com. The Association's comprehensive website has detailed summaries of and links to most hotels in Chicago and throughout Illinois.

League of Chicago Theaters ⓦ www .chicagoplays.com. Provides details on venues, showtimes and ticket prices for plays being performed in Chicago. Includes a link to a list of half-price theatre shows (under "Hot Tix").

Mayor's Office of Special Events ⓦ www.ci.chi .il.us/SpecialEvents. The best source for information on festivals, parades, holidays and sporting events, as well as any films that are currently being shot in Chicago. Updated regularly.

National Weather Service ⓦ weather.noaa .gov/weather/IL_cc_us. The organization's Illinois page provides up-to-the-minute reports on weather conditions on the roads and at O'Hare, Midway and regional airports.

Sports Illinois ⓦ www.sportsillinois.com. Part of the Illinois Bureau of Tourism's extensive site, covering every conceivable sport and where to participate, throughout the state.

The City

The City

The Loop

A s the city's central business district, **the Loop** is Chicago at its most iconic: a forest of steel, glass and masonry skyscrapers packed tightly together and encircled by an elevated train – **"the El"** – that rattles perilously along rusted trestles on Lake Street, South Wabash Avenue, Van Buren Street and Wells Street. Many people think the El forms the boundaries of the Loop but for practical purposes the district extends from the south branch of the Chicago River all the way east to Lake Michigan and from the central branch of the river all the way south to Congress Parkway. Walking around here at night, after the office workers have cleared out, you can see why director Christopher Nolan chose it to double as **Gotham City** in the Batman movie, *The Dark Knight* – it's rife with homely, neon-fronted diners that evoke the comic-book era, while at the same time its high-rises are built on a scale that suggest unimaginable, vaguely sinister power.

That said, if you can only visit the area once, you should visit on a weekday, when you can appreciate the district's street life and, even better, its formidable **architecture**, ideally on a walking tour or river cruise with the excellent Chicago Architecture Foundation (see p.44). The Loop was, after all, the **birthplace of the skyscraper** in 1885, and since then has become home to one of the finest collections of commercial buildings in the country, ranging in style from the vernacular Chicago School straight through to Postmodernism. From the the relatively diminutive **Rookery** on LaSalle Street, via the **Carson Pirie Scott** and **Reliance** buildings on State Street, to Wacker Drive's gigantic **Sears Tower** – which stands head and shoulders above the rest in height though it is not everybody's favourite building – the variety of Chicago's architecture never fails to impress. If you can't make a tour, be sure to drop by the free **Chicago Cultural Center** for a glimpse of one of the city's finest interiors, as well as some excellent exhibits. In a canny bit of urban planning, the city has also had a policy since the 1960s of setting aside a percentage of all public construction funds to buy **public art**, so in plazas throughout the Loop and elsewhere you'll come across startling works by Picasso, Calder, Miró, Dubuffet, Nevelson and Chagall, among others.

As big as these names are, however, not one of their sculptures rivals the current popularity of *Cloud Gate*, by the British artist Anish Kapoor. Nicknamed **"the Bean"** for its kidney bean shape, this extraordinary 110-ton mirrored stainless-steel structure was unveiled at **Millennium Park**'s opening in 2004 and has since become the most celebrated work of art in the city, with snap-happy visitors mobbing it at all hours to play in its fun-house reflections. Likewise, the park itself – created from a formerly bleak section of Grant Park, just north of the renowned **Art Institute of Chicago** – is now Chicago's most dynamic public space, with Jaume Plensa's mesmerizing Crown Fountain doubling as a splash pool for rambunctious tots and concerts taking place nearly ever summer evening at Frank Gehry's spiffy **Jay Pritzker Pavilion**.

Millennium Park's success has spilled over to the Loop proper, with a rash of new condominium towers, restaurants and hotels in the blocks just west of **Michigan Avenue** (the avenue itself is protected by law from intrusive development), making it for the first time worthy of your consideration as a **place to stay**. Even if you bunk elsewhere, the Loop demands at least one full day to appreciate, and at least two if you intend to fully explore the enormous Art Institute.

Some history

The oldest non-native settlement in the Loop – and the second oldest in the city – was **Fort Dearborn**, built in 1803 by the US Army on the south bank of the Chicago River, near what is now Michigan Avenue. Despite the government's intention to use it to retain control of the area in the wake of the War of Independence, the British won over the local Potawatomie Indians and during the War of 1812 members of the tribe killed several dozen Americans as they were evacuating the fort and burnt down the fort itself three days later. A second fort was built in 1816 and was garrisoned intermittently according to the state of affairs with the Indians. In 1857, a fire destroyed virtually all that remained of it.

Meanwhile, the tiny settlement of Chicago took root in the area just south of the fort, in the northern portion of the Loop, and, with just 350 residents, formally declared itself a city under Illinois state law in 1833. By then, the Great Lakes had already been linked to New York Harbor for eight years by the Erie Canal, and the race was on between Midwestern cities to determine which one would be the preeminent port of call in the heartland. The prize went to Chicago, whose leading lights presciently sponsored the digging of the **Illinois and Michigan Canal** in 1848, which created a continuous waterway between New York and New Orleans via the Mississippi River. With most ships now stopping in Chicago, it was a natural next step that all the major railroads would also use the city as a hub. With the influx of cross-country trains – specifically the invention of the refrigerated railcar – came the **meatpacking industry**, which turned the Loop into a spectacularly filthy and smelly place for most of the nineteenth century, albeit a thriving one.

By 1870 about 300,000 people called themselves Chicagoans, and such was the momentum of the city's growth that even the **Great Chicago Fire of 1871** – which reduced 18,000 buildings to rubble, including almost all of the Loop, and left 90,000 souls homeless – proved barely a hiccough in the rush of progress. With the rabble of wooden buildings wiped away by the blaze, men like **Louis Sullivan**, who arrived from Boston in 1873, along with locals such as **William LeBaron Jenney** and **Daniel Burnham**, were able to stretch their considerable design and engineering skills to fill the void and, in

In the Loop

Though it's a widely held belief that the Loop was named after the elevated train lines encircling the district, the moniker actually preceded the arrival of the El by fifteen years. In the 1860s, a cable-car line was set up to shuttle residents of the newly created suburbs on Chicago's South Side to and from downtown stores like Field, Palmer & Leiter (which later became Marshall Field's and is now Macy's). The consensus is that **the Loop name** came from the circular turnaround where the cable car would reverse direction for the return journey.

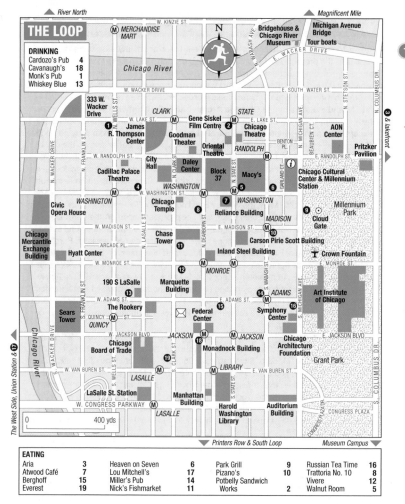

▲ River North   ▲ Magnificent Mile

THE LOOP

DRINKING

Cardozo's Pub	4
Cavanaugh's	18
Monk's Pub	1
Whiskey Blue	13

1

THE LOOP

❸ & lakefront

The West Side, Union Station & ❶⑦

EATING							
Aria	3	Heaven on Seven	6	Park Grill	9	Russian Tea Time	16
Atwood Café	7	Lou Mitchell's	17	Pizano's	10	Trattoria No. 10	8
Berghoff	15	Miller's Pub	14	Potbelly Sandwich		Vivere	12
Everest	19	Nick's Fishmarket	11	Works	2	Walnut Room	5

the process, usher in the modern architectural age with the world's first skyscrapers. By a stroke of luck, the pioneering German architect **Ludwig Mies van der Rohe**, director of the Bauhaus in the early 1930s, moved to Chicago in 1939 to teach. He stayed on for thirty years until his death, leaving an indelible mark on the city with his austere International-style designs, including the Federal Center complex in the heart of the Loop. In the years since, other great architects, from Skidmore, Owings and Merrill, Helmut Jahn and Philip Johnson in the 1970s and 1980s to Renzo Piano and Frank Gehry in the 2000s, have helped shape the Loop into one of the most enticing urban architectural landscapes in the world. (See *Chicago Architecture* colour section for more details.)

Unlike many US city centres, the Loop remained relatively robust as a place to do business throughout the 1960s to the 1980s, even as **State Street**, once

Architectural tours of the Loop

Taken together, the buildings of the Loop tell the story of the skyscraper from its origins to the present day, but it can be tricky to stitch together the tale on your own: some significant structures don't look very special, others are known for just one small detail, and while they're all within walking distance of one another, the buildings are by no means situated in chronological order. That's where a tour guide comes in handy, and the tours by the **Chicago Architectural Foundation** (CAF) are by far the best in town. There are 85 to choose from, but if you must pick only one, opt for the exceptional ninety-minute **architectural river cruise**. Offered from May through November, with between three and thirteen outings per day, depending on the day of the week and the season, the cruise brings you up the north branch of the river, around the perimeter of the Loop on the south branch and then almost to the lake and back on the main stem. A knowledgeable docent offers nonstop commentary on all the buildings you see along the way, including the Sears Tower, 333 W Wacker Drive, the Merchandise Mart, the Wrigley Building, Tribune Tower, Marina City and the Chicago Spire. Not all structures are in the Loop proper (those on the north side of the river are in Near North), but you'll get a good overview of the architectural scene, along with some terrific views. Advance reservations are strongly advised. Purchase tickets at Chicago's First Lady Ticket Window at the base of the stairs at the southeast corner of the Michigan Avenue Bridge at Wacker Drive (where all cruises depart); at the CAF ArchiCenter Shop, 224 S Michigan Ave; at any HotTix/Ticketmaster box office location; or by phone or internet, though be advised that a service fee is charged on any order not made in person (Sat, Sun & holidays $30 per person, Mon–Fri $28 per person; ⊤312/902-1500, ⊛www.ticketmaster.com/rivercruise or ⊛www.architecture.org).

For a little more depth on the evolution of Chicago's high-rises, consider taking one of the CAF's brisk, informative **walking tours** of the Loop: "Historic Skyscrapers (1885–1935)" and "Modern Skyscrapers (1950–present)" are both first-rate, with tour guides bringing you from CAF's ArchiCenter, 224 S Michigan Ave, to and (when possible) through the city's most significant buildings (2hr each; 1–3 tours per day depending on the day of the week and the season; $15; discounts are available for seniors and students; ticket-purchasing information same as above). Many other thematic tours, as well as bus tours, are available. For more information, visit ⊛www.architecture.org.

---

the city's main shopping thoroughfare, lost its edge to upper Michigan Avenue – "the Magnificent Mile" – in Near North (see p.76). The district is now poised, however, to become the city's **next great neighbourhood**, largely thanks to Millennium Park's success and Mayor Richard M. Daley's vision of turning the Loop into a 24-hour district like Times Square in Manhattan. An estimated 200,000 revellers turned out for the first two all-night Looptopia festivals in May 2007 and 2008 to give the concept a spin, though whether this energy can be sustained throughout the year has yet to be seen.

Along Michigan Avenue

Although the stretch of Michigan Avenue north of the river is the part that's known as "the Magnificent Mile" (see p.76), the section south of the river, here in the Loop, is hardly shabby. In fact, exploring this mile-long corridor – flanked by two of the city's most important cultural institutions, several historic buildings, and the city's best park – could easily take up a day or more of your time. It leads straight into the **South Loop** (see p.64), where the Museum Campus will consume another day.

Prior to the 1871 fire, the west side of the street was lined with posh industrialists' mansions and the east side bordered the lake. Afterwards, high society decamped for **Near North** (see p.76), and much of the debris from the blaze was dumped into the harbor, with the city adding to the heap over subsequent decades to create Grant Park. The Neoclassical **Art Institute** was the only structure allowed in the park and it remains Chicago's one unmissable sight, presenting a monumental collection of nineteenth-century European art and an iconic body of twentieth-century American art. Carved out of Grant Park just north of the Art Institute in 2004 is **Millennium Park** (the rest of Grant Park is discussed in Chapter 2, "South Loop and Near South"); across from the park, the **Chicago Cultural Center** houses art exhibits, a staffed tourist information centre and the world's largest Tiffany-glass dome. Musical inspiration comes in the form of **Symphony Center**, headquarters of the revered Chicago Symphony Orchestra, and the **Auditorium Building**, built by Dankmar Adler and Louis Sullivan in 1889, which now hosts the Joffrey Ballet and big-name concerts. Finally, at the south end of this stretch, the **Santa Fe building**, designed by Daniel Burnham in 1904, is home to the **Chicago Architecture Foundation** (see box, p.44), whose tours of the city are without peer.

McCormick Tribune Bridgehouse and Chicago River Museum

The seasonal **McCormick Tribune Bridgehouse and Chicago River Museum** (May–Oct Thurs–Mon 10am–5pm; $3, children under 5 free; ☏312/977-0227, ⊛www.bridgehousemuseum.org), located in the southwestern bridge tower of the Michigan Avenue Bridge, at Wacker Drive, is as interesting for its architecture as for its exhibits on the death and rebirth of the Chicago River. While the structure looks no bigger than a family crypt at street level, it in fact measures five stories. The outside is covered with ornate bas-reliefs depicting the massacre at **Fort Dearborn**, which once stood on the site. Within, a basement-level gear room filled with the cogs, wheels and counterweights that raise the bridge about one hundred times a year between April and November (Wed and Sat mornings) to make way for sailboats and other tall vessels travelling between the river and Lake Michigan.

The four upper floors contain photographs and text panels describing how the river was despoiled, then later brought back to life. Used as a **municipal toilet and garbage dump** throughout the nineteenth century, the Chicago River was, not surprisingly, the source of a cholera epidemic that killed one in ten residents in the 1880s. Subsequent feats of engineering not only reversed its flow – a controversial move that sent the waste downstream to St. Louis – but led to its eventual cleanup. Though it's still famously dyed green every St. Patrick's Day, the waterway now manages to support seventy species of fish, up from just ten in the 1970s. The upper-story porthole windows offer beautiful views of the river and surrounding buildings.

Chicago Cultural Center

Among the finest of Michigan Avenue's buildings is the **Chicago Cultural Center**, 78 E Washington Blvd, at Michigan Avenue (Mon–Thurs 8am–7pm, Fri 8am–6pm, Sat 9am–6pm, Sun 10am–6pm; free; ☏312/744-6630 or/346-3278,

Ⓦ www.chicagoculturalcenter.org). An 1897 Beaux-Arts-style palace intended as the original Chicago Public Library and a Civil War monument, it now houses several **art galleries**, glorious interior spaces and the Loop's main **visitor information center** (see p.37), with a play area for kids, counters for various tour agencies, rack upon rack of brochures and local publications, as well as helpful staff, including a thoughtful restaurant adviser.

Based on classical Greek and Italian Renaissance models, the Washington Street lobby drips with Carrara marble and glimmers with mosaics of rare Favrile glass. In the Preston Bradley Hall on the third floor – site of many **free concerts** (visit the Center's website for calendar) – you'll see intricate mosaic scrolls and rosettes spanning the arches under a stunning, 38-foot-wide **Tiffany dome** containing some 30,000 pieces of glass within an ornate iron frame. The biggest dome of its kind in the world, it underwent a major cleaning and restoration in 2008, to dazzling effect.

The largest of the Center's galleries are the **Exhibit Hall** and **Sidney Gates Gallery** on the fourth floor and the **Michigan Avenue Galleries**, both containing museum-quality contemporary work. Other art and history installations are tucked here and there throughout the centre; ask for a map at the Randolph Street information desk for locations. Free tours of the building take place on Wednesday, Friday and Saturday at 1.15pm, beginning in the Randolph Street lobby. No reservations are necessary.

Millennium Park

The lakefront area between Michigan Avenue and Columbus Drive from Randolph south to Monroe Street forms 24.5-acre **Millennium Park** (daily 6am–11pm; free; Ⓣ 312/742-1168; Ⓦ www.millenniumpark.org), the city's most dazzling public space. Officially opened in July 2004 – four years late and $250 million overbudget – it's an arresting display of contemporary architecture and design, lauded by *New York Times* architecture critic Paul Goldberger as "one of the great new models for a kind of urban park". Embraced by locals and visitors alike, it's widely regarded as Chicago's most impressive public-works project since the 1893 World's Columbian Exposition (often known as the World's Fair).

As the storey goes, the park was conceived by the mayor himself, **Richard M. Daley**, as he sat in his dentist's chair across the street and looked out on the sprawl of parking lots and railyards that occupied the site until the late 1990s. The original plan, by the internationally renowned firm Skidmore, Owings and Merrill – which is based in Chicago – was in accord with the rest of Grant Park, with formal fountains and gardens, but the private donors who had already pledged to supplement public funds for the park's construction rejected the design as too conservative. Chicago philanthropist **Cindy Pritzker**, wife of the late Jay Pritzker, founder of the Hyatt hotel chain and architecture's renowned Pritzker Prize, eventually convinced Frank Gehry (a former Pritzker Prize winner) to build the centerpiece pavilion for the park, as well as a bridge leading over Columbus Avenue to the lake. With Gehry on board, other top-shelf talent signed on, eventually creating an impressively diverse but coherent whole.

Welcome Center, Harris Theater for Music and Dance and McDonald's Cycle Center

If you plan to explore the park in depth, start out at the park's **visitor center**, located in the solar-powered Northeast Exelon Pavilion, 201 E Randoph St (late May to mid-Oct daily 9am–7pm, rest of the year daily 10am–4pm; same

▲ Millennium Park

contact details as park), which has maps, daily schedules of events, and staff to help you plan your time here. Free 45-minute guided walking tours of the park are offered daily in high season (late May to mid-Oct) at 11.30am and 1pm, starting at the centre. You can also download an MP3 audio tour and map of the park from the website Ⓦwww.millenniumpark.org, or grab a map at the Chicago Cultural Center.

Next door to the Welcome Center stands the **Harris Theater for Music and Dance** (Ⓣ312/334-7777, Ⓦwww.harristheaterchicago.org), looking much smaller than it actually is. Because of long-standing limitations on the size of buildings permitted on public land, all you see above ground, in the glass rectangle, is the lobby; the 1500-seat theater lies underground, 30ft below the water table in an architectural steel bathtub to prevent leaks. Programming ranges from folk and classical music to ballet and contemporary dance.

It's well worth considering biking as the best way to see the beaches, parks and museums along the lake, a little to the east, with terrific views of the looming skyline. **McDonald's Cycle Center**, 239 E. Randolph St, provides bike rentals and tours to visitors, sparing you a visit to other rental outlets at hyper-touristy Navy Pier should you decide to bike the lakefront.

Jay Pritzker Pavilion, BP Bridge, and Lurie Garden

The **Jay Pritzker Pavilion**, an open-air concert hall, is the park's anchor. It's trademark Frank Gehry: twelve billowing ribbons of steel-plated aluminum form the stage's whimsical, 120-foot-high "headdress", while a mammoth trellis of steel pipes soars over the 4000-seat amphitheater and 7000-capacity Great Lawn, supporting a state-of-the-art sound system. There are free concerts here throughout summer and early fall, from the classical Grant Park Music Festival (Ⓦwww.grantparkmusicfestival.com), featuring the resident Grant

Park Orchestra, to world music, blues and jazz. Gehry also designed the snaking, stainless-steel **BP Bridge**, which connects Millennium Park to Daley Bicentennial Plaza on the east side of Columbus Drive. The only Gehry-designed bridge in the world, the 960-foot-long structure was reputedly inspired by the live carp the architect's Jewish grandmother used to buy at the fishmarket in Toronto.

Just south of the Great Lawn, the 2.5-acre **Lurie Garden** represents a radical departure from both formal garden design and the free-flowing landscape architecture promoted by Frederick Law Olmstead in the late nineteenth century. It instead relies on 130 species of native plants to create a richly textured, serene prairie in the heart of the city. The centrepiece of the collaboration between Kathryn Gustafson of Seattle, Piet Oudolf of the Netherlands, and Robert Israel of Los Angeles is a 15-foot-high, dramatically lit "shoulder hedge" – a nod to Carl Sandburg's characterization of Chicago as the "stormy, husky, brawling, City of the Big Shoulders". Guided tours of the garden are offered on Sundays from mid-May through September, leaving from the BP Bridge every fifteen minutes between 10am and 1pm.

Cloud Gate, Millennium Monument and Crown Fountain

Anish Kapoor's first public installation in the US, *Cloud Gate* was dubbed **"the Bean"** by Chicagoans who couldn't wait for the sculptor's own title, and the name stuck. The work was forged from 168 quarter-inch-thick steel plates, initially attached to a steel frame but now largely disconnected to allow the sculpture to expand and contract with Chicago's widely varying temperatures. Though today you can't see the seams between the plates, you could at the park's inauguration in 2004, when it was unveiled incomplete; not until the next year did workers painstakingly polish the Bean to appear as a seamless whole. In the words of Kapoor, the sculpture represents "a gate to the city, a poetic idea about the city it reflects". Indeed, walking around it you get reflections of all sorts: the Michigan Avenue skyline, the park and, if you stroll underneath it, yourself, in a fantastically warped, fun-house swirl.

At the base of the Bean is **McCormick Tribune Plaza**, which doubles as a 16,000-square-foot **ice rink** from November to March (daily 10am–10pm, weather permitting; free; rental skates available for $9; ☎312/742-5222) and an **open-air bar/restaurant/café** in summer. North of the plaza is Millennium Park's most old-fashioned work, **Millennium Monument**, an 80 percent replica of the classical peristyle that stood here between 1917 and 1953, when it was ripped down to make way for a parking lot. Etched in its base are the names of all the individuals, foundations and companies that coughed up nearly $300 million for the park's construction. South of the plaza, two 50-foot-tall glass towers facing one another across a granite plaza form **Crown Fountain**, the work of renowned Spanish architect Jaume Plensa. Underneath the glass blocks on the surface are LED screens showing a rotating array of 1000 Chicagoans' faces in close-up. Drawn from communities throughout the city, the subjects were told to pretend they were blowing on a feather and filmed. Now, when their digital likenesses pucker their lips, water spurts from their mouths to the glee of frolicking children.

The Art Institute of Chicago

One of the top museums in the world, the **Art Institute of Chicago**, 111 S Michigan Ave (summer Mon–Wed 10.30am–5pm, Thurs & Fri 10.30am–9pm, Sat & Sun 10am–5pm; rest of the year Mon–Wed & Fri 10.30am–5pm, Thurs

10.30am–8pm, Sat & Sun 10am–5pm; $12; seniors, students & children over 12 $7; under-12s free; free after 5pm and for the month of Feb; ☎312/443-3600, ⓦwww.artinstituteofchicago.org), is one of Chicago's must-see sights, with renowned collections of Impressionist and Postimpressionist paintings, bolstered by an ambitious body of modern and contemporary work that's shown in the **new Modern Wing** by Italian architect Renzo Piano. The Medieval and Renaissance painting collections are also excellent and a new layout shows them to best advantage with contemporaneous decorative arts. The African, Native American and Asian art galleries are undergoing a makeover as well, with a projected completion date of 2010. The institute is located in Grant Park just south of Millennium Park on Michigan Avenue, with the old entrance, flanked by lions, on Michigan at Adams Street and the new one on Monroe Street between Michigan and Columbus.

Some history

After the original home of the Art Institute was razed in the Great Chicago Fire of 1871 – it had stood on the southwest corner of State and Monroe streets – its founders looked to rebuild on a larger scale. The ideal spot, they decided, was not in the Loop itself but on the detritus that had been dumped in the harbour on the east side of Michigan Avenue after the blaze. Though this new land had already been set aside as a public park, civic leaders agreed to let the Art Institute build its new headquarters there if the city could use the facility during the world's fair. Completed in 1893, the Beaux-Arts design, by the Boston firm Shepley, Rutan and Coolidge, hewed to the "White City" aesthetic of the **World's Columbian Exposition** (see p.258) that enchanted some 25 million visitors to the South Side of Chicago that same year.

Still today the original Art Institute building oozes turn-of-the-twentieth-century opulence, noticeable in its Corinthian columns, limestone facade and soaring archways. The first major additions came in the 1920s, when the museum decided to expand eastward toward the lake, spanning the Illinois Central railroad tracks with a long, thin gallery (Gunsaulus Hall) and then constructing a new complex of buildings on the other side. Two other bursts of construction – in the 1960s and the 1980s – added still more rooms, enabling the museum to show more of its growing collection even as visitors got more and more disoriented in the endless tangle of hallways, sculpture courts and galleries.

Recently, the Art Institute has taken huge steps to remedy the situation, commissioning architect Renzo Piano to build an enormous new Modern Wing to house its vast modern and contemporary art collections. Slated to open in May 2009, the three-storey wing, made of limestone, steel and glass with a moveable aluminum "flying carpet" roof that filters sunlight into the galleries, faces Monroe Street and is linked to Millennium Park via the Nichols Bridgeway, an elevated footbridge. In mid-2010 the museum will also complete the largest renovation and reinstallation project in the Art Institute's history, updating galleries throughout the complex. While this will entail more than the usual closures over the next year – be sure to grab an up-to-date **free map** and ask about closures at the ticket desk – the result should be a much more unified and contemporary feel to the whole place. Among the changes: 35 percent more gallery space for non-Western art and a new design centre for American and European decorative arts, along with a reconfiguration of the painting galleries to include contemporaneous decorative arts, updated textiles galleries and a new children's gallery.

School of the Art Institute of Chicago

The Art Institute of Chicago started life as the **Chicago Academy of Design**, a small art school founded in 1866 by a group of artists who wanted to provide top-notch education in studio arts and showcase student works. After outgrowing several rented facilities and losing its first permanent home to the 1871 Chicago Fire, the school changed its name to The Art Institute and eventually settled into its current location at 37 S Wabash Ave, in a modern building adjacent to the magnificent Beaux-Arts pile that houses the school's now formidable art holdings.

Today, the School of the Art Institute of the Chicago is one of the largest independent schools of art and design in the US, and one of the best (it was ranked third for its fine-arts graduate school by US News and World Report in 2008). Alumni include Georgia O' Keeffe and Walt Disney (although both failed to graduate), Playboy founder Hugh Hefner (who studied anatomy), sculptors Claes Oldenburg and Jeff Koons, painter Joan Mitchell, writers Sarah Vowell and David Sedaris, plus political satirist Herblock. Student work is frequently on display in the school's galleries.

Impressionism and Postimpressionism

The Art Institute has works recording more than 5000 years of human expression but is most famous for its collection of **Impressionist** and **Postimpressionist** paintings, exhibited on the second floor of the main building. Many of these works were donated by **Bertha Honoré Palmer** (see p.101), who was passionate about collecting art – she purchased 25 Monet paintings in 1891 – and reinventing Chicago, hitherto regarded as a cultural backwater. In 1893, she organized a seminal exhibition of Modern European paintings at the World's Columbian Exposition. Among the highlights of the collection are **Gustave Caillebotte**'s striking masterpiece, *Paris Street, Rainy Day* (1887), which plays with focus and perspective using his careful mathematical techniques, and **Renoir**'s *Acrobats at Circus Fernando* (1879), Bertha Palmer's favourite painting, which she carried with her everywhere, even on trips abroad. You'll also see what is considered the first truly Impressionist landscape, an early **Monet** from 1868, *On the Bank of the Seine, Bennecourt*, which has a free, bold energy that his calculated later pictures can lack.

The feeling of motion is conveyed in **Degas'** *Millinery Shop* (1884/90), a painting cropped in such a way as to give the viewer the perspective of a passerby looking into a shop window. The artist's passion for the human body in motion is apparent in his meticulously composed sculptures *Retiring* (1883), *Young Spartans* (1860) and *Spanish Dance* (1883). The museum's most famous painting is **Georges Seurat**'s *La Grande Jatte* (1884). It took 28-year-old Seurat two years to paint this Pointillist masterpiece, and that perfectionist instinct is evident even in the white frame, which he specially designed.

Shortly after Seurat exhibited *La Grande Jatte*, **van Gogh** arrived in Paris from Holland. In his painting *The Bedroom*, van Gogh employed Seurat's Pointillist "dot" technique to create an energetic surface, which in van Gogh's own words demonstrated a "Seurat-like simplicity". Also look for **Henri de Toulouse-Lautrec**'s famed *At the Moulin Rouge* (1892/95) and its lurid greenish-yellow face of May Milton. Monet resurfaces in this later period with his seemingly psychedelic London paintings of Waterloo Bridge in which the smog and grime of nineteenth-century London appear to dissipate all traces of urban life, transforming the image into a timeless poetic vision. The fifteen canvasses which form the calmer *Grain Stacks* series (1891) demonstrate Monet's fascination with temporality as he explores the emotional and visual consequences of capturing the light and atmosphere at different times of the day, month and year.

American modern art: 1900–50

Also on the second floor is the museum's lauded collection of **American modern art**. The most famous of these may well be **Edward Hopper**'s *Nighthawks* (1942). While the composition – three people lost in thought in an all-night diner in New York – suggests a narrative, Hopper's stated intent was to present a fleeting moment in time, "unconsciously, probably I was painting the loneliness of a large city".

Another show-stopper is **Grant Wood**'s *American Gothic* (1930), in which Wood's sister and dentist posed with a pitchfork to create one of the most reproduced (and parodied) images in American art. It's one of the best examples of Regionalism, a movement that rejected avant-garde European art in favour of simple rural themes.

The pioneering Modernist **Georgia O'Keeffe** is also well-represented. Look out for her ominous *Black Cross, New Mexico* (1929). On a visit to New Mexico, O'Keeffe recalled the great frequency with which she encountered mystifying crosses, which represented to her the "dark veil" of Catholicism. She worked right up to her death, aged 98, in New Mexico, where she had lived since 1949.

European modern art: 1900–50

The museum's excellent collection of **European modern art** is now displayed on the top floor of the Modern Wing. Among the works to look for are **Marc Chagall**'s *Praying Jew* (1923), in which the holy figure is a nomadic beggar posing in the black-and-white prayer shawl that belonged to Chagall's father.

One of the best-known pictures from **Picasso**'s Blue Period is his melancholy *The Old Guitarist* (1903), whose contorted features are representative of the growing artistic trend of the early twentieth century to convey the subject's mental state through his physical being. **Paul Gauguin**'s colourful evocations of the local scenery in Tahiti reveal the artist's emphasis of the intuitive over the intellectual, the primitive over the refined. **Henri Matisse**'s first original sculpture, *The Serf* (1900–03), is also on display.

Among the later works of this period to keep an eye out for are **Dalí**'s *Visions of Eternity* (1936) and **Magritte**'s *Time Transfixed* (1938), which fulfils the characteristic Surrealist device of placing commonplace objects in unusual contexts. According to the artist, this image of a locomotive juxtaposed with a living-room fireplace was intended to stir in the viewer a meditation on the mysteries of thought.

Contemporary art

Reflecting the increasing globalization of the art world following World War II, the **Contemporary art** displays show European and American work side by side on the second floor of the new Modern Wing. Highlights include the **David Hockney** canvas *American Collectors* (1968), all pinched profiles and pink kaftans bathed in dazzling California light, and the monumental fifteen-foot high *Mao* (1973) by **Andy Warhol**. The most influential and renowned of the Pop artists, Warhol used irony with aplomb to examine the impact of consumerism and the cult of personality – themes which have particular resonance in today's celebrity-obsessed society.

Roy Lichtenstein's *Brushstroke with Splatter* (1968) is one of a series in which the artist moves from comic-book-style parodies of popular culture to irreverent send-ups of fine art; the supposed spontaneity and intuitive nature of Abstract Expressionism is undermined by Lichtenstein's deliberate and precise evocation of the style's basic elements – the brushstroke and its splatter.

Other collections

While the vast majority of visitors will probably confine their visit to the museum's most famous collections, listed above, there are plenty of other things to see here. Fine works predating the Impressionists abound in the section of the museum devoted to **European paintings before 1900**, including **Tintoretto**'s *Tarquin and Lucretia* (1580–90), a terrific example of Mannerism's obsession with distortion and *contrapposto* (the twisting of a figure on its own vertical axis), and Spanish master **El Greco**'s *Assumption of the Virgin* (1577), which exemplifies the artist's religious preoccupations while showcasing his unique, distended style. **Rembrandt van Rijn**'s *Old Man with Gold Chain* (c.1631) contrasts the craggy subject's furrowed face with his gleaming jewels, and the four paintings in **Giambattistta Tiepolo**'s sensual *Torquato Tasso* series (1740) are a paradigm of his dream-like technique, where it often seems like he's painting with pastel-hued ice cream.

The museum's **photography** collection is renowned as well and includes 15,000 works by pioneering photographer **Alfred Stieglitz**. At least a few of these pictures are often included in the rotating themed exhibits that the museum mounts in the Modern Wing.

In December 2008 the Alsdorf Galleries of Indian, Southeast Asian, Himalayan and Islamic Art completed the extension of the **Asian art** galleries. This new space – previously a windowless walkway filled with European arms and armour – was renovated by Renzo Piano to include three large windows cut out of the limestone walls, facing north to Millennium Park, as well as higher ceilings and wood floors. Here the museum presents, in chronological order, five millennia of Asian art, including works from Japan, Korea, China, the Himalayas, India, Southeast Asia and the Near and Middle East.

And while their new arrangement was still to be determined as this book went to press, the galleries for **African Art and Indian Art of the Americas** will devote over 35 percent more room to these works than the old layout did. The African collection focuses on masks, sculpture, beadwork, furniture, regalia and textiles of sub-Saharan Africa, while the Indian collection is particularly known for its Mesoamerican and Andean ceramics, sculpture, textiles and metalwork.

Symphony Center and Santa Fe Center

Opposite the Art Institute, the 2600-seat **Orchestra Hall**, 220 S Michigan Ave, forms the core of **Symphony Center**, home of the renowned **Chicago Symphony Orchestra**. Designed by Daniel Burnham in 1904, the Georgian-style brick-and-stone facade bears the names of great composers, while the hall itself is a magnificent space that makes going to hear the symphony, which will be led by the charismatic Italian conductor Riccardo Muti beginning in 2010, all that much more rewarding. See p.197 for ticketing information.

Next door, the **Santa Fe Center**, 224 S Michigan Ave, has a rich architectural history. It, too, was designed by Daniel Burnham in 1904; Burnham later conceived his 1909 city plan in a top-floor office here. The **Chicago Architecture Foundation (CAF)** has since set up shop in the building, which also holds the headquarters of Skidmore, Owings and Merrill, Chicago's largest

The men who built Chicago

Remarkably, many of the breathtaking buildings in the Loop were the work of just a handful of gifted architects. While **Frank Lloyd Wright** (1867–1959) and **Ludwig Mies van der Rohe** (1886–1969) are the most famous and influential among the Chicago architects, several other architectural luminaries designed major works in the Loop.

Known as the "father of the skyscraper", **William Le Baron Jenney** (1832–1907) came to Chicago from Massachusetts in the 1860s to work on urban planning projects; after the Great Fire, though, he became heavily involved in the rebuilding of downtown. Jenney's 1885 **Home Insurance Building** – widely regarded as the world's first skyscraper because it used a metal skeleton to help support the exterior wall – no longer stands, unfortunately, but his 1891 **Manhattan Building**, 431 S Dearborn (see p.59) remains a good example of his strong, practical constructions.

The wildly creative, high-strung **Louis Sullivan** (1856–1924) spawned the revolutionary tenets that were the foundation of the Chicago School of architecture. Born in Boston, and trained at MIT and in Paris, Sullivan came to Chicago after the Great Fire to put into practice his maxim "form follows function", which soon had many adherents. Often working with brilliant engineer **Dankmar Adler** (1844–1900), Sullivan covered masterpieces like the **Carson Pirie Scott** building at 1 S State St (see p.55) with elaborate, nature-inspired ornamentation.

A forward-thinking architectural giant with an evangelical zeal for city planning, **Daniel H. Burnham** (1846–1912) designed and oversaw the wildly successful 1893 World's Columbian Exposition on Chicago's South Side and later formulated Chicago's master plan, which established the lakefront park system. His best construction in the Loop – designed with his partner John Wellborn Root – is the show-stopping **Rookery**, 209 S LaSalle St (see p.60), known for its gorgeous light court, in 1888. Burnham was also the mastermind behind the **Reliance Building**, 32 N State St (see p.55), finished in 1895: it's considered a forerunner of today's giddying skyscrapers due to the unprecedented use of glass in its facade, made possible by the advent of the internal steel frame pioneered by Jenney. Compare this structure to Burnham and Root's 1891 **Monadnock Building**, 53 W Jackson Blvd (see p.59), a rather dour construction with thick, load-bearing masonry walls, and you can clearly see how revolutionary the steel frame was to modern architecture.

William Holabird (1854–1923) and **Martin Roche** (1855–1927) met while working together in Jenney's offices. Together, they are credited with popularizing the "Chicago window" – a fixed central pane flanked by moveable sash windows. The pair are remembered for the **Marquette Building**, 140 S Dearborn St (see p.58); with its open facade and steel frame, it was the prototype for many modern office buildings. After the architects' deaths, the firm was taken over by Holabird's son John (1886–1945), who, together with John Wellborn Root's son, designed the one major Art Deco masterpiece downtown, the **Chicago Board of Trade**, at 141 W Jackson Blvd (see p.59).

Though both **Helmut Jahn** (1940–) and **Ludwig Mies van der Rohe** were German expatriates drawn to Chicago by the Illinois Institute of Technology (the former to study there, the latter to help found it), their work could not be more different. Whereas Mies' constructions, such as the **Federal Center complex**, 219 S Dearborn St (see p.59), were rather stark and sombre, Jahn's buildings, including his local masterpiece, the **James R. Thompson Center**, 100 W Randolph St (see p.60), convey a sense of energy and fun with curving reflective glass and colourful ornamentation. Both men's styles reverberated through the Chicago architectural community: Skidmore, Owings and Merrill's **Sears Tower**, 233 S Wacker Drive is a direct descendant of Mies' International style, while Frank Gehry's **Pritzker Pavilion** (see p.47) continues Jahn's legacy of making architecture that doubles as outlandish sculpture.

architecture firm, responsible for the John Hancock Center (1969), the Sears Tower (1974) and many famous buildings around the world. Step inside to see the CAF's **ArchiCenter** (Tues–Sun 9am–4.30pm), featuring rotating design exhibits in the skylit atrium and a scale model of the city in a separate gallery, as well as its fabulous gift shop (Mon–Sat 9am–6.30pm, Sun 9am–6pm), where most of the CAF's tours (see p.44) convene.

The Auditorium Building

The stately Chicago School **Auditorium Building**, 430 S Michigan Ave, is best known for its 4000-seat **Auditorium Theatre**, whose entrance is at 50 E Congress Parkway (℡ 312/922-2110, ⊛ www.auditoriumtheatre.org). The near-perfect acoustics and four massive, flamboyantly trimmed arches moved Modernist Frank Lloyd Wright to call it the "greatest room for music and opera in the world". The Auditorium Building itself was built by Louis Sullivan and Dankmar Adler in 1889 and included a hotel and office, but after less than a decade, the building had fallen into disrepair; at its lowest point it served as a recreation center for soldiers, who turned the stage into a makeshift bowling alley. Roosevelt University eventually bought the building in 1946, but it wasn't until the 1960s that the structure was fully restored and reopened. In 1989, the Auditorium Building celebrated its 100th birthday with the opening of *Les Misérables.* A comprehensive restoration project was initiated in 2001 with extensive paint analysis to bring back the original colour patterns, stencilling detail and a lovely mural that once graced the interior. In 2002, the theater's 113-year-old stage was removed and reconstructed in time to play host to the Bolshoi Ballet, which performed to sell-out crowds and received critical eulogy. Sullivan fans note: if you can't make a concert, then come for a tour (Mon 10am & noon; $8; reservations recommended; ℡ 312/431-2389).

Along State Street

Immortalized by Frank Sinatra as "That Great Street" in his musical tribute to the city, the iconic **State Street** is still one of the city's prime retail and entertainment corridors. Over the years State Street's fortunes have ebbed and flowed, from its apotheosis as a major shopping enclave at the turn of the twentieth century to a neo-urban wasteland in 1979 when Mayor Jane Byrne transformed the street into a pedestrian mall. In 1996, Mayor Daley set about breathing life back into State Street, opening it to cars again, widening the sidewalks and adding planter boxes and vintage streetlamps. While these measures didn't prevent 100-year-old department store **Carson Pirie Scott** from closing its Louis Sullivan-designed doors in 2006, they have contributed to the upsurge of interest in the Loop as a place to live and cavort after dark.

Harold Washington Library

Anchoring the lower Loop is the main branch of the Chicago Public Library system – the nine-storey **Harold Washington Library Center**, 400 S State St (Mon–Thurs 9am–9pm, Fri & Sat 9am–5pm, Sun 1–5pm; ℡ 312/747-4300,

Ⓦ www.chipublib.org). The largest public library building in the world, filling a whole city block, it holds more than two million volumes, filling 71 miles of shelves, and the largest **blues archive** in the country, with audio, video, demo, and promotional recordings from such blues legends as Willie Dixon, John Lee Hooker and Buddy Guy. Casual visitors, however, will be more drawn to the hundreds of paintings on display (ask at the front desk for a brochure describing the works found on each floor), as well as frequent big-name readings.

The library was completed in 1991 in honour of Chicago's first black mayor, Harold Washington, an avid reader who died unexpectedly in office in 1987. Designed by Tom Beeby of the firm Hammond Beeby Babka, the library deliberately recalls some of the Loop's most famous buildings – in particular, the Romanesque arches of the Rookery – though its most eye-catching features are the outsize acroteria on the roof: the ornament facing State Street depicts an owl, symbolizing knowledge, perched in foliage. Inside, on the north wall of the main lobby, look for the blue Jacob Lawrence **mosaic mural** depicting key moments from Washington's life. If you look down through the circular opening into the lower lobby, you'll see *DuSable's Journey*, created by Houston Conwill, a map that traces the routes of **Jean-Baptiste Point du Sable** – Chicago's first settler, also black – through the waters he navigated between his homeland of Haiti and Chicago; the quotations around the map's edges are taken from Washington's inaugural speeches.

Carson Pirie Scott building

Four blocks north of the library, the building that once held the **Carson Pirie Scott** department store, 1 S State St, was Louis Sullivan's last major work in Chicago and the exuberant cast-iron ornamentation at street level, especially on the rounded corner of State and Madison, is a testament to his original melding of naturalistic and geometric design. Look for his initials, LHS, worked into the tracery over the main entrance. In May 2008 the gourmet grocer *Fox & Obel* announced that it would open a market and café in the building – great news for the Loop's culinary fortunes, as F&O's flagship café at 401 E. Illinois in Streeterville serves some of the best sandwiches, soups and salads in town. The Australian retailer Billabong and the stir-fry restaurant *Flat Top Grill* were also expected to move in.

The Reliance Building

Lauded as the forerunner of the glass-and-steel skyscrapers that sprung up everywhere in the middle of the twentieth century, the thin, cream-coloured **Reliance Building**, 32 N State St, lies one block north from Carson Pirie Scott, on the corner of W Washington Street. It was designed by Daniel Burnham in 1891 and construction was completed in 1895 by Charles B. Atwood. Preceding modern glass-and-steel towers by some sixty years, the pioneer of the Chicago School of Architecture appears almost to defy gravity; the entirely interior steel-frame construction supports wide flat and bay windows, flanked by moveable sash windows – a style subsequently referred to as "the Chicago window". By the 1960s, this historic treasure had fallen from glory and the City of Chicago began a $30-million restoration. Exuding old-world grandeur, the European-style *Hotel Burnham* opened here in 1999 (see p.150); step inside for a look at the lobby and decorative trimmings, or get a bite to eat or a cocktail at the charming *Atwood Café* (see p.164).

Macy's and Block 37

When New York department-store giant **Macy's** bought Chicago institution **Marshall Field's and Co.** in 2005, locals panicked that the store, at 111 N. State St (Mon–Thurs 10am–8pm, Fri 9am–9pm, Sat 9am–10pm, Sun 11am–6pm; ☎312/781-1000, ⓦwww.macys.com), would lose its charm and traditions. So far, that hasn't been the case, and it remains a bastion of bourgeois propriety, complete with the *Walnut Room* – ground zero for ladies who lunch – and ornate Christmas windows. It's housed in a nine-storey Neoclassical building that was built in stages between 1892 and 1914 by Daniel Burnham. Taking up an entire city block, it's hard to miss, adorned by two huge, bronze (now green) clocks, one of which has been keeping time for over a century. The clock at the corner of State and Washington streets cemented its status as a Chicago symbol when a painting of it by Norman Rockwell landed on the cover of the *Saturday Evening Post* in 1945: in it a repairman sets the time on the big clock using his pocket watch. Flanking the State Street entrance are two **granite pillars**, constructed in 1902, and only surpassed in height by the pillars on the Temple of Karnak in Egypt.

Step inside to check out the glistening **Tiffany ceiling** in the north atrium, the first ever built of Favrile iridescent glass (1.6 million pieces to be precise). Completed in 1907, the ceiling – considered the largest Tiffany mosaic in existence – covers six thousand square feet and took more than eighteen months to create. And if you're in the market for a souvenir or take-home gift redolent of old Chicago, it's hard to beat a box of Frango Mints – these tasty boxed chocolates are now made by Macy's with organic ingredients but look and taste pretty much the same as the Marshall Field's originals.

Across the street, at 108 N State St, **Block 37** is finally shaping up into a viable development after more than twenty years of assorted real-estate shenanigans. The glass-sheathed, mixed-use complex already houses the local CBS affiliate's studios on the ground floor; a mall with retailers including Aveda and Steve Madden, a high-end food court and an eight-screen cineplex is expected to open in spring 2009. Also in the works: condominiums, a luxury hotel and a CTA transit hub with express service to Midway and O'Hare airports. With the economy in the doldrums, however, no one would be surprised by more delays or reversals.

Gene Siskel Film Center

Run by the Art Institute of Chicago, the **Gene Siskel Film Center**, 164 N State St (☎312/846-2600, ⓦwww.siskelfilmcenter.org), brings a much-needed shot of high culture to the Loop, with an ambitious programme of classic, foreign and indie films shown daily in top-notch facilities. There's also a small gallery and café where you can hang out before or after screenings. The Center is named after *Chicago Tribune* film critic Gene Siskel, who became one of the most famous and influential film critics in America when he teamed up with the *Sun Times'* Roger Ebert to review movies on television in the 1970s. Siskel died in 1999 at the age of 53 of complications arising from a brain tumour; Ebert, generally regarded as the less nuanced critic of the two, is still going strong with new partner Richard Roeper.

The Theatre District

Located on the north end of the Loop on and around Randolph Street, the **Theatre District**, such as it is, consists of a small assemblage of turn-of-the-twentieth-century jewel-box theatres, along with the powerhouse Goodman Theatre's sparkling glass complex, completed in 2000. With the exception of the Goodman, most venues here specialize in mainstream Broadway fare which, though not especially groundbreaking, has succeeded in bringing nightlife to this previously forlorn part of the city.

A quick look around should begin at the 1926 **Oriental Theatre/Ford Center for the Performing Arts**, 24 W Randolph St, whose famously bizarre interior – a riot of sculptured sea horses, goddesses and elephants, all designed to resemble, however obliquely, an Asian temple – underwent an extensive renovation in 1996. The iconic vertical "C-H-I-C-A-G-O" sign and marquee of the **Chicago Theatre**, 175 N State St, is all but impossible to miss, as is the facade, styled after the Arc de Triomphe. The theatre is better known, however, for its opulent interior – exquisite murals, crystal chandeliers and bronze light fixtures, all modelled on Versailles. Forty-five-minute **tours** (usually Tues, Thurs & Sat at noon but check ahead as times vary by season; $10; ☎312/462-6300, ⓦ www.thechicagotheatre.com), led by docents, cover all the highlights, including the theatre's magnificent Wurlitzer pipe-organ (demonstrated on Saturdays) and dressing rooms.

The **Goodman Theatre**, 170 N Dearborn St, offers the most ambitious programming in the district, with new plays alternating with star-studded revivals. The state-of-the-art complex, lit up in Times Square-style rainbow lights, puts on performances in its two auditoriums and outdoor amphitheatre. Two blocks west of the Goodman stands the 1926 **Cadillac Palace Theatre**, 151 W Randolph St, whose staid exterior hides an absurdly ornate interior dripping with huge mirrors, crystal chandeliers and gold fixtures. It has been hosting Broadway musicals since a major renovation was completed in 1999.

To see some of the grand interiors without attending a show, hop on to one of Broadway in Chicago's **tours**, beginning in the Oriental Theatre's lobby every Saturday at 11am ($10; ☎312/977-1700; ⓦ www.broadwayinchicago .com). For **ticket information**, see p.205.

Along Dearborn Street

The north–south artery **Dearborn Street** cuts through the core of the Loop, sporting some of the neighbourhood's best-known art and architectural landmarks. At the corner of Dearborn and Washington, you'll come upon the concrete expanse of **Richard J. Daley Plaza**, whose focal point is an untitled cubist **Picasso sculpture**, which – depending on your orientation – will look like a giant angry bird, a woman's face or, as one youngster told Chicago writer Studs Terkel, a giant red hot-dog. The fifty-foot creation was unveiled in 1967 and has transcended initial waves of derision to become one of the city's most beloved symbols. Picasso was 82 and living on the French Riviera when he completed the design model, which was later to be built by US Steel in Gary, Indiana. The artist never made it to Chicago to view the completed work and returned the $100,000 commission fee sent by Mayor Richard J. Daley, saying the sculpture was a "gift for the people of Chicago". At various times during the year the plaza hosts **performances**, and around the winter holidays, an enormous twinkling Christmas tree.

Across Washington Street stands the **Chicago Temple Building**, home to the First United Methodist Church of Chicago, among other tenants. Besides a French Gothic sanctuary on the ground floor, the building's main highlight is the **Chapel in the Sky**, located in the eight-storey spire, which, from afar, looks like an elf's hat plopped onto a staid office-tower; **half-hour tours** of the chapel leave from the church's office on the second floor (Mon–Sat 2pm, Sun 9.30am & 12.15pm; free; T312/236-4548). Beneath the building, you'll spot yet another piece of public art, this one a sculpture by Picasso's contemporary **Joan Miró**. This 39-foot statue, made of concrete, steel and ceramic tiles, is supposed to represent a "great Earth mother", topped with a star.

Walk south on Dearborn Street until you reach **Chase Tower**; designed by C.F. Murphy and Associates, the sixty-storey high-rise curves gracefully skyward with a stunning inward sweep that recedes 105 ft from its 200-foot-wide base. On the Dearborn Street side of the plaza stands Marc Chagall's renowned *Four Seasons* mosaic, a 3000-square-foot wall of glass-and-stone tiles in 250 different shades, all painstakingly applied to give shape to whimsical dancers, musicians, animals and angels floating above cityscapes, as if carried by the wind.

Across Dearborn at 30 W Monroe St, the winsome blue-glass and stainless-steel **Inland Steel Building**, designed by Skidmore, Owings and Merrill in 1957, is an exuberant example of Mid-Century Modern architecture. The nineteen-storey building was the first skyscraper built on pilings (steel columns), and the first to use external steel beams for structural support. It's now partially owned by Frank Gehry and home to a number of architecture firms.

The Marquette Building and south

To the south, the 1895 **Marquette Building**, 140 S. Dearborn St, is a classic of the Chicago School. Designed by Holabird and Roche, its terracotta facade is punctuated by Chicago-style windows. The bronze reliefs over the main door depict scenes from the 1674 expedition of Chicago's European discoverer Jacques Marquette, from the launching of his canoe to his local burial. But the exterior pales beside the glittering lobby, whose shimmering bronze fixtures are offset by a **Tiffany glass mosaic**, running around the atrium on the first floor. Designed by J.A. Holzer, it too retells the story of the French exploration of Illinois. Continue back through the lobby to see a display on the history of the

Crash and Byrne

Daley Plaza provided the setting for the climactic scene of the quintessential Chicago movie **The Blues Brothers** (1979). In a classic movie moment, misfit brothers Elwood and Jake, played by Chicago natives Dan Aykroyd and John Belushi, drive their Bluesmobile across the plaza, smashing into the glass lobby of Daley Center. While such antics were frowned on by former mayor Richard M. Daley ("The Boss"), Belushi and Aykroyd thought they might get away with it under newly elected **Mayor Jane Byrne**, and they were right. Having pledged during her campaign to quash Daley's political machine, Byrne agreed to close the plaza for the film shoot, seeing the opportunity to destroy Daley's namesake building – if only briefly – as highly symbolic. "I said, 'Be my guest'," Byrne recalls. "I was fighting the Machine. I felt like, 'Knock it all down'."

building and its recent restoration, courtesy of the MacArthur Foundation, a prominent tenant.

Between Jackson Boulevard and Adams Street, the triumvirate of black steel buildings that constitute the **Federal Center complex** – a courthouse, government office building and single-storey US post office – are the work of Ludwig Mies van der Rohe, founder of the International Style of modern architecture. The US General Services Administration commissioned the complex in 1959, but budgetary strife delayed its completion until 1974. All three governmental buildings are geometrically perfect and their steel frames brought to the surface, resulting in a highly linear and orderly construction that is beautiful in its simplicity. Even the grid lines of the rectangular concrete blocks that form the plaza floor were carefully designed to line up with the building's vertical axis – hardly surprising for an architect who is said to have stood over the architectural model for hours, as if in meditative trance, before moving something an eighth of an inch in a flash of recognition. His motto, fittingly, was "God is in the details".

In the plaza, providing a counterbalance to the "Miesian" aesthetics of almost religious exactitude is **Alexander Calder**'s precocious *Flamingo*. Standing 53-ft high and painted in vivid vermilion, the steel sculpture was completed in 1974, just three years before the artist's death.

The hulking **Monadnock Building**, 53 W Jackson Blvd, runs south along Dearborn for a full city block. Designed by Daniel Burnham and John Wellborn Root, it was completed in 1891 and remains the tallest commercial masonry building in the world – its walls are six feet thick to support the structure's immense weight. Though relatively devoid of ornamentation, it has some fine touches, like painstakingly chamfered corners.

The bay-windowed **Manhattan Building**, 431 S Dearborn St, erected in 1891, is the oldest surviving building by William Le Baron Jenney, "father of the skyscraper". The world's first entirely iron-frame structure, it was briefly – at sixteen stories – also the world's tallest.

Along LaSalle Street

Chicago's Wall Street, the Midwest's financial fulcrum, occupies the six blocks of **LaSalle Street** between Lake Street and Jackson Boulevard. For the most part, the area is a prosaic strip of money-making functionality, strewn with the requisite chain coffee shops and takeout lunch spots, but there are a few very notable exceptions, listed here from south to north.

The Chicago Board of Trade

The **Chicago Board of Trade** building, 141 W Jackson Blvd at S LaSalle St, is one of the rare examples of Art Deco anywhere in the city. The gorgeous, 1930 monolithic tower is topped by a thirty-foot high stainless-steel statue of *Ceres*, Roman goddess of grain, symbolizing the board of trade's history trading agricultural products. The thirteen-foot high clock on the facade, above the main entrance, can be seen from almost fifteen blocks away on LaSalle Street. The board of trade no longer exists as an independent entity – it was purchased in 2007 by its longtime rival, the **Chicago Mercantile Exchange**, which in turn merged with the New York Mercantile Exchange in 2008 – but the building is busier than ever. In May 2008 the Mercantile Exchange moved from its headquarters at 30 S Wacker Drive to the Board of Trade Building, which is more spacious. You can no longer watch the traders in the cacophonous open-outcry "pit" – a dying custom in any case, as computers take over the business – but be sure to step inside to see the fine detailing in the lobby and a small history exhibit on trading in Chicago.

The Rookery

The massive red brick, stone and terracotta building at 209 S LaSalle St, known as **The Rookery**, was built between 1885 and 1888, and while topping out at only twelve stories was the tallest building in the world at the time of its construction. The seminal work of two leading Chicago architects, Daniel Burnham and John Wellborn Root, it is one of the city's most celebrated and photographed edifices: its forbidding Moorish and Romanesque exterior gives way to a wonderfully airy **lobby**, decked out in white-glazed terracotta and intricate iron tracery in 1905, during a major remodelling by Frank Lloyd Wright. The spiral cantilever staircase rising from the mezzanine must be seen to be appreciated. The building takes its name from the City Hall that occupied the site in the aftermath of the Great Fire in 1871, which became a favoured roost or "rookery" for pigeons.

190 S LaSalle

On the corner diagonally across from the Rookery is the blandly named **190 S LaSalle**, by Philip Johnson and John Burgee. Johnson's only Chicago work and the first local skyscraper by native son Burgee, the forty-storey tower is best viewed from a few blocks away, where you can most easily see its distinctive **gables**, an homage to Burnham and Root's 1892 Masonic Temple, which once stood at Randolph and State Streets – sadly, it was demolished in 1939. Johnson and Burgee traded red brick for red granite but duplicated other old-world features of Burnham and Root's design: the grand, seemingly endless lobby brings to mind a Gothic cathedral, with millions of dollars' worth of gold leaf on the ceiling, individual elevator banks decorated in their own shades of marble, and the intriguing **bronze sculpture** on the lobby's north end (Alfred Carel's *Fugue*). Hanging in the adjoining side room is a **tapestry** of Daniel Burnham's 1909 plan of Chicago, a chance to see the tremendous vision and plans he had for this city.

James R. Thompson Center

Seven blocks north of 190 S LaSalle, the **James R. Thompson Center**, 100 W Randolph St, is the state's headquarters in Chicago. Helmut Jahn's iconoclastic glass building was completed in 1985, its bevelled wedge shape and exuberant, if now somewhat dated, colour scheme standing out amid the neighbouring office towers. Inside, transparent elevator shafts shuttle office-workers between the sixteen floors of the silver-red-and blue-toned rotunda. More than fifty state agencies are housed here, as well as an art gallery, three floors of restaurants and shops. It also gathers the expected parade of gawkers. The sculpture standing in the building's foreground, looking like a cross between an iceberg and a ten-ton plaything, is Jean Dubuffet's *Monument with Standing Beast*. The mass of white fibreglass and black trim was taken from the artist's "Art Brut series", an attempt to divorce art from culture. According to Dubuffet, the piece contains four motifs: an animal, a tree, a portal and a Gothic church. Good luck finding them.

The Sears Tower and Wacker Drive

Perched on the western edge of the Loop, the **Sears Tower** is the **tallest building in the US** and the most famous skyscraper in Chicago. You can see it from just about everywhere in this flat city, but getting up close has its benefits: gazing up the facade from street level as the clouds soar overhead is a head-spinning experience, while travelling up to its 103rd-floor observation deck offers views of four states on extremely clear days. Afterward, head north on Wacker Drive to see other noteworthy buildings such as the **Hyatt Center**,

▲ Sears Tower

then cross the river to River North (see p.85) or take the River Walk back to the Michigan Avenue Bridge.

The Sears Tower

Measuring 1451 feet from the sidewalk to the roof, the **Sears Tower** was the tallest building in the world from 1973 until 1997, when Malaysia's Petronas Towers, while much shorter in terms of habitable space, controversially nudged it from the number-one spot with their long spires. Only if you count the Sears Tower's massive 280-foot-tall antennae does the building maintain its status as the world's tallest structure, but even that distinction is soon to fall with the new crop of super-skyscrapers, including Burj Dubai, slated for completion in 2009 with more than 160 storeys, and Santiago Calatrava's **Chicago Spire** in Near North (see p.76) – at 150 floors on track to be the world's tallest residential building.

Bruce Graham of **Skidmore, Owings and Merrill** designed the Sears Tower, which opened in 1973. Though it takes up an entire city block and contains more than four million square feet of interior space, it took only three years to build and was technologically innovative, consisting of nine enormous steel "tubes", varying in length from 50 to 110 stories, bundled together to provide strength and flexibility – it's said that Graham conceived of the different levels when he watched someone shake cigarettes out of a pack. The tower was originally built to house up to 13,000 employees of the department store Sears Roebuck & Co. but was sold in 1989 to three property developers and is now filled with a variety of commercial renters. It contains one hundred elevators and 16,000 windows – all, thankfully, equipped with automatic window-washers.

To get to the **103rd-floor observatory**, enter on Jackson Street through the specially marked door. Feel free to skip the cursory introductory movie and head straight for the ear-popping elevator ride, which takes about seventy seconds to reach the skydeck (daily: April–Sept 10am–10pm, Oct–March 10am–8pm, closed occasionally due to high winds; $12.95, children 3–11 $9.30, under-3s free; ☎875-9696 or 875-9447, ⓦ www.searstower.com). Once there, you'll have good views of the city's east and north sides, though even on a clear day you'll be squinting to see the neighbouring four states (Michigan, Illinois, Indiana and Wisconsin), as touted in the tower's literature: call to check the visibility index before turning up – if it's under five miles, come another time. The handy touch-screen computers mounted on the rails will help identify what you see, and you can read fascinating stories from the city's history on the walls. The least-crowded times to visit are first thing in the morning or after 6pm, though keep in mind that you can get similar (some say better) views atop the John Hancock Building in Near North for the price of a cocktail (see p.81).

The Hyatt Center and further north

At 71 S Wacker Drive, just north of Sears Tower, stands the striking 49-storey **Hyatt Center**, designed by Henry Cobb of New York-based Pei Cobb Freed & Partners in 2005. While its serene curves, slicing through the skyline like a ship's prow, form a graceful aberration, its blunt vertical-end walls imbue it with that formidable edge that defines the no-nonsense Chicago street-grid and skyline. Cobb, whose mantra is that a building needs to be a "good citizen", made the security features integral to the design; the planter boxes in the plaza are tough enough to protect the building's supporting columns from a truck bomb. This sense of fortification without compromising beauty has made the building one of the most prestigious office addresses in the city, and a symbol of architectural innovation since September 11, 2001.

As you continue north you'll come to the massive **Civic Opera House**, at 20 N Wacker Drive, home to the Lyric Opera of Chicago. Conceived as a monument to culture and commerce and completed in 1929, the Neoclassical building was designed with a grand two-storey portico running its entire length, making it look like a giant armchair from the river. For further information on performances, see p.209.

Walking north from here to where the river bends eastward, you'll spot **333 W Wacker Drive** on your right, a curving, wafer-thin building covered in a skin of reflective green glass. Built in 1983 by New York-based Kohn Pederson Fox, it was designed to mimic the contour and colour of the Chicago River, and is best viewed from the opposite bank in **Near North** (see p.85) or from an **architectural river cruise** (see p.44).

2

South Loop and Near South

With its pitch-perfect vistas of the Loop's unmistakeable skyline, the lakefront portion of the **South Loop** is best known for the triumvirate of superb attractions on what's now known as **Museum Campus**: the standout **Field Museum**, the **Adler Planetarium**, and the **Shedd Aquarium**, all housed in beautiful classical buildings and worthy of several hours' consideration apiece, especially if you have kids in tow. The campus anchors the south end of rambling **Grant Park**, a legacy of Daniel Burnham's 1909 plan for Chicago and now a major outdoor-festival site. The inland portion of the South Loop centres on **Printers Row**, an atmospheric little district that runs along S Dearborn Street, between Congress Parkway and Polk Street. There are also a couple of small museums in the South Loop on South Michigan Avenue.

The **Near South**, extending from Roosevelt Road to the Stevenson Expressway (I-55), just below 24th Street, is the first clear sign most visitors will see of Chicago's urban problems. Aside from the historic **Prairie Avenue Historical District**, which preserves the palatial mansions of Chicago's former elite, the one safe, intriguing neighbourhood out this way is Chicago's **Chinatown**. Filled with markets and restaurants, it makes a great place for a cheap meal. Though the South Loop is safe for visitors, be aware that the area surrounding Chinatown is still rather iffy: take public transportation and you should be fine, but make sure not to wander outside the district's ten or so buzzing blocks.

The South Loop

Depending on your enthusiasm for walking, most of the sights in the **South Loop** – especially the area around Printers Row – can be reached on foot from the Loop. If you want to make a beeline for the Museum Campus, consider taking a **water taxi** from the Michigan Avenue Bridge, Sears Tower or Navy Pier (late May to early Sept daily 10am–6pm; ☎312/222-9328, Ⓦ www.shorelinesightseeing.com). It's a bit pricey, but worth it for the speed and the views of the skyline. Another good way to get there is by **bicycle**

EATING

Chicago Firehouse Restaurant	10
Edwardo's Natural Pizza	13
Eleven City Diner	6
Gioco	9
Hackney's	5
Manny's Deli	7
Mercat a la Planxa	4
Orange	2
Penang	12
Tamarind	3
Three Happiness	11
Zapatista	8

ACCOMMODATION

Hyatt Regency McCormick Place	B
Wheeler Mansion	A

DRINKING

Alcock's Bar	1

along the lakefront; for bike rental information, see p.237. CTA **bus** #146 also connects the Museum Campus with downtown via Michigan and State streets, as does a **free trolley** (May–Sept daily; rest of the year weekends only; ⊕877/244-2246). A cab ride from the Loop will set you back $7–10.

Printers Row and around

From the late nineteenth century to the mid-twentieth century, the brick enclave of **Printers Row** thrived as the last stop on most railroad lines and the centre of the Midwestern printing industry. Though it fell on hard times in the 1970s, it has, like most other neighbourhoods within a stone's throw of the Loop, recently been revitalized with a proliferation of loft apartments flanked by cafés, shops and restaurants, ranging from hole-in-the-wall stalwarts like *Manny's Deli* (see p.167) – a symbol of grittier days gone by – to chi-chi newcomers like *Mercat a la Planxa* (see p.168) on South Michigan Avenue, where the small **Museum of Contemporary Photography** and the **Spertus Museum** are also located.

The area's literary connections are most evident during the lively **Printers Row Book Fair**, held each June (see p.246), and in the smattering of terrific **bookstores** here (see p.227). Be sure to take a look at renowned muralist Oskar Gross's terracotta panels on the **Franklin Building**, 720 S Dearborn, presenting the history of the publishing industry.

Dearborn Station

At the southern end of Printers Row stands the handsome Romanesque Revival pile of **Dearborn Station**; built in 1885, it was the oldest of Chicago's six rail terminals but closed in the 1970s as rail services declined. After standing empty for a decade, the station's interior has been done over as a moderately successful office and retail complex, and the railyards stretching south from the station have been replaced by a public park. The most famous tenant in Dearborn Station – and the only one really meriting a visit – is the *Jazz Showcase* (see p.199), a staple of Chicago's live jazz scene for over fifty years, which relocated here in 2008.

The Museum of Contemporary Photography

A few blocks east of Printers Row, the **Museum of Contemporary Photography**, 600 S Michigan Ave (Mon–Sat 10am–5pm, Thurs until 8pm, Sun noon–5pm; free; ☎312/663-5554, ⊛www.mocp.org), feels less like a museum than a small gallery, with high-quality, thought-provoking exhibits mounted in a few whitewashed rooms. Recent shows have explored themes such as "On the Road", in honour of the fiftieth anniversary of Jack Kerouac's famous work, and "Beyond the Backyard", in which photographers poked their lenses into Americans' private little fiefdoms and found all sorts of odd contradictions. The museum also displays a small, rotating selection of works from the permanent collection of 8500 photographs and photography-related objects by American artists including Dorothea Lange, Gregory Crewdson, Sally Mann and Mary Ellen Mark.

The Spertus Museum

Some 3500 years of Jewish history, art, tradition and ethnology are presented next door at the **Spertus Museum**, 610 S Michigan Ave (Sun–Wed 10am–6pm, Thurs until 7pm, Fri 10am–3pm; $5, students and seniors $5, free Tues 10am–noon & Thurs 3–7pm; ☎312/322-1700, ⊛www.spertus.edu). Be aware, however, that the museum itself takes up only a tiny bit of the vast new ecofriendly building, which also houses a college, library, kosher café, theatre, shop and administrative offices.

You can see about a tenth of the museum's 15,000-piece collection of art and artefacts – including Torah scrolls, jewellery, textiles, photographs and keepsakes from victims of the Holocaust – on the ninth floor in "**viewable storage**" format, which is to say, in tall glass cases without the usual explanatory text. To get the most of the exhibit, including the fascinating stories behind some of the objects, coordinate your visit with one of the daily gallery talks (daily except Sat 12.30pm) or pick up an audio guide at the front desk; both are free with museum admission. Consistently impressive temporary shows on the tenth floor usually focus on more contemporary work and themes. **Kids** needn't feel left out: a Children's Center opened in October 2008 on the fourth floor, where visitors between the ages of 2 and 12 can listen to stories, explore a "Wall of Doors and Drawers", and even climb through a rope tube (parental monitoring required).

Grant Park

Due east from the Spertus Museum, **Grant Park** (daily 6am–11pm) is a sculpture-dotted greensward edging the lake from the Art Institute (see p.48) south to Roosevelt Road. While it provides some respite from the downtown urban grid, wide strips of high-speed road and railroad slice through it, so casual rambling can be frustrating. The creation of snazzy Millennium Park (see p.46) from its northwest corner in 2004 has also lowered the profile of Grant Park, which now feels quite stodgy in comparison. Still, its vast size – 300 acres – and lakefront locale make it the city's most popular spot for large protests and festivals. Two of these have grabbed the attention of the world. During the Democratic National Convention of 1968, the park was the site of highly publicized clashes between antiwar protesters and police, earning Mayor Daley and Chicago itself a reputation for barbarism. Forty years later, on November 4, 2008, the scene could not have been more different. On that uncommonly balmy night, **Barack Obama** held his election-night party here, an event that drew 125,000 jubilant spectators, including famous locals Jesse Jackson and Oprah Winfrey, as well as untold millions of television viewers, to watch the Illinois senator accept the post of President of the United States and present the new First Family to the world.

Major renovations to the park have been proposed but put on hold due to the nation's economic woes. For the time being, the main attractions are, at the north end, the **Petrillo Music Shell** and adjoining Hutchinson Field – where the Taste of Chicago food festival is held every summer (see box below) – and immense **Buckingham Fountain**, sitting amid colonnades of trees and thousands of rose bushes a few blocks south.

Some history

Grant Park dates back to the city's beginnings. In 1835, just two years after Chicago was incorporated, civic leaders proposed to keep this swathe of lakefront free of development. Named Lake Park in 1847, the land was soon eroded almost all the way west to Michigan Avenue, and in 1852, the Illinois Central Railroad was allowed to build a trestle across the watery expanse so that trains could reach the river. Ungainly as it was, the trestle buffered Michigan Avenue and its mansions from both floods and violent storm-driven waters. Over the years, the land between the rail tracks and the shore gradually filled in, especially after debris from the fire of 1871 was dumped here. In the wake of the fire, many local businessmen and city officials considered the land fit for development and a source of revenue for the city, but **Aaron Montgomery Ward**, who started the world's first mail-order business in Chicago, fought to keep the land for the people, filing four lawsuits against developers, and eventually prevailed.

Summer festivals in the park

As Chicago's de facto backyard, Grant Park plays host to festivals and events – most of them free – all summer long. Among the most famous is the **Grant Park Music Festival**, which presents top-notch classical-music rehearsals and performances at the Jay Pritzker Pavilion in Millennium Park (see p.47) from mid-June to mid-August. Over the same period, **Chicago Summerdance** offers free dance lessons, live music, and dancing Thursday through Sunday nights in the Spirit of Music Garden, at 601 S Michigan Ave in Grant Park, with styles ranging from Jewish klezmer to tango. In the area around the Petrillo Music Shell in late June or early July, the **Taste of Chicago** festival attracts some four million people to a week-long feeding frenzy, garnished with concerts and other live entertainment. Classic films are screened al fresco near the corner of Monroe Boulevard and Lake Shore Drive every Tuesday night from mid-July through August at the **Chicago Outdoor Film Festival**. For details on these and other park events, see p.244.

In 1893, Ward allowed the Art Institute to be built within the park's borders as part of that year's World's Fair, and in 1901, the patch of green was renamed Grant Park after the nation's 18th president. Most of the landscaping took place in the 1910s and 1920s, in accordance with Daniel Burnham's city plan of 1909.

Buckingham Fountain and around

Southeast of Millennium Park and the Art Institute, **Buckingham Fountain** was donated to Grant Park in 1927 and modelled after a fountain at Versailles. An ornate pile of stacked pink marble, the fountain provides a spectacle from May to October when it shoots more than a million gallons of water up to 150ft in the air. It also plays host to popular light and water shows daily from dusk to 11pm.

A few statues nearby are worth noting: across Columbus Avenue to the west of the fountain is the seated **Lincoln statue**, surveying the park from atop a pedestal. Like its counterpart in Lincoln Park, the statue, created by Augustus Saint-Gaudens, was unveiled in 1926, although it is more subdued. Flanking Congress Parkway near Michigan Avenue, *The Bowman and the Spearman* is an impressive pair of 17-foot-high bronze Indian warriors, created by sculptor Ivan Mestrovic.

Museum Campus and around

Museum Campus – the 57-acre landscaped park that holds the Field Museum of Natural History, the Shedd Aquarium and Adler Planetarium – was created in 1998, when city planners finally decided to reroute the northbound lanes of Lake Shore Drive west of Soldier Field and the museums so that culture-hungry tourists wouldn't have to risk their lives scampering between these attractions. If it's summertime, bring your bathing suit: just south of the planetarium, pleasant **12th Street Beach** offers good swimming along a rarely crowded crescent of sand, along with a café and changing rooms.

The Field Museum of Natural History

The **Field Museum**, 1400 S Lake Shore Drive at Roosevelt Rd (daily 9am–5pm, last admission 4pm; $14, students and seniors $11, free on the second Monday of each month and select weeks, free highlights tours Mon–Fri 11am & 2pm, Sat 11am & 1pm, Sun 1pm; a variety of self-guided tours may also be downloaded from the website; ☎312/922-9410, ⓦwww.fieldmuseum.org), is one of the most impressive natural history museums in the world, and one that strikes an elusive balance by engaging adults with surprisingly up-to-date and in-depth science, while captivating kids with dazzling artefacts and hands-on exhibits. It's yet another legacy of the 1893 World's Columbian Exposition, where department store magnate **Marshall Field** had endowed many of the natural history displays. Originally housed in the Palace of Fine Arts on the South Side fairgrounds, the Field Museum's collections were moved to the present building – an enormous Greek Revival pile – in 1921 have been and greatly expanded in the years since.

The museum presents more than twenty million objects across six acres on three levels, but don't let that daunt you, as with comfortable shoes and a plan of the museum (available at the information booth), it's easily navigable. On the main floor, on the building's north side, is the *Tyrannosaurus rex* **Sue** (see box opposite), the most complete *T-rex* fossil ever found, missing only one foot, one

T-rex Sue and the custody battle of the century

Sue's discovery on a Cheyenne River Sioux Indian reservation in the badlands of South Dakota by fossil hunter Susan Hendrickson in 1990 was the spark for one of the greatest custody battles in the history of paleontology. The reservation property was held in trust by the government for a Sioux Indian, **Maurice Williams**, who was paid $5000 by fossil hunters to renounce all claims.

The government soon got wind of the discovery and in 1992 the US Justice Department quickly dispatched FBI agents to seize the skeleton pending a decision on ownership (the *T-rex* was found, after all, on government land). Eventually, the court ruled in Williams' favour – the 1906 Antiquities Act doesn't cover fossils. Thus, **Sue's bones** were auctioned off to the highest bidder at Sotheby's in New York in October 1997; thanks to the combined corporate muscle of McDonald's and Disney, the Field was able to outbid its rivals for the skeleton, ultimately paying $8.4 million. On May 17, 2000, after two and a half years spent assembling the 13-foot-tall, 14-foot-long fossil, the Field Museum revealed to the world the crown jewel of its collection.

"hand", and a few back bones. Paleontologists speculate that the body of Sue (actually, "her" gender is officially undetermined) was most likely buried by an avalanche or mudflow, which kept her bones intact for millions of years. Take the stairs to the upper level to see Sue's skull: too heavy to mount, the original is presented on its own, while the one you see in context on the main floor is a replica cast. There's also a virtual journey inside Sue's head and touchable bone casts that reveal the life-threatening wounds inflicted upon the great flesh-devouring monster some 65 million years ago.

Adjacent to the Sue Store, where you can buy all manner of Jurassic memorabilia, **Evolving Planet** is a sleek walk-through exhibit covering four billion years of evolution – from the dawn of Earth to the arrival of man – that includes an impressive Cambrian underwater scene, re-created from fossil finds in the Burgess Shale, a patch of soft rock in the Canadian Rockies that was sea floor about 505 million years ago. It continues through the eras with an amazing collection of Permian-period tetrapods and ends with an expanded Dinosaur Hall, where kids can play the role of a paleontologist, using interpretive screens to examine a dinosaur's anatomy.

Opened in May 2008, the **DNA Discovery Center** is also on the upper level. Largely geared toward older kids and adults, the small exhibit comprises a five-minute film explaining the basics of genetics, a few hands-on displays and a glass-fronted lab where evolutionary biologists conduct research; you can ask them about their work (Mon–Fri 11am–noon).

On the main floor, aside from ogling Sue, take time to explore the top-notch **Ancient Americas** exhibit, a maze of connected galleries that, taken in sequence, relate 13,000 years of history on the American continents, from the arrival of the first humans to the present day. It is an exemplary work of museum science, seamlessly blending film and video, artefacts, audio recordings and wall panels so that all types of visitors can find something of interest here – without being overwhelmed by the all-too-frequent cacophony that results from a multimedia approach. Particularly interesting are the rooms exploring the leadership structures of ancient superpowers like the Aztecs and Incas; the gallery filled with exceptionally accomplished pottery of the Moche people; and the "Past Meets Present" documentary videos, in which descendants of indigenous Americans talk about their heritage.

Ground-floor exhibits are aimed squarely at families. Of these, the **Crown Family PlayLab**, opened in September 2007, is by far the most popular, with six hands-on play areas that children aged 2 to 10 go wild about: an Illinois Woodland, which invites kids to dress up as animals and star in a play about nature; the Scientists' Lab, where children can measure, sort and magnify specimens; the Dinosaur Field Station, where little ones can dig for a bone and play in a dinosaur nest; the Rhythm Section, which features percussion instruments from around the world; an Art Studio, where museum docents guide children in creative projects; and the Pueblo, a pueblo home and plaza, where kids can make coil baskets and grind corn. Across the hall in the trippy **Underground Adventure** exhibit, visitors are "shrunk" to one hundredth of their size and set on a pathway under the earth, surrounded by soil, giant roots and oversized fibreglass insects, including a Cadillac-sized crayfish.

The Shedd Aquarium

On the lakefront just a few hundred feet northeast of the Field Museum, the **Shedd Aquarium** (summer daily 9am–6pm; rest of year Mon–Fri 9am–5pm, Sat & Sun 9am–6pm; Mini Pass $15.95, $11.95 children 3–11 and seniors; Total Experience Pass $17.95, $13.95 children 3–11 and seniors, includes a 12- to 15-minute "4-D" movie; visit website for list of Community Discount Days, when admission is free; ☎312/939-2438, ⓦwww.sheddaquarium.org), is the largest indoor aquarium in the world, with tanks that extend underneath the octagonal marble structure and jut out into the lake. In 2007 it was the most popular tourist attraction in Chicago, with two million visitors.

The central exhibit is a 90,000-gallon recreation of a **Caribbean Coral Reef**, complete with 500 aquatic species, including sharks and thousands of rainbow-coloured tropical fish. The undisputed star is the green sea-turtle **Nickel** – named after the 1975-nickel coin found lodged in her oesophagus when she arrived at Shedd in 2003 from Clearwater Marine Aquarium in Florida. On the south side of the Caribbean reef, the **Amazon Rising** exhibit reveals the impact of the changing seasons on one of the world's most ecologically diverse environments. In addition to red-bellied piranhas and green anacondas, look out for the wattled jacanas – the feminist icons of the bird world, defending huge swathes of territory and being entertained by a harem of up to five males, who kindly take care of the incubation and parental care after hatching. On the north and east sides of the main hall, the otherwise lacklustre **Waters of the World** exhibit features an endangered **blue iguana** from Grand Cayman (less than thirty remain in the wild), the largest lizard in the western hemisphere.

At the back of the museum, the three-million-gallon **Oceanarium** provides a modern lake-view home for marine mammals such as Pacific dolphins, beluga whales (which consume nearly 600lb of seafood daily) and delightfully playful sea otters. Undergoing renovation until summer 2009, it also functions as a carefully disguised amphitheatre for demonstrations of the animals' "natural behaviour", such as jumping out of the water and fetching plastic rings. Performances take place four times daily (summer 10.30am, 11.30am, 1.30pm & 4.30pm; rest of the year Mon–Fri 10.30am, 11.30am, 1.30pm & 3.30pm, Sat & Sun 10.30am, 11.30am, 1.30pm & 4.30pm) but at other times you can watch from underwater galleries as the animals cruise around the tank, and listen to the clicks, beeps and whistles they use to communicate with each other.

Also on the lower level (below Amazon Rising), **Wild Reef** consists of 26 interrelated habitats that together re-create a Philippine coral reef. Among the five hundred species of fish you'll see gliding through the live coral are mangrove rays, blue spotted stingrays and more than fifty kinds of shark.

The Adler Planetarium and Astronomy Museum

At the eastern end of the Museum Campus, jutting out into Lake Michigan, is the beloved **Adler Planetarium and Astronomy Museum** (daily: summer 9.30am–6pm; winter 9.30am–4.30pm; first Fri of each month until 10pm; $23, $21 seniors $19 children, including 2 shows; $19, $17 seniors, $15 children including 1 show; see website for discount days and weeks; ☎312/922-7827, Ⓦwww.adlerplanetarium.org). Quirky and old-fashioned-looking from the outside, the twelve-sided planetarium was built in 1930, with each side representing a sign of the zodiac. Major renovations in the 1990s brought the interior up to date, with permanent exhibits including **Bringing the Heavens to Earth**, an examination of the impact of astronomy on ancient cultures, and **CyberSpace**, where "Cyberclassrooms" linked by high-velocity broadband networks enable two-way telecasts with NASA, whose "feeds" project breaking space-related news across plasma displays.

In honour of the planetarium's 75th anniversary in 2005, American space hero Captain James A. Lovell contributed his personal collection to Adler, including personal space artefacts (note the fecal collection bag), documents, and memorabilia. Lovell became a national hero in 1970, when he and his crew successfully modified the Apollo 13 lunar module into a lifeboat when the oxygen system failed. Unveiled in 2006, the **Shoot for the Moon** exhibition features the restored Gemini 12 spacecraft, one of four spacecraft flown by Lovell, and thirty related items, in an enthusiastic pitch for further manned space travel.

Bear in mind that the Adler is relatively small and often mobbed by school groups, making the dark and calm confines of its **space theatres** all the more appealing. Two – the Sky Theater and the Definiti Space Theater – are traditional, domed planetarium theatres in which high-definition images of the stars, planets, and other cosmological phenomena are projected onto the ceiling. The lower-level 3-D Universe Theater shows movies on a flat screen, with subject matter more suited to young children. Tickets for all shows are available only at the box office on a first-come, first-served basis.

Soldier Field

Just south of Museum Campus, the 100ft Doric colonnades of **Soldier Field** (tours by reservation only Mon–Fri 9am–5pm; $15, $10 students, $7 seniors, $4 children 4–12; ☎312/235-7244, Ⓦwww.soldierfield.net) marked it as a sports palace of a bygone age before its controversial renovation in 2002. Designed by Holabird and Roche, who pioneered the Chicago School, the original seven-acre stadium was built in the 1920s as a memorial to American soldiers who died in battle. Since then, some of the most famous battles in sports have been staged here, including the 1927 heavyweight boxing rematch between Jack Dempsey and Gene Tunney that ended with the famously controversial "long count". Dempsey knocked down Tunney but lost five precious seconds by heading to the wrong corner before the referee started his count. On the count of nine, Tunney staggered to his feet and proceeded to beat Dempsey.

Home to the Chicago Bears since 1971, Soldier Field closed in 2002 for a $600-million facelift. The new stadium was unveiled on Sept 29, 2003, and was received with scorn and derision by an overwhelming majority of Chicagoans: the once-grand classical colonnades of the original stadium are now dwarfed by a glass "bowl" that looms up from behind them like an oversized toilet. As a result of the debacle, Soldier Field was removed from the National Register of Historic Places in 2004 and de-listed as a landmark in 2006. When all is said and done, though, the Bears will remain and packs of loud, bare-chested men, seemingly numb to the sub-zero temperatures, will continue to brave the arctic winds off the lake to watch them (see p.234 for ticket information).

The Near South

The **Prairie Avenue Historic District** and **Chinatown** are the primary highlights of the Near South, which tends to be dominated by somewhat anonymous condo developments and some traces of old-school industry. The walk from the South Loop isn't terribly interesting, so if you want to make the trip to the Prairie Avenue Historic District, you'd be best off jumping on a #4 Cottage Grove bus or taking the Metra to the 18th Street station and walking over to Prairie Avenue. Chinatown is a bit more accessible via public transportation, as visitors who take the Red Line to the Cermak/Chinatown stop will find that it's only about ten minutes from the Loop. Either way, each of these areas can be thoroughly explored in a couple of hours, transit time included.

The Prairie Avenue Historic District and around

The city's first elite neighbourhood, **Prairie Avenue**, was for a brief time the most expensive street in America outside of New York's glitzy Fifth Avenue. Some of Chicago's first homes were built around Prairie Avenue in the mid-eighteenth century, and it came to be known as "Millionaire's Row" – the most coveted property in town. George Pullman (see p.257), creator of the Pullman railroad car, and some twenty industrial magnates settled here following the Chicago Fire, building extravagant mansions along S Prairie Avenue. Though a handful of their homes have survived, only **Glessner House** and **Clarke House** are open to the public, providing a glimpse of Chicago's Gilded Age.

By the beginning of the twentieth century, the rich had moved on to the lakefront north of the Loop to join millionaire Potter Palmer (see p.101). Subsequently, the area around Prairie Avenue plunged into decades of seediness, helped along by the saloons and brothels that had sprung up nearby following the success of the railroads leading into the South Loop. In recent years, the city has made considerable strides in transforming what was previously an unsafe and down-at-heel semi-industrial area into a fashionable loft neighbourhood.

Walking tours of Prairie Avenue

Walking tours, put on from June through October by Prairie Avenue House Museums, point out the avenue's prominent residents, the architecture of the homes, and the history of the district's decline and renewal.

The only way to see inside **Clarke House** and **Glessner House** – the most visited of the bunch – is on a guided tour, which leaves from the Tour Center (the Glessners' former stables) on the 18th Street side of the house (Wed–Sun, tours of Clarke House noon & 2pm, tours of Glessner House 1pm & 3pm; $15, $12 seniors & $8 children for both houses, $10, $9 seniors & $6 children for one house; free Wed; ☎312/326-1480, ⓦwww.glesserhouse.org. Tours (one hour in each house) are on a first-come, first-served basis and are limited to twelve people for Glessner House, seven for Clarke House. To see both houses, be sure to show up at the Tour Center no later than 2pm.

The blocks around Michigan and Prairie avenues are attracting young professionals with spruced up commercial and leisure amenities, ranging from prosaic chain stores and fast-food restaurants to health clubs, outdoor cafés and bars. The area has also benefitted from easy access to the Loop, a feature not lost on real estate agents and city developer types, and convenient downtown access.

You're best off **getting here** by cab, bus, or train, as the route from downtown is confusing. It's about a $6 cab ride from the Loop, or a short hop on the Michigan Avenue CTA buses (#1, #3, and #4), all of which stop at the corner of 18th Street and Michigan Avenue, in front of the Prairie Avenue House Museums (see box opposite).

Clarke House

Built in 1836, **Clarke House**, 1855 S Indiana Ave, is Chicago's oldest house and seems more suited to a New England town than a masonry-heavy city like Chicago. Even as far back as the 1850s, the house was reason enough to make an excursion here; city-dwellers used to come by carriage to see this white, timber-frame Greek Revival structure with its white colonnade, built in what was then a forest. Later, the house spent many years as a community centre before being gussied up as a minor museum of interior decor in the late 1970s.

Although the building has been moved twice to avoid demolition (it's now just two blocks from its original location), in 2004 the interior was remodelled to reflect its appearance in the 1850s as the Clarke family home. All of the interior decoration, from the wallpaper to the furniture, is a faithful reproduction of the Victorian era – none of the originals survived. Guided tours amply evoke the pioneer existence during the early days of industrialization and the American migration west.

The neutral sandstone colour of the Greek Revival exterior is attributed to the taste of the wealthy classes during the 1850s who eschewed the conspicuousness of bright white in favour of more earthy tones that would complement the surrounding landscape.

The Glessner House Museum

One of the few structures to have survived the neighbourhood's decline is the Romanesque 1886 **Glessner House**, standing sentry on the southwest corner of Prairie Avenue and 18th Street. It is Chicago's only remaining house designed by one of the most important architects of the nineteenth century, Henry Hobson Richardson, whose Romanesque-revival features inspired both Frank Lloyd Wright and Louis Sullivan. Commissioned by John and Frances Glessner, its unadorned structure was a departure from the more decorative traditional Victorian architecture, causing outrage among the neighbours, especially industrialist George Pullman (see p.257). "I do not know what I have ever done", he reportedly said, "to have that thing staring at me in the face every time I go out my door". Behind the forbidding facade, the house opens onto a large garden court, its interior filled with Arts and Crafts furniture and swathed in William Morris fabrics and wall coverings; it is also generously panelled in oak. Today, it exists almost entirely furnished as the Glessners left it, crammed with the family's collection of ceramics, delicate Art Nouveau and Venetian glass, plus intricate hand-carved furniture and ornamental pieces by Chicago artisan Isaac Scott.

Between Glessner House and Clarke House, the **Chicago Women's History Park** makes for a nice little walk along a curving path lined with a hundred plaques commemorating Chicago's famous women.

The National Vietnam Veterans Art Museum

Next door to the Glessner House, the 1981 **National Vietnam Veterans Art Museum**, 1801 S Indiana Ave (Tues–Fri 11am–6pm, Sat 10am–5pm,; $10, students $7; ⊤ 312/326-0270, ⓦ www.nvvam.org), focuses on the war from a personal point of view. The only museum of its kind in the United States, it contains more than five hundred works by 125 American Vietnam veterans and, to a lesser extent, soldiers from Australia and North and South Vietnam. The sombre and at times gut-wrenching exhibits include a mix of paintings, photographs, sculptures, drawings, diaries and other artefacts.

One of the most powerful works hangs from the ceiling above the front desk: *Above and Beyond*, a 10ft by 40ft sculpture consisting of 58,000 dog tags representing Americans killed in the war. Each stainless-steel tag is imprinted with a soldier's name, branch of service and casualty date and is hung in chronological order. The solitary black dog-tag hangs in memory of soldiers who died from their injuries after the war.

Veterans are on hand to lead discussions for the visiting school groups; ask if you can join one of these groups in order to experience a powerful firsthand account.

The Blues Heaven Foundation

As you head a couple of blocks southwest, the next place of note is the **Blues Heaven Foundation** museum at 2120 S Michigan Ave, inside the building that once housed the legendary **Chess Records**, the greatest of all blues labels.

Started in 1957 by brothers Leonard and Phil Chess, the studio launched so many top blues musicians – everyone from Willie Dixon and Bo Diddley to Muddy Waters, Koko Taylor and even Chuck Berry – that it became a shrine of sorts, nowadays run by the Willie Dixon Blues Heaven Foundation for the preservation of the blues. The Rolling Stones, who took their name from a Muddy Waters tune, even cut an album here and commemorated the place in their song *2120 South Michigan*.

▲ On Leong Building

You can take a **tour** of the renovated studio, though unless you're a real blues aficionado or simply want to say you've been to the site, you're better off skipping it altogether – you won't see much beyond a sterile recording studio and there's little in the way of informed commentary by guides. Tours last 30 to 45 minutes (call ahead to book a place) and end with a short *Keepin' the Blues Alive* video (Mon–Fri noon–4pm, Sat noon–2pm; $10 donation; ☎312/808-1286, ☯www.bluesheaven.com). For more on Chicago blues music, see p.267.

Chinatown

Half a mile southwest of the Blues Heaven Foundation and best accessed on either the Red Line to Cermak-Chinatown or bus #24 to E Cermak Road and S Wentworth Avenue, the narrow, ten-block area of Chicago's **CHINATOWN** has maintained a decidedly authentic feel. The distinctive green and red **gate** at Wentworth Avenue and Cermak Road marks the beginning of the district, and once through here you could just as well be in downtown Hong Kong as central Chicago.

Chicago's first Chinese immigrants began arriving in the 1870s, after the completion of the first transcontinental railroad when many of them found themselves out of work and without a place to live. They soon carved out an area around Cermak Road and Wentworth Avenue, two miles south of the Loop, though in time overcrowding threatened to strain the budding neighbourhood's infrastructure, and construction of city highways in the area restricted further growth. Even so, Chinatown has managed to survive and remains almost entirely Chinese.

There's nothing in the way of traditional sights around here, except the **On Leong Building**, 2216 S Wentworth Ave, easily identified by its large green and red pagodas – formerly the Chinese city hall and long the heart of the bustling commercial district. Today it houses, among other things, the only indigenous Chinese shrine in the Midwest. In 2005, the **Chinese-American Museum of Chicago** opened at 238 W 23rd St, but regrettably the building sustained serious fire damage in September 2008, so it's probably worth checking out their website (☯www.ccamuseum.org) before making a special trip. **Chinatown Square** is an offshoot just to the northwest, with more shops and restaurants, plus the Chamber of Commerce. It's fun to poke around the little groceries filled with exotic spices, myriad teas, medicinal herbs and exotic-looking vegetables, but the real attraction here is the food: you'll be spoiled for choice among the more than forty **restaurants** serving inexpensive Mandarin, Szechuan, Shanghai and Cantonese cuisine; for reviews of restaurants in the area, see p.168.

A few boisterous **festivals** also make the neighbourhood worth checking out if you are in town: July boasts the popular Lantern Festival and February sees the vibrant Chinese New Year Festival take over the local streets (for more information, see p.245).

3

The Near North Side

While the Loop is more important as a centre of business and finance, Chicago's **Near North** has established itself as the most energetic downtown area, with its four very different districts – **the Magnificent Mile**, **Streeterville**, **River North** and the **Gold Coast** – each offering different reasons to visit.

The "Mag Mile" (North Michigan Avenue) is best known for its **world-class shopping**, with nearly every major international chain store having some kind of presence here. Reaching east from Michigan Avenue to the lake, Streeterville, by contrast, is a mostly residential neighbourhood of high-rises, with a couple of notable exceptions: the small but compelling **Museum of Contemporary Art** and **Navy Pier**, an unabashedly commercial entertainment complex. The hippest bit of Near North is River North, west of Michigan Avenue, where many former warehouses have been turned into **art galleries**, clubs and restaurants. Extending north from the Magnificent Mile to Lincoln Park (p.92), the Gold Coast is, as its name suggests, one of Chicago's wealthiest enclaves, with smart boutiques on its south end, posh mansions to the north and a clutch of party-hardy bars in the middle.

The Magnificent Mile

Walking along the wide swathe of Michigan Avenue north of the Chicago River is the one thing that almost every visitor to the city will do. One of the world's most famous shopping districts, **the Magnificent Mile** is well stocked with mainstream retailers (Niketown, Forever 21, Banana Republic, Crate & Barrel and the like), major department stores (Saks and Neiman Marcus), and malls (900 N Michigan Ave, Chicago Place, and Water Tower Place) – for more information on these and other stores, see "Shopping", p.225. But even if you don't want to shop, there's plenty of interest here: the strip is anchored at the south end by the **Wrigley Building** and **Tribune Tower** and at the north end by the 100-storey **John Hancock Center**, with the famous **Water Tower** in between.

Some history

Although South Michigan Avenue was an early addition to the city plan (1836), its northern stretches were not developed until the **Michigan Avenue Bridge** was finally constructed in 1920, allowing expansion across the Chicago River. Inspired by the Alexander III Bridge in Paris, the bridge is decorated with four forty-foot pylons – two at either end – each of which features a sumptuous relief

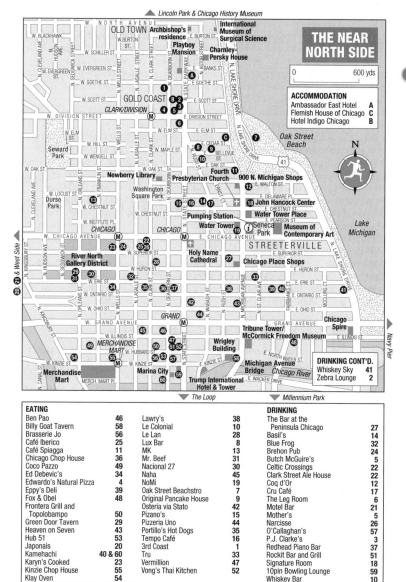

Lincoln Park & Chicago History Museum

THE NEAR
NORTH SIDE

| 0 | 600 yds |

ACCOMMODATION
Ambassador East Hotel	A
Flemish House of Chicago	C
Hotel Indigo Chicago	B

OLD TOWN
Archbishop's residence
International Museum of Surgical Science
Playboy Mansion
Charnley-Persky House

GOLD COAST
CLARK/DIVISION

Oak Street Beach

N

Newberry Library
Washington Square Park
Fourth Presbyterian Church
900 N. Michigan Shops
John Hancock Center
Water Tower Place

Durso Park

CHICAGO
Pumping Station
Water Tower
Seneca Park
Museum of Contemporary Art

Lake Michigan

River North Gallery District

STREETERVILLE

Holy Name Cathedral
Chicago Place Shops

GRAND

Chicago Spire

MERCHANDISE MART

Wrigley Building

Tribune Tower/
McCormick Freedom Museum

DRINKING CONT'D.
| Whiskey Sky | 41 |
| Zebra Lounge | 2 |

Merchandise Mart
Marina City
Michigan Avenue Bridge
Trump International Hotel & Tower
Chicago River

The Loop

Millennium Park

Navy Pier

20, 21 & West Side

EATING					DRINKING	
Ben Pao	46	Lawry's	38		The Bar at the	
Billy Goat Tavern	58	Le Colonial	10		Peninsula Chicago	27
Brasserie Jo	56	Le Lan	28		Basil's	14
Café Iberico	25	Lux Bar	8		Blue Frog	32
Café Spiagga	11	MK	13		Brehon Pub	24
Chicago Chop House	36	Mr. Beef	31		Butch McGuire's	5
Coco Pazzo	49	Nacional 27	30		Celtic Crossings	22
Ed Debevic's	34	Naha	45		Clark Street Ale House	22
Edwardo's Natural Pizza	4	NoMi	19		Coq d'Or	12
Eppy's Deli	39	Oak Street Beachstro	7		Cru Café	17
Fox & Obel	48	Original Pancake House	9		The Leg Room	6
Frontera Grill and		Osteria via Stato	42		Motel Bar	21
Topolobampo	50	Pizano's	15		Mother's	5
Green Door Tavern	29	Pizzeria Uno	44		Narcisse	26
Heaven on Seven	43	Portillo's Hot Dogs	35		O'Callaghan's	57
Hub 51	53	Tempo Café	16		P.J. Clarke's	3
Japonais	20	3rd Coast	1		Redhead Piano Bar	37
Kamehachi	40 & 60	Tru	33		Rockit Bar and Grill	51
Karyn's Cooked	23	Vermillion	47		Signature Room	18
Kinzie Chop House	55	Vong's Thai Kitchen	52		10pin Bowling Lounge	59
Klay Oven	54				Whiskey Bar	10

depicting a key event in the city's history: the city's discovery by French explorers in the seventeenth-century; its settling by nineteenth-century pioneers; the Fort Dearborn Massacre during the War of 1812; and the city's regeneration after the Great Fire. The southwest tower now houses the seasonal **McCormick Tribune Bridgehouse & Chicago River Museum** (see p.45).

The Michigan Avenue Bridge is composed of two levels, or "leaves", which are raised independently of one another to allow boat traffic to pass beneath.

The lower level was expressly designed to service the *Chicago Sun-Times* and *Chicago Tribune* newspapers, which were both written and printed nearby (now only the *Tribune's* editorial offices remain, in Tribune Tower). The design, which came to be known as a Chicago-style bascule bridge, was replicated on fifty bridges along the river, but mastering its operation apparently took a little practice. On opening day, a bridge tender raised the Michigan Avenue Bridge for a boat, unaware that four cars were parked on it, and dumped the vehicles into the river. These days the bridge is lifted – uneventfully – on Wednesday and Saturday mornings in summer.

After the bridge was completed, developers renamed hardscrabble Pine Street – at that time, an unpaved road of soap factories, breweries and warehouses – North Michigan Avenue, capitalizing on existing Michigan Avenue's cachet. Next, they persuaded two local businesses to establish banner headquarters at the grand new avenue's southernmost end: the Wrigley Building (1924) on the west, the Tribune Tower (1922) to the east. Still, it wasn't until real-estate entrepreneur Arthur Rubloff christened the strip "The Magnificent Mile", then set about making good this claim of magnificence in the 1960s, that the area truly came to life.

With the wholehearted support of Mayor Richard J. Daley, the Magnificent Mile exploded with shops, but only in the past decade has it come into full flower, literally – Daley's son, the current mayor, has poured millions of taxpayers' dollars into beautification projects around the city, but few are as striking as the **lush flowerbeds** lining this renowned corridor.

The Wrigley Building and around

Flanking the southern entrance of the Magnificent Mile is the **Wrigley Building**, 400 N Michigan Ave, sometimes called the "Jewel of the Mile". The nickname is especially fitting at night, when hundreds of floodlights across the river bathe the glazed white terracotta facade and huge clocktower in sparkling light. Composed of two towers linked by enclosed walkways, the building's shape was modelled on the Giralda Tower of the Cathedral of Seville, but the ornamentation was done in French Renaissance style. It holds the headquarters of the Wrigley chewing-gum company (now owned by Warren Buffett's Berkshire Hathaway investment group) and a variety of tenants. Step inside the building's lobby, open during regular business hours, to see its extensive brasswork.

Next door, at 401 N Wabash Ave, the mirrored oval **Trump International Hotel & Tower** topped out in September 2008 at 92 storeys, making it the second-tallest building in the US after the Sears Tower. Originally Donald Trump had planned to make it the tallest building in the world, but plans were scaled back after the September 11, 2001, terrorist attacks. Surprisingly sensitive to its context, echoing the curve of the river and the Wrigley Building, the structure contains a hotel (see p.155), the obligatory luxury condos and a restaurant. Adrian Smith, formerly of Skidmore, Owings and Merrill, was the chief architect.

Just north of the Wrigley Building stands the pensive-looking statue of **Benito Juarez**, president of Mexico from 1861 to 1872, and a contemporary of Illinois native Abraham Lincoln. Indeed, Juarez was often referred to as the "Mexican Abraham Lincoln", and the two shared a regular correspondence and friendship, perhaps owing to their backgrounds in law and their similar paths from poverty to presidency. For a memorable bite to eat in the area, head down the stairs to the venerable grease-pit *Billy Goat Tavern* (see p.172), tucked away beneath the statue and Michigan Avenue.

The Tribune Tower

Across the road from the Wrigley Building, the **Tribune Tower**, 435 N Michigan Ave, rises like a Gothic cathedral from the riverbank, complete with flying buttresses and ornate scrollwork. The tower was built in 1925 as headquarters for the *Chicago Tribune*, supported by the deep pockets of the newspaper's eccentric editor-publisher Robert "The Colonel" McCormick. Dapper McCormick and his scruffy co-publisher, Joseph Patterson, launched a contest in 1922 to mark the 75th anniversary of the founding of the *Chicago Tribune*, offering $100,000 in prizes to architects around the world willing to submit designs for the "most beautiful office building in the world". The winning entry was by the American team John Mead Howells and Raymond Hood, with second place going to Finnish-born Modernist Eliel Saarinen.

Like Louis Sullivan, Howells and Hood were heavily influenced by Britain's Arts and Crafts movement, which rebelled against angular, mass-produced decoration; hence, most of the detail features plants and animals, as well as figures from Aesop's fables, woven into the scrollwork in the stone screen above the main entranceway. Don't miss the **main lobby**, which has notable decorative features of its own: quotations serving as propaganda in support of a free press are chiselled over almost every inch of marble. There's a massive relief map of North America on the main wall; strangely, it's made from plaster mixed with old dollar bills, since tough currency paper enhances durability. The planned image included much of South America, too; but the slightly batty and very patriotic Colonel decided to make the United States more prominent by chopping two feet off the bottom of the design.

The *Chicago Tribune* still has offices in the building, and its subsidiary **WGN radio** (its call letters stand for "World's Greatest Newspaper" – see p.30) still broadcasts from here; you can watch DJs at work most weekdays from 9am to 9pm, and some weekends, in the ground-floor studio facing Michigan Avenue.

Fragments of history

The most famous feature of the Tribune Tower are the 120 **fragments of famous buildings** dotting the facade; they include pieces from the Houses of Parliament in London, St Peter's in Rome, the Taj Mahal and the Forbidden City in Beijing. The tradition began with the Colonel himself who, while working as a war correspondent during World War I in France, grabbed a chunk of Ypres cathedral that had been knocked from the wall by German shells. Soon, the Colonel was instructing his far-flung network of newshounds (by honourable means) to create a display that would underscore his claim that the *Trib* was the "World's Greatest Newspaper". Of course, many reporters chose to risk the wrath of local lawmakers rather than the anger of their ornery boss, so no one can be sure how many of the souvenirs were purloined rather than purchased. Their activities became so well known that one journalist arrived in Reims, France, to see the local newspaper blaring warnings about his intentions across its front page.

These days, new (legal) acquisitions are set aside for ten years to gauge their true historic value before being mounted on the walls – exceptions include a piece of the Berlin Wall added in 1990, and the moon rock on long-term loan from NASA that's displayed in its own glass case. To identify the fragments, pick up one of the superb free **leaflets** available inside the main lobby.

McCormick Freedom Museum

Opened in 2006, the **McCormick Freedom Museum**, 445 N Michigan Ave (Wed–Mon 10am–6pm; ☎ 312/222-4860, ⓦ www.freedommuseum.us), occupies a two-level space at the base of Tribune Tower and is dedicated to examining the role of the First Amendment in American life. It's not much of a museum in a formal sense, with only a few artefacts, but the numerous multimedia displays on the history of democracy, the US Constitution and the various controversies that have erupted over the First Amendment's interpretation provide a rousing civics lesson. They cover hot-button issues like hate speech, immigrants' rights and eminent domain.

The Chicago Water Tower and Pumping Station

Chicago's past and present collide at the intersection of Michigan Avenue and Pearson Street, where the sky-scraping mall and condominium **Water Tower Place** (Oprah Winfrey's home as of 2008) faces off against one of the last remnants of Old Chicago, the **Chicago Water Tower**.

An awkward-looking limestone structure surrounded by low turrets – Oscar Wilde described it as "a castellated monstrosity with pepper boxes stuck all over it" – the water tower was built in 1869 to house a standpipe that equalized the pressure of water from the **Pumping Station** across the street. Both structures were part of a major effort by the city to supply safe drinking water to its swelling population, a goal that was really only reached in 1900, when the city reversed the course of the Chicago River, flushing the city's waste south toward St. Louis. Because the buildings withstood the Great Fire of 1871 that engulfed the rest of downtown, they became symbolic of Chicago's survival and remain among the city's best-known landmarks.

Today, the tiny interior of the Water Tower, 805 N Michigan Ave, houses temporary photo exhibitions on Chicago themes, while the Pumping Station, 163 E Pearson St, contains the **Chicago Water Works Visitor Center** (Mon–Thurs 8am–7pm, Fri 8am–6pm, Sat 9am–6pm, Sun 10am–4pm; ☎ 1-877/244-2246, ⓦ www.choosechicago.com), whose staff can provide tons of maps and brochures, plus details on the latest cultural events throughout the city. A recent addition to the pumping station is a 270-seat theatre that hosts productions by the **Lookingglass Theatre Company**, an acting ensemble that boasts former *Friends* star David Schwimmer as a founder and active member (see p.206 for more information).

The John Hancock Center and around

Sleek and muscular, the **John Hancock Center**, 875 N Michigan Ave, is a tapered, quarter-mile-high construction of cross-braced steel, black aluminum skin and bronze-tinted windows, topped by two massive spires. Though it appears imposing from its base, viewed from afar the building is beautifully austere, a splendid example of the International style that Mies van der Rohe (see p.53) so effectively championed.

Upon its completion in 1969, the Hancock Center, designed by Skidmore, Owings and Merrill, was the tallest building in Chicago, but it was surpassed in height by the Sears Tower (another SOM design) in 1974. In spite of its slightly lower elevation, the Hancock Center's 94th-floor **observatory** (daily 9am–11pm; last observatory ticket sold at 10.45pm; $15, seniors $13, children 4–11

Chicago architecture

In an architectural prizefight between America's biggest cities, there's little question that Chicago would win by a knockout. Not only are the city's grand buildings diverse in style, but most of them stand within a few blocks of one another, inviting comparison and study that's impractical or even impossible in other urban cores. Unique structures ranging from the rugged limestone Water Tower to the sleek and futuristic IBM Building will give you an idea of the spectrum of architectural genius that has been cultivated here over the past 150 years.

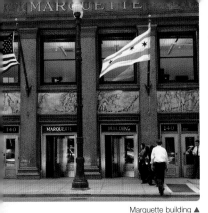

Marquette building ▲

Manhattan building ▼

The Chicago School

After the Great Fire of 1871 razed downtown Chicago, ambitious architects flocked to the city to take advantage of a once-in-a-lifetime combination: hundreds of clients clamouring for new designs and virtually no architectural context that would inhibit bold experimentation. Even before the debris was cleared, William Le Baron Jenney, Louis Sullivan, James Holabird, Martin Roche, Charles Atwood, Daniel Burnham and John Wellborn Root were beginning to define what would come to be known as the **Chicago School of architecture**. Jenney, the elder statesman of the group, made the most important contribution to the style, and to the future of the skyscraper, by being the first to use an internal steel frame, rather than thick external walls, to support a building's weight. Compare his steel-framed **Manhattan Building** (1891) to Chicago's tallest masonry structure, the **Monadnock Building** (also 1891) by Burnham and Root, and you can see how much lighter the building feels. Just four years later, the team of Holabird and Roche created the **Marquette Building**

Window dressing

The Chicago School of architecture is marked by its innovative window treatments that fused form with function. **Oriel windows** are a type of bay window that run the height of a structure to emphasize its verticality, while **Chicago windows** contain three sections: a huge, fixed central pane and two smaller sashes on either side. Excellent examples of Chicago School windows can be found on the Fisher Building and the Marquette Building.

and Atwood and Burnham designed the **Reliance Building**, both clear forerunners to the modern skyscraper with their bountiful windows and strong vertical lines.

From City to Prairie

The Chicago School's innovations weren't just technical. After working briefly with Jenney, **Louis Sullivan** studied for a year at the École des Beaux-Arts in Paris and returned with a love of ornamentation that would mark some of the finest Chicago School designs. Like the Reliance Building, Sullivan's 1899 **Carson Pirie Scott department-store building** boasts a steel frame and hundreds of Chicago-style windows, but it's best known for the riotous cast-iron ornamental work surrounding the curved entryway at the corner of State and Madison streets. Sullivan's most famous protégé, **Frank Lloyd Wright**, picked up some tips and tricks from the master, whose influence can be detected in the ornate lobby of **The Rookery**, which Wright renovated in 1905. But it was their collaborative design of the 1892 **Charnley-Persky House**, in the Gold Coast neighbourhood, that really shows where Wright was headed in his career. While his predecessors looked skyward, Wright turned to the wide, flat grasslands around Chicago for inspiration, eventually inventing the **Prairie style**. His low, horizontal buildings feature open interiors, long stretches of windows, and a connection to their surroundings through native stone and wood. There is a clutch of Wright homes in the suburb of **Oak Park**, including his home and studio, but the masterpiece of this movement is the **Robie House** (1910) in Hyde Park.

▲ 333 Wacken Drive

▼ Frank Lloyd Wright house in Oak Park

▼ Marquette building lobby

John Hancock Center ▲

Tribune Tower ▼

The International style

There's a smattering of other architectural styles on display in Chicago – among them **Beaux Arts** (the Art Institute), **Art Deco** (the Chicago Board of Trade) and **Gothic Revival** (the Tribune Building) – but it wasn't until German émigré **Ludwig Mies van der Rohe** arrived in 1938 that Chicago regained its place at the cutting edge of architecture. Mies took the modernist ideals of the first Chicago School a step further in his groundbreaking new **International style**, which eliminated all historical references and ornamentation and celebrated neutral, rectilinear forms of glass and steel. Two of Mies' most notable creations are the **Federal Center** (1959–74) and the **IBM Building** (1971). Mies still looms large over Chicago, notably in the firm of **Skidmore, Owings & Merrill**, whose designs for the **John Hancock** and **Sears Tower** owe a considerable debt to the man who famously quipped, "Less is more".

Five of the finest

▶▶ **The Rookery** (1888). Seminal work in red-brick and terracotta with a surprisingly light and airy lobby.
▶▶ **The Reliance Building** (1895). Precursor of the modern skyscraper, its fourteen storeys feature an almost entirely glass facade.
▶▶ **Tribune Tower** (1925). Majestic Gothic skyscraper, with flying buttresses.
▶▶ **The John Hancock Center** (1970). This 100-storey black steel-frame building features exterior steel columns braced by X-shaped steel diagonals.
▶▶ **Jay Pritzker Pavilion** (2004). The centrepiece of Millennium Park boasts twelve "ribbons" of steel-plated aluminium framing the stage and an acoustic-enhancing steel trellis.

$9; ☎312/751-3680 or ☎1-888/875-8439, ⓦwww.hancock-observatory.com) is a better perch from which to view the city.

As with the Sears Tower, you'll see as far as Indiana, Michigan and Wisconsin on a clear day, but the Hancock offers 360-degree views (rather than 180), stays open later, and is generally less crowded (come before 11am or after 6pm for the shortest queues). And if the views alone aren't diverting enough, you can listen to an audio tour (free with admission) or check out one of the talking telescopes that point out what you're seeing. There's a wall devoted to city history and a bit about the construction of the building itself.

If you just want the view, though, skip the observatory and head straight to the **Signature Room** on the 96th floor, where you can take in the scenery for the price of a drink (see p.190). One floor down, the *Signature Room* **restaurant** also has terrific views, but the American fare is overpriced and uninspired; you're better off fueling up before or after your trip. Elsewhere in the building there are a couple of well-regarded art galleries (see p.216).

Opposite the John Hancock Center is the English and French Gothic **Fourth Presbyterian Church**, at 126 E Chestnut St, built in 1914. Peek inside at the elegantly understated interior and the peaceful courtyard – a surprisingly quiet spot just a stone's throw from Michigan Avenue.

Streeterville

Stretching north of the river and east of the Magnificent Mile to the lake, **Streeterville** was hardly a place to visit until the city revamped **Navy Pier** in 1995, creating the city's largest amusement park and one of its top attractions. The arrival of the **Museum of Contemporary Art** a year later helped raise the neighbourhood's profile another notch, and nowadays even locals are likely to venture here for the swanky hotel bars and restaurants that dot the landscape. Streeterville's stretch of **lakefront** makes for a pleasant stroll or a bike ride; the path is accessible through tunnels at Chicago Avenue, Ontario Street and Ohio Street, and bikes can be rented at Navy Pier.

George Wellington Streeter

More than any Chicago neighbourhood, Streeterville had a shaky start. The land east of Michigan Avenue and north of the Chicago River came into being through a bizarre set of circumstances. On July 11, 1886, **George Wellington Streeter**, a captain and a spitfire of a man, ran his makeshift boat aground on a sandbar some 400ft offshore of today's Streeterville. After obtaining permission from one of the landowners to let him keep his boat there, he persuaded city contractors to dump refuse around his boat. In a short time, the rubbish had filled in the space between his boat and shore and could be called "land", a designation that Streeter would use to great advantage. He declared this previously nonexistent plot of over a hundred acres the "Free District of Lake Michigan", a territory independent of both Chicago and neighbouring Illinois, and then sold chunks of it to unscrupulous buyers. For the next three decades, Streeter guarded this illegal shanty area with dubious legal claims and a shotgun. Somehow he survived through all of this but the courts eventually overruled him in 1918, paving the way for development to begin in earnest west of his plot.

The Museum of Contemporary Art

Specializing in work that's provocative, offbeat, seductive or divisive, the **Museum of Contemporary Art (MCA)**, 220 E Chicago Ave (Tues 10am–8pm, Wed–Sun 10am–5pm; suggested donation $10, students and seniors $6, free 5–8pm on Tues; ☎312/280-2660, ⓦwww.mcachicago.org) occupies a squat, boxy building designed by German architect Josef Paul Kleihues. There's usually some sort of public art installation on the platforms flanking the stairs that lead up to the second-floor entrance.

Museum facilities take up all four levels. The ground floor is home to the lower level of the gift shop and the auditorium. The second floor contains the upper level of the gift shop, a large space for temporary exhibitions and the rather antiseptic café, *Puck's at the MCA*, best visited in summer when the terrace is open.

Pieces from the permanent collection are displayed on a rotating basis on the third and fourth floors. On the third, you're almost certain to find some Modernist mobiles of **Alexander Calder**; a local art collector has lent the museum fifteen of his bobbing, abstract sculptures on indefinite loan, among them the monochromatic *Black 17 Dots* and *The Ghost*, especially eye-catching given Calder's penchant for using rainbow colours.

On the fourth floor, expect to find work by modern-art stalwarts like **Jasper Johns**, **Sol LeWitt** and **René Magritte** as well as more contemporary offerings. There will probably be at least a few pieces by **Bruce Nauman** on view, as the MCA owns one of the largest collections of his work. Nauman's best known for his flashing neon slogans like *Life Death Love Hate Pleasure Pain,* but he also dabbled in creating video and audio environments, photography, sculpture and drawing. Photographer **Cindy Sherman** is represented by a number of her own self-dramatizing portraits and is the subject of a painting by **Chuck Close**, in his customary passport-photo style. The museum also possesses works by the controversial photographer **Andres Serrano** – look for prints from his *Morgue* series, in which deceased subjects are identified not by name but by the manner of death.

Navy Pier

Navy Pier, jutting into Lake Michigan at the end of East Ohio Street, may be Chicago's top tourist attraction, and is certainly family-friendly, but it has the feel of commercialism run amok – everything in sight is sponsored to within an inch of its life. Navy Pier could also be anywhere – aside from one museum, which touts its local connection, this pier makes little reference to its hometown or its history. Built as Municipal Pier No. 2 in 1916 under Burnham's Chicago plan (see box, p.53), it was quickly appropriated during World War I by the Navy, after which it was renamed in 1927. Navy Pier then served various civil and military purposes until the city decided to smarten up the ramshackle structure in the 1970s, and pumped massive investment into its refurbishment; it opened in its current incarnation in 1995. Note that it's fairly confusing to get around, thanks to the enormous parking garages and convention centre in its mid-section: stop at the information desk inside the western entrance, or at the kiosk just south of the pier, and grab a **free map** – you'll need it.

Pier attractions

Just inside the main entrance to your right is the popular, often chaotic **Chicago Children's Museum** (Sun–Wed & Fri 10am–5pm, Thurs & Sat

Navy Pier practicalities

Navy Pier hours are mid-May–Aug: Sun–Thurs 10am–10pm, Fri & Sat 10am–midnight; Sept–Oct & April–mid-May Sun–Thurs 10am–8pm, Fri & Sat 10am–10pm; Nov–March Mon–Thurs 10am–8pm, Fri & Sat 10am–10pm, Sun 10am–7pm. Admission to the park is free, but some attractions charge a fee. Fireworks are exploded over the pier from late May through August every Wednesday night at 9.30pm and Saturday night at 10.15pm, with additional times added throughout the year. For further details, contact ☎312/595-7437 or 1-800/595-7437 or visit ⓦwww.navypier.com, which has a full entertainment calendar.

Getting there and around

Getting to Navy Pier on **public transportation** is easy. Four bus lines stop at the pier's front entrance every day – the #29-State St, #65-Grand Ave, #66-Chicago Ave, and #124-Navy Pier Express – with three more stopping here during weekday rush hour (the #2, #120 and #121). There's also a convenient **free trolley** that runs between State Street and the pier along Grand Avenue (westbound) and Illinois Street (eastbound) every twenty minutes (Sun–Thurs 10am–11pm, Fri & Sat 10am–1am). Walking to Navy Pier is by no means cumbersome, but the free trolley will save you at least fifteen minutes. Snag a bus map and a trolley map at the Water Works Visitor Center (p.80) or the Chicago Cultural Center (p.45) or go to Navy Pier's website to download maps.

If you're **driving** to Navy Pier, you can park at one of the three **parking garages** inside the pier (Mon–Thurs $19 per day, Fri–Sun $23 per day); if they're full, head back to one of the many parking lots on Ohio, Illinois and Grand avenues just west of Lake Shore Drive.

Boats and bicycles

While the Michigan Avenue Bridge is the place to go for cruises of the Chicago River, Navy Pier's Dock Street (the path that runs along the southern side of the pier) is where most tours of the lakefront begin. The **Shoreline Sightseeing Co** (☎312/222-9328, ⓦwww.shorelinesightseeing.com) runs standard, thirty-minute cruises along the lakeshore, as well as a water taxi service to Museum Campus, from May to October, while other companies offer specialty tours. **Seadog Cruises** (☎312/822-7200, ⓦwww.seadogcruises.com) conducts its thirty-minute tours on speedboats, while ninety-minute sightseeing tours are given on the **Tall Ship Wendy** (☎312/595-5555, ⓦwww.tallshipwendy.com), a four-masted schooner. The **Spirit of Chicago** (☎312/836-7899, ⓦwww.spiritofchicago.com), **Odyssey** (☎1-800/947-9367, ⓦwww.odysseycruises.com) and **Mystic Blue** (☎1-888/330-4700, ⓦwww.mysticbluecruises.com) are all sleek mini-cruise ships that offer meals, drinks, and dancing on longer outings.

If you'd rather get around under your own steam – and this means biking *from* the pier, not *on* the pier, which is usually too crowded for cyclists – head to **Bike Chicago**'s kiosk on the south side of the pier, near the *Shoreline* boats, and rent a set of wheels; they also organize lakefront tours. For details, see "Sports and outdoor activities", p.234.

10am–8pm; $9, free to children under 1; free to all Thurs 5–8pm; free to children under 15 first Mon of the month, when hours are extended to 8pm; ☎312/527-1000, ⓦwww.chicagochildrensmuseum.org), which plans to stay here until 2012, when it will move to a new facility across from Millennium Park. Exhibits include a large archeology pit, where would-be fossil hunters can dig for treasure, and a model of the city of Chicago, resized for toddlers, including a fourteen-foot-high model of the Sears Tower made from more than 50,000 Lego bricks. Outside the museum, in the **Family Pavilion**, a troupe of

▲ Navy Pier Ferris wheel

actors dressed as pirates or other colourful characters performs skits for kids three or four times daily; see the posted schedule or check online for details.

Navy Pier's main attraction, **Pier Park**, is a mini-amusement park on the pier's upper deck. It's here that you'll find the soaring, 148-foot-high **Ferris wheel** (same hours as pier, weather permitting; $6), which offers great views of downtown, though it doesn't add much if you've already been to the John Hancock Center observatory and pales in comparison to the original Ferris wheel created for the World's Fair of 1893, which was 260ft tall and carried 2000 people at a time. Close by, there's an **old-fashioned carousel**, aimed at very young kids, with painted horses and the like (same hours as pier, weather permitting; $5).

At the southeast corner of the Pier Park, the glass and steel **Chicago Shakespeare Theater** (☎312/595-5600, ⓦ www.chicagoshakes.com) feels a bit incongruous amid the hot dog vendors and cruise ship docks, but it manages to turn out some fabulous drama by the Bard and others, winning the 2008 Tony Award for being the best regional theatre in the country. The eye-catching building contains two intimate venues, seating 200 and 500. For further details, see "Performing arts and film", p.204.

The only other cultural offering on the pier is the free **Smith Museum of Stained Glass** (opening hours the same as Navy Pier; tours held most Thursdays at 2pm; for information, call ☎312/595-5024), an 800ft-long series of galleries running along the south side of the exhibition halls, across from the *Mystic Blue* dock. Among 150 stained-glass panels dating from 1870 to the present day are Louis Sullivan's octagonal ceiling panels, rescued from the original Chicago Stock Exchange building before it was demolished, and Frank Lloyd Wright's *Avery Coonley Pool House Window*. Unfortunately, the dim hallway-like setting detracts significantly from the work.

River North

The once industrial wasteland of **River North**, due west of Streeterville on the other side of Michigan Avenue, has seen its fortunes rise ever since the 1970s, when artists first began staking out affordable studio space in the abandoned warehouses and factories. While most artists are long since gone and the cutting edge has moved to the West Loop, there's still quite a lot of good art to see in the **River North Gallery District**. But what the area's better known for these days are the bars, restaurants and clubs that have moved in around the outskirts of the gallery district, many with sidewalk seating, which makes it a good area to saunter around in the summertime. **Hubbard Street** is especially jam-packed with trendy spots, but you can find good places, ranging from cosy to cavernous, throughout the area (see the "Eating" and "Drinking" chapters for reviews).

The Merchandise Mart and around

While they don't merit a special trip (you can see them all on an architectural river cruise, p.44), there are a few buildings worth noting along the north bank of the river, just across from the Loop. The monumental **Merchandise Mart**, 300 N Wells St at Merchandise Mart Plaza (60–90min tours held throughout the year; $12; call for times: ☎312/527-7762), houses six hundred private showrooms of home furnishings that are open to trade buyers only, as well as a food court and two floors of shops dedicated to home design, construction and renovation that are open to the public.

With 4.2 million square feet of space, the Mart takes up the whole block from N Orleans to N Wells Street and Merchandise Mart Plaza to W Kinzie Street. It was constructed for Marshall Field in 1931 as a showroom and administrative headquarters. When the department store faced tough economic times after World War II, Kennedy patriarch Joe – who knew a good bargain when he saw one – snapped up the building for a fraction of its value simply by paying its back taxes. The Kennedys completed the flip in 1998, selling the place for over $500 million. Joe's unmistakable – if oddball – 1953 addition to the building was the row of **eight bronze busts** on marble pillars at the Mart's main entrance, grandly titled "the Merchandise Mart Hall of Fame" and paying tribute to the patron saints of shopping, including F.W. Woolworth, Edward A. Filene and, of course, Marshall Field himself.

The River North gallery district

River North's **gallery district** doesn't generate quite the excitement that it did during its heyday in the 1980s, now that some galleries have had to pack up and move to cheaper neighbourhoods (like the West Loop, p.114), but it still accounts for a sizeable chunk of the city's art scene, notably around Huron, Superior, and Wells Street, where you'll find some well-established places.

Galleries usually host receptions for new shows on Friday evenings (5–8pm), with the artists themselves and cool crowds on hand for great people-watching. For information on current events and occasional free trolleys that run between the River North galleries and the Michigan Avenue museums, pick up a copy of the free glossy *Chicago Gallery News*, available from some hotels and most galleries, or visit its helpful website, ⓦwww.chicagogallerynews.com. For additional gallery reviews, see chapter 18, "Galleries".

Walking three blocks east to Dearborn Street will bring you to the twin towers of **Marina City** (entrance at 300 N State St) – look for the buildings that resemble corncobs – a monument to the combined power of late-1960s paranoia and the Chicago winter. Bertrand Goldberg designed the complex to be completely self-contained, offering just about everything you could need in your life (doctor, dentist, mall, even an undertaker) under one roof. Since most residents do need to get out and about once in a while, the bottom twenty storeys are used as parking garages: the cars peeking out at the edge of each floor look surreal and not altogether secure hundreds of feet high in the air. Most visitors to the city, though, will only stop by to check out the *House of Blues* nightclub (see p.199), which opened here as part of a massive modernization programme in the late 1990s.

One block north stands the future home of the **Museum of Broadcast Communications** (℡312/245-8200, ⓦwww.museum.tv), 400 N State St at Kinzie, an energy-efficient glass box of a building that will hold 15,000 square feet of exhibits on the history of TV and radio, as well as studios where you can try your hand at broadcasting, a shop and a café. The projected opening date is 2009, but check first, as delays have plagued the project since its inception.

Holy Name Cathedral and around

Heading north on State Street for eight blocks or so will bring you to **Holy Name Cathedral**, 735 N State St (tour information ℡312/787-8040), currently undergoing a massive restoration. The seat of the Roman Catholic archdiocese of Chicago, the grand, Gothic Revival church was designed in 1875 by Patrick Charles Keely, who, by that time, had a remarkable six hundred churches and sixteen cathedrals under his belt. The interior features several striking examples of contemporary spiritual art, from the sculpted resurrection crucifix suspended from the ceiling to the bronze-cast Stations of the Cross on the walls of the nave. Note the red decorations hanging high above the sanctuary – cardinals' hats (*galeros*), each one representing one of the city's past cardinals.

A few blocks further on is the Romanesque **Newberry Library**, 60 W Walton St, between N Clark and N Dearborn sts (exhibit gallery open Mon, Fri & Sat 8.15am–5.30pm, Tues, Wed & Thurs 8.15am–7.30pm; free building tours Thurs 3pm & Sat 10.30am; free gallery walks Thurs 5.45pm; ℡312/943-9090, ⓦwww.newberry.org). This sumptuously appointed research library, whose wide-ranging collection covers Western Europe and the Americas from the Middle Ages, includes a few oddities as well, such as the only bilingual text of *Popol Vuh*, the Mayan creation myth first written down in Guatemala during the sixteenth century. What's more likely to draw you here, though, are the exhibitions in the downstairs galleries, where you can linger over artefacts, photographs and paintings from its collection.

Across from the library, **Washington Square Park** is one of the prettiest vest-pocket parks in the city, with a central fountain, bursting flower beds, walking paths and benches. It wasn't always this way. Known as Bughouse Square from the 1910s to the 1960s for the neighbouring flophouses, the park became a famous public forum where everyone from established authors to editors to anarchists, struggling artists, hack writers and street performers had their say on the soapboxes. The spirit of the soapboxers lives on in the Newberry Library's annual Bughouse Square Debates, held on a Saturday afternoon in July, when residents try their hand at public oration (and heckling). There's also live music and a book sale.

The Gold Coast

Roughly bounded by Oak Street, North Avenue, Lake Shore Drive and Clark Street, the **Gold Coast** is split between its urban southern half and its serene and residential northern half. During the day, most activity is centred on and around **Oak Street**'s swanky boutiques and **Rush Street**'s sidewalk cafes, just a few short blocks from the Magnificent Mile, while after dark, crowds can be found in the myriad bars of **Division Street**, where hordes of twenty-something singles congregate in boozy packs.

Above Division Street, the Gold Coast enters its most exclusive stretch; a stroll along N Astor Street towards Lincoln Park will take you past some of the city's most palatial digs, like the elegant Philip B. Maher-designed Art Deco high-rise at **1260 N Astor St**, once home to famous Chicago names such as Potter Palmer II, Robert Hall McCormick III and Morton Salt Company chairman Sterling Morton.

Getting here is easy by train or bus. Take the Red Line to Clark/Division or hop on the #151-Sheridan bus, running up Michigan Avenue and Lake Shore Drive to Division Street.

Oak Street and around

On the border between Near North and the Gold Coast, **Oak Street** is filled with ultra-chic shops like Prada, Jimmy Choo and Jil Sander as well as the slightly more accessible Bebe, Juicy Couture and Mac. If you've got the dough, it's a pleasant enough place to shop, though it generally lacks the energy of the Magnificent Mile.

By contrast, running at an angle from Chicago Avenue to Elm Street, **Rush Street** is lined with bars, sidewalk cafés and old-school steakhouses that are packed at all hours. Most places are touristy and overpriced, but there are a couple of exceptions (see "Eating", p.173). Just one block north of Elm, **Division Street** is home to a string of raucous bars that overflow with drunken college students and young professionals on weekend nights, with the addition of middle-aged men on the prowl giving the whole area the nickname "the Viagra Triangle" (see "Drinking", p.190, for reviews).

Follow Oak Street east and then take the pedestrian tunnel under Lake Shore Drive to reach **Oak Street Beach**, a small stretch of sand that's packed on summer weekends with toned and tanned residents from the Gold Coast's high-rise condos. The beach evolved when this area was a resort – the famed **Drake Hotel** (for review, see p.157) opened in 1920 as a beachfront property, where guests could wander from the changing rooms on the arcade level out onto the sand. Unfortunately, the construction of Lake Shore Drive severed the beach from the neighbourhood, but it's easy enough to access via the tunnel and remains a great place to throw down your towel and take a dip. Among its facilities are changing rooms and bathrooms, volleyball courts, and the *Oak Street Beachstro* (see p.172), a restaurant right on the beach that offers a casual, albeit overpriced menu, along with stellar lake and skyline views.

North of Division Street

The northern half of the Gold Coast is predominantly residential, with a mix of architecturally varied mansions, most from the late nineteenth century, and luxury high-rises predating the 1975 landmark designation of the district, which curtailed construction. Wander the side streets – especially

North State Parkway and North Astor Street – to get a feel for this tranquil part of town.

At the south end of N State Parkway, the **Pump Room**, in the *Ambassador East Hotel* (see p.157), milks its movie-star associations for all they're worth – the foyer is covered with photos of celebrity patrons from Humphrey Bogart and Frank Sinatra to Lauren Bacall and Elizabeth Taylor – but it's still a fun place to linger over a drink and soak up the swank atmosphere.

Further up the street, the unassuming red-brick mansion at no. 1340 was once the famed **Playboy Mansion**, home and office of publisher and Chicago native Hugh Hefner, whose lavish parties for the glitterati are renowned. Hefner is long gone from here (he moved out in the early 1970s), as is the door plate inscribed *Si non oscillas, noli tintinnare* ("If you don't swing, don't ring"), and the mansion has since been converted into million-dollar apartments.

A couple of blocks north, just below Lincoln Park, the conspicuous octagonal tower, nineteen chimneys and numerous gables, turrets and dormers mark the Queen Anne-style red-brick Roman Catholic **Archbishop's Residence** at 1555 N State Parkway. The mansion was built in 1880 on the former site of a cemetery; soon after, the archdiocese sold off the surrounding plots of land – keeping a sizeble yard to themselves, of course – to wealthy Chicago families, who proceeded to construct their dream homes in the neighbourhood.

Charnley-Persky House

A block west of N State Parkway, on Astor Street, stands the **Charnley–Persky House**, no. 1365 (℡312/573-1365, ⓦwww.sah.org), an austere three-storey building of brick and limestone that's considered a forerunner of modern residential architecture. Louis Sullivan and his then assistant Frank Lloyd Wright built the house between 1891 and 1892, adopting the low-lying, symmetrical style that would later become the hallmark of Wright's Prairie School architecture (see *Chicago Architecture* colour section) and herald the move away from Victorian design trends. Inside, the stairwell and mantelpieces feature beautifully carved woodwork, including Louis Sullivan's signature pointed-seedpod and circle-and-square motifs, while the entrance is a skylit atrium panelled in burnished oak. The Society of Architectural Historians, which has its headquarters here, runs 45-minute **tours** of the sparsely furnished house on Wednesday at noon (free) and on Saturday at 10am, with an additional tour offered from April to November on Saturday at 1pm. Saturday tours of the house cost $5, or $10 if you choose to continue on the 45-minute guided walk along Astor Street and inside the nearby **Madlener House**, 4 W Burton Place, the work of architect Richard E. Schmidt and designer Hugh M. G. Garden.

International Museum of Surgical Science

A few blocks to the northeast, at 1524 N Lake Shore Drive, is one of the city's quirkier sights, the **International Museum of Surgical Science** (May–Sept Tues–Sun 10am–4pm; Oct–April Tues–Sat 10am–4pm; $9, students/seniors $5; tours included with admission Sat 2pm; ℡312/642-6502, ⓦwww.imss.org). Set in a historic 1917 mansion modelled on a chateau on the grounds of Versailles, the museum boasts 22 galleries stuffed with art and artefacts that illustrate the history of surgery around the world. Among the highlights are a polio exhibit featuring a rare iron lung from the 1930s; a shoe-fitting fluoroscope made in the days before radiation's dangers were known; a molded plywood leg splint by furniture makers Ray and Charles Eames; and reproductions of paintings and murals showing doctors performing surgeries before anesthetics were invented, their patients' faces contorted with unimaginable pain.

4

Old Town and Lincoln Park

Though it's just a few blocks northwest of the dandified Gold Coast, you won't see manicured hedges and white-gloved doormen in **Old Town**: the neighbourhood has a distinctly more lived-in feel, with brick row houses and, in the **Old Town Triangle**, charming wooden residences jumbled along its narrow tree-lined streets. It's a fine place for a stroll, but the main reason you'll probably visit is to see a show at the legendary comedy club **Second City** or the **Steppenwolf Theatre**, widely considered Chicago's finest theatrical venue.

Snooty hipsters deride **Lincoln Park**, just north of Old Town, as a yuppie haven, filled with weekend rollerbladers working up a sweat before grabbing a latte. While it's certainly true that the area is upscale, middle-class, and rather mainstream, its gorgeous namesake park – home to the free **Lincoln Park Zoo** and **Lincoln Park Conservatory** – is a powerful lure for any visitor, as are the verdant avenues of the neighbourhood itself. Lincoln Park's one offbeat section centers on **DePaul University**: this enormous Catholic institution, better known for hard partying than devout prayers, has created a small but funky scene in the surrounding blocks.

Some history

Prior to the fire of 1871, **Old Town** was nothing but pasture for local cows. Afterwards, thousands of German immigrants, displaced from their downtown homes, began to arrive, and the nickname "German Broadway" for North Avenue soon stuck. It was never a wealthy place – as is clear from the modest houses everywhere – but the government's decision in the 1940s to raze seventy acres of southwest Old Town and build a massive low-income housing project in its place proved disastrous for what remained of the neighbourhood.

Over the course of thirty years, **Cabrini Green**, as the project is known, grew to encompass 15,000 residents in high-rise and mid-rise towers that by the 1960s had become shamefully neglected by the city as well as by those who lived there. Many law-abiding tenants moved out, leaving the complex to be taken over by drug dealers and criminals. In an effort to show her commitment to the area, **Mayor Jane Byrne** moved into a Cabrini Green apartment in 1981; she lasted three weeks. Old Town residents fled to the suburbs as property values plummeted and street crime rose. Hippies and artists filled the void,

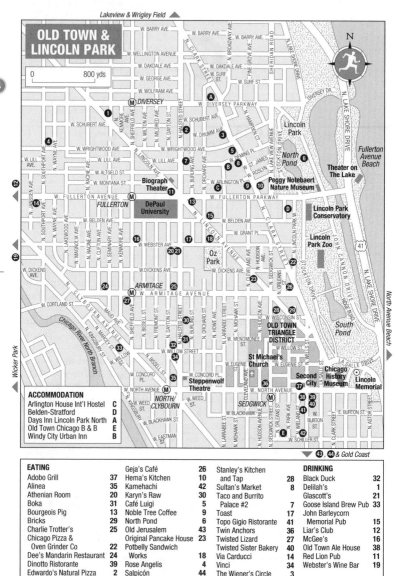

OLD TOWN & LINCOLN PARK

0   800 yds

Lakeview & Wrigley Field ▲

W. BARRY AVE.
W. BARRY AVE.
W. WELLINGTON AVENUE
W. OAKDALE AVE.
W. GEORGE AVE.
W. WOLFRAM AVE.
Ⓜ DIVERSEY
W. SCHUBERT AVE.
W. WRIGHTWOOD AVE.
W. LILL AVE.
W. ALTGELD ST.
W. MONTANA ST.

Biograph Theater

W. FULLERTON AVENUE Ⓜ FULLERTON
DePaul University
W. BELDEN AVE.
W. WEBSTER AVE.

Oz Park

W. DICKENS AVE.
ARMITAGE
W. ARMITAGE AVENUE

OLD TOWN TRIANGLE DISTRICT

St Michael's Church

Steppenwolf Theatre

SEDGWICK

Lincoln Park
North Pond
Peggy Notebaert Nature Museum
Lincoln Park Conservatory
Lincoln Park Zoo
South Pond
Theater on The Lake
Fullerton Avenue Beach
North Avenue Beach

Second City
Chicago History Museum
Lincoln Memorial

▼ ⑬, ⑭ & Gold Coast

ACCOMMODATION

Arlington House Int'l Hostel	C
Belden-Stratford	D
Days Inn Lincoln Park North	A
Old Town Chicago B & B	E
Windy City Urban Inn	B

EATING						DRINKING	
Adobo Grill	37	Geja's Café	26	Stanley's Kitchen		Black Duck	32
Alinea	35	Hema's Kitchen	10	and Tap	28	Delilah's	1
Athenian Room	20	Kamehachi	42	Sultan's Market	8	Glascott's	21
Boka	31	Karyn's Raw	30	Taco and Burrito		Goose Island Brew Pub	33
Bourgeois Pig	13	Café Luigi	5	Palace #2	7	John Barleycorn	
Bricks	29	Noble Tree Coffee	9	Toast	17	Memorial Pub	15
Charlie Trotter's	25	North Pond	6	Topo Gigio Ristorante	41	Liar's Club	12
Chicago Pizza &		Old Jerusalem	43	Twin Anchors	36	McGee's	16
Oven Grinder Co	22	Original Pancake House	23	Twisted Lizard	27	Old Town Ale House	38
Dee's Mandarin Restaurant	24	Potbelly Sandwich		Twisted Sister Bakery	40	Red Lion Pub	11
Dinotto Ristorante	39	Works	18	Via Carducci	14	Webster's Wine Bar	19
Edwardo's Natural Pizza	2	Rose Angelis	4	Vinci	34		
		Salpicón	44	The Wiener's Circle	3		

buying up places on the cheap and establishing countercultural hangouts like Second City, but the neighbourhood remained marginal until the mid-1990s when the city began demolishing Cabrini Green, tower by tower, and replacing it with mixed-income, low-rise housing, a plan that's supposed to be finished by 2010. As crime has decreased, Old Town has surged in popularity, and it's now one of Chicago's more expensive districts.

Originally filled with orchards supplying produce to the city farther south, the area that would become **Lincoln Park** was converted into Chicago's first cemetery in the mid-nineteenth century. The local dead rested in peace for only a few years before city bigwigs had their bodies moved elsewhere to make room for a massive, prairie-inspired greenspace fit for the unofficial capital of the Midwest. Established in 1864 and named in honour of President (and Illinois native) **Abraham Lincoln**, it is a staggering slab of greenery, stretching more than 1200 acres along the lakefront. The adjacent neighbourhood of Lincoln Park, first settled by German farmers, remained a working-class immigrant enclave well into the 1980s but has since been gentrified to the hilt.

Old Town

Old Town has only a couple of cultural sights – the **Steppenwolf Theatre** (see p.206), on the western fringe of the district, and **Second City**, right in the centre of it – but the neighbourhood's streets are still worth exploring for their rows of Victorian homes, offbeat shops and friendly restaurants. **North Wells Street** – Chicago's answer to San Francisco's Haight-Ashbury District in the late 1960s – is the neighbourhood's main drag, and though hardly bohemian nowadays, the short stretch between North Avenue and Schiller Street is mellow and quaint, its sidewalks lined with flower planters, historical markers and plenty of cafés and restaurants offering outdoor seating. If you want a glimpse of Old Town's beatnik past, head to the top of the strip, where the grizzled *Old Town Ale House* (see p.192) sits at the corner of North Avenue and Wieland Street. The bar sees a share of Second City comics (the club is

The Second City

"To be, to be... sure beats the shit out of not to be."

John Belushi as Hamlet, *Second City*, Chicago, 1971

John Belushi may not have taken these words to heart, considering his untimely end in 1982 at the age of 33, but **The Second City improv club** that launched his career is still going strong. Taking its name from a biting *New Yorker* profile about Chicago's second-rung status, it evolved from a drama troupe formed by students at the University of Chicago (*The Graduate* director Mike Nichols and *Tootsie* writer Elaine May among them), becoming the improvisational Compass Players, who settled into the club's present location in 1959. Since then, the facility has expanded to include two theatres (the main stage and the adjacent *Second City e.t.c.*) and has spawned training centres in several locations across the continent, including LA, Toronto, Las Vegas and Detroit, where comedians-in-training are schooled in the unique mix of improvisation and writing of smart, satirical sketches that have become the company's trademark.

But it's Chicago's club that remains the most established, feeding talent to TV's long-running sketch-comedy show *Saturday Night Live* as well as to loads of sitcoms and movies. Alan Alda, Alan Arkin and Ed Asner all got their start here in the 1960s, followed by the likes of Bill Murray, Gilda Radner, Dan Aykroyd and John Belushi in the 1970s. Mike Myers and Chris Farley came up in the 1980s, while Amy Sedaris, Tina Fey and Stephen Colbert made their mark in the 1990s. Years may go by without the club producing any stars of note but, with that kind of track record, it's no wonder people come with high expectations. For details on seeing a show, see p.208.

right across the street), but it's also a Chicago institution in its own right, a dignified old dive with book-lined shelves, bouffant-haired bartenders and a motley crew of yuppies, old-timers, artists and loners. To get to Old Town take the Brown Line El to Sedgwick.

❹ The Old Town Triangle

Spreading north from Second City, the **Old Town Triangle** feels like a town within the city thanks to its narrow streets, lush trees and gardens, as well as an eclectic assortment of wood-frame homes and row houses. Built in the years immediately following the Great Fire, these "workers' cottages" were built mostly in wood and designed with front-facing gable roofs, rectangular floor plans and little ornamentation. Since then, they've been restored with varying degrees of authenticity; you can see some good examples at 215–219 Eugenie St. Keep heading west on Eugenie and you'll hit another great, old-timey bar and restaurant, *Twin Anchors* (see p.175), a favourite of Frank Sinatra's.

If you happen to be in town on the second full weekend of June, be sure to stop by the **Old Town Art Fair** (see p.247), a sixty-year-old fest that brings 250 exhibitors and more than 50,000 art lovers to the neighbourhood, along with food vendors and musicians.

St Michael's Church

Massive **St Michael's Church**, 1660 N Hudson Ave, rises up nearly 290ft and marks the centre of the old German Catholic community that existed here during the mid- to late 1800s. It was for years the tallest building in Chicago, even after the 1871 fire that left only the charred walls and belltower standing. Built in its place in 1873, the new church is a handsome example of the Romanesque style, with ornate murals, stained-glass panels and steeply pitched gables. It continues to be a focal point for the community, with several summer and autumn festivals (including the popular Oktoberfest in late Sept), which raise funds to preserve the building.

Lincoln Park

Extending some six miles from North Avenue to Hollywood Avenue along the lakefront, **Lincoln Park** is, to many, the city's best park. Less urban than Grant Park, less commercial than Millennium Park, it offers wide-open lawns, lush gardens, jogging paths and – best of all in summer – **beaches**, where throngs of locals come to sunbathe, swim and play volleyball. Lincoln Park also has several noteworthy attractions: the excellent **Chicago History Museum** at the south end, and the **Lincoln Park Zoo**, **Lincoln Park Conservatory** and **Notebaert Nature Museum** in the middle of the park.

Spreading west from the park all the way to Damen Avenue, the **neighbourhood** of Lincoln Park is a vast, gentrified zone full of college students (around **DePaul University**), professional twenty-somethings and young families. Though the area doesn't have any formal sights, its spiffed-up rowhouses and mansions make for tantalizing eye-candy on an afternoon stroll, and its commercial drags have some of the most original boutiques, record stores, thrift shops, restaurants and bars in the city – all of which get progressively cheaper as you near DePaul.

The park

Because Lincoln Park is so large – 1200 acres – it's probably best not to try to tackle it all on foot in a day, especially if you plan to stop at the zoo and other sights. The #151-Sheridan bus provides direct access along the park's west side, making stops along Stockton Drive every ten minutes or so (every 15–30min during off-peak times) – you can catch it in front of Millennium Park and take it all the way north to Devon Avenue, famed for its Indian restaurants and markets (see p.134).

Cycling is an ideal way to get around the park, allowing you to get to sights quickly (locks are free with rentals) and also enjoy the scenery. Bike paths lace Lincoln Park, but the most popular by far is the **Lakefront Trail**, which stretches from Hollywood Avenue at the north end of the park to the South Side fourteen miles away, offering great views and easy access to beaches along the way. **Bike Chicago** rents bikes from the **North Avenue Beach House** in Lincoln Park (May–Sept only) for $8–10 per hour or $25–35 per day and will allow you to drop them off at one of four other locations (including Foster Avenue on the north end of the park and Millennium Park in the Loop) for a small fee. See p.237 for details.

The Chicago History Museum and around

At the park's southwest edge, the recently expanded and refurbished **Chicago History Museum**, 1601 N Clark St (Mon–Wed, Fri & Sat 9.30am–4.30pm, Thurs 9.30am–8pm, Sun noon–5pm; $14 includes audio tours, $12 seniors and students 13–22, children under 12 free; free Mon; ☎312/642-4600, ⍟www .chicagohistory.org), founded in 1852, is the city's oldest cultural organization and the only one solely dedicated to documenting its history. The entry fee is steep, but it's worth it for the overview you'll get of the city's history, engagingly related in Smithsonian-style exhibits drawing from the museum's 22-million-piece collection.

On the **first floor**, behind the snazzy 1978 Chevrolet lowrider that's the centrepiece of the lobby, "Lincoln Treasures" presents artefacts related to the Illinois senator-turned-president's assassination in Washington DC, including the bed, engravings and some floorboards from the room in which he died. Opening off this gallery, "Imagining Chicago" is a surprisingly interesting series of old-fashioned dioramas tracing Chicago's growth from a frontier outpost in 1804 to an international tourist destination as the host of the World's Fair of 1893. Be sure to press the buttons to get the light and sound. Elsewhere on the first floor are a children's gallery, where kids can make their own postcards, among other activities, and a costume and textile gallery presenting clothes made and worn by Chicagoans.

You could easily spend a couple of hours on the **second floor**, which is crammed with fascinating exhibits. At the top of the stairs, "**World's Fairs Treasures**" covers both of Chicago's World's Fairs – the seminal 1893 fair and the nearly forgotten 1933–34 fair – including scale models of the futuristic Art Deco buildings that temporarily stood on the grounds of the latter. Behind this exhibit, the **Chicago Room** contains architectural fragments and furniture by some of the city's greatest designers, from William Le Baron Jenney to Louis Sullivan to Frank Lloyd Wright. A corner of the floor's main gallery, "**Chicago: Crossroads of America**", is set up as a jazz and blues club, with TVs showing some of the city's great performers on stage, while nearby there's a display about Chicago native Hugh Hefner's first Playboy Club, opened in the Loop in February 1960 to much public consternation. Elsewhere in "Crossroads" are displays about the May 1886 Haymarket affair, when four anarchists were hanged for allegedly setting off a bomb that killed seven policemen at a rally in support of the eight-hour workday; the 1915 Eastland disaster, when the Eastland passenger steamer capsized in the Chicago River, killing an unbelievable 844 passengers and crew (it's still Chicago's most deadly catastrophe); and the 1968 Democratic National Convention, when Chicago police viciously beat up protesters in Grant Park with Mayor Daley's consent, tarnishing the city and the mayor's reputation for decades. Be sure to get the 45-minute audio tour accompanying "Crossroads", narrated by members of the Second City comedy troupe; it's free with admission.

In the park just east of the museum, **The Standing Lincoln**, by Augustus Saint-Gaudens, is widely regarded as the finest statue this eminent sculptor ever created. Though the larger-than-life-size scale of the work evokes Lincoln's heroism, Saint-Gaudens depicts the sixteenth president in an attitude of humble reflection, standing in front of an ornate claw-foot chair, head slightly bowed, as if gathering his thoughts before giving a speech.

Continue two blocks east on North Avenue and proceed through the tunnel beneath Lake Shore Drive to reach **North Avenue Beach**, a popular patch of sand in the summertime. The centre of activity here is the 22,000-square-foot **North Avenue Beach House**, which resembles an ocean liner. Dedicated in 2000, it has outdoor showers; a lifeguard station; rental offices for bikes, chairs and volleyball equipment; and a rooftop restaurant with great views of the city skyline.

The Lincoln Park Zoo and Lincoln Park Conservatory

In the heart of the park sits renowned **Lincoln Park Zoo** (Nov–March 9am–5pm, buildings and farm 10am–4.30pm; April–Oct Mon–Fri 9am–6pm, buildings and farm 10am–5pm; free; parking $14–20 depending on length of

---

The Couch Mausoleum

On a grassy flat surrounded by trees behind the Chicago History Museum stands the last visible sign of the park's history as a cemetery: the **Couch Mausoleum**. But who's actually buried inside the tomb and why it's even there is something of a mystery. As the story goes, Ira Couch moved to Chicago in the early 1830s, building a fortune as a hotelier. When he died in 1857, his family had a white limestone crypt shipped from his native New York and placed in the City Cemetery, which occupied the southern portion of what's now Lincoln Park. Unfortunately for them, the cemetery's days were already numbered, with local residents complaining that the 20,000 bodies buried there spread cholera and other diseases.

In the early 1860s the city agreed to convert the cemetery to parkland and began moving bodies to nearby cemeteries, clearing everything but the Couch Mausoleum. Why did this one monument remain? Well, no one really knows. Some say that the family used political connections to keep it there, while others assert that the city was too cheap to move it. No record exists that the family brought the matter to the Supreme Court, as has often been alleged. There's no record, either, of who is actually inside. One Couch descendant said there were thirteen family members within; another believed there were only two, plus a friend. Both counted Ira among those interred, but Ursula Bielski, author of the book *Chicago Haunts*, discovered records at Rosehill Cemetery in Ravenswood showing that he is buried there with the rest of his family. So unless the City Council passes a resolution to have the vault opened (which is highly unlikely), we may never know who's inside the tomb – if indeed anyone is.

▲ Lincoln Park Zoo

stay; ☎312/742-2000, ⓦwww.lpzoo.org), which you can enter at 2200 N Cannon Drive, just west of Lake Shore Drive at the Fullerton Parkway exit, or through several gates along Stockton Drive, where the #151-Sheridan bus stops. Opened in 1868 with the gift of two swans from New York's Central Park, the zoo is the oldest in the country, and with winding paths crisscrossing its 35 acres, it's a nice enough place to spend a few hours, especially if you have kids in tow (and the free admission ensures that there are always lots of kids). But if you're used to seeing animals in vast naturalistic environments, you may be a bit put off by the tight outdoor quarters and old stone buildings that a thousand or so creatures call home. Indeed, all has not been rosy recently at the zoo, which came under intense scrutiny in the spring of 2005 after the deaths of several animals – including three langur monkeys, a gorilla, and all three of the zoo's African elephants – occurred in less than a year and a half. After extensive investigation, the zoo was found not to be at fault. Zoo officials insist that they are dedicated to keeping the animals happy and healthy, and most enclosures have been brought up to modern standards, but there's still something a bit nineteenth-century about the place.

The zoo is best known for its collection of great apes, now housed in the state-of-the-art new **Regenstein Center for African Apes**, boasting 29,000 square feet of indoor and outdoor living space, dozens of trees and 5000ft of artificial vines for climbing. Monkey-lovers should check out the **Primate House** for the smaller lemurs and howler monkeys. Other highlights are the **Kovler Lion House**, with its impressive collection of big cats and the interactive **Farm-in-the-Zoo**, a five-acre replica of a Midwestern farm, where kids can milk cows, churn butter and groom goats. Another attraction aimed squarely at little ones is the **Pritzker Family Children's Zoo**, full of interactive exhibits that teach toddlers about bears, wolves, beavers and otters.

Faintly reminiscent of London's bygone Crystal Palace on a far smaller scale, the **Lincoln Park Conservatory** stands just south of Fullerton

Parkway on Stockton Drive (daily 9am–5pm; free; ☎312/742-7736, ⊚www .chicagoparkdistrict.com), only a few hundred feet from one of the zoo's western exits. Built between 1890 and 1895, this steamy indoor oasis is divided into four areas (Palm House, Show House, Orchid House and Fern Room), which have thousands of exotic plants on display.

The Peggy Notebaert Nature Museum and around

Across Fullerton Parkway, the **Peggy Notebaert Nature Museum**, 2430 N Cannon Drive (Mon–Fri 9am–4.30pm, Sat & Sun 10am–5pm; $9; ☎773/755-5100, ⊚www.naturemuseum.org), is mainly geared toward educating children about the benefits of natural ecosystems and what can be done to protect them from human meddling. However, full-grown nature buffs will find some compelling stuff here too, including "Mysteries of the Marsh", which explains how wetlands (the habitat of two-thirds of Illinois' endangered species) work; a "Wilderness Walk" through simulated prairie, savannah and dune environments; and a 17,000-square-foot "green" rooftop that demonstrates how this popular ecofriendly technology works to reduce fuel costs and combat climate change. The highlight for visitors of all ages, though, is the **Judy Istock Butterfly Haven**, a glass enclosure containing an artificial rainforest populated by 75 species of **butterflies**, numbering about 1500 in all.

Just north of the museum on Cannon Drive, in an arts-and-crafts-style park building dating from 1912, *North Pond* (see p.176) is a fantastic spot for lunch or Sunday brunch. Alternatively, heading east on Fullerton Avenue from the museum will bring you to **Fullerton Avenue Beach**, 2400 N Lake Shore Drive, a pleasant strip of sand that's less of a scene than the North Avenue (see p.93) and Oak Street (see p.87) beaches to the south but still has concessions and (one block south) restrooms. Nearby, the red-brick **Theater on the Lake** (☎312/742-7529, ⊚www.chicagoparkdistrict.com) hosts annual summer performances by top local theatre groups like Steppenwolf and Second City (for more on these companies, see Chapter 17, "Performing arts and film").

Northern Lincoln Park

About two miles north of the theatre, off Waveland Avenue, the crowded, nine-hole **Sydney R. Marovitz Golf Course** (see p.240) has good views of the city, but if you're looking to hit a few balls you're better off heading elsewhere (such as the public **driving range** at 141 W Diversey Parkway, which is tucked a block east of the intersection of Diversey and Sheridan; for details, see p.240). Beyond here, there's more rolling park and space for a few outdoor pursuits, such as **archery** on Belmont Harbor Drive and **birdwatching** at the **Magic Hedge**, an area of trees and shrubs at Montrose Point to the far north. The best time to visit the hedge – accessible only by car – is during spring and fall migrations, but on any given day you're likely to spot up to fifty-odd species, including warblers, swallows and falcons; especially eye-catching are the thousands of purple martins that flock here in early August. From Montrose Avenue, east of Lake Shore Drive, take a right on Montrose Harbor Drive, then follow the first curve in the road to the small hill to the east.

The Lincoln Park neighbourhood

Loosely bordered by North Avenue, Diversey Parkway, Damen Avenue and Lincoln Park, the **Lincoln Park neighbourhood** was first settled in the early to mid-1800s by German farmers. Like Old Town, it boomed after the Great Chicago Fire, with waves of new residents moving into newly constructed brick row houses

The St Valentine's Day Massacre

One of the bloodiest moments in Chicago's gangland history took place in Lincoln Park on February 14, 1929, when five men – three dressed as cops, two as civilians – visited the garage of **Al Capone**'s rival **Bugs Moran** at 2122 N Clark St, surprising seven of his henchmen. Announcing a bust, the men in uniform promptly lined Moran's men up against the back wall of the garage, gunned them down execution-style and sped off into the night, an event that came to be known as the **St Valentine's Day Massacre**. The "cops" were widely believed to be Capone's men in disguise, sent to avenge the deaths of two of Capone's heavies as well as the theft of his booze shipments from Canada. Although Moran had taken cover at the first sight of the "cops" and escaped unharmed, the massacre effectively put him out of business.

While the police could never pin the deed on Capone (in fact, no one was ever charged for the crime), who was vacationing in Florida at the time, the FBI arrested him for tax evasion a few years later and shipped him off to Alcatraz. The garage was demolished in 1967; these days, there's just a patch of lawn and a few trees where the garage once stood – the lawn of a public housing project for the elderly – though spooked passers-by have claimed to hear screams and machine-gun fire in the vicinity. For more on Capone, see p.262.

after their homes downtown were destroyed. But despite its proximity to the park, Lincoln Park remained solidly working class well into the 1980s, thanks largely to residents' resistance to city-sponsored gentrification schemes. Ironically, the neighbourhood's pristine architecture – over half of the buildings here were built between 1880 and 1904 – is just what made it so appealing to yuppie fixer-uppers, who began arriving in the 1980s and have since displaced most of the old-timers. Now they, in turn, have their hands full fending off the developers who want to replace their beloved brick row houses with high-rise condos.

Lincoln Park is well served by public transportation: just hop on the Brown, Red or Purple El lines and get off at the Fullerton stop, and you'll be in the middle of **DePaul University**, founded in 1898. With 20,000 students, it's the largest Catholic university in the country, and while its campus doesn't offer much of interest to the casual visitor, the nearby stretches of Lincoln Avenue and Clark Street are dotted with the expected rash of sports bars, pizza places and cafés. Most are pretty generic, with the exception of the pleasantly rumpled and literary *Bourgeois Pig* (see p.175), near the intersection of Lincoln and Fullerton avenues. Just up the street, at 2433 N Lincoln Ave, the 1915 **Biograph Theater** marks the site where bank robber John Dillinger met his end in a shootout with the FBI in 1934. Declared a national landmark in 2001, the old movie house has since been bought and refurbished by the **Victory Gardens Theater** (see p.207), which now produces new plays here, many by local playwrights.

The neighbourhood's charms are more apparent south of Fullerton on **Armitage** and **Webster** avenues, where you'll pass upscale boutiques and shops of every kind, from women's fashion to outdoor-equipment stores. **Halsted Street** is the focus of the area's nightlife, with countless bars overflowing with Abercrombie & Fitch-clad twenty-somethings and their girlfriends. Away from these streets, the area is pleasantly residential and tranquil, especially in leafy **Oz Park**, at the corner of Webster and Lincoln avenue. Named after the mythical land dreamed up by L. Frank Baum, who wrote *The Wonderful Wizard of Oz* while living in nearby Humboldt Park, the thirteen-acre park boasts a yellow-brick road and three sculptures by John Kearney: a shiny Tin Man made entirely of chrome car-bumpers, a bronze cowardly lion and a scarecrow, the last of which was dedicated in the summer of 2005.

5

Lakeview, Wrigleyville and Andersonville

While the North Side area of **LAKEVIEW** was for a long time little more than the poor man's version of its southern neighbour Lincoln Park, in recent years, rising real-estate prices and increased congestion have turned the area into a similar yuppie haven, although some of its rough edge remains. Though there isn't much to see or do here besides window-shop, hang out in cafés or have a tipple, it's still pleasant to browse **Clark Street**, the main thoroughfare, on a weekend afternoon or stroll along the lakefront parkway. Incorporated as a township in 1857 by a group of German celery-farmers, Lakeview takes its name from the long-since-vanished *Lakeview Inn*, a local hotel with sweeping vistas of Lake Michigan. This chunk of land north of Fullerton Avenue remained a separate town (much like Hyde Park on the South Side, which was annexed by Chicago at around the same time) until 1889, when it was swallowed whole by the growing city.

As the settlement rapidly grew, its neighbourhoods took on individual identities, none more so than **Wrigleyville**, which in 1914 became home to the newly built Wrigley Field, stadium of the Chicago Cubs. Wrigleyville anchors more nebulous Lakeview, which rambles between Chicago's two most gay-friendly neighbourhoods. To the south, the "pink triangle" of **Boystown** occupies the blocks between Halsted Street, Broadway, and Belmont Avenue. Once a haven for silent-film cineastes and speakeasy patrons, **Uptown**, north of Wrigleyville, still has a few traces left of its Jazz Age past. Further north, **Andersonville** is a former Swedish settlement that, while holding onto its Scandinavian roots, has become another centre for the city's gay and lesbian community. Clark Street is the common thread that links all the neighbourhoods mentioned here, from Boystown in the south to Andersonville in the north.

Transport links grow spottier the further north you travel; the best option is to hop on the Red El line train that bisects the area. Remember to check the sports schedules before planning a trip – during home games, Wrigleyville transforms into a boozy, frat-boy packed nightmare, where it's often impossible to find **parking** (or an empty barstool, for that matter). As there are no major highways around these parts, and virtually no parking to be found, the El trains to the Red Line Addison stop nearby become moving sardine-cans.

Boystown

The rainbow-coloured Art Deco pylons lining Halsted Street let you know you're in **BOYSTOWN**, the hub of Chicago's sizeable gay community. Along with the Castro in San Francisco and Chelsea in New York, Boystown is one of the most welcoming, gay-friendly districts in the US. The neighbourhood is most alive during the summer, when events like the **Gay Pride Parade** in late June (see p.223) and **Northalsted Street Market Days** in early August (see p.223) draw thousands upon thousands of gay, lesbian, bisexual and transgender folks to party in the streets. With its excellent restaurants and lively

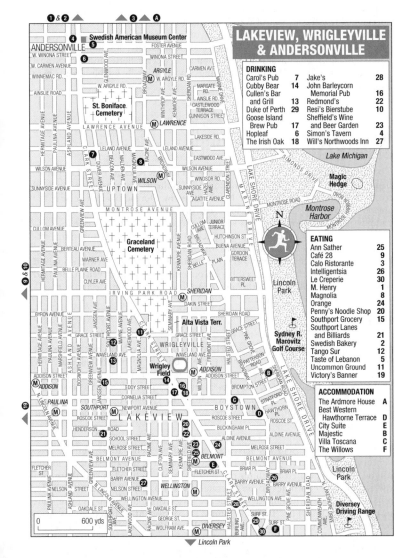

LAKEVIEW, WRIGLEYVILLE & ANDERSONVILLE

DRINKING

Carol's Pub	7	Jake's	28
Cubby Bear	14	John Barleycorn	
Cullen's Bar		Memorial Pub	16
and Grill	13	Redmond's	22
Duke of Perth	29	Resi's Bierstube	10
Goose Island		Sheffield's Wine	
Brew Pub	17	and Beer Garden	23
Hopleaf	6	Simon's Tavern	4
The Irish Oak	18	Will's Northwoods Inn	27

EATING

Ann Sather	25
Café 28	9
Calo Ristorante	3
Intelligentsia	26
Le Creperie	30
M. Henry	1
Magnolia	8
Orange	24
Penny's Noodle Shop	20
Southport Grocery	15
Southport Lanes	
and Billiards	21
Swedish Bakery	2
Tango Sur	12
Taste of Lebanon	5
Uncommon Ground	11
Victory's Banner	19

ACCOMMODATION

The Ardmore House	A
Best Western	
Hawthorne Terrace	D
City Suite	E
Majestic	B
Villa Toscana	C
The Willows	F

99

cafés, the neighbourhood buzzes most on **Halsted Street** and **Broadway** between Belmont Avenue and Irving Park Road – studded with trinket shops, rare-book stores and leather markets. Recent years have seen something of an exodus to Uptown and Andersonville to the north, but the intersection of Roscoe and Halsted is still a central gathering place for the gay, lesbian and transgender community.

Most of the action centres on the long-standing bars here – *Sidetrack* and *Roscoe's Tavern*, in particular, are both classics (see p.222), prone to long queues on busy weekend nights. In the 1980s, the neighbourhood had a seedy feel, with men openly cruising each other on Halsted and soliciting for sex on the side streets but, for better or for worse, ubiquitous condo development and rising real-estate prices have transformed the 'hood into another polished yuppie corridor. A few blocks east of Wrigley Field, the much-anticipated **Center on Halsted** opened in 2007. The first facility of its kind in the Midwest, the centre caters to the city's gay, lesbian, bisexual and transgender community, with gay youth schemes, mental health and community services, galleries and recreational and social space. See p.218 for more listings on gay-friendly establishments here and elsewhere.

Wrigleyville and around

The neighbourhood that surrounds Wrigley Field, **WRIGLEYVILLE**, got its name from savvy developers, hoping to trade on the park's immense popularity to sell the new houses they were building nearby. During baseball season, the area is overrun by **Cubs fans**, loyally bedecked with blue-and-white team paraphernalia and crowding into the many local bars or spilling out into the streets and even onto the rooftops. It quietens down somewhat during the off-season, but not much – on weekends, the neighbourhood's twenty-something residents pack into **sports bars** on the stretch of Clark Street between Addison and Roscoe, and the stadium itself has become a sort of Mecca: even in the dead of winter, tourists will hop off the train at Addison to stand outside and contemplate the coming baseball season.

Wrigley Field

At the centre of it all, ivy-covered **Wrigley Field** itself remains one of the best places to get a real feel for baseball – the Cubs are so traditional that they fought the installation of floodlights until 1988. Even if you know nothing about baseball, there are few more pleasant ways to spend an afternoon than drinking beer, eating hot dogs, and watching the Cubs struggle to win a ball game (they haven't won a World Series since 1908, though they did top their division in 2008).

Built in 1914 and named after Cubs owner and chewing-gum bigwig Philip Wrigley, the stadium has been extensively renovated over the past century, but some things haven't changed: the field is still the smallest in the league, the ivy planted to climb the outfield walls in 1937 is still there and the scoreboard continues to be operated by hand. Equally enduring is the tenacious loyalty of its fans; despite heavy losses, the Cubs manage to sell out nearly every game. The "Bleacher Bums", a contingent of raucous fans, have been a fixture ever since they first staked their claim to the outfield bleachers back in 1966. One of their traditions is to toss home-run balls hit by the opposing team back onto the field. For more information on the Cubs and seeing a game, see p.235.

If you can't make it to the ballpark during a game, there's a ninety-minute **tour** of the stadium that will take you through the clubhouses, suites, dugouts, press box, bleachers and playing field ($25, must be purchased in advance; call for schedule ☏773/404-2827).

Alta Vista Terrace

Nicknamed the "Street of Forty Doors", this charming oddity, tucked away northwest of the stadium, is well worth a detour. In the 1890s, after a trip to London's chic Mayfair district, local real-estate developer Samuel Eberly Gross decided to create his own version of the area's stately townhouses back home in Chicago. It took him four years to build his vision, **Alta Vista Terrace**, a single block of row houses wedged between N Sheridan Road and N Grace Street, but by 1904 they were complete and have remained refreshingly untouched ever since. Indeed, thanks to the close-set homes' unique, high-Victorian style and the unusual narrowness of this one-way street, Alta Vista is unlike any other street in Chicago.

Architecturally, the houses may seem eclectic and far from uniform at first; doorways are painted a variety of colours, from bright red to slate grey, and the buildings feature various ornate gables and windows that set them apart from one another. Look more closely, though, and you'll notice a curious thing: each house on the block has an identical twin that is diagonally opposite it across the street. These houses were designed to be exactly the same, from the shape of their ornate gables and garland moulding to the striking round bay windows that adorn several on the block.

Graceland Cemetery

The final resting place of Chicago's old-time elite, the lush **Graceland Cemetery** (8am–4.30pm) makes for a pleasant ramble across its 120 rolling acres, which spread from W Irving Park Road to Montrose Avenue. Opened in 1860, Graceland was created to replace the overcrowded municipal cemetery in what's now Lincoln Park (see p.92), a move brought on by fears that the lakeside cemetery posed a serious health risk. The main entrance is at Clark Street and Irving Park Road, where you can pick up a map as well as a copy of the Chicago Architecture Foundation's *A Walk Through Graceland Cemetery* ($9.95), though only fanatics looking to search out every marker might need this.

You'll spot a wide variety of memorials here, everything from fussy Gothic graves to veritable temples, all laid out among a lush landscape of giant oak, elm and maple trees. Socialites **Potter** and **Bertha Palmer** lie inside a massive Neoclassical mausoleum held up by sixteen columns. Less ostentatious are steel tycoon **Henry Getty**'s grave – a subdued stone cube designed by Louis Sullivan – and the headstone of **Daniel Burnham**, which sits on a small island linked to the shore by a narrow walkway.

Two of Chicago's most influential architects have surprisingly unremark-able tombs: **Ludwig Mies van der Rohe** lies beneath a polished stone slab set into the ground, while **Louis Sullivan**'s is only slightly more conspic-uous. Sullivan, in fact, died in 1924 in poverty and lacked a gravestone for several years.

Chicago shopping magnate **Marshall Field** is commemorated here with the Daniel Chester French-designed monument *Memory*, a contemplative seated figure that bears more than a passing resemblance to the Lincoln Memorial, which French also designed. One of the more whimsical gravesites is that of **William Hulbert**, founder of professional baseball's National League, who is memorialized with a large baseball-shaped marker. Other sites not to be missed include the tomb of wealthy hotelier **Dexter Graves**, whose grave is marked by the eerie, hooded bronze figure *Eternal Silence* (also known as the "Statue of Death"), which stands in front of a polished black-marble slab; the pyramid-shaped mausoleum of Prussian-born brewery owner **Peter Schoenhofen**, guarded by a male sphinx and a female angel holding a bronze key; and the life-sized statue enclosed in Plexiglas of 6-year-old Inez Clark, who, local ghost stories attest, can sometimes be seen walking through the cemetery in nineteenth-century garb.

To **get here**, take the Red Line to the Sheridan stop and walk a few blocks west on Irving Park Road.

Southport Avenue and around

Outside its specific neighbourhoods, sprawling Lakeview holds a few pockets of interest along its commercial thoroughfares. One of the more popular strips is **N Southport Avenue** between Belmont Avenue and Irving Park Road, along which cluster shops, restaurants and bars, minus the crowds and sales gimmicks. One of the strip's long-standing novelties is **Southport Lanes** (see p.238), at no. 3325, a four-lane bowling alley that opened in 1922 and still uses human pinsetters to this day – one of the posted rules says "Remember, if you see legs, don't bowl!" Several blocks north, it's hard to miss the large pink neon sign and old-fashioned marquee of the **Music Box Theatre** (see p.211), at no. 3733, a refurbished movie house built in 1929. Step inside to see the twinkling stars on the ceiling – it's accessible and worth a look, even if there's not a show on. Further east, both **Belmont Avenue** and the central section of **N Clark Street** contain more excellent **restaurants**; for reviews see p.178.

Uptown

The curtain of nondescript high-rises between Lakeview and Andersonville forms the backdrop for **UPTOWN**, once the playground of Prohibition-era mobsters and pre-Hollywood-era filmmakers (see box opposite). Mostly untouched until the late 1890s, the area was swampy and undesirable. As wealthy Chicagoans continued to move north, however, this "suburb" became more attractive and by the early 1900s Uptown was one of the city's fastest-growing neighbourhoods, with dozens of high-rise apartment buildings, hundreds of shops, and an active nightlife centred around the area's many restaurants and speakeasies. After World War II, Uptown ceased to be a dominant centre of nightlife and entertainment, and thousands of migrants from the American South poured into the area's increasingly affordable apartments. By the 1960s, Uptown was an ethnically diverse community, although middle-class residents were beginning to move away to the distant suburbs.

Hollywood in Chicago

Back in the early 1900s during the heyday of silent movies, the epicentre of the film industry wasn't LA or New York – it was Chicago, whose Uptown-based **Essanay Studios** were a powerful force in bringing cinema to the masses.

Founded in 1907 by **George K. Spoor** and actor **G.M. "Bronco Billy" Anderson**, Essanay ("S and A") was based in a warehouse at 1333–45 W Argyle St. It was in this building's studios and outdoor courtyard that the pair made hundreds of silent films starring Anderson (who created the first cowboy hero in Bronco Billy), legendary actress **Gloria Swanson**, and, most famously, **Charlie Chaplin**, who made *His New Job*, *A Woman*, and the classic short *The Tramp*, for the studio. The studio was a bona-fide smash, and Spoor and Anderson soon set up Essanay-West in Los Angeles, where the industry was gaining a foothold thanks to more reliable weather and an infinite pool of star talent.

Soon, though, the tides turned on Essanay: Chaplin defected to Metro Films (soon to become MGM), and disputes between Spoor and Anderson led to the collapse of the studio in 1917, less than ten years after it was established. Eventually, Anderson and Spoor would go on to win honorary Academy Awards in 1948 and 1958, respectively, for their contributions to the development of film. The studio warehouse itself was declared a Chicago landmark in 1996, and the company's logo – a terracotta Native American head – is still visible over the entrance of the building, now home to St Augustine College.

The area grew increasingly run-down in the 1970s and 1980s, though in recent years, there has been increased gentrification. These days, Uptown retains a rather curious mix of new condo construction, Starbucks, halfway houses and public housing projects. Most of the action happens around the intersection of Broadway and Lawrence; **to get here**, take the Red Line to Lawrence and walk a block west to Broadway.

Uptown's colourful past survives at *The Green Mill* (see p.199), a former speakeasy that was once Al Capone's favourite watering hole and still Chicago's best **jazz club**. Just north of *The Green Mill* is one of the neighbourhood's greatest monuments, the ornate **Uptown Theater**, at 4816 N Broadway, a majestic movie and stage palace. The theatre was built in 1925 in the Spanish Revival style, with elaborate roof parapets, twisting columns and terracotta ornamentation; with seating for 4300 people it was the second-largest movie palace in the country after New York's Radio City Music Hall. Shuttered in the 1970s, the theatre was designated a Chicago landmark in 1991; the building was purchased by a concert promoter in 2008, and plans have been announced for a major restoration.

Lincoln Square

A little over a mile to the west, in upcoming **Lincoln Square**, the **Old Town School of Folk Music**, at 4544 N Lincoln Ave, hosts hundreds of concerts a year, which reflect the school's exhaustive course offerings – everything from blues guitar to Djembe and Aztec ceremonial dances. Take the Ravenswood El line to Western Station, then walk east to Lincoln Avenue and turn south to the school or else catch the Lincoln (#11) or Western (#49) bus lines to their Wilson Avenue stops and from there walk south on Lincoln Avenue.

Andersonville

Perched north of Lakeview and Uptown, **ANDERSONVILLE** is as small-town as Chicago gets, with independent shops and cafés, a friendly, neighbourly feel and a lingering Scandinavian heritage. Beginning in the 1840s, many Swedes began to immigrate to Chicago to escape overpopulation in their home country. After the Great Fire, wooden homes were outlawed in Chicago, so the Swedish poor moved north of the city, transforming a cluster of celery farms into a bustling centre along **Clark Street** between Foster and Bryn Mawr, still the commercial heart of the neighbourhood today.

Although Swedes continued to emigrate here well into the twentieth century, by the 1960s their community had begun to disperse, many returning to their homeland or moving to the suburbs. Despite the exodus, Andersonville still has one of the highest concentrations of Swedes in the US, and Clark Street does still boast several thriving Swedish shops, bakeries and a museum. Preserving that heritage becomes ever more challenging, though, in the face of a burgeoning influx of professionals (including a sizeable gay and lesbian community) moving north to escape the escalating costs of Lakeview and Lincoln Park.

To **get here**, take the CTA Red Line to Berwyn or Bryn Mawr or hop on bus #22 (Clark), #36 (Broadway), or #92 (Foster).

Clark Street and around

Lined with shops, restaurants and bustling cafés, the northern stretch of **Clark Street** is the heart of Andersonville, and everything worth visiting in the neighbourhood is on or nearby it in the few blocks north of Foster Avenue. Chief among these is the engaging **Swedish American Museum Center**, 5211 N Clark St (Tues–Fri 10am–4pm, Sat & Sun 11am–4pm; $4; ☎773/728-8111, Ⓦwww.samac.org), devoted mainly to Chicago's Swedish-American heritage but with enough broad appeal to please anyone interested in the immigrant experience. Officially dedicated in 1976 by Swedish king Carl Gustaf, the museum began as a modest storefront with collections of family histories; three decades, a move and several renovations later, the collection encompasses several floors of historical and cultural exhibits, from displays of works by contemporary Swedish artists to maps, artefacts and a hands-on children's museum that teaches kids about the immigration experience using a 20ft model steamboat and a replica of a Swedish farmhouse.

During the winter holidays, residents of nearby states make the pilgrimage to Andersonville for the **Swedish food**: traditional *rosette* and *spritz* cookies, Swedish meatballs, Göteborg sausage and pickled herring. Any of Clark Street's handful of establishments devoted to Swedish cuisine are worth a try, particularly cozy café *Svea*, at no. 5236, or extremely popular *The Swedish Bakery* (see p.178) at no. 5348.

One of the last great **city taverns**, *Simon's*, at 5210 N Clark St, is thick with dark, divey atmosphere and history, helped along by the worn mahogany bar, the steamship motif, and the Viking paraphernalia. During the 1930s, the original owner began a free cheque-cashing service for Swedish labourers, throwing in free sandwiches to boot – an ingenious idea, as most of the money he doled out to his workers never left the bar. If you're lucky, the present owner will show you the bullet-proof cheque-cashing station under the stairs or the original basement door to the speakeasy, which was run on the premises during Prohibition.

▲ Swedish Bakery

Around the corner from *Simon's* at the intersection of Ashland and Foster is the **Neo-Futurarium**, where fringe theatre group the Neo-Futurists have staged their play *Too Much Light Makes the Baby Go Blind* every weekend night since December of 1988, making it the longest-running show in Chicago today (see p.208). A cult favourite for college students, the production features thirty plays performed in sixty minutes, and admission price is determined by the roll of a die (5153 N Foster Ave; ☎773/275-5255, Ⓦwww.neofuturists.org).

Away from Clark Street, the neighbourhood holds little of interest, though the quiet, narrow side streets to the east are lined with rows of charming early twentieth-century brownstone houses and make for a pleasant stroll.

Bucktown, Wicker Park and Ukrainian Village

Located about three miles northwest of the Loop, the **Bucktown** and **Wicker Park** neighbourhoods are home to a lively alternative music scene, numerous thrift stores and a thriving bohemian culture of cafés and clubs. **Ukrainian Village**, the area's younger sibling further south, is grittier and less affected, but not by much: though still dominated by the Eastern European immigrants who settled here a hundred years ago, it is also in the midst of a massive gentrification process by young hipsters and condo dwellers.

While there are no big-ticket sights in any of these locales, you'll find a couple of rewarding pockets of historic nuance, such as the quiet streets of the **Wicker Park historic district** (especially Hoyne and Pierce aves), lined with some of the city's finest examples of Victorian-era architecture and a striking contrast with the modern, concrete low-rises on the neighbourhood's main drags; many of these old houses have been superbly, if a little self-consciously, restored.

The best way to see these neighbourhoods, however, is after dark; the **nightlife** here is, hands down, the best in the city, centred on the boisterous "six corners" intersection of **Milwaukee**, **North**, and **Damen** avenues. The other commercial hubs – **North Avenue**, **Division Street** and **Chicago Avenue** – run east–west and serve as the informal dividing lines for Bucktown, Wicker Park and the Ukrainian Village, respectively. While there are some **dicey areas** west of Western Avenue, the main thoroughfares are well travelled, and are safe. If you keep an eye out as you walk around, you should be fine.

Some history

While today Milwaukee Avenue is the central artery of these three neighbourhoods, in the early 1800s it was an unpaved Indian trail that ran from Chicago to Milwaukee, Wisconsin. The area was sparsely populated by **Polish immigrants**, many of them farmers. After the Great Chicago Fire of 1871, displaced Chicagoans started moving here in large numbers, and the Polish population continued to swell, augmented by an influx of **Ukrainians**. These

BUCKTOWN, WICKER PARK & UKRAINIAN VILLAGE

0   600 yds

N

Holstein Park

BUCKTOWN

WESTERN Ⓜ

DAMEN Ⓜ

Wicker Park

Wicker Park Historic District

Nelson Algren House

Division Street Russian Bathhouse

WICKER PARK

Clemente Park

Holy Trinity Orthodox Cathedral

St Stanislaus Kostka Church

DIVISION Ⓜ

Polish Museum of America

St. Nicholas Ukrainian Church

Ukrainian Institute of Modern Art

Sts. Volodymyr & Olha Church

Eckhart Park

UKRAINIAN VILLAGE

Ukrainian National Museum

Old Town ▶

Gold Coast ▶

River North ▶

ACCOMMODATION
House of Two Urns   **B**
Wicker Park Inn   **A**

EATING				DRINKING			
Adobo Grill	**22**	Le Bouchon	**6**	California clipper	**25**	Northside Bar & Grill	**11**
Bongo Room	**19**	Letizia's Natural Bakery	**20**	Club Lucky	**10**	Quencher's	**2**
Café Absinthe	**12**	Margie's Candies	**4**	Gold Star Bar	**24**	Rainbo Club	**23**
Earwax Café	**17**	Piece	**16**	Hideout	**8**	Subterranean	**15**
Handlebar	**13**	Spring	**14**	Map Room	**5**		
Hot Chocolate	**9**	Toast Two	**3**	Marie's Rip-Tide Lounge	**7**		
Jerry's Restaurant	**21**	Vienna Beef Factory	**1**	Nick's Beergarden	**18**		

Eastern European communities were largely centred on the area's many churches, the most influential of which was (and still is) the looming **St Stanislaus Kostka Church**. The church exerted such influence over the area that locals initially referred to the neighbourhood as "Stanislawowo" and later, in the twentieth century, as the slightly more anglicized "Kostkaville".

After World War II, many Poles moved to less crowded areas further northwest up Milwaukee Avenue (still a Polish stronghold today), and this area of the city became more ethnically diverse, attracting large numbers of **Latinos** (mostly Puerto Ricans). In the 1960s and 1970s, a rise in gang activity and violence led to the abandonment of the neighbourhood by many residents, and the area fell into disrepair. Factories closed, arson fires raged, and drug addicts and prostitutes roamed the streets.

The process of urban renewal began in Bucktown, the northernmost of the three areas, and has gradually spread south over the past twenty years. Largely ruled by Latino gangs since the 1960s, Wicker Park remained a staunch no-go zone until the housing prices in Bucktown skyrocketed and displaced artists made the leap south over the railroad tracks at North Avenue and established homes in Wicker Park. Today, much of the original Polish community, along with the more recent Hispanic residents, has been pushed north and west, to the other side of Western Avenue. With gentrification edging ever westward, it's a safe bet that this will be the next boundary to be crossed.

Bucktown

Much like many of the city's inner suburbs, **BUCKTOWN** began life as an immigrant hub: Germans, Poles and other Eastern Europeans who arrived in the mid-nineteenth century settled on and around Milwaukee Avenue. In the 1800s, the area was dominated by open fields where Polish settlers raised goats; the male goat is called a buck, which is how the neighbourhood most likely got its name.

Bucktown spreads just north of the six corners, bounded on either side by the Kennedy Expressway and Western Avenue. Above this sprawling intersection are a bevy of restaurants and cafés, plus a few galleries, located mostly on Damen and Milwaukee avenues, south of Armitage. Of special interest are the neighbourhood classic *Club Lucky*, at 1824 W Wabansia Ave, where the former Polish banquet hall and bar has been restored to its 1930s glory and currently packs 'em in as a casual Italian joint (see p.193), and old-fashioned ice cream parlour *Margie's Candies* (see p.180), a few blocks west on Western Avenue. Its quaint booths have seen everybody from Al Capone and Sinatra to the Beatles and Princess Di – the Smashing Pumpkins even wrote a song about tables six and seven.

Restaurants and bars aside, it's worth a wander around Bucktown's quieter streets for a look at the variety of architecture. The stretch of Wabansia Avenue from Milwaukee to Ashland has a good representation of Chicago housing styles, including 1920s walk-up apartment buildings, highly decorated nineteenth century Victorian homes, and a clutch of modern condominium buildings. The cornerstone of Bucktown's development sits just west of here at no. 2300. The handsome, four-storey, red-brick-and-glass building housing the **Clock Tower Lofts** was built around 1900 and originally occupied by curtain makers and tailors. The building was entirely gutted in the early 1990s and converted into airy lofts; within a few years their value had doubled, with waves of development spreading from here in all directions.

Concord Street and around

Skip over to **Concord Street**, where many of the houses were built from stone by wealthy, late nineteenth-century industrialists and so have weathered well. The only thing disrupting the old-world, suburban calm is the El, which now rumbles along the street's eastern reaches. Look out for the graphic, stained-glass features in the windows of **no. 2140**. Also note the houses that have suffered stylistic alterations, from the stone cladding that smothers **no. 2121** (the original detailing is still visible above the dormer window) to the Queen Anne mansion, **no. 2138**, whose rounded turret windows have been replaced by flat panes to save money.

Be sure not to miss the wonderful building at **2041 North Ave**, behind whose delicate white terracotta facade once stood the 1923 **Luxor Bathhouse**, a relaxing haven for Turkish and Russian immigrants. This structure has since been converted into the upscale restaurant *Spring* (see p.182), but the fish reliefs above each window bear witness to its original use.

Wicker Park

While slightly truer to its Eastern European roots than nearby Bucktown, **WICKER PARK** is also facing the encroaching forces of urban renewal. Immigrant communities coexist with the artsy types who've been driven here by rising rents elsewhere in the city, creating an eclectic mix of artists, elderly women in babushkas and black-clad youth, all sharing the sidewalk en route to a café, deli, Polish Roman Catholic church or the nearest poetry slam. Though yuppies have started to move in (bringing with them a few generic sports bars that horrify longtime locals), the neighbourhood retains an anti-establishment feel. In 2001, when MTV filmed its popular series, **The Real World** here, the producers faced protests from angry locals upset at the area's commodification.

Though it's not much to look at, there is an eponymous **park** here, just south of the six corners, named after brothers **Joel** and **Charles Wicker**, who donated it in 1870. In its heyday the park held a small swan pond and a shelter, but the pond was long ago filled in and there's just a plain-looking fountain breaking up this little patch of green. Writer **Nelson Algren** (see box, p.111) once lived in one of the pretty Victorian homes south of the park – but beware: after sundown it's best to steer clear of the park, as it's a known haven for drug dealers.

In a city full of ornate churches, the **St Stanislaus Kostka Church**, 1351 W Evergreen Ave (☎773/278-2470), west of Wicker Park, still stands out. Towering more than two hundred feet tall, the church has a stunning Baroque interior, complete with chandeliers and stained-glass windows, which you can view by appointment. Built in 1876, the church was for many years the stronghold of the city's Polish Catholic community, once the heart of "Stanislawowo" and later "Kostkaville". With the increasing gentrification and the building of the Kennedy Expressway, much of the Polish community moved away; these days, masses are given in English and Spanish as well as Polish, reflecting the area's changing demographics.

6

The Wicker Park historic district

Chicago's architectural blockbusters, whether pioneering skyscrapers or modern engineering marvels, tend to be crammed into the Loop, but the northwest district of Wicker Park has its own immaculately maintained gems – nineteenth-century Victorian homes spared Chicago's wrecking ball to become a designated **historic district**.

This area, bounded by N Damen Avenue and N Leavitt Street, stretching from Caton to Division streets (a sliver of it falls in neighbouring Bucktown), is one of the most gentrified segments of this up-and-coming area.

Start a walking tour of the area on **N Hoyne Avenue**, once known as "Beer Baron Row" for the number of brewing tycoons who built their homes here in the late 1800s. Of the many eye-catching old buildings, the two most prominent are **nos. 1407** and **1520**. The former is set on the corner of Schiller Street, its onetime grandeur evident from the adjoining coach-house and enormous octagonal tower. It is currently being renovated to its former grandeur, which is certainly a positive step forward. The latter (a block north) is in better condition: note the elaborate, wrought-iron scrollwork and table-leg columns, as well as the massive ornamental canopy over the entrance. The Queen Anne period house, topped by a turret with a witch's-hat roof, also preserves the expensive curved glass that was made possible late in the nineteenth century by industrial innovations. It's also worth stopping by **no. 1558**, at the junction with North Avenue, whose elaborately restored exterior features ironwork on its tower, leaded windows, and lime paint with dark green contrasts.

Head back to **W Pierce Avenue** for more fine Victorian homes. The most famous is the **John D. Runge House** (no. 2138), built in 1884 and one-time residence of the Polish consulate; the house was also paid a visit by the famed Polish pianist Ignacy Paderewski, who gave a performance on its porch. Today, it's still one of the grandest in the area, a double-fronted mansion with a veranda even outside its dormer windows. Across the street is the unmistakeable **Gingerbread House**, at 2137 W Pierce Ave, so named because of the look of its intricate, machine-cut mouldings. Built in 1888, this late Victorian masterpiece is painted in an eye-popping gold, ochre and blue colour scheme – a far cry from the sober paint that would have graced it when it was built. **Nos. 2118** and **2046** further down are also notable: the former for its faux-Gothic decorative elements above the upper windows, the latter for its rounded-glass bay windows.

Division Street and around

Division Street was made famous by Studs Terkel's *Division Street America* (see box opposite), a penetrating portrait of Chicago's hardscrabble urban life. In recent years, the street's rough reputation has been softened somewhat with the arrival of lounge-style restaurants and lower crime rates, but there's still enough grit left here – from empty storefronts to shady alleyways – to merit caution, especially after dark. Division and the surrounding side streets are not particularly well lit, and pedestrian traffic thins out after 10pm.

For a one-of-a-kind Chicago experience, head to the **Division Street Russian Bathhouse** at no. 1914 (Mon–Sat 4pm–10pm, Sun 7am–11am; $20 for all-day admission, massages start at $30 for 30min; ☎773/384-9671, ⓦwww.chicagorussiansauna.com), a throwback to Chicago's stockyard days, when residential indoor plumbing wasn't as common as it is today. One of the few remaining *schvitz* (Yiddish for "sweat") places left in the country, the humble bathhouse has traditionally seen folks from all walks of life unwind in its blistering 180°F steam rooms, ice-cold pools, massage rooms and showers. These include more than a few celebrities, from Jesse Jackson to Mike Ditka (check out the signed photos on the wall). A separate women's side of the bathhouse offers waxing, facials, massages and a eucalyptus-scented wet sauna. Afterwards a stop at **Letizia's Natural Bakery**, just up Division at no. 2144, will replenish whatever you've sweated out. After a visit to *Letizia's* you can wander around the multitude of the restaurants, bars and shops that are ubiquitous around this corner of Chicago. See the relevant Listings chapters for reviews.

Ukrainian Village

South of Wicker Park, **UKRAINIAN VILLAGE** has been home to Chicago's Polish and Ukrainian communities since the late 1800s, when a steady stream of Eastern European immigrants settled west of Damen Avenue between Chicago Avenue and Division Street. These days, the neighbourhood is more of a melting pot, with yuppies joining the city's growing Hispanic community in the developing area as the Eastern European influence dwindles. But stroll along Chicago Avenue, and you'll still pass delis selling pillowy *pierogi* (stuffed dumplings) and hear local Poles chatting in their native tongue (you may hear them refer to the Village as *Helenowo*, after the area's sizeable Polish Roman Catholic parish). Off the main drag, rows of simple red-brick two-flats are centred on the orthodox **churches** that are still the focal points of the community. The neighbourhood celebrates its heritage at the annual **Ukrainian**

Division Street's literary legacy

Two of Chicago's most beloved native sons, writers **Nelson Algren** (1909–81) and **Studs Terkel** (1912–2008), found inspiration on **West Division Street**. Having grown up poor on the South Side, Algren lived in Wicker Park (at 1958 W Evergreen St) for nearly twenty years after studying journalism in college and serving in the Army. At that time, the neighbourhood wasn't just a bit rough around the edges, as it is today – it was a veritable skid row for drunks, pimps, prostitutes and hoods. Algren was fascinated by the city's underbelly, and wrote about it eloquently in controversial works like *Chicago: City on the Make*, and *The Man with the Golden Arm*, which depicted ex-con Frankie Machine's descent into heroin addiction and was subsequently made into a 1955 movie starring Frank Sinatra and Kim Novak. After Algren's death in 1981 at the age of 72, the city of Chicago renamed Evergreen Street Algren Street – but soon changed it back after complaints from local residents.

For Terkel – who was one of Algren's closest friends – Division Street epitomized life in the United States, with people of all walks of life, all ethnic backgrounds and all classes coming together in one neighbourhood. A popular TV actor and radio host in the 1940s, Terkel turned to writing after being blacklisted in 1953 for refusing to co-operate with Joseph McCarthy's House Un-American Activities Committee. Intrigued by the lives of the "anonymous millions", the writer set out to preserve the oral history of normal, everyday citizens, interviewing seventy city residents for his 1967 book *Division Street: America*. Terkel talked to immigrants, ambitious locals and streetwise kids, compiling their views and beliefs to show that, across lines of class and race, each subject had "pertinent comments to make on urban life in the twentieth century". Terkel passed away on October 31, 2008, and his writings remain an integral part of the conscience of Chicago, and in a very real way, the conscience of the United States.

Village Fest, held in September and featuring a beer garden, live music, traditional dancing, food and games.

St Nicholas Ukrainian Cathedral and around

The dominant feature of the low-rise skyline of Ukrainian Village is the ornate, onion-domed roofs of **St Nicholas Ukrainian Catholic Cathedral**, 2238 W Rice St, at N Oakley Blvd (tours by appointment; ☎773/276-4537, ⓦwww .stnicholascathedralukrcath.org), which was built in 1913 when the surrounding area was little more than pasture. Almost one hundred years later, the church remains the hub of the local Ukrainian community and all services, except one on Sunday, are held in the native language.

The cathedral is a scaled-down model of St Sofia in Kiev, with thirteen rather than the original's 32 domes, but it's a magnificent replica nonetheless, all beige brick and greenish copper. The mosaic in the main loggia above the entrance was installed in 1988 to commemorate the 1000th anniversary of Christianity's arrival in Ukraine and features the king who ushered in its acceptance, St Volodymyr. It's well worth calling ahead to arrange a tour of the dazzling, Byzantine-style **mosaics** in the interior, as well as the largest **chandelier** in North America, which holds a blinding 480 bulbs.

More modern but less intriguing than the neighbouring cathedral, the squat and monumental **Sts Volodymyr and Olha Ukrainian Catholic Church** (☎773/276-3990), 739 Oakley Blvd, stands on the southeast corner of Chicago Avenue. The sapphire-blue and ochre-yellow ceiling paintings in the interior are striking, but the real reason to stop by is the enormous, glittering mosaic above the main entrance, which depicts the church's namesake saints, St Volodymyr and his mother St Olha, accepting Christianity into Ukraine.

▲ St Nicholas Ukrainian Cathedral

Another hidden neighbourhood gem, the small **Ukrainian Institute of Modern Art** (Wed–Sun noon–4pm; free; ☎773/227-5522, Ⓦwww.uima-art .org), 2320 W Chicago Ave, at Western Ave, highlights the works of contemporary Ukrainian and Ukrainian-American artists, from religiously themed oil paintings to abstract sculptures in forged steel.

The Polish Museum of America

Preserving the heritage of the city's more than one million Poles, the long-standing **Polish Museum of America**, 984 Milwaukee Ave, at Augusta Blvd (daily except Thurs 11am-4pm; $5 donation; ☎773/384-3352, Ⓦwww .polishmuseumofamerica.org), has an eclectic mix of art and artefacts, mainly from Poland but relating to Polish Americans as well, and is worth a visit for those intrigued by the Polish-American experience. Known for its holdings of the personal effects of renowned pianist, statesman and former Polish prime minister Ignacy Paderewski, the collection also features several exhibits sent from Poland for the city's 1939 World's Fair. One rather striking item was an exhibit for which the museum's thirty-foot-high stained-glass windows were made. World War II intervened, and all of these "temporary" exhibits became permanent, as they could not be returned safely. Other displays feature Polish folk costumes, military uniforms, hand-carved Easter eggs and religious relics; be sure to check out the huge painting in the Great Hall of Revolutionary War hero Casimir Pulaski.

The West Side

Comprising the neighbourhoods of Greektown, Pilsen, Little Italy and the West Loop, Chicago's **West Side** was the gateway for Chicago's myriad ethnic groups, who flocked to the city during its late nineteenth-century boom years and congregated in its now distinct neighbourhoods. Since then, many of the Greek, East European and Italian residents have moved to the suburbs or been displaced by large-scale development (notably the campus of the University of Illinois-Chicago), a shift especially evident in **Greektown**, where these days you'll struggle to find many Greek Americans other than those running the local restaurants.

Little Italy, conversely, is one of the few immigrant communities that *is* flourishing, as young hipsters move in alongside older residents. South of Little Italy sits the **University Village**, which is a massive new development built around the former home of the Maxwell Street Market. Chicago's Mexican-American community is booming as well; the city has one of the largest Hispanic populations in the country, found in pockets across the city but clustered most heavily in the former Eastern European neighbourhood of **Pilsen**. Here the buildings are covered with brightly painted murals and tile mosaics paying homage to important Mexican and Chicano figures from Frida Kahlo to Carlos Santana.

Between these residential areas and downtown stands the **West Loop**, where warehouses thrown up in the nineteenth century were converted into trendy loft apartments a hundred years later. Aside from these and the popular restaurant row along W Randolph Street (sometimes referred to as the Randolph Street Corridor), the West Side is a solid, working-class area with few official sights – a visit here is more about soaking up ethnic flavours than hopping between museums.

The best **public transport** option to reach these neighbourhoods is the El Blue Line, which hugs the Congress Expressway; but make sure to stick to main streets, especially at night. Pilsen especially is a safe enclave stuck amid blocks of urban blight: get off at the 18th Street stop or just grab a cab.

The West Loop

Crossing the Chicago River from the Loop into the **WEST LOOP**, the first thing you'll notice are the gleaming new office towers and the tips of construction cranes poking into the sky, all signs of economic spillover from the Loop. This is where the West Side proper begins, bounded by Ashland Avenue to the

THE WEST SIDE

South Side

EATING						DRINKING	
Al's #1 Italian Beef	18	Green Zebra	2	Parthenon	14	Betty's Blue Star Lounge	1
Blackbird	9	La Vita	17	Red Light	5	Jaks Tap	13
Café Jumping Bean	20	Marche	7	Rodity's	12	Matchbox	3
Francesca's on Taylor	15	Mario's Italian Ices	16	Sushi Wabi	8	Plush	10
Greek Islands	11	Nuevo Leon	19	Twisted Spoke	4	Tasting Room	6

ACCOMMODATION
Crowne Plaza
Chicago-Metro **A**

west, the river to the east, Grand Avenue to the north and 16th Street to the south, a sprawl of tired-looking low-rises that continues on, flat and unchanging, for miles.

Close to the river are the city's two main train stations. You can get a whiff of the grand days of railway travel inside **Union Station**, at 500 W Adams St, through which almost every cross-country Amtrak train passes. During the 1940s and 1950s, more than 100,000 people filed across the pink marble floors of the Great Hall daily or sat under its airy, vaulted ceilings on the wooden benches; now that number has been halved, and most travellers bypass the hall and buy their tickets on board the trains instead. The climactic baby carriage shootout scene in the movie *The Untouchables* was filmed on the marble steps.

The more contemporary **Ogilvie Transportation Center**, also known as North Western Station, serves the Metra commuter-rail network three blocks north at 500 W Madison St. The train station is housed beneath the striking **Citicorp Center tower** – the blue glass of Helmut Jahn's Postmodern skyscraper cascades down its north and south sides like a waterfall.

You'll find the city's oldest church standing a couple of blocks west of Union Station, at 700 W Adams St: **Old Saint Patrick's** has fifteen magnificent stained-glass windows inspired by Celtic art from the World's Fair and the *Book of Kells*. Each July, the restored Romanesque building, completed in 1856, hosts the self-styled "World's Largest Block Party", a fundraiser that doubles as a singles' event (see p.247). Just west of North Western Station you'll find **Claes Oldenburg's** playful *Batcolumn*, a slender 100-foot-long cage shaped to resemble an oversized baseball bat planted in front of the Social Security Administration Building, at 600 W Madison St. A short walk northwest of here will bring you to the area's top **restaurants**, who've set up shop on artsy-industrial W Randolph Street; for reviews, see "Eating", p.182).

The only other place of note around the West Loop is **Harpo Studios**, at 1058 W Washington Blvd (Mon–Fri 9am–5pm; ☎312/633-1000, ⓦwww .oprah.com), a former armoury where the enterprising **Oprah Winfrey** tapes her phenomenally popular talk shows. **Tickets** to the shows are free. They're generally made available for one month at a time and are snapped up within days, so check the website for updates on schedules and availability. Keep in mind that on the day of taping, you'll have to stand outside until the doors open, and it will likely be cold, given that the show takes June to August off. Of course, you can also just visit the Oprah Store next door at 37 N Carpenter St, which sells all types of Oprah-related products, including embroidered velour pajamas and tote bags. For more information, see p.31.

Greektown and around

The first Greek immigrants arrived in Chicago in the mid-1800s, mostly seamen whose plan was to work, save money and then return to the homeland. Many did indeed return to Greece and spread the word about the opportunities available in Chicago (particularly after the Great Fire), resulting in new waves of immigrants to the city. By the 1900s, a full-fledged **GREEKTOWN** had grown up around Harrison and Halsted streets around the former intersection with Blue Island Avenue. Known as "the Delta", the area had developed into a bustling little community by the 1950s but the building of the Eisenhower Expressway and the UIC campus eventually pushed Greektown a few blocks north to its present location, centred on the intersection of Halsted and Madison streets.

Today, the surrounding neighbourhood has been transformed into a yuppie haven of lofts and high-end restaurants but the stretch of Halsted Street between Madison and Van Buren is still staunchly Greek. Despite the tacky Greek temples and pavilions on the street corners – misguided attempts to beautify the neighbourhood for the 1996 Democratic National Convention – this pocket of the city has avoided becoming too touristy, and you'll still hear the mother tongue spoken in the area's shops, cafés, and boisterous restaurants (*tavernas*), where families and large groups chatter away and cries of "Opa!" fill the air as plates of *saganaki* (flaming feta cheese) are set alight.

The highlights of the neighbourhood calendar are the annual **Greek Independence Day Parade** in late March (see p.245) and a weekend in August when the tempting aromas of the **Taste of Greece** festival fill the air.

The United Center

The polished **United Center**, at 1901 W Madison St, replaced the old Chicago Stadium in 1995, a famously loud space that saw just about every kind of event, from hockey and basketball to Elvis concerts and speeches by Franklin D. Roosevelt (the phrase "New Deal" was first uttered here). Home to the **Bulls** (see p.235) and ice hockey's **Blackhawks** (see p.236), the new stadium has been called "the House that Michael Built", after the Bulls' Michael Jordan, who led his team to dominate the NBA during the 1990s.

There's nothing special about the stadium to make the one-hour backstage **tour** worthwhile (for groups of 15–40 only, by reservation; $20, includes lunch; ☎312/455-4500), but if you're here for a game or a concert, be sure to check out the **bronze statue** of Jordan at the front. Bear in mind that the surrounding neighbourhood is gang-ridden, desolate and **dangerous** (particularly west of here on Madison St and on nearby Damen Ave), so take a cab there. If you have a car, the stadium has plenty of monitored parking.

The Garfield Park Conservatory

Unfolding across 185 acres four miles west of Greektown, **Garfield Park** has exotic flower gardens and a lagoon, as well as facilities for all kinds of sports (tennis, basketball, soccer and baseball), a playground and a pool. Inside the park is one of Chicago's least-known and most underrated attractions, the **Garfield Park Conservatory**, 300 N Central Park Ave (Fri–Wed 9am–5pm, Thurs 9am–8pm; free; ☎312/746-5100, ⓦwww.garfield-conservatory.org; Green Line to Conservatory–Central Park), sister to the Lincoln Park Conservatory but the bigger and better of the two. Billing itself as "landscape art under glass", the current conservatory sits in the surrounding park. It was built between 1906 and 1907 to replace the original glasshouse designed by William Le Baron Jenney (see box, p.53), which fell into disrepair and was demolished.

Winding your way through banana trees, a deliciously arid desert section (more fun during a Chicago winter), and the masterful Fern Room by noted landscape designer Jens Jensen can occupy several hours. Kids will enjoy the hands-on displays in the **children's garden**, turning a crank to guide a giant "bee" into a flower, among other things. There's also an outdoor sensory garden where you can hold and smell fragrant flowers and fruits. Visitors can take self-guided **tours** (guided tours are for members only) through the well-marked and easily navigable gardens, which are almost never crowded.

Little Italy and around

Many of Chicago's first Italian immigrants came to the city in the 1890s as temporary workers, intending to return home with money earned from hard work on the railways, but those who settled in this poor enclave quickly turned it into **LITTLE ITALY**, a lively, restaurant-packed community. The name for this 'hood is a bit of a misnomer, as Italians never constituted a statistical majority within this hardscrabble area west of the Loop. Now, the charming old row houses that fill most of the backstreets like Aberdeen and Carpenter – as well as the construction of fancy new condominiums and lofts in pockets of land which was once populated by small factories and large parking lots – have seduced young professionals into moving here. The neighbourhood's relative seclusion (it's tucked away in a pocket just west of Interstate 90/94 and south of Interstate 290) has thus far protected it from being completely gentrified.

To catch the full flavour of Little Italy, you'll need to amble down Taylor Street, from Halsted to Ashland. Look out for *Mario's Lemonade* (see p.182), the

▲ Mario's Lemonade

little red, green, and white shack at 1068 W Taylor St, which has been selling delectable **Italian ices and lemonade** for more than thirty years. Among the last of Little Italy's old-fashioned, family-owned businesses, *Mario's* draws long lines in summer that give the place a friendly, block-party atmosphere. Across the street at no. 1079, *Al's Number 1 Italian Beef* (see p.182) has been doing similarly brisk business since 1938. For pure Chicago-style gluttony, their "dipped" **Italian beef sandwiches** are hard to beat.

If you're here during the day, head for the blocks around **Arrigo Park**, a patch of green just north of the intersection of Taylor and Loomis streets, which has some lovely turn-of-the-century townhouses all along its northern edge. The park has a baseball field and is a popular gathering spot for local Ultimate Frisbee players.

For the record, the place where Mrs O'Leary's poor cow supposedly kicked over a lantern and started the massive **fire of 1871** (see p.256) was in a barn at what's now the intersection of Jefferson and Taylor streets, just short of a mile from the centre of Little Italy, and east of the John F. Kennedy Expressway. There's really nothing to see here, other than the ironically situated **Chicago Fire Academy**, where trainee firefighters learn to extinguish smaller blazes.

Maxwell Street Market

If you're in Little Italy on a Sunday, poke around the **Maxwell Street Market**, a couple of blocks away at the intersection of Roosevelt Road and Desplaines Street. This giant **open-air flea market** happens every Sunday, rain or shine, from 7am to 3pm, and boasts **live blues music**, tortilla stands and around 500 vendors who hawk everything from car repair kits to boxes of fresh produce.

Locals still moan that it's only a shadow of the original Maxwell Street Market, which held court on Maxwell Street from the late 1800s till 1994, when the city forced the market to relocate to Canal Street. The Market moved once again in the fall of 2008, and while the naysayers may be right, you can still come away with a bargain or two, or sample the wide variety of food stalls that sell everything from Polish sausages, tacos and empanadas to thick, tortilla-like Salvadoran *pupusas*.

Jane Addams Hull-House Museum

Just west of Little Italy, you'll run smack into a concrete pile of Modernist architecture known as the campus of the 25,000-strong **University of Illinois-Chicago** (UIC). The university, which made headlines in the 1960s when its construction commenced (with the blessing of Mayor Richard J. Daley), brought much-needed money into the area but at the same time displaced many of the residents and altered the West Side's landscape for good. You will, however, find a piece of the area's history preserved in the form of the **Jane Addams Hull-House Museum**, 800 S Halsted St, at Harrison St (Tues–Fri 10am–4pm, Sun noon–4pm; free; ℡312/413-5353, Ⓦwww.uic.edu/jaddams /hull/), which makes for a rewarding visit if you're in the area.

Hull-House was an innovative settlement house (or neighbourhood social welfare agency) founded in 1889 that provided much-needed services to children, women and immigrants on Chicago's struggling West Side, where many of them lived in appalling conditions. **Jane Addams**, a social reformer who went on to win the Nobel Peace Prize in 1931, founded the house with fellow reformer Ellen Gates Starr after being inspired by a visit to Toynbee Hall, an influential settlement house in London's East End. By 1907, Hull-House had grown to fill several buildings, with day-care programmes for the children of working mothers, employment centres for immigrants, an art studio and gallery, a labour museum, a public kitchen and even a coffeehouse.

The organization, still a force for social welfare in the city, has moved on to headquarters in the Loop. Two of the original Hull-House buildings have survived, though, and are owned and run by the university: both Hull Mansion and the dining hall have been restored to their original appearance. Inside Hull Mansion, you'll see some of Addams' original furniture, paintings and photographs, plus rotating exhibits and memorabilia from famous supporters and Hull-House visitors such as Carl Sandburg, Ida B. Wells, Frank Lloyd Wright, W.E.B. Dubois, Clarence Darrow, Gertrude Stein and William Butler Yeats. On the second floor of the dining hall, a fifteen-minute film explains how Hull-House tackled the West Side's entrenched social problems. For an excellent firsthand account of Hull-House, read Addams' *Twenty Years at Hull-House* (see p.278).

Pilsen

In summer especially, you could easily mistake **PILSEN** for a neighbourhood on the outskirts of Mexico City, with radios blaring mariachi music from apartment windows and residents congregating around the *fruterías* (produce markets), *panaderias* (bakeries), and Mexican restaurants. The bustling centre, focussed a mile south of Little Italy along 18th Street, west of Racine Avenue, is home to the city's large Latino community and, since the 1960s, has been a haven for local artists. The authentic **Mexican cuisine** to be found in the area's restaurants – many along 18th Street between Racine and Ashland avenues – is reason enough to come here, as is the **National Museum of Mexican Art**, the largest Latino cultural institution in the US. Much art can be found out of doors as well, courtesy of local muralists who have covered the walls of local buildings with tributes to Mexican culture. Good examples of this artwork can be found at the Blue Line 18th Street El station at 18th and Paulina, as well as at 1645 W 18th St, where the Jose Clemente School is alive with **colourful mosaics**.

The first **Mexican immigrants** began arriving in Chicago in the mid-1800s, their numbers growing steadily until World War I, when labour shortages in the

US brought thousands of Mexicans to Chicago seeking work. Many found jobs in the steel mills, railyards and stockyards and settled on the near West Side, where the immigration services of Hull-House (see p.119) did much to ease their way. However, much like the West Side's Greek and Italian communities, urban renewal and the building of expressways eventually forced the Mexican immigrants to settle here, a neighbourhood originally settled by **Czech émigrés** in the early 1800s, who named it after the town of Plzen in West Bohemia in 1870 (the neighbourhood of Pilsen East, centred on 18th and Halsted streets, still retains some vaguely Czech flavour). Today, roughly one million Mexicans live in Chicago, and census figures estimate that by 2010, Mexicans will be the largest ethnic group in Chicago.

Getting here on public transportation is possible, though in most cases time-consuming. On weekdays, take the Cermak Branch of the Blue El Line to the 18th Street stop; bear in mind that this branch doesn't run on weekends. Your best bet on weekends is to take a taxi. The buses that run along Halsted Street, Blue Island Avenue and the other main streets into Pilsen are slow and irregular.

The National Museum of Mexican Art

Pilsen's main attraction is the engaging **National Museum of Mexican Art**, at 1852 W 19th St and Wolcott Ave (Tues–Sun 10am–5pm; free; ☎312/738-1503, ⓦwww.nationalmuseumofmexicanart.org/), dedicated to the arts of Mexico as well as US Mexican communities. The small but wide-ranging exhibits are presented in five rotating galleries, with thoughtful captions in both Spanish and English. On display is a history of Mexican art from ancient times to the present day, shown through pre-Columbian artefacts, charming Talavera de Puebla pottery (glazed Spanish-influenced earthenware) and contemporary photos of the Mexican experience in Chicago. You might also spot a few sketches by famed muralist Diego Rivera, as well as etchings by Jose Clemente Orozco and the politically charged work of David Alfaro Siqueiros.

The museum is known locally for its annual, month-long **Day of the Dead exhibit** – the nation's largest – which commemorates the holiday with paintings, folk art, sculpture and mixed-media pieces that explore the theme of death and dying. The museum also puts on performing arts festivals twice a year, in the spring and fall.

Free guided **tours** of the main gallery are offered to groups of ten or more in English or Spanish. There's also a **gift shop** stocked with distinctive black Oaxacan pottery and hand-woven rugs, silver jewellery, and a wide selection of posters and books. The museum's only drawback is its somewhat remote location on the lower West Side; you could make a day of it by combining a visit here with a trip to nearby Chinatown (see p. 75) or to the historic homes further east on S Prairie Avenue.

8

The South Side and Hyde Park

S prawling from south of the South Loop all the way to the city limits, the **South Side** of Chicago is a case study in urban contrasts, as it contains the very affluent and those who are struggling the most in the Second City. The area includes the neighbourhoods of Hyde Park, Kenwood and Bronzeville, and you can wander through the hushed, neo-Gothic quadrangles of the University of Chicago, famous for snagging Nobel Prizes. Just a few blocks away from this tweedy academic enclave you can find yourself in some of the most dangerous and run-down districts of the city, where windows are boarded up, garbage is scattered across empty lots, and a sense of hopelessness predominates.

The story of **Hyde Park**, the main target for most visitors heading to the South Side, is intertwined with Chicago's apogee in the 1890s, when it was the site of the city's two greatest civic projects. The first, the **University of Chicago**, rose out of the mucky and marshy centre of Hyde Park in 1892 and quickly achieved academic fame; it's perhaps best known as the site of the first nuclear reaction (see p.263). A year after the university was founded, Hyde Park served as the site of the **World's Columbian Exposition**, a mammoth civic scheme that was arguably Chicago's finest moment: remnants from that spectacular success include the building that houses the **Museum of Science and Industry** and the Midway Plaisance greenspace. Hyde Park also holds one of the hands-down most important (and most intriguing) structures in the city, Frank Lloyd Wright's **Robie House**.

Flanking the western fringes of the university campus is **Washington Park**, expansive and rugged, with people out playing soccer, football and cricket. The historic district of **Kenwood**, located north of Hyde Park Boulevard stretching to E 47th Street, is full of turn-of-the-twentieth-century grandeur, with an eclectic display of Gothic, mock Tudor and Queen Anne-style homes designed by Frank Lloyd Wright and other great twentieth-century American architects.

Outside Hyde Park and Kenwood, the South Side is a predominantly African-American neighbourhood: racial tensions run high and many locals feel that the area's been unfairly left to decay while white districts like Lincoln Park have been aggressively smartened up. However, the **Bronzeville** neighbourhood, a cradle of opportunity from the 1920s to the 1950s, when it was birthplace to legendary jazz musicians, civil rights leaders, and entrepreneurs, contains enough vestiges of its former vibrance to reward a visit.

To **get to** Kenwood, take the Metra to 47th Street and for Hyde Park, take the Metra to 55th, 56th, 57th, or 59th street stations or the #6 Jeffrey Express bus; avoid the Green Line El. For the South Side sights and entertainment we've highlighted outside Hyde Park and Kenwood, the safest option is to take a cab.

Some history

The South Side has seesawed between swanky mansions and gritty industry since Chicago first exploded as an industrial powerhouse in the mid-nineteenth century. It was home to many of the local railway and manufacturing magnates until Potter Palmer decamped to the Gold Coast (see p.87) in the 1880s and the rest of the elite followed. The South Side was also the site of the city's heavy industry, including the monumental slaughterhouses known as the **Chicago Stockyards**, whose stench wafted over the area until closing up shop for good in 1971.

But the South Side is best known as the crossroads between black and white Chicago. Labour shortages in the early twentieth century forced owners to look to African-American workers from the South to fill their factories. The newly arrived employees then settled close by their jobs, in Chicago's South Side. The South Side's African-American population grew, partly owing to the city's **segregation policy** (see p.260), which sequestered most African Americans along a southerly strip of State Street. Isolated

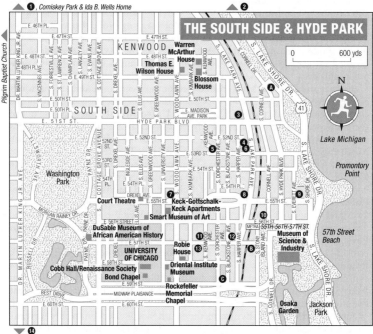

THE SOUTH SIDE & HYDE PARK

EATING				DRINKING		ACCOMMODATION	
Caffé Florian	12	Mellow Yellow	6	The Cove Lounge	9	International House	
Dixie Kitchen and Bait Shop	4	Negro League Café	1	Jimmy's Woodlawn Tap	7	of Chicago	C
Edwardo's Natural Pizza	11	Original Pancake House	3	Keegan's Pub	14	Ramada Inn Lakeshore	A
La Petite Folie	8	Pearl's Place	2			Wooded Isle Suites	B
Medici on 57th	13	Piccolo Mondo	10				
		Ribs 'n' Bibs	5				

Comiskey Park and the 1919 World Series

The thoroughly modern and desperately sterile **Comiskey Park Stadium** sits immediately west of the Dan Ryan Expressway in the unpolished South Side neighbourhood of **Bridgeport**. It was here in 1919 that the most famous scandal in baseball history occurred. Despite having some of the best players ever assembled on one team – one that outclassed the rest of the league in regular season, en route to a 110-win season – the White Sox played uncharacteristically sloppily in the final game of the **1919 World Series**, which they were heavily favoured to win, losing 10–5 to the Cincinnati Reds. Suspicion fell on eight of the White Sox players, who were soon accused of throwing the game in exchange for cash. Although all eight players, notable among them star **Shoeless Joe Jackson**, were ultimately acquitted of criminal activity after a lengthy investigation. However, they were banned from baseball for life, and the team itself was disgraced with the nickname "**the Black Sox**". John Sayles' evocative film *Eight Men Out* (1988) offers a good introduction to the incident. For information on the current – and untainted – Chicago White Sox, see p.235.

geographically, politically and culturally from the city as a whole, Chicago's black community developed a singular identity – and its association with blues music and jazz clubs was truly cemented, especially in the entertainment district known as **The Stroll** (see p. 260), which began at S State and 31st streets.

While a distinct African-American culture was developing here, so was a simmering resentment of local whites' treatment of blacks – there were six consecutive days of **race riots** across the city in July 1919 that resulted in the deaths of twenty-three African-Americans and fifteen whites. This anger only worsened as the largely white local government paid little attention to the economic impact Chicago's crumbling industrial backbone had on the South Side. The area has never truly recovered from the incident, and a casual trip by car down S Stony Island Drive will take you past low-rise buildings covered in barbed wire, and heavy iron grilles on most shop windows.

Bronzeville

South of the McCormick Place Convention Center at 26th Street lies the primarily African-American neighbourhood of **BRONZEVILLE**. During the late nineteenth and early twentieth centuries, Bronzeville was a thriving "Black Metropolis", a land of opportunity for African Americans who had fled the South during the "Great Migration". Lively streets lined with stately homes, Art Deco theatres, jazz clubs and blues bars nurtured musical icons, legendary activists and pioneers of the twentieth century: Andrew "Rube" Foster, founder of the Negro National Baseball League; Ida B. Wells, a civil rights activist, journalist and organizer of the NAACP; former Nation of Islam leader Elijah Muhammad; Bessie Coleman, the first African-American woman pilot; and Louis Armstrong, the legendary trumpeter. By 1929, Bronzeville's population had generated over $100 million in real estate and the Regal Theater, Savoy Ballroom and Metropolitan Theater all ranked alongside the city's most prestigious entertainment venues. Nowadays, the story is very different, a depressing landscape of run-down streets, vacant lots, derelict buildings, segregation and urban blight.

While resentment simmers that Mayor Daley has neglected the South Side in favour of "vanity" projects like Millennium Park, there are signs that with investment and local initiatives Bronzeville is making a comeback. Around 47th Street, restaurants, cafés, galleries and bookstores are opening and attracting visitors from other neighbourhoods. The eye-catching **Harold Washington Cultural Center**, unveiled in 2004 at 4701 S Martin Luther King Drive (box office 8am–4pm; ☎773/373-1900), has since become the focus of plans to develop the Bronzeville community. A swish arts, music and educational complex, with a staircase that looks like a winding piano, the Cultural Center plays host to the occasional jazz legend.

There are a few other sights of minor note, but it's really Bronzeville's historical resonance that provides the area's interest. The **Bronzeville Walk of Fame**, on Martin Luther King Drive between 25th and 47th streets, features 91 bronze plaques engraved with the names of Bronzeville's famous residents. Close by, the 15-foot-statue, **Monument to the Great Northern Migration** (1996), depicts a travel-worn man pointing north, his feet resting upon a mound of soles, symbolizing all those who fled the South in search of the northern "Promised Land". One of the oldest African-American churches in Chicago, built by Louis Sullivan in 1890, the **Pilgrim Baptist Church**, 3301 S Indiana at 33rd Street, is a gospel-music landmark. Regrettably, the building suffered a devastating fire in January 2006, and it is currently being rebuilt. At 35th Street and Martin Luther King Drive, the **Victory Monument** pays tribute to the Eighth Regiment of the National Guard, an African-American unit that fought in France during World War I. Further south, at 3624 S Martin Luther King, is the former home of **Ida B. Wells**, who lived here between 1919 and 1930.

This part of the South Side has quite a crime problem and care should be taken at all times. Take taxis everywhere and avoid the area at night.

Kenwood

The historical district of **KENWOOD** extends east from S Drexel Boulevard to S Blackstone Avenue, and south from E 47th Street to Hyde Park Boulevard. When Kenwood became part of Chicago in 1889, the city's business, scholarly and fashionable elite made Kenwood their suburban oasis, building grandiose homes along its leafy tree-lined boulevards; Kenwood exuded classical grandeur. Meatpacker Gustavus Swift, lumber merchant Martin Ryerson and Sears Roebuck executive and philanthropist Julius Rosenwald were the kings of Kenwood and they commissioned the city's visionary architects to build their castles in a flamboyant array of styles. By the 1920s, many homes had been subdivided into multi-family apartments and new monolithic high-rises began to dilute its vintage aura.

It's not worth going out of your way, but if you happen to be in the area, there is a crop of landmarks here, including two of Frank Lloyd Wright's "bootlegged" houses. **Blossom House**, at 4858 S Kenwood, was built in 1892 in Queen Anne style; all buttercup yellow with a neat white trim and Palladian windows, it may not be signature Wright, but the fluid interior (access not permitted) betrays some Prairie School influence. Next door, the Dutch-style colonial house at **4852 S Kenwood** was commissioned by manufacturer Warren McArthur in 1892. Built with a gambrel roof and featuring a dado with Roman brick to create a horizontal plane, it was the first structure in which Wright used leaded windows.

Howard van Doren Shaw, described as, "the most rebellious of the conservative and the most conservative of the radical", built 21 homes in the Hyde Park and Kenwood areas. His eclectic style ranged from Tudor Gothic to Georgian and beyond. Examples include the **Oskar Bolza house** at 5533 S University Ave and the **Thomas E. Wilson** house at 4815 Woodlawn.

Hyde Park

Seven miles south of downtown, **HYDE PARK**, the most attractive and sophisticated South Side neighbourhood, is an island of middle-class prosperity surrounded by urban poverty. Fitting into less than two square miles between 51st Street and 59th Street and from S Cottage Grove Avenue to the lake, it's also one of the most racially integrated areas of the city, strikingly evident in its array of ethnic eateries and its mix of low-income housing and mansions. Likewise it's among the more erudite, with the **University of Chicago** at its centre and the popular **Museum of Science and Industry** in Jackson Park.

For a glimpse of collegiate Hyde Park – and a smattering of terrific second-hand bookstores – head for **57th Street**: it bisects the main campus and passes a short distance from the **Robie House** at 58th Street and Woodlawn Avenue. Otherwise, Hyde Park's commercial hub is **53rd Street**, where there are traces of the urban blight that looms outside the area, with cheap cafeterias standing alongside chic houseware shops. Though the area is mostly safe, you should remain aware of your environment at night, and avoid less travelled streets during the evening hours.

Promontory Point

For a change from Hyde Park's busy storefronts and crowded sidewalks, you can visit the small headland at the east end of 55th Street, **Promontory Point**. This open, grassy spot on the rocky shores of Lake Michigan usually teems in summertime with picnicking families, sunbathers and joggers, all of whom come for the spectacular view northward to downtown Chicago. The view south towards industrial Indiana is much less appealing. A dip in the lake around

Hyde Park parakeets

Perhaps the neighbourhood's most unique populace is the local flock of some hundred *Myiopsitta monachus* – better known hereabouts as Hyde Park **parakeets**. Native to Argentina and Brazil, these bright-green monk parakeets, sporting grey underbellies and blue wing feathers, were first sighted in the area in the 1970s nesting in huge tangles of twigs in the treetops or electrical poles. Unlike their South American counterparts, the Hyde Park parakeets aren't considered agricultural pests, but are known for their loud, high-pitched squawking.

How these tropical birds came to trade their sultry southern homeland for Hyde Park is not known, though it's commonly thought that the birds escaped from a cage at a Chicago airport. Despite the bitingly cold winters here, they have managed to thrive; threats of elimination by the US Department of Agriculture in the late 1980s eventually faded after local protests.

Nicknamed "Parrot Park", the corner of **Harold Washington Park** at Lake Shore Drive and 53rd Street is the most popular nesting site for the birds.

the Point is refreshing, but take care to avoid swimming from the generally unclean and crowded 57th Street Beach to the south.

The Museum of Science and Industry

The monumental **Museum of Science and Industry**, 57th Street and Lake Shore Drive (Mon–Sat 9.30am–4pm, Sun 11am–4pm; $13, $12 seniors, $9 children, free during Jan, Sept and the first week of June; ☎773/684-1414, ⓦ www.msichicago.org), is a textbook example of how terrific fun can be integrated with higher learning; it will entrance even the most reluctant child, thanks mostly to the genuinely enthusiastic and question-friendly staff. The Beaux Arts building itself was originally designed as the Palace of Fine Arts for the World's Columbian Exposition in 1893; the only structure salvaged at the exhibition's end, it was painstakingly dismantled before a stone frame was rebuilt around its steel skeleton. A massive refurbishment in 1997 made the place more navigable: visitors now enter through the subterranean entrance hall, surfacing under the main rotunda, and can plan a visit from there. You'll still need one of the free maps, however, to get around the three sprawling levels.

On the main floor, whatever you do, don't miss the **Coal Mine**: here, hardhat-sporting staffers take you through a thirty-minute coal-miner training session, which includes a rickety ride on an underground trolley (expect long queues at the weekend). Close by, there's also the mesmerizing **Chick Hatchery**, divided into two habitats. In one, you can watch fluffy chicks running around and eating; in the other, you can witness the damp, awkward-footed baby birds pecking their way out of a shell and then slumping down to rest after all the effort. Also on this floor, the **Great Train Story** is a wonderful reincarnation of the museum's original model railroad that for over sixty years had re-created the journey between Chicago and Seattle. Imaginatively and ingeniously, the new train travels over steel trusses, through the Rocky Mountains, over the Grand Canyon, and past cotton gins, coal mines, and lumber mills.

Continuing the train theme, **All Aboard the Silver Streak** is a tour of the pioneering *Zephyr* train, which completed the longest and fastest non-stop railroad run in 1934. Travelling from Denver to Chicago, it averaged 77.6 miles per hour, slashing twelve hours and forty minutes off the previous record. Known as "shovelnose" streamline trains, nine more were built between 1934 and 1939.

Other popular stopoffs on the ground floor include the enormous, exhaustively detailed dollhouse known as the **Fairy Castle**, created by silent film star Colleen Moore. The actress employed movie set designers and art directors to create her fantastical vision. No expense was spared: there's Royal Doulton china in the kitchen, Viennese tapestries in the dining room, platinum chairs encrusted with diamonds and emeralds, as well as a mother-of-pearl floor in the Princess' bedroom.

There's a fifteen-minute "captained" tour ($5) of the **U–505 Submarine**, captured from Germany in 1944 by forces led by a Chicago native. Interactive features, simulated sound effects and atmospheric lighting make the experience feel very immediate as you manoeuvre through the warren-like spaces of the engine room, captain's quarters (whose bed was just thirty inches wide) and the torpedo room. Claustrophobics should steer clear.

Upstairs on the balcony, check out the **HIV exhibit**, which explains the virus in easy-to-understand, comic-book style, and the walk-through **human heart**. As you make your way through the museum, make sure to take the **blue stairs** at least once, which hold perhaps the most startling exhibit of all – a pickled human being, sliced into wafer-thin sections using a band saw in the 1930s, preserved in formaldehyde, and wedged between sheets of glass. A bit macabre perhaps, but still oddly compelling.

The Robie House

Perched on the edge of the University of Chicago, the **Robie House**, 5757 S Woodlawn Ave (access by tour only; $12, $10 seniors and children 11–18, $5 children 4–10, children under 4 free; ☎708/848-1976, ⓦwww.wrightplus.org), is one of Frank Lloyd Wright's masterpieces, and its location in Hyde Park makes it a more convenient alternative to his better-known homes in Oak Park west of Chicago (see p.140). Commissioned by local businessman Frederick Robie in 1908, the red-brick house is a prime example of Wright's **Prairie School style** (see *Chicago Architecture* colour section). Drawing inspiration from the flat Midwestern prairie, and attempting to carve out a distinctly American style, Wright gave Robie an overwhelmingly horizontal house. The cantilevered roof seems to levitate over the building and extends 20ft from its supports. The main floor is a fluid space with no walls or partitions; the fireplace serves as a "screen" between the living and dining room areas.

Sacrificing practicality to achieve aesthetic consistency, he didn't even include downspouts in the building's drainage system, which resulted in ninety years' worth of water damage to the pavements. Wright wanted every element unified – which meant that he designed everything: building, plants, light fittings, chairs, even the clothes the Robies' two children would wear – and was known to show up unannounced at any time to make sure that all the furniture was still in its proper place. The Robies learned to hold him off at the door, rearrange the rooms, and then invite him in.

The house passed through several families' hands in quick succession after the Robie family lost its fortune. In 1926, the house was bought by the Chicago Theological Seminary, which promptly converted it into student accommodation. As if the damage this caused wasn't enough, by 1957 the Seminary had raised enough money to carry out its original plan of demolishing the building completely. It took the philanthropy of another businessman, William Zeckendorff, to save the house, which he then donated to the University of Chicago in 1963.

Though the Frank Lloyd Wright Preservation Trust completed work on the exterior in 2003, a further $4 million is still needed to finish the interior renovations. Until the restoration is completed in late 2009, tours will be conducted only on Saturdays.

The University of Chicago

Perhaps the top institution in the Midwest, the **University of Chicago** is interested in proving itself worthy to the east coast Ivy League crew: the intensely studious 14,000-strong student body is one symptom, as are T-shirts sold in the campus bookstore that read "The U of C: Where Fun Comes to Die". Previous alumni include Saul Bellow, Nobel Prize-winning author of *Herzog*; Nobel Laureate Milton Friedman, hailed for his study of monetary policy; Nathanial Kleitman, who identified REM sleep; Saul Alinsky, noted community activist and author; and John Hope Franklin, the country's most esteemed scholar of African-American history. It was also the base for several postwar decades of influential neoconservative professor Leo Strauss, who

taught many prominent members of the discredited George W. Bush administration. Of course, these days, much of the talk is about United States President
Barack Obama. While not an alumnus of the University of Chicago, he taught
at the Law School here from 1992 to 2004, while cutting his political teeth and
starting a family.

For the most impressive introduction to the university, either walk or drive
west down the **Midway Plaisance**, a long green strip that was the site of the
World's Columbian Exposition. The Midway was then filled with full-sized
model villages from around the globe, including an Irish market town and a
mock-up of Cairo complete with belly dancers. These days, it's used mainly by
joggers and students tossing Frisbees.

To explore the campus, consider taking one of the student-led **tours** that
depart from the Office of College Admissions, 1101 E 58th St (March–Nov
Mon–Fri 10.30am & 1.30pm; Dec–Feb Mon–Fri 10.30am; Sept 25–Nov 22
9am & 11am; ☏773/702-8650). Intended primarily for prospective students
and their parents, these one-hour walking tours cover the entire campus and
offer some campus history and architectural commentary, as well as some quirky
anecdotes.

The Rockefeller Memorial Chapel and around

If you'd rather see things on your own, a good place to start is the **Rockefeller
Memorial Chapel**, at 5850 Woodlawn Ave, philanthropist John D. Rockefeller's last, and major, architectural contribution to the university. Dedicated in
1928, the austere limestone chapel's most impressive feature is its tremendous
size, which you can take in by walking its length all the way to the altar,
admiring the stained-glass windows and numerous religious figurines.

The chapel is, fittingly, home to the world's second-largest musical instrument
– the tuned bells of the Laura Spelman **Rockefeller Carillon**. If you have the
time and the gumption to climb the 274 steps of the stone spiral staircase for
the complete carillon tour, you will be rewarded with a spectacular view of the
city and Lake Michigan, plus the chance to stand inside one of the larger bronze
bells and even pound out a couple of notes on the keyboard that will be heard
for blocks. A single person controls the carillon's 72 bells by pressing large oak
keys with his or her fists, as well as using foot pedals. **Tours** are offered during
the academic year by appointment only (9am–4pm; ☏773/702-9202, ⓦwww
.rockefeller.uchicago.edu). The carillon is played weekdays at noon and 6pm
and at noon only on Sundays.

One block away from the chapel's entrance, book lovers cherish the **Seminary
Co-op Bookstore**, housed in the cozy basement of the Chicago Theological
Seminary at 5757 S University Ave. Reminiscent of an over-crowed small-town
library, the store has over 100,000 volumes of academic and mainstream books
on religion crammed in its cellar. See p.227 for more details and other Hyde
Park bookstores.

The Oriental Institute

Just north of the chapel, the **Oriental Institute**, 1155 E 58th St (Tues &
Thurs–Sat 10am–6pm, Wed 10am–8.30pm, Sun noon–6pm; suggested donation
$5; ☏773/702-9520, ⓦwww.oi.uchicago.edu), is well worth an hour's visit for
its superb collection of artefacts from the ancient Near East, notably Egypt,
Mesopotamia, Iran and Anatolia. It's not a museum in the traditional sense, but
a research institute that shows off just a fraction of its world-class holdings. The
institute has recently unveiled its new galleries, including **Empire in the**

▲ Oriental Institute

Fertile Crescent: Ancient Assyria, Anatolia, and Israel. The institute's archeological teams excavated most of the Fertile Crescent artefacts seen here.

One of their greatest finds is a collection of bronze figurines discovered in Tell Judaidah in southeast Turkey. Dated 3000 BC, they are considered the earliest bronze artefacts discovered in the world. Other noteworthy artefacts include a fragment of the Dead Sea Scrolls – one of the few fragments of the ancient Hebrew manuscript, hidden around 100 AD, on display in the US. Another exhibit presents the finds from the institute's dig at **Megiddo** (the place referred to in the Bible as Armageddon and considered the cradle of archeology in Israel): don't miss the beautifully carved Megiddo ivories, dated 1300 BC. Especially worthwhile is the **Egyptian Gallery**, which houses more than 30,000 artefacts, one of the largest collections in the US. The most impressive piece is the "Colossal Statue of King Tutankhamun", which dates from 1334 BC (though it's hardly colossal, it's still pretty tall at 17ft). Also look out for the elaborately decorated "Mummy and Coffin of Meresamun", which shows scenes of the hoped-for afterlife.

Many of the artifacts in the **Persian Room** were excavated by the Oriental Institute during the 1930s, when the U of C was at its peak in the field of archeology. Among the highlights is the robust-looking "Colossal Bull Head" from Iran, one of a pair of beautifully carved stone statues dating from 486 to

424 BC. There is also a lavish collection of Achaemenid art, found during excavations at **Persepolis** (the ceremonial capital of the Persian empire from 612–330 BC) in the 1930s.

The Quads

At the heart of the university, between 57th and 59th streets and Ellis and University avenues is the **Main Quadrangle**, or "The Quads". Surrounded by neo-Gothic offices and libraries, its footpaths and lawns are the busiest part of the campus, usually buzzing with students heading to and from classes. The best ways to enter the quadrangle are from the east at the intersection of 58th Street and University Avenue or through the gate directly across from Regenstein Library on 59th Street. In the southeast corner, you'll find the peaceful **Social Science Quad**, which makes a good spot to contemplate the periodic sounding of the bells.

Lying in the shadow of the much grander Rockefeller Chapel is the quaint and detailed **Bond Chapel**, in the Classics Quadrangle in the southwest corner of The Quads. The chapel is frequently the site of small weddings, and you might just happen in during a practice sermon by a student from the nearby Divinity School.

Just west, at 5811 Ellis Ave, the English Gothic–style **Cobb Hall** is the University's oldest building, built in 1892 by Henry Ives Cobb. The hall is home to the **Renaissance Society** (Tues–Fri 10am–5pm, Sat & Sun noon–5pm; free; ✆773/702-8670, Ⓦwww.renaissancesociety.org), which presents some of the country's most provocative contemporary art. Founded in 1915, the society gained an international reputation in the 1930s for its displays of avant-garde European art, including paintings by Picasso and Miró sourced directly from the artists' studios. In 1934, the society held the first solo exhibition of Alexander Calder's "mobiles," and it was the first Chicago gallery to exhibit Bruce Nauman and Julian Schnabel in the 1980s.

Cobb Gate, at the north end of the quads, forms the gateway to the University. Also designed by Henry Ives Cobb, the gargoyles that adorn the ornate Gothic gate are said to represent the progression of every University of Chicago student; the gargoyles at the bottom represent the impeding figures of the Admissions Counselor and Examiner, while the figures at the top symbolize the fourth-year students who have successfully climbed the ivory tower.

If only for its sheer oddity, pass by Henry Moore's bronze *Nuclear Energy* sculpture, located on the east side of S Ellis Avenue between 56th and 57th streets. The university was the site of the Manhattan Project research, and the heavy, mushroom-shaped work commemorates the moment that "…man achieved here the first self-sustaining chain reaction and thereby initiated the controlled release of nuclear energy".

Smart Museum of Art

The small, scholarly collection at the **Smart Museum of Art**, 5550 S Greenwood Ave (Tues, Wed & Fri 10am–4pm, Thurs 10am–8pm except during summer break, Sat & Sun 11am–5pm; free; ✆773/702-0200, Ⓦsmartmuseum .uchicago.edu), is where the majority of the U of C's art collection – which spans more than five thousand years and contains more than nine thousand pieces – is stored and displayed. Perhaps because of the museum's modest size, there's a lot of attention paid to detail, from the impeccable displays and unique themes down to thoughtful captions and quotes from artists. Though you'll find a little bit of everything here – Old Master paintings, Frank Lloyd Wright's dining-room furniture and twentieth-century paintings ranging from Rothko to Diego Rivera – the museum is perhaps best known for its works by the Chicago Imagists. Emerging from Hyde Park during the 1960s, the Imagists created playful neon, cartoon-like art which referenced non-Western and Surrealist art as well as drawing on images from popular culture. Look out for the work of Ed Paschke (1934–2004), one of the genre's leading exemplars. A graduate from the Art Institute of Chicago, Paschke was influenced by the photo-based works of Andy Warhol. Further highlights in the **Modern Art and Design** section (room 1) include the painting *Money is the Reason for Work* (1949) by French Dada artist Francis Picabia, and *Je m'arche* (1949), by Chilean artist Roberto Matta Echaurren, who whipped the New York art world into a frenzy during the 1940s by stating that emotions could be expressed through an abstract vocabulary.

Round out your U of C tour by grabbing a beer or a greasy lunch just north of campus at **Jimmy's Woodlawn Tap** (see p.195), at 1172 E 55th St, a shabby, fifty-year-old local bar that has seen the likes of Dylan Thomas, Margaret Mead and Saul Bellow. Stop by on Sundays to hear free jazz and talk about the state of world affairs.

Washington Park

One of the social linchpins of the Southside, the rugged expanses of **Washington Park**'s 372 acres stretch west from Cottage Grove Avenue between 51st and 60th streets. The park was laid out by Frederick Law Olmsted (1822–1903) in the 1870s. The "father of American landscape architecture", Olmsted is best known for landscaping New York's Central Park. During the 1920s, racial tensions soared in Washington Park when the area's population changed dramatically from mostly white to mostly African American. Despite the threats and intimidation by white gangs, semi-professional African-American baseball teams continued to play on the baseball fields at Washington Park during the 1920s.

Daniel Burnham's firm designed several buildings in the park, including the **Refectory**, at Morgan and Martin Luther King Drive, built in 1881, and the limestone **Roundhouse Stables**, built in 1880, in the southeast corner of the park; after their recent multi-million-dollar renovation, the stables now form the expanded galleries of the **DuSable Museum of African American History** (see p.132).

At the west end of the Park, don't miss Lorado Taft's sculpture **Fountain of Time**, based on poet Austin Dobson's lines: "Time goes, you say? Ah no, Alas, time stays, we go". The fountain is composed of the figure of Father Time watching over the flow of humanity in the form of one hundred human figures. It took Taft twelve years to complete the sculpture, which also contains a reflecting pool integral to the sculpture's symbolism. The Chicago weather and piecemeal restoration have done little to allow the sculpture to steal time; a massive restoration project was completed in 2005.

Long-time denizens and newer South Side residents flock to Washington Park as it provides a range of sports amenities and hosts many festivals and events during summer. The city's only public **cricket pitch** is here and on Sunday mornings, six teams of Washington Park residents can be seen decked out in their spick-and-span cricket whites, playing in Chicago's only organized cricket league. The park is full of facilities including basketball courts, racquetball courts, baseball diamonds, children's playground areas and a lagoon. In 2003, a mini-arboretum was created between 51st and 55th streets and Martin Luther King Drive and Payne.

The **neighbourhood** of Washington Park, west of the park stretching west from Cottage Grove to Wentworth Avenue and south from 51st Street to 63rd Street, holds little of interest for the visitor. It's one of Chicago's poorest neighbourhoods and the area can be a bit dicey in the evening.

DuSable Museum of African American History

On the west edge of Hyde Park and a ten-minute walk from the centre of the U of C campus, the **DuSable Museum of African American History**, 740 E 56th Place (daily 10am–5pm, Sun from noon; $3, seniors & students $2, children 6–13 $1, children under 6 free, free on Sun; ☎773/947-0600, Ⓦwww.dusablemuseum.org), is the oldest American institution devoted to collecting and preserving the heritage of Africans and African Americans. With such an ambitious mission, it's almost impossible for the museum not to fall short – which it does on several fronts – but there's still enough here to make a visit worthwhile if you're in the area; it's not necessarily something you'd journey out specifically for, though.

Start by picking up a map at the entrance and head past the bust of **Jean-Baptiste Point DuSable** (see p.253), the museum's namesake, to reach *The Ames Mural* (also known as *The Roots Mural*) – Robert Ames' mural of carved oak (1965), which powerfully brings to life the African-American struggle by way of key scenes and figures from history, from Harriet Tubman to civil rights marches on Washington.

In a small corridor in the main leg of the museum, you'll find traditional African art displayed in the **Africa Speaks** exhibit, mostly carved pieces such as stools, dolls and combs from early West African kingdoms; the Mossi dance masks are especially playful. An ornate exhibit entitled The Red, White, Blue & Black pays homage to the role of blacks in the U.S. Armed Forces over the past 225 years. It's an effective and compelling mix of militaria, photographs and other items of historical ephemera and worth more than a passing glance.

The **main hall**, the largest space of all, is usually reserved for upbeat temporary exhibits. Beyond the main hall is a re-creation of the office of Harold Washington, Chicago's first black mayor.

A $25 million expansion, completed in 2007, added additional exhibition space, cultural amenities and research facilities housed in the Roundhouse building, a former limestone horse-stable and Historic Landmark, designed by Daniel Burnham.

9

Rogers Park and the North Shore

Nearly ten miles north of the Loop at the northeast corner of the city, the tree-lined, residential neighbourhood of **Rogers Park** is Chicago's most diverse enclave, with more than eighty languages spoken among the area's sixty thousand-odd residents. Home to the Jesuit-affiliated **Loyola University**, active Indian and Pakistani communities and an increasing number of young professionals claiming condos along the city's last stretch of affordable lakeside housing, this neighbourhood welcomes a hodge-podge of ethnic and economic backgrounds – though not many visitors, as there is little for tourists to see or do.

Cross north over Juneway Terrace and you've entered the entirely different world of **the North Shore**, a series of affluent lakeside suburbs that are home to a mix of CEOs, college professors and wealthy financiers. From the college town **Evanston** (home of **Northwestern University**) to picturesque **Wilmette** with its breathtaking **Baha'í Temple**, the streets of these idyllic suburbs are lined with beautiful houses surrounded by manicured lawns – you might recognize the terrain from John Hughes's 1980s teen movies *Ferris Bueller's Day Off* and *Sixteen Candles* or Paul Brickman's *Risky Business*, which launched Tom Cruise's career. While there's not much here for an out-of-town visitor to see, a drive up lakeside **Sheridan Road**, lined with the multi-million-dollar mansions of various corporate bigwigs, makes for an intriguing glimpse into how the other half lives, and presents a striking contrast with adjacent Rogers Park.

This region of Chicago is best visited by car. The best **public transport** option to reach Rogers Park is the El Red Line Loyola stop, at Loyola University; from here, you can take the #155 bus to explore Devon Avenue. To visit Evanston, drive north on Sheridan Road from Chicago, or take the El Purple Line to the Davis or Foster stops; for Wilmette, continue north on Sheridan or get off at the last Purple Line stop, Linden.

Rogers Park

Eight miles north of the Loop, **ROGERS PARK** was established in the mid-1800s by Irish, German and Luxembourgian immigrants and that diversity has been one of the neighbourhood's marked characteristics ever since. From Jamaican and Korean to Vietnamese, Latino, Peruvian and African, this area north of Devon Avenue (6400N) and east of Ridge Boulevard (1800–2200W) to the lake is a true melting pot. Aside from the few small **beaches**, there are no real sights to speak of here; the main north–south drags are **Clark Street** to the west and the lake-hugging **Sheridan Road** to the east, both with a smattering of ethnic cafés and shops, from Peruvian restaurants and burrito counters to bike shops and run-down video arcades. Fans of Indian food should make tracks to **West Devon Avenue**, a treasure-trove of authentic Indian and Pakistani fare.

The neighbourhood also has a significant student population, courtesy of the Jesuit-affiliated **Loyola University**, whose grassy, pleasant main campus covers several city blocks at the intersection of Sheridan Road and Broadway. The area is safe for the most part, but **gangs and drug dealers** are still active in this part of the city, particularly near the Red Line Howard stop, which should be avoided after dark.

Loyola University

One of the nation's foremost Catholic colleges, **Loyola University**, located at 6525 N Sheridan Rd, was founded in 1870 by the Society of Jesus, a Catholic order reputed for its passion for learning and intellectual curiosity. Spread out over a few blocks overlooking the lake, the picturesque campus is a mixture of architectural styles, from the hushed beauty of the Art Deco **Madonna della Strada Chapel**, which overlooks the lake at the campus's eastern end, to the 1996 **Joseph J. Gentile Center** basketball facility in the centre of campus. If you're looking for action in this area, however, the couple of blocks of Sheridan north of Devon Avenue are the place to head; they're home to a few college hangouts, as is the stretch of **Broadway** south of Devon.

Rogers Park beaches

Though they'll never be mistaken for the expansive swaths of sand at Oak Street or North Avenue, Rogers Park also boasts several **beaches** that draw crowds of local families for sunbathing and swimming. The largest and most popular of these is at **Loyola Park**, a 21.5-acre facility stretching from Pratt Boulevard to Chase Avenue with a baseball field, an athletics centre, a walking trail and a tennis court as well as a fine – if crowded – stretch of beach.

Most of the neighbourhood's other beaches are small, facility-less affairs at the eastern end of residential streets, like **North Shore Beach Park**, at 1040 W North Shore Ave, and the tucked-away **Rogers Avenue Beach and Park**, just south of Evanston at 7800 N Rogers Ave.

Along West Devon Avenue

Chicago's thriving **South Asian community** – one of the largest in the US – buzzes less than two miles west of Loyola University on Devon Avenue. Here, centred on Western Avenue (2400W), the street is lined with Indian and Pakistani shops: video stores hawk the latest Bollywood films; colourful saris are draped in the front windows of traditional clothing stores; and the heady smell of curry wafts through the air from the doors of the neighbourhood's myriad restaurants.

Historically, the street has always attracted a diverse ethnic and religious mix. In the mid-nineteenth century, it was a centre of commerce for Chicago's Jewish community and later attracted a number of Croatian Catholics; since the mid-1960s, though, West Devon has become a haven for a burgeoning Hindi, Muslim and Sikh population from India, Pakistan and, to a lesser extent, Bangladesh and Sri Lanka, benefactors of the abolishment of racial quotas in immigration laws. Sights are few and far between along the strip; West Devon is worth visiting mostly for the authentic South Asian sounds and smells, and, of course, for the excellent **restaurants**, which serve some of the finest Indian food in the Midwest (see p.186 for reviews).

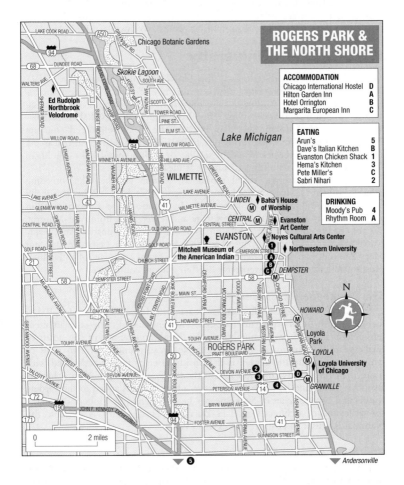

Evanston

Follow Sheridan Road north from the city as it winds through Rogers Park and you'll shortly end up in lakeside **EVANSTON**, best known as the home of **Northwestern University**. With its wide, shaded streets and grand, early twentieth-century homes, the town has a prosperous, small-town feel and a comparatively tranquil atmosphere. Casual but lively with families, thirty-something condo-owners, and local college and high school students, the several blocks that make up **downtown Evanston** are a relaxed alternative to downtown Chicago's hectic shopping and dining scene – its charming **shopping** district, centred around Church and Davis streets, bustles with bookstores, clothing shops and cinemas, plus several notable **restaurants**. The town also boasts several lovely **beaches** just off Sheridan Road, as well as an active **arts** scene, including the highly regarded **Evanston Arts Center** and **Noyes Cultural Arts Center**, as well as the **Mitchell Museum of the American Indian**.

Evanston is easily accessible via the CTA's Purple Line; get off at the Davis stop for the downtown shopping district, or Noyes for Northwestern University.

Northwestern University

While not quite as prestigious as the University of Chicago (see p.127), **Northwestern University** (ⓦ www.northwestern.edu) is nonetheless considered one of the Midwest's elite universities. The campus is a bit of an architectural hodgepodge – styles range from the handsome Italian Renaissance **Lunt Hall**, 2033 Sheridan Rd, to the boxy reinforced-concrete **Nathaniel Leverone Hall**, just south at 2001 Sheridan Rd – but it scarcely seems to matter given its beautiful setting on 240 acres of Lake Michigan shoreline. Plenty of winding paths make it ideal for a stroll.

Among Northwestern's several prominent schools are the CEO-breeding grounds of the Kellogg School of Management as well as the nationally renowned Medill School of Journalism. In addition, the Communication programme has turned out countless stage and screen stars, from Ann-Margret, Warren Beatty and Charlton Heston to more recent graduates like *Friends*' David Schwimmer and Tony Award-winners Denis O'Hare (*Take Me Out*) and Mary Zimmerman (*Metamorphoses*). NU's sports teams compete valiantly, albeit mostly fruitlessly, in the powerhouse Big Ten athletic conference.

The Shakespeare Garden

One campus highlight is the **Shakespeare Garden**, 2121 Sheridan Rd, a formal English Tudor-style garden designed by renowned Prairie-style architect Jens Jensen in 1915 to commemorate the 300th anniversary of the death of Shakespeare. The intimate 70ft-by-100ft plot is surrounded by two rows of hawthorn trees, and the garden itself consists of eight flower beds filled with more than fifty plants common in the Bard's day, including rosemary, hyssop, lavender, thyme and lemon balm. In 1929, a fountain was added to the garden, featuring a bronze relief of Shakespeare's head designed by Hubert Burnham, son of legendary architect Daniel H. Burnham. The garden was added to the National Register of Historic Places in 1989.

The Mary & Leigh Block Museum of Art

A ten-minute walk to the southeast, the lakeside **Mary & Leigh Block Museum of Art**, 40 Arts Circle Drive (Tues 10am–5pm, Wed–Fri 10am–8pm,

Sat & Sun noon–5pm; free; ☎847/491-4000, ⓦ www.blockmuseum .northwestern.edu) owns an impressive collection of art dating from the thirteenth century to the present, with a focus on works on paper. Standouts include Old Master drawings, German Expressionist prints, and American photographs, shown in rotating exhibitions. The museum's collection of twentieth-century American and European sculpture is also one of the finest in the Midwest, with sixteen works showcased in the adjacent outdoor **sculpture garden**. Among them are prized works like Joan Miró's *Constellation*, a free-swinging flattened sphere embedded with a golden pearl and Henry Moore's sexy, sinuous *Interior Form*; there are also pieces by Hans Arp, Barbara Hepworth and Chicago-born Northwestern alumnus Irwin Kremen.

Downtown Evanston and around

Much of the action in **downtown Evanston** happens in the vicinity of Church and Davis streets between Maple and Hinman avenues, close to the Davis CTA stop. Here you'll find grad students bent over books in funky cafés, couples pushing strollers along brick-lined sidewalks and a surprisingly sophisticated **dining scene** (see reviews, p.185).

Shopping and entertainment are the focus of this area, but there are several worthy cultural sites nearby as well. The **Evanston Art Center** (Mon–Thurs 10am–10pm, Fri & Sat 10am–4pm, Sun 1–4pm; suggested donation $3; ☎847/475-5300, ⓦ www.evanstonartcenter.org), 2603 Sheridan Rd, presents frequent exhibitions of local and Midwestern artists working in paint, photography, sculpture and other media. Near the Noyes train station at 927 Noyes St, the **Noyes Cultural Arts Center** (Mon–Sat 10am–7pm, Sun 10am–6pm; ☎847/448-8260) is the centre of Evanston's artistic community, with two art galleries showcasing the work of area artists plus a 190-seat theatre space. It also acts as the headquarters for several local arts organizations, including Light Opera Works, the Actors Gymnasium Circus and Performing Arts School, and the Piven Theater and Workshop, whose alumni include John and Joan Cusack, Lili Taylor, Jeremy Piven and Lara Flynn Boyle.

A couple miles to the northwest of downtown, the **Mitchell Museum of the American Indian** (Tues, Wed, Fri & Sat 10am–5pm, Thurs 10am–8pm, Sun noon–4pm; suggested admission $5; ☎847/475-1030, ⓦ www.mitchellmuseum .org), 2600 Central Park Ave, offers an in-depth look at the history and culture of Native American tribes of the Woodlands, Plains, Southwest and Northwest coast. The collection includes more than 3000 objects, from an authentic full-sized birchbark canoe to glass beads, quillwork, carved bowls and even a twentieth-century walrus-intestine parka from western Alaska. Each gallery includes a "touching table" with artefacts and raw materials – caribou fur, snakeskin and buffalo skin among them – that visitors can handle. To get here by public transport, take the Metra commuter rail to Central Street, then walk or catch the #206 westbound bus to the museum, a mile away.

North of Evanston

Curving beyond Evanston, Sheridan Road hugs the lake and arrives in **WILMETTE**, a quiet, affluent suburb of expansive lawns and even larger lakefront mansions. There are few attractions to make the trek this far north worthwhile to the average visitor, but those who do will be rewarded with the breathtaking sight of the majestic **Baha'í House of Worship**. Cyclists, too, will want to explore the paved, well-maintained **Green Bay Trail**, which extends nine miles north toward the **Chicago Botanical Garden** in **Glencoe**. To **get to** Wilmette, follow Sheridan Road north of Evanston, or take the El Purple Line to its final stop (Linden); the Baha'í temple is three blocks east of the station. To reach Glencoe, take the Metra commuter rail's Union Pacific North line to Glencoe and walk one mile west on Lake Cook Road.

The Baha'í House of Worship

Rising 135ft in the air, the pristine, ivory-hued **Baha'í House of Worship,** 100 Linden Ave (daily 6am–10pm, visitor centre daily 10am–5pm; free; ⊤847/853-2300; ⓌÂ www.bahai.us/bahai-temple), is a breathtaking – if unexpected – lakeside sight in this quiet North Shore suburb. The North American centre of the Baha'í faith, the nine-sided, domed temple was completed in 1953 and is made entirely of cast concrete, with lace-like ornamentation covering the dome and two levels of elaborate spires that emphasize the building's height. All around it are fountains, gardens and broad

▲ Baha'í House of Worship

lawns – ideal for quiet reflection. The Baha'í faith was founded in Iran in 1844 on the tenets of racial unity, gender equality, a strong family unit and world peace. The religion now claims to have about five million adherents in 236 countries. Brief devotional programmes are held in the auditorium Monday through Friday at 5.15pm, and on weekends at 9.15am, 12.30pm and 5.15pm.

The Chicago Botanic Garden and around

Spreading over 385 acres (much of it wooded), the **Chicago Botanic Garden**, 1000 Lake Cook Rd, Glencoe (daily 8am–sunset; free; ☎847/835-5440, ⓦwww.chicagobotanic.org), features 26 beautifully landscaped gardens, from a secluded, romantic English garden and a rose garden brimming with more than 5000 rose bushes to a Zen-like Japanese garden set on three islands. These lush displays are wild with dahlias, daylilies, sunflowers and coneflowers – well over two million plants in all – and attract nearly 800,000 visitors each year. The best way to explore is to take a motorized tram **tour**, offered April to October only. Options include the Grand Tram Tour of the grounds' perimeter and the Bright Encounters Tour, focussed on the gardens of the main island. Both last 35 minutes and cost $5 (children $3).

An excellent route to the botanic garden is the **Green Bay Trail**, a favourite route for local cycling enthusiasts. This nine-mile asphalt and crushed-stone trail begins near the intersection of Lake Avenue and Green Bay Road in Wilmette and then continues north through the similar northern suburbs of Winnetka and Kenilworth. Skirting the east side of the botanic garden in Glencoe, the trail continues past the Ravinia Festival grounds – the summertime home of the Chicago Symphony Orchestra and other music and dance ensembles (see p.208 for details) – to end in downtown Highland Park.

Oak Park

Chicago's most famous suburb, **Oak Park**, ten miles west of the Loop, is the prime excursion in the outlying area. Revelling in the moniker of the "largest village in the world", the town prides itself on nurturing artistic genius: **Ernest Hemingway** was born and spent his youth in Oak Park, and **Frank Lloyd Wright** lived and worked here for twenty of his most productive years, designing twenty-five homes in the area and defining his architectural philosophy. Today Oak Park is at its most bohemian in the small **arts district** on Harrison Street, between Austin Boulevard and Ridgeland Avenue, which has a dozen or so galleries as well as cafés, restaurants and boutiques. But elsewhere the suburb is solidly bourgeois, with prettified Victorian homes fronted by English-style gardens. Hemingway famously referred to his hometown as a "place of wide lawns and narrow minds", and Wright's Byron esque attire – flowing capes and ascots – hardly endeared him to his conservative neighbours.

Still, local residents are proud of these two world-famous men, and do a brisk business showing visitors their legacy here. The **Ernest Hemingway Home**, where Big Ern was born and raised till the age of six (when he moved to a house nearby), may be visited along with a small but satisfying **museum** dedicated to one of America's greatest twentieth-century writers. You can also tour the **Frank Lloyd Wright Home** and **Studio**, the Wright-designed compound where the architect lived and worked from 1889 until 1909; before or after the tour, be sure to rent the audio tour of the neighbourhood, which describes the architectural history of the surrounding blocks, including several designs by the master himself. Wright's **Pleasant Home**, one of the earliest and most opulent examples of the Prairie style, and **Unity Temple**, an illustration of his concept of the sacred, are both a short walk away and may be toured as well.

Oak Park practicalities

To reach Oak Park by **car**, take the Eisenhower Expressway (I-290) west from downtown to Harlem Avenue and exit north; there's a large parking garage above the visitor centre (below) that's free for the first two hours on weekdays (and cheap after that) and all day on weekends and holidays. If you don't have a car, don't worry – the town is well served by public transportation. Both the Green and Blue **El** lines stop in Oak Park: the Green Line is marginally more convenient, letting you off at the corner of Oak Park Avenue and South Boulevard. Four blocks away the **Oak Park Visitors Center**, 158 Forest Ave (daily: Jan–Feb 10am–4pm, rest of the year 10am–5pm; ☏708/848-1500 or 1-888/625-7275, ⓦ www.visitoakpark.com), offers a wealth of town-related

OAK PARK

EATING
Geppetto's Pasta and Pizza	3
Great Harvest Bread Company	2
Khyber Pass	1

ACCOMMODATION
Carleton Hotel	C
Longwell Hall Bed and Breakfast	A
Write Inn	B

gifts and information and is the departure point for the two-hour **self-guided "Heart of Oak Park" audio tour**, describing the evolution of architecture from the early Victorian period through the Art Deco era (daily 10am–3.30pm; $10, $5 youth & seniors). You can also check your bags and buy discount combination tickets here.

As for **getting around**, Oak Park is easy to navigate on foot, with all of the Hemingway and Wright sights within walking distance of the visitor centre. The small downtown area – centred on the intersection of Harlem Avenue and Lake Street, is just a few blocks further west. From here, it's about a mile and a half to the Harrison Street arts district, a hefty walk, but you can get there more easily on the **free shuttle bus** that connects all of the main sights on an hour-long looped route. Beginning at the Green Line El's Oak Park stop, shuttles run daily every thirty minutes between 10am and 5.30pm, with service extended to 9pm in summer (℡708/343-4830).

Frank Lloyd Wright Home & Studio and around

The slick operation at the **Frank Lloyd Wright Home & Studio**, 951 Chicago Ave at Forest Ave (guided tours only, Mon–Fri 11am, 1pm & 3pm, Sat & Sun every 20min 11am–3.30pm; $12, $10 children 11–18 & seniors, $5 children 4–10; ℡708/848-1976, Ⓦwww.gowright.org), adopts the officious approach of its former owner: visitors are frequently warned to touch nothing. If you can resist the temptation, you'll be rewarded with an up-close look at Wright's surroundings in his Oak Park years, along with titillating stories about his family life and hard-charging business practices. To ensure you get on the tour of your choice, either arrive early (around 10am) or buy advance tickets through the website or by calling ℡1-800/514-3849, as tours often sell out, especially in the summer and fall.

The complex stands at the edge of a residential **historic district** full of beautifully restored homes, including some that were designed or remodelled by Wright himself. An informative, hour-long **self-guided audio tour**, describing 25 homes in the district as well as the basic precepts of **Frank Lloyd Wright's Prairie style**, is available for rent at the gift shop (Mon–Fri 10am–3.30pm; $12, $10 childrens 11–18 & seniors, $5 childrens 4–10). Guided tours, are offered on weekends for the same price (March–Oct 11am–4pm every hour on the hour; Nov–Feb noon, 1pm & 2pm; 1hr).

Clad in brick and brown shingles, with deep eaves and Asian influences throughout, Wright's home-and-studio complex is one of the highlights of a visit to Oak Park, standing as a forerunner to the revolutionary **Prairie style** that he developed while in residence here from 1889 to 1909. Wright borrowed $5000 from his boss Louis Sullivan to build the house and while the shingles and steeply pitched roof aren't typical of the Prairie style, other elements of the house are. In sharp contrast to the brightly painted Victorians that were popular at the time – Ernest Hemingway's Birthplace (see p.144) being a prime example – Wright used earth tones both on the exterior and in the interior of the house, blurring the boundaries between the built and natural environments. In lieu of wallpaper, rooms are panelled in natural oak; built-in shelves abound, reducing clutter. The layout, too, is unusual for the time: Wright dispensed with the symmetrical, boxy floor plan of the typical Victorian house, instead creating rooms that flowed into one another. In 1898 he added the studio where he would design the Unity Temple (p.145) and Robie House (p.127). The octagonal drafting room here is one of the most striking in the complex, with its clerestory windows and wraparound balcony. His adjoining office (also octagonal) and waiting room are painted gold, supposedly to impress clients who might balk at his high fees and routine cost overruns. In 1909 Wright closed the office and travelled to Europe with a client's wife, leaving his own wife, Catherine Tobin, to raise their six children on her own. After settling in his native Wisconsin, he remodelled his former Oak Park studio as their living quarters and converted the house to rental units to provide them with income. The house and studio

Frank Lloyd Wright

The building as architecture is born of the heart of man, permanent consort to the ground, comrade to the trees, true reflection of man in the realm of his own spirit. His building is therefore consecrated space where he seeks refuge and repose for the body, but especially for the mind.

Frank Lloyd Wright

Without a doubt the most influential American architect of the twentieth century, **Frank Lloyd Wright** influenced generations of architects with his philosophies concerning space and interior design and the harmonious relationship between interior and exterior. Wright's signature **Prairie style** is evident in over 25 private residences that he designed in Oak Park between 1889 and 1915, but perhaps the best example of his style is the **Robie House** (1908), on the University of Chicago campus in Hyde Park (see p.127), where low horizontal lines, projecting eaves and ribbons of art glass blend seamlessly with the landscape.

Born in June 8, 1867, in Richland Center, Wisconsin, Wright studied engineering at the University of Wisconsin before moving to Chicago in 1887 to work as an apprentice on a building commissioned by his uncle, who was a Unitarian pastor. After his year-long apprenticeship with J. Lyman Silsbee, he signed a five-year exclusive contract with the firm of Adler & Sullivan, working with Chicago School pioneer Louis Sullivan on residential designs, including the **Charnley-Persky House** (see p.88). When Sullivan discovered that Wright had been accepting his own commissions on the side, however, he asked him to leave the firm.

In 1894, Wright opened his own office in the Schiller Building in downtown Chicago, and in 1898, tired of the commute to the city, expanded his Oak Park home to accommodate his growing business. Incidentally, several of the "bootleg" projects he designed while working for Sullivan are located nearby.

Wright was the first architect to use concrete for non-commercial structures, the first to create open-plan interior spaces, and the first to view interior design as integral to the construction; at the **Dana Thomas House** in Springfield, Illinois, one of the best-preserved of the Prairie-style constructions, there are more than one hundred pieces of Wright-designed white oak furniture. Wright's desire for total control over his buildings' interiors is even said to have extended to the dress code of his clients' children.

Wright's pioneering views of "organic architecture", the idea that a building is never really completed but an integral part of the setting, is embodied in the design of the **Frank Lloyd Wright Home** in Oak Park, where a willow tree formed an integral part of the building's design by connecting the hallway of the house to the studio. Sadly, the willow tree died several years ago and an artificial replacement doesn't quite provide the natural effect.

have, however, been restored to their appearance the year before the conversion.

South along Forest Avenue, which is lined with Victorian mansions, two Wright buildings display the contrast between the architect's pre- and post-Prairie styles: the **Huertley House** (1902), at no. 318, and the **Nathan Moore House** (1895; rebuilt 1923), directly opposite on the corner of Superior Street. The former, a low-slung, heavily horizontal, brown-brick home is a proto-Prairie building. The latter, a mustard-coloured mock Tudor monstrosity, is a rare instance of the ornery architect following a client's brief rather than his own designs – understandable when you consider that it was one of Wright's first independent commissions and he couldn't kick and scream to get his way as he later would.

The Hemingway Birthplace Home and Museum

It shouldn't come as much of a surprise that Ernest Hemingway, passionate lover of women, blood sports, revolution, guns and cocktails, escaped Oak Park as soon as he could and even lied about his upbringing to avoid being associated with a place so quaint. What is striking is how little Oak Park's residents seem to care; rejected by him throughout his life, they have embraced him after his death, and nowhere more so than at the **Hemingway Birthplace Home**, 339 N Oak Park Ave (Sun–Fri 1–5pm, Sat 10am–5pm; $8, $6 students & seniors, includes admission to museum, below; ☎708/848-2222, ⓦwww.ehfop.org), where ninety-minute guided tours shed light on the odd family dynamics that shaped Hemingway's imagination and undoubtedly spurred his globe-trotting.

The Queen Anne-style house, built in 1890 by Ernest's maternal grandparents and restored to the tune of $1 million a century later, drips with the kind of Victorian finery that Frank Lloyd Wright and, one suspects, Ernest himself despised: aggressively cheerful carpeting and wallpaper, watered-silk settees, doilies, gilt picture frames and the like. The few family possessions here are evocative – stuffed animals shot by Ernest's dad, an avid hunter, and Ernest's first "book" penned at the age of two and a half – but even more compelling are the stories about Ernest's family, including Grandfather Abba, who lived with the family and delivered nightly sermons; Great-Uncle Tyley, a tippling travelling salesman, who occasionally roomed here and regaled the family with stories; and especially Ernest's mother, Grace, an amateur opera singer turned music teacher who dressed Ernest and his older sister, Marcelline, as twins well into their toddler years. Guides spin these stories as evidence of a colourful and

▲ Hemingway Birthplace Home

"warm" childhood, but you can't help but feel that Ernest's later rejection of the clan had some basis in reality.

Down the street, the small but engaging **museum**, two blocks south at 200 N Oak Park Ave (same hours as Birthplace Home; entry included), is housed in an old Christian Science church. The exhibits inside are old-fashioned but excellent: picture- and text-heavy panels trace Hemingway's life (and troubled relationships) from Chicago to Paris to Havana. The photographs from the Hemingway family album are especially revealing – look for the 1910 image of 11-year-old Ernest feeding a nut to a (stuffed) squirrel – as are the original manuscripts, among them a report Ernest wrote on a high school football game that earned him a "D" for bad penmanship, some angsty early poetry ("Cover my eyes with your pinions/ Dark Bird of Night ..."), and a draft of the first page of *For Whom the Bell Tolls*.

The Unity Temple

The **Unity Temple**, 875 Lake St at Kenilworth Ave (Mon–Fri 10.30am–4.30pm, Sat & Sun 1–4pm; guided tours Sat & Sun 1pm, 2pm & 3pm; $8, $6 seniors & students, children under 5 free; ☎708/383-8873, ⓦwww.utrf.org), is one of Frank Lloyd Wright's lesser-known masterpieces. Though Wright himself wasn't especially religious, his mother was a Unitarian and, through her friendship with the local minister, helped her son snag the commission to build this church for the Unitarian congregation in Oak Park. Wright's intent was to create a space of purity and simplicity, reminiscent of an ancient temple. Built from concrete, the structure an evolution in ecclesiastical architecture and represented a seminal moment in Wright's career; some fifty years after the building's completion Wright expounded upon his theories: "Unity Temple is where you will find the real expression of the idea that the space within the building is the reality of that building."

From the outside, the temple resembles a forbidding column-encased concrete box; Wright deliberately made it hard to find the entrance, so that worshippers would have to "interact" with the building as soon as they arrived. Slipping through the doors on Kenilworth Avenue, you find yourself in an atrium that leads, through a low-ceilinged passageway, into the main auditorium.

The sanctuary is illuminated from above – symbolizing the divine ideal – by a crown of leaded-glass windows, which extend around the building beneath the projecting roof, and by recessed amber skylights beneath a glass ceiling. The exposed electrical cords of ornate Japanese-style hanging lights are wrapped in gold silk, an early example of Wright's intent to express function without compromising luxury. The temple appears to be bathed in a heavenly, golden glow; Wright ensured that the predominant yellow hue would diffuse the earthy palette of greys, browns and greens.

Wright created a serene space in the centre of the square room, filled with pews; each of the two balconies overlooks this area and assures a sense of intimate community, despite its seating capacity of more than four hundred. By enclosing the stairs, the two balconies appear to be floating bridges that flow into the windows, producing a fluid horizon of light and space. Another feature that fosters a sense of community is the placement of the exit doors: unlike most traditional churches, where the congregation turns its back on the pastor to leave, Wright wanted worshippers to pass the pastor as they left (and chat with him) – hence the hidden doors on either side of the pulpit through which you must leave.

If the clunky pews seem out of place, that's not unexpected – Wright designed his own, but as the cost of the building spiralled to one and a half times its projected budget, the congregation opted for cheaper alternatives. Note, too, the radiators everywhere: Wright's ingenious, but short-lived, forced-air heating system broke down almost as soon as the building was put to use and these radiators had to be grafted on to keep worshippers warm. One feature that still functions beautifully is the auditorium's superb acoustics: fund-raising concerts are regularly held here – highly appropriate given Wright's belief that designing a building is similar to composing music.

The Historic Pleasant Home and south Oak Park

It's a shame that the **Historic Pleasant Home**, 217 S Home Ave, located in Mills Park south of the Metra train line, is so often skipped by visitors coming to see Wright's Home and Studio (see p.142), as a visit here is every bit as interesting (guided tour only: March–Nov Thurs–Sun 12.30pm, 1.30pm & 2.30pm; Dec–Feb 12.30pm & 1.30pm; $5, $3 students 5–18 years, children under 5 free; Fri free; ☎708/383-2654, ⊛www.pleasanthome.org). The enormous thirty-room building was designed by Prairie School architect **George Maher** in 1897 for investment banker and philanthropist John Farson. Farson died in 1910, and the house was sold to Herbert Mills, the inventor of vending and slot machines; in turn it was sold to the local park service in 1939 for use as a community centre. A few years ago the home was reclaimed and slow restoration continues.

There's not much furniture inside yet, other than the monolithic dining table Maher designed (too heavy ever to be moved), but the rooms themselves provide an intriguing early hint of how the Prairie style would evolve. Unconstrained by walls, the rooms flow into one another (a signature Prairie motif), while the huge windows open onto a wraparound porch (blurring the line between indoors and outside). In the library, the gigantic, curved-glass sash windows – which recede 6ft into the wall above when lifted – underline the money-is-no-object opulence of the place. Maher was also determined to achieve balance in design, whatever the obstacle: see the fake door to the left of the onyx fireplace in the Great Hall; it's only there to even out the entranceway to the right. Ask to stop by the women's bathroom on the first floor, which contains one of Maher's original marble sink designs, complete with built-in, shell-shaped soap dish.

Tours spend time on the second floor at the small, ragtag museum of the **Historical Society of Oak Park**: it's small, but there's a detailed room dedicated to the history of the area and filled with old photographs.

South Oak Park

The final architectural pit-stop on a tour round Oak Park is just east of here, where you'll find the heaviest concentration of preserved **Victorians** in town, along Pleasant Street between Clinton and Oak Park avenues. The five **Burton Row Houses**, on the corner of Pleasant and Clinton, show how developers here were eager to offer affordable housing to middle-class refugees from the city: the shared partition walls lessen privacy as well as price.

Listings

Listings

Accommodation

n recent years, tourism to Chicago has grown quickly; since 2007, the total number of visitors staying here (including business travellers and those from abroad) has topped 34 million. The city maintains an abundance of **accommodation**; indeed, there are more than 100,000 rooms in the metropolitan area, though, in truth, many of these are in large, rather soulless hotels catering to business people and conventioneers. Even so, you shouldn't have too hard a time finding reasonable and affordable, if often unexciting, options in the city centre. Most basic accommodation (save hostels and perhaps B&Bs) will run you a minimum of $100 a night, especially if you need a room at the last minute, while rooms at better hotels average $160–185 per night. It's also worth noting that there's a heavy seasonal variation in hotel pricing, as June through September people flock to Chicago in tremendous numbers. If you can make your way through the snow and cold, consider a trip in the winter.

A preponderance of hotels is concentrated in just a few pockets around downtown, the largest of which is **Near North**, where several dozen expensive hotels cluster in River North and around N Michigan Avenue. The more business-oriented **Loop** has a few pricey hotels, but also the city's best hostel, as well as some mid-range boutique options. Besides being close to many of the downtown attractions, the Loop offers easy access to O'Hare International Airport (45min by El train) – a cumbersome trip from other parts of the city unless you're willing to shell out around $40 for a taxi.

Outside the most central areas, accommodation choices thin out considerably, although there's more variety in terms of B&Bs versus business hotels and rates are generally lower. Most of the city's B&Bs and guesthouses are located in **Old Town** and **Lincoln Park**, while **Lakeview** has some budget options and arty boutique hotels, as well as gay-friendly accommodations (see p.218). Staying this far north may not be practical for extended downtown exploration – but all will do if you want to get a better feel for the city's residential neighbourhoods. **West and south of the Loop**, you'll find a few big-name chains, but again, these aren't particularly close to most of the major attractions or public transportation options. We've also included a list of **airport hotels**, which are worth considering only if you need to catch an early-morning flight.

Even in a major city like Chicago, where you'll find some of the top hotels in the country, it's still possible to find excellent rooms at drastically reduced prices, either through one of the popular **booking agencies** like Hot Rooms (☎773/468-7666 or 1-800/468-3500, ⓦwww.hotrooms.com) or an **internet search site** like ⓦwww.orbitz.com, ⓦwww.expedia.com or ⓦwww.hotwire.com. In fact, unless you want to stay at a B&B or one of the hostels, you should do your pre-trip bargain-hunting **online**. Many hotels offer web-only specials or guarantee that their online rates are the lowest out there; if you find a great rate at a discount site, chances are the hotel's website will match or beat it. Since there are so many hotels in the city, even the top hotels are forced to slash rates during the week and at off-peak times, with many offering package deals for couples with tours and meals included. All in all, it's generally easy to find a $300 room at luxury places like the *W* hotels or at the *Drake* for under $200.

Alternatively, going through a **B&B service** like Chicago Bed and Breakfast or At Home Inn Chicago (see box, p.158) will get you a room, or a full apartment, in a private residence or guesthouse, priced from around $90 to usually not more than $175, unless the B&B is exceedingly precious or historic. Corporate **discounts** and those for AAA (American Automobile Association) members can bring down the price significantly, so make sure to enquire about them before making your reservation. Keep in mind, however, that all Chicago hotels will add a 15.4 percent room **tax** to your bill. It's also wise to arrange for a room ahead of your visit, especially around holidays and in spring and summer; note that Chicago can also get overrun by conventions, some of them big enough to fill every available room in the city.

If you're arriving by car, **parking** at the Loop and Near North hotels will be unavoidable and costly ($25–45 per night).

Hotels

See Central Chicago Accommodation map opposite for hotel locations, unless otherwise indicated.

The Loop

Hotel Allegro 171 W Randolph St, at N LaSalle St ☎312/236-0123 or 1-800/643-1500, ⓦwww .allegrochicago.com; all lines to Clark St. This chic, recently restored 1920s business hotel, right in the Theatre District, has almost 500 rooms that blend contemporary decor – striped, upholstered headboards, walls painted in bold reds and oranges – with Art Deco accents and offer amenities like flat-screen TVs and Aveda bath products. The staff's professionalism is a selling point and there's a free wine hour every evening (5–6pm), as well as an on-site fitness center and access to a nearby pool. $159–299

Hotel Burnham 1 W Washington St, at S State St ☎312/782-1111 or 1-877/294-9712, ⓦwww .burnhamhotel.com; Red or Blue Line to Washington; Brown, Green, Orange or Purple Line to State/Lake. Located in one of the world's first glass-and-steel skyscrapers, the *Burnham* is an intimate boutique hotel where everything – from the romantic ambience to the exemplary service – strives to create a luxurious oasis amid the heavily trafficked business hotels of downtown. The one hundred rooms and twenty-odd suites all come with turn-down service and twice-daily housekeeping. There's a free wine reception in the lobby (daily 5–6pm), plus free coffee and tea (6–9.30am). Prices fluctuate wildly depending on availability and the season, but internet prices, last-minute and package deals (dinners, tours) can make this place affordable even if it's out of your immediate range. The excellent *Atwood Café* is located on the first floor (see p.164). $199–509

Congress Plaza Hotel 520 S Michigan Ave, at W Congress Parkway ☎312/427-3800 or 1-800/635-1666, ⓦwww.congressplazahotel.com; Red Line to Harrison; Blue Line to LaSalle; Brown or Orange

ACCOMMODATION | Hotels

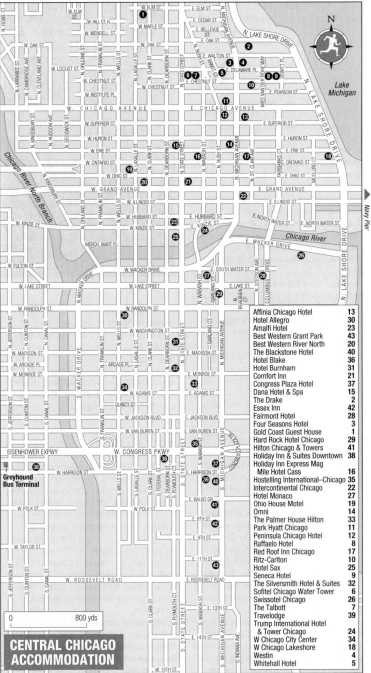

Lincoln Park

N

Lake Michigan

Navy Pier

Chicago River

Affinia Chicago Hotel	13
Hotel Allegro	30
Amalfi Hotel	23
Best Western Grant Park	43
Best Western River North	20
The Blackstone Hotel	40
Hotel Blake	36
Hotel Burnham	31
Comfort Inn	21
Congress Plaza Hotel	37
Dana Hotel & Spa	15
The Drake	2
Essex Inn	42
Fairmont Hotel	28
Four Seasons Hotel	3
Gold Coast Guest House	1
Hard Rock Hotel Chicago	29
Hilton Chicago & Towers	41
Holiday Inn & Suites Downtown	38
Holiday Inn Express Mag	
Mile Hotel Cass	16
Hostelling International–Chicago	35
Intercontinental Chicago	22
Hotel Monaco	27
Ohio House Motel	19
Omni	14
The Palmer House Hilton	33
Park Hyatt Chicago	11
Peninsula Chicago Hotel	12
Raffaelo Hotel	8
Red Roof Inn Chicago	17
Ritz-Carlton	10
Hotel Sax	25
Seneca Hotel	9
The Silversmith Hotel & Suites	32
Sofitel Chicago Water Tower	6
Swissotel Chicago	26
The Talbott	7
Travelodge	39
Trump International Hotel	
& Tower Chicago	24
W Chicago City Center	34
W Chicago Lakeshore	18
Westin	4
Whitehall Hotel	5

CENTRAL CHICAGO ACCOMMODATION

0   800 yds

Greyhound Bus Terminal

Hyde Park   McCormick Place

Line to Library-State/Van Buren. Huge hotel (over 800 rooms) and convention centre that was built for the 1893 World's Columbian Exposition and has seen better days. Many of the rooms tend toward the small and are sometimes rough around the edges but afford great views of Buckingham Fountain and Lake Michigan. The hotel is a decent alternative to some of the better-restored and modern boutique hotels in the Loop, which are generally the first to fill up. $99–359

Fairmont Hotel 200 N Columbus Drive, at E Lake St ☎312/565-8000 **or 1-866/540-4408,** ⓦwww .fairmont.com; **Red Line to Lake; Brown, Green, Orange or Purple Line to Randolph/Wabash.** In addition to luxurious rooms and suites, the *Fairmont* features a pleasant art-filled lobby, two swank ballrooms and a fitness club. The food and service are top-notch and, while not as splashy as the *Peninsula* or the *Park Hyatt*, it's just as plush and provides a somewhat more personalized touch. $149–549

Hard Rock Hotel 230 N Michigan Ave, at E Lake St ☎312/345-1000 **or 1-866/966-1566,** ⓦwww .hardrockhotelchicago.com; **Red Line to Lake; Brown, Green, Orange or Purple Line to State.** The Loop's landmark 40-storey Art Deco Carbide and Carbon Building was transformed into the city's hottest new hotel, when it opened in 2004. The location is convenient – walking distance from Millennium Park, the Mag Mile, the Art Institute and the Theatre District – and the rooms and suites are stylishly appointed, with sweeping city views, 27-inch flat-screen TVs, and complimentary high-speed internet access. Downstairs, live DJs spin nightly in the *BASE* bar and a beautiful crowd gathers in the pricey but impressive Asian-fusion restaurant *China Grill*. $219–299

Hotel Monaco 225 N Wabash Ave, at E Lake St ☎312/960-8500 **or 1-866/610-0081,** ⓦwww .monaco-chicago.com; **Red Line to Lake; Brown, Green, Orange or Purple Line to State/Lake.** Plush boutique hotel decorated in French Art Deco style and close to the Mag Mile. Though some of the amenities, like the "companion" goldfish – which guests who are missing their pets can take to their rooms – are gimmicky, the hotel itself is far nicer than any of the nearby business hotels charging similar prices. The rooms, some of which come with Jacuzzis, are stylish, and there are even some special "Tall" rooms,

▲ Hotel Monaco

with longer-than-average beds and raised showerheads. Prices vary depending on availability; your best bet is to check their website for promotions and last-minute discounts. $159–449

The Palmer House Hilton 17 E Monroe St ☎312/726-7500 **or 1-800/445-8667,** ⓦwww1 .hilton.com; **Red or Blue Line to Monroe, all other lines to Adams/Wabash.** The oldest continuously operating hotel in the US and the sister hotel to New York's famed *Waldorf-Astoria*, the *Palmer* is a good bet if you want to be in the Loop but close to the Mag Mile. There is an enclosed shopping arcade, a health club, small indoor pool and four restaurants, along with the *Potter's Lounge*, which is a 1940s style bar in the main lobby. The rooms are generally smallish but kept to *Hilton* standards. Though the larger rooms and suites can be pricey, it's possible to book one of the smaller rooms at highly discounted rates (as low as $120) that can work out to be cheaper than some budget chains. Free morning paper delivered to your door. $119–259

The Silversmith Hotel & Suites 10 S Wabash Ave, at W Madison St ☎312/372-7696 **or 1-800/979-0084,** ⓦwww.silversmithchicagohotel .com; **Blue or Red Line to Monroe, all other lines to Madison.** This recently remodelled, ten-storey business hotel, inside the 1897 Daniel Burnham-designed Silversmith Building, has simple but tasteful rooms. The bright, cheery (though sometimes small, given the hotel's age) rooms come with a CD player and there's also a fitness centre. Also, there's a complimentary dessert reception on weekdays. $99–399

Swissotel Chicago 323 E Wacker Drive, at N Columbia Drive ☎312/565-0565 or 1-800/637-9477, ⓦwww.swissotel.com; Red Line to Lake; Brown, Green, Orange or Purple Line to Randolph/Wabash. Stylish and better run than most other business hotels in town, the towering *Swissotel* has superb city views from its location on the Chicago River and Michigan Ave, as well as a 42nd-floor health club with pool. Each of the rooms has marble bathrooms and is fairly spacious. Rooms with the better views cost $15–35 more, and like other business-oriented hotels, rates tend to go down on weekends. $199–289

W Chicago City Center 172 W Adams St ☎312/332-1200 or 1-877/946-8357, ⓦwww.whotels.com; Red or Blue Line to Jackson; Brown, Orange or Purple Line to Quincy. Ultra-chic chain hotel in the heart of the Loop, with beautifully decorated and comfortable rooms. The lobby – a two-storey space called "The Living Room" – is sumptuously ornate and equipped with its own DJ. Best to ignore published prices and search for deals online instead. The second-floor hotel bar, *Whiskey Blue*, is a slick, retro after-work hot spot (see p.189). $249–469

Near North

Affinia Chicago Hotel 166 E Superior St, at N Michigan Ave ☎312/787-6000 or 1-866/246-2203, ⓦwww.affinia.com; Red Line to Chicago. With its elegant glass-enclosed lobby, the *Affinia Chicago Hotel* includes a few perks that are a bit unusual. For starters, there's a pillow "menu" that includes a buckwheat filled pillow or a "magnetic therapy" pillow for aching joints and such. The hotel also offers up a welcome drink for each guest and there are special treats for pets, who are made to feel quite welcome. $149–329

Amalfi Hotel 20 W Kinzie St, at State St ☎312/395-9000 or 1-877/262-5341, ⓦwww.amalfihotelchicago.com; Red Line to Grand. This sleek, new 215-room hotel with great city views just north of the river has spacious rooms, 316-thread-count Egyptian cotton linens, multi-head showers, and complimentary high-speed internet in every room. In their Ravello Lounge, guests can also sit back every night from 5.30 to 7 pm to enjoy complimentary hors d'ouevres and cocktails. Pets welcome. $139–339

Best Western River North 125 W Ohio St, at N LaSalle St ☎312/467-0800 or 1-800/727-0800, ⓦwww.rivernorthhotel.com;

Airport hotels

Hilton O'Hare Airport O'Hare International Airport, directly across from the terminals ☎773/686-8000 or 1-800/445-8667, ⓦwww.hilton.com/hotels/CHIOHHH; Blue Line to O'Hare. This busy, 900-room hotel is nice enough and reasonably priced. Facilities include restaurants, a sports bar and a health club. $119–239

Hyatt Regency O'Hare 9300 W Bryn Mawr Ave, Rosemont ☎847/696-1234, ⓦwww.ohare.hyatt.com; take the free hotel shuttle from baggage claim at O'Hare. The most likely reason you'd stay here is if you're stranded at O'Hare and the comparable, but slightly less expensive *Hilton* is full. The hotel has a pool and fitness center. $119–189

Sofitel O'Hare 5550 N River Rd ☎847/678-4488 or 1-800/221-4542, ⓦwww.sofitelchicagoohare.com; take the free hotel shuttle from O'Hare. Three miles from O'Hare, this plush hotel, with 300 immaculate rooms, includes a superb restaurant, a pool, sauna and fitness centre (all with 24hr access), a bakery, reasonable parking ($18/night), and 24hr free shuttles to the airport every 20 minutes. Rates are almost always cheaper on weekends. $140–180

Wyndham O'Hare 6810 N Mannheim Rd ☎847/297-1234 or 1-877/999-3223, ⓦwww.wyndham.com/hotels/ORDAP; take the 24hr shuttle from baggage claim at O'Hare. Two miles from O'Hare, the *Wyndham* is the best value among the airport hotels, with basic rooms, indoor and outdoor pools, plus a small fitness centre. $99–129

Red Line to Grand; Brown or Purple Line to Merchandise Mart. This refurbished *Best Western*, in a great River North location close to many attractions is the only downtown hotel that provides guests with free parking. Rooms are spacious, while facilities include a fitness centre and an indoor pool on the roof. Close to transportation. $89–319

Comfort Inn 15 E Ohio St, at N State St ☎312/894-0900 or 1-888/775-9223, ⓦwww .chicagocomfortinn.com; Red Line to Grand. Basic high-rise budget chain hotel. though with a more glamorous-looking lobby than most and amenities such as a fitness room, whirlpool and sauna. Suites feature wet bar, microwave, refrigerator and an extra area with a sleeper sofa and desk. $149–299

Dana Hotel & Spa 660 N State St, at W Erie St ☎312/202-6000, 1-888/301-7952, ⓦwww .danahotelandspa.com; Red Line to Grand. Done up in the very popular boutique hotel style, this new River North lodging establishment features natural woods in the rooms and a mix of pleasures that include relaxing bathrobes and European coffeemakers. If you're coming to celebrate a special event, the in-room wine chiller might be a real bonus. $225–290

Four Seasons Hotel 120 E Delaware Place, at N Michigan Ave ☎312/280-8800 or 1-800/819-5053, ⓦwww.fourseasons.com; Red Line to Chicago. The service is unbeatable at this majestic 343-room hotel, which offers sumptuous rooms with superb views, a spa, fitness club, skylit pool and top-notch restaurants and lounges. You pay for what you get, however, and you'll rarely find a reduced rate here. $375–550

Holiday Inn Express Mag Mile Hotel Cass 640 N Wabash Ave, at E Ontario St ☎312/787-4030 or 1-800/799-4030, ⓦwww.casshotel.com; Red Line to Grand. Recently remodelled, the *Hotel Cass* features flat-screen televisions in every room, along with complimentary wireless internet access. In the mornings, guests can also take advantage of the free breakfast buffet and work some of the meal off later at the fitness centre. $119–219

InterContinental Chicago 505 N Michigan Ave, at E Illinois St ☎312/944-4100 or 1-800/628-2112, ⓦwww.chicago.intercontinental.com; Red Line to Grand. Originally built in 1929 as a luxury men's club, this classic hotel features over 800 festively decorated rooms on 42 floors. Best to stay in the Tower as opposed to the lower floors, despite the slight extra cost, as the views are spectacular. The recently renovated rooms are impressively modern, with minibar, coffeemaker and terry bathrobes. Hotel amenities include laundry valet service and a gorgeous, junior Olympic-sized swimming pool. Rates vary widely; best to check for deals on the website. $279–499

Ohio House Motel 600 N LaSalle St, at W Ohio St ☎312/943-6000 or 1-866/601-6446, ⓦwww .ohiohousemotel.com; Red Line to Grand; Brown or Purple Line to Merchandise Mart. If you're on a tight budget, this two-floor roadside motel is usually available, though its down-at-the-heels air makes it a last-resort budget option. And, of course, parking is free, which is a real rarity in this area. $100–140

Omni 676 N Michigan Ave, at E Erie St ☎312/944-6664 or 1-800/843-6664, ⓦwww .omnihotels.com; Red Line to Grand. The *Omni* (which is used by the *Oprah Winfrey Show* for its guests) is pricey but worth the money. Each of the rooms features complimentary internet access, two TVs, and plush terry robes. Health-conscious travellers can check into one of their "Get Fit Rooms" which feature a treadmill, dumbbells, and healthy snacks. There's also an indoor heated pool and two rooftop sundecks. $219–369

Park Hyatt Chicago 800 N Michigan Ave, at Chicago Ave ☎312/335-1234, ⓦwww .parkchicago.hyatt.com; Red Line to Chicago. Professional but not obtrusive, sophisticated, yet perhaps a touch arrogant, the *Park Hyatt* is one of the newer entries to vie for the title of top Chicago luxury hotel. The list of amenities goes overboard – each room has CD and DVD players, four phones, and Mies van der Rohe-designed chairs – and the prices tend to as well. Hard to find reduced rates here, as occupancy remains high in its 200 rooms. Has a magnificent gourmet restaurant, *NoMi* (see p.172), that faces onto Water Tower Park. $375–465

🏃 **Peninsula Chicago Hotel 108 E Superior St, at N Michigan Ave** ☎312/337-2888 or 1-866/288-8889, ⓦwww.chicago.peninsula .com; Red Line to Chicago. Everything you've ever wanted from a hotel and then some is available at the hip *Peninsula Chicago*. The 300-plus plush guest rooms are equipped with every conceivable amenity, including TVs beside the bathtubs. The spa on the

19th and 20th floors offers spectacular views of Lake Michigan and N Michigan Ave, while *The Bar* is popular with the martini-drinking set. $450–575

Raffaello Hotel 201 E Delaware Place, at N Mies van der Rohe Way ☎312/943-5000 or 1-888/560-4977, ⓦwww.chicago raffaello.com; Red Line to Chicago. Just behind the John Hancock building in Streeterville, this superbly located boutique hotel offers nice, larger-than-average rooms, affordable rates, free continental breakfast and friendly service. $149–380

Red Roof Inn Chicago 162 E Ontario St, at N St Clair St ☎312/787-3580 or 1-800/733-7663, ⓦwww.redroof-chicago -downtown.com; Red Line to Grand. Better than you might expect from a budget motel chain, the *Red Roof*'s rooms are close to the Mag Mile and the River North galleries and restaurants. Though slightly worn, the motel is a solid budget pick for the area, often going for $100 or less. Weekends generally see a moderate increase in rates. $93–149

Ritz-Carlton 160 E Pearson St, between N Michigan Ave and N Mies van der Rohe Way ☎312/266-1000, ⓦwww.fourseasons.com /chicagorc; Red Line to Chicago. Connected to Water Tower Place and a block from the Mag Mile, this is the place to stay if you want to feel like royalty. *The Ritz* has giant, richly appointed rooms, several top-notch restaurants, a health club, lap pool and spa. The airy café off the lobby makes for a great place to soak up the luxurious atmosphere. $425–570

Hotel Sax 333 N Dearborn St at Carroll Ave, River North ☎ 312/245-0333, ⓦwww.hotels axchicago.com. Red Line to Grand or Red Line to Lake. The new *Hotel Sax* (on the grounds of the former *House of Blues Hotel*) has been reinvented to feature a variety of lifestyle amenities (such as in-room spa services) and colourful interiors that bring together mustard coloured and muted pink throw pillows. Perhaps the most intriguing thing about the *Hotel Sax* is "The Microsoft Experience", which brings together Zune mp3 players and Xbox game stations in select guestrooms. Of course, every guest can get in on this modern form of media immersion in "The Studio", which is on the sixth floor. $161–$309

Seneca Hotel 200 E Chestnut St, at N Mies van der Rohe Way ☎312/787-8900 or 1-800/800-6261, ⓦwww.senecahotel.com; Red Line to Chicago. Plush boutique hotel, next to the John Hancock building, with spacious rooms for those wanting to stay near N Michigan Ave, but away from the crowds. Frequent special deals (standard room, full breakfast included) make this a sensible option. All rooms have free wireless Internet access. There are two excellent restaurants: the romantic *Saloon Steakhouse* and *Chestnut Grill & Wine Bar*. $169–269

Sofitel Chicago Water Tower 20 E Chestnut St, at N Rush St ☎312/324-4000, ⓦwww.sofitel chicago.com; Red Line to Chicago. This sleek glass tower is one of the more striking hotels in Chicago. The 400-plus rooms are minimally decorated yet chic, the service is impeccable, and many of the rooms – especially the suites – have lake views. Equally stylish is the street-level hotel hangout *Le Bar*. $225–325

Trump International Hotel & Tower Chicago 401 N Wabash Ave ☎ 312/588-8000 or 1-877/458-7867, ⓦwww.trumpchicagohotel.com; Red Line to Grand. New York's favourite realtor-turned-reality show host finally landed in Chicago in 2008 with this 92-storey hotel and condo tower. Each of the 339 guest rooms has ten foot floor-to-ceiling windows, combined with a fully equipped kitchen and free wireless internet access. Younger visitors can take advantage of the kid-friendly offerings, such as kid's robes and several popular video game systems. $395–575

W Chicago Lakeshore 644 N Lake Shore Drive, at E Ontario St ☎312/943-9200 or 1-888/846-8357, ⓦwww.whotels.com; Red Line to Grand. The lakefront location is this chic hotel's biggest asset, followed by rooms with down-stuffed beds and high-end amenities. The luxurious first-floor lounge and bar are immensely popular with

Rooms with a view

The Drake p.157
Park Hyatt Chicago see opposite
Ritz-Carlton see above

Swissotel Chicago p.153
W Chicago Lakeshore see above

Chicago's crowd, as is the rooftop bar, *Whiskey Sky*. One of the closest hotels to Navy Pier and with an infinitely more relaxed setting than its sibling in the Loop (see p.153). $139–249

Westin 909 N Michigan Ave, at W Delaware Place ☎312/943-7200, ⓦ www.starwoodhotels .com; Red Line to Chicago. Over 700 rooms in this large luxury chain hotel right across from the John Hancock Building. The recently renovated rooms are plush, with *Westin's* signature pillow-top Heavenly Beds, and great views of the area. Has a pricey and excellent steakhouse *The Grill on the Alley* on the first floor. Can't beat it for location, and they often have discounted rates, especially in winter. $149–289

Whitehall Hotel 105 E Delaware Place, between N Rush St and N Michigan Ave ☎312/944-6300 or 1-866/753-4081, ⓦ www .thewhitehallhotel.com; Red Line to Chicago. Boutique hotel just off Mag Mile that achieves a sort of non-snooty European ambience. Guests have use of the fitness center as well as complimentary car service within a two-mile radius of the hotel. One of the top choices for those who want to stay in the area but try to avoid the chains. $159–259

South Loop and Near South

Best Western Grant Park 1100 S Michigan Ave, at E 11th St ☎312/922-2900 or 1-800/416-8752, ⓦ www.bwgrantparkhotel.com; Green, Orange or Red Line to Roosevelt. Located in the South Loop near the Museum Campus, this chain hotel has 173 rooms – all devoid of any sort of style, yet clean enough – an outdoor pool and sundeck, and complimentary coffee and newspapers. Popular with convention and tour groups; weekends tend to book up. Lake-view rooms fetch $10–20 more. $88–210

The Blackstone Hotel 636 S Michigan Ave, at Balbo Ave ☎312/447-0955 or 1/800-468-3571, ⓦ www.marriott.com; Red Line to Harrison. Built in 1908, the *Blackstone Hotel* reopened in 2008 after a very ambitious restoration. With 328 guest rooms, the hotel has taken on a boutique air and the hotel is peppered with over 1400 pieces of contemporary art by local artists. The lobby and other public spaces are a bit cramped, but the views of Grant Park and Lake

Michigan from the upper floors are outstanding. $161–305

Hotel Blake 500 S Dearborn St, near W Congress Parkway, South Loop ☎ 312/986-1234, ⓦ www .hotelblake.com. Red Line to Harrison or Blue Line to LaSalle. This new addition to the South Loop hotel scene offers 162 guest rooms, along with six suites. Located in a former printing press building, the hotel's amenities include free wireless internet, high-end spa products in each room, and iPod docking stations for those who can't bear to be without their tunes. Finally, the hotel also has a 24hr business centre and a fitness facility that has free weights and cardio equipment. $119–$299

Essex Inn 800 S Michigan Ave, at E 8th St ☎312/939-2800 or 1-800/621-6909, ⓦ www .essexinn.com; Red Line to Harrison. Fifteen-storey, 255-room South Loop hotel that's favoured by many travellers for its cheapish rates, clean (if somewhat spartan) rooms, and convenient location to Loop attractions. $119–259

Hilton Chicago and Towers 720 S Michigan Ave, at E Balbo Drive ☎312/922-4400 or 1-800/445-8667, ⓦ www.hilton.com; Red Line to Harrison. Unless you need to be here for a convention or want to stay near Grant Park, you might not find much reason to stay at this 1500-room hotel. Still, the rooms are kept up well enough, there are stunning lakefront views, and rates are more reasonable than Loop hotels. There's an indoor pool, fitness room, and all the business-traveller amenities you'd expect. $159–329

Holiday Inn & Suites Downtown Chicago 506 W Harrison St, at S Canal St ☎312/957-9100 or 1-800/972-2494, ⓦ www.hidowntown.com; Blue Line to Clinton. A reasonable-value chain hotel just southwest of the Loop, near the Sears Tower, the two main Metra train stations, right underneath the inn. Easy access to Greektown and Little Italy. Rooms are spacious, staff are pleasant, and there's a small restaurant on site, as well as a fitness room and outdoor pool. $91–327

Hyatt Regency McCormick Place 2233 S King Drive, at E Cermak Rd ☎312/567-1234 or 1-800/492-8804, ⓦ www.mccormickplace.hyatt .com; bus #35. The place to be for convention-eers, this handsome hotel towers incongruously over the empty acres just west of the convention centre. Although it's a bit isolated, it's possible to find some good deals here when there's not a huge convention in town.

The 800 rooms are colourfully decorated and each offers complimentary high-speed Internet access. There is also an impressive array of on-site services like printing, shipping and computer work stations. $119–249

Travelodge 65 E Harrison St, at S Wabash Ave T312/427-8000 or 1-800/578-7878, Wwww .travelodge.com; Red Line to Harrison. No-frills chain in the South Loop near Grant Park that's clean and has comfortable enough beds and bathroom furnishings, but overall it's a bit worn. Basic amenities include coffeemaker, complimentary paper, and high-speed internet access. $125–190

Wheeler Mansion 2020 S Calumet Ave, at E 18th St T312/945-2020, Wwww.wheelermansion .com; Metra 18th St. Probably the city's most luxurious B&B, housed in a beautifully restored 1870s mansion, with the amenities of a small luxury hotel (Egyptian-cotton sheets, towels, robes and turn-down service). Popular with conventioneers meeting at McCormick Place, the B&B is also just a block from the historic Glessner House (see p.73) and the rest of S Prairie Ave. Rates include breakfast and there's a classy first-floor dining room where you can also order in the evening. Minimum stays usually apply on weekends. You can choose from standard rooms and junior or master suites; prices include tax. $230–365

Gold Coast

Ambassador East Hotel 1301 N State Parkway, at W Goethe St T312/787-7200 or 1-888/506-3471, Wwww.theambassadoreasthotel.com; Red Line to Clark/Division. Great hotel in a prime Gold Coast location, offering surprisingly affordable room rates for the area. Considering its age, the rooms are very spacious, comfortable, and well kept. Built in the 1920s, the *Ambassador* was a favourite haunt of Frank Sinatra and the Rat Pack during the 1950s; its famed *Pump Room* bar is still here, and its clubby old-school feel makes it worth a trip. See map on p.77 for location. $155–349

The Drake 140 E Walton Place, at N Michigan Ave T312/787-2200 or 1-800/553-7253, Wwww.thedrakehotel.com; Red Line to Chicago. If it didn't occupy the most coveted piece of property in the city and have such history, Chicago's elegant *Drake* might have been surpassed years ago by its high-powered competitors.

Across from Oak Street Beach and with outstanding views of Lake Shore Drive and Lake Michigan, the hotel has 535 renovated rooms, which still feel a bit aged and are smallish, especially compared to some of the newer hotels in the area. Some rooms start from $400 a night, but most cost half that, and a few rooms even less (check the hotel website for the best deals). $199–315

Gold Coast Guest House 113 W Elm St, at N Clark St T312/337-0361, Wwww.bbchicago .com; Red Line to Clark/Division. This converted 1873 row house, run by a wonderful host, includes continental breakfast and evening refreshments in their rates and usually requires a two-night stay on weekends. Each of the four guest rooms comes with air conditioning and private bath – a couple even have a whirlpool – and bed sizes vary by room. There's also a charming garden outside and the lake is just a 10min walk away. No smoking. $129–229

Hotel Indigo Chicago – Gold Coast 1244 N Dearborn Parkway, at W Goethe St T312/787-4980 or 1-866/521-6950, Wwww.goldcoast chicagohotel.com; Red Line to Clark/Division. Bright, cheerful, completely renovated hotel that's a great deal in one of the city's most expensive neighbourhoods. Very central – a few blocks from the lake and near the Mag Mile, as well as dozens of restaurants and bars. Rooms are well appointed but on the small side. See map on p.77 for location. $113–261

The Talbott 20 E Delaware Place, at N State St T312/944-4970 or 1-800/825-2688, Wwww .talbotthotel.com; Red Line to Chicago. Striving for (and mostly achieving) old English country club style, the *Talbott* is a small Gold Coast boutique hotel built in 1927. The rooms are small but comfortable, the service impeccable and the lobby, with its leather armchairs and dark-wood walls, a wonderful escape. Just steps off Michigan Ave but utterly relaxing. $199–315

Old Town and Lincoln Park

See map on p.90 for hotel locations.
Belden-Stratford 2300 Lincoln Park West, at W Fullerton Ave T773/281-2900 or 1-800/800-8301, Wwww.beldenstratfordhotel.com; bus #74. One of the city's most elegant old hotels, this landmark inn and residence building in the heart of Lincoln Park boasts a gorgeous lobby with gold chandeliers and

a painted sky-motif ceiling, plus stylish rooms and suites with nine-foot high ceilings, plush carpeting and comfortable furnishings. Other amenities include a rooftop sundeck, beauty salon, spa and two stellar on-site restaurants: the seafood-based *L20* and the casual, buzzing *Mon Ami Gabi*. Great location overlooking the lake close to Lincoln Park Zoo. $99–147

Days Inn Lincoln Park North 644 W Diversey Parkway, at N Clark St T 773/525-7010 or 1-800/654-7871, W www.lpndaysinn.com; **Brown or Purple Line to Diversey.** A budget-friendly place to crash in accommodation-starved Lincoln Park. Not necessarily the most inspired atmosphere, but rooms are bright and clean, and rates include complimentary continental breakfast (6.30–11am), as well as passes to Bally's health club next door, which has an indoor track, lap pool, sauna and whirlpool. $121–219

Old Town Chicago B&B Inn 1442 North Park Ave, at Schiller St T 312/440-9268, W www.oldtown chicago.com; **Brown or Purple Line to Sedgwick.** Lavishly decorated wing of a multimillion-dollar Art Deco town house in Old Town. The four guest rooms, all suites with luxurious queen beds, each come with private bath and cable TV. Breakfast plus 24hr snacks are included in rates. There's also a nice roof deck. A three-night minimum stay is generally required for weekend stays reserved more than a week in advance. One of the nicer B&B options in the city. $185–275

Windy City Urban Inn 607 W Deming Place, at N Clark St T 773/248-7091 or 1-877/897-7091, W www.windycityinn.com; **Red, Brown, or Purple Line to Fullerton.** Cozy and friendly B&B in a restored Victorian mansion, with charmingly

decorated rooms and suites named after local literary lights (Saul Bellow, Studs Terkel, Gwendolyn Brooks), none of which seem to have much to do with the author chosen. All rooms have private bath and rates include a breakfast buffet. Weekends tend to book up quickly. $115–325

Lakeview and Wrigleyville

See map on p.99 for hotel locations.

Best Western Hawthorne Terrace 3434 N Broadway, at W Hawthorne Place T 773/244-3434 or 1-888/860-3400, W www.hawthorne terrace.com; **Red Line to Addison; Red, Brown or Purple Line to Belmont.** Located in Boystown, one block from the Lincoln Park lakefront, this budget option – formerly a hotel for transients, though you'd never know it – has about sixty clean rooms (including some junior suites) that come with complimentary continental breakfast and newspaper. Facilities include a fitness centre with a sauna and whirlpool. Two-night minimum stay on some weekends in high season. $125–199

City Suites 933 W Belmont Ave, at N Willow Ave T 773/404-3400 or 1-800/248-9108, W www .cityinns.com; **Red, Brown or Purple Line to Belmont.** A smallish, old-fashioned hotel on busy Belmont Ave, perfect for younger people who want to explore the area's bars and stagger home or just to walk around some of the city's less-explored neighbourhoods. Rooms (double rooms and office suites) are basic but clean and it's a dependable option in a non-touristy location. $115–218

Majestic 528 W Brompton Ave, at N Lake Shore Drive T 773/404-3499 or 1-800/727-5108, W www.cityinns.com; **Red Line to Addison.** This old business hotel in Wrigleyville, with country-manor decor, has charming features like vintage elevators and radiators. A solid choice in an area not exactly overflowing with hotels and close to Lakeview's nightlife. It's a bit of a hike from the Loop but there are many buses that head in that direction on nearby Lake Shore Drive. $122–257

The Willows 555 W Surf St, at N Broadway ☎773/528-8400 or 1-800/787-3108, Ⓦwww .cityinns.com; Brown or Purple Line to Diversey. Well-kept and affordable boutique hotel, located in a border zone between Lincoln Park and Lakeview, just two blocks from Lake Michigan. Renovated in nineteenth-century French country style, the hotel's rooms and suites have an easy elegance, with antique furniture, patterned wallpaper, and soothing peach and light green colours. Complimentary breakfast is included in rates. Sister to the *Majestic* and *City Suites* hotels, the *Willows* is the most romantic of the three. $122–262

Wicker Park

See map on p.107 for hotel locations.
House of Two Urns 1239 N Greenview Ave, at W Division St ☎773/235-1408 or 1-877/896-8767, Ⓦwww.twourns.com; Blue Line to Division/Milwaukee. Charming, quiet B&B in Wicker Park with five creatively decorated and unusual rooms (the "Alice Room" has a Lewis Carroll vibe, with a jewel-toned, custom-made bed set high atop a stack of painted mattresses, a la *The Princess and the Pea*). Amenities go beyond the usual B&B offerings to include DVD rental, private phone lines and answering machines. Take in some spectacular views of the downtown skyline from the roof deck. The only drawback is that most guest rooms share a bathroom with another guest room. Advance bookings usually require a minimum two-or-three night stay. A 10–15 percent discount is usually offered in Jan & Feb. $79–185

Wicker Park Inn 1329 N Wicker Park Ave, at N Wood St ☎773/486-2743, Ⓦwww .wickerparkinn.com; Blue Line to Damen. Three-room B&B in a two-storey 1890s row house, a few blocks from the El. It's nothing extraordinary, and not as quaint as *Two Urns* (see above), but it does book up quickly – for weekend stays, call two months ahead. Rooms are bright but small – think your first post-college apartment.

Breakfast is included and is served daily in the small dining area. Smoking is not permitted, and cats are on the premises. The inn charges a flat rate and accepts most major credit cards as well as traveller's cheques. $129–189

The West Side

See map on p.115 for hotel location.
Crowne Plaza Chicago – Metro 733 W Madison St, at S Halsted St ☎312/829-5000, Ⓦwww .ichotelsgroup.com; Green Line to Clinton; Blue Line to UIC/Halsted. Stylish, contemporary hotel close to Greektown and the United Center and not far from the Sears Tower – a smart option for those wanting to be near the Loop and the West Side, but not wanting to pay Loop prices. The 398 rooms and 42 suites are done up in rich taupes and reds, with CD players and flat-screen TVs. Fitness centre and restaurant on site. Valet parking is steep at $35, but worth it in this somewhat gritty neighbourhood. Pets welcome. $161–270

Hyde Park

See map on p.122 for hotel locations.
Ramada Inn Lakeshore 4900 S Lake Shore Drive, at E 51st St ☎773/288-5800 or 1-888/298-2054, Ⓦwww.ramada-chicago.com. Four-storey no-frills motel in Hyde Park, with an outdoor pool and sweeping views of the lake. Affordable and good-sized rooms – if you're visiting the University of Chicago, it's one of the only hotels in the area. Offers a direct shuttle to airports, a lifesaver for a hotel this far south. $79–179

Wooded Isle Suites 5750 S Stony Island Ave, at E 57th St ☎773/288-6305 or 1-800/290-6844, Ⓦwww.woodedisle.com; bus #6. Simple, pleasantly furnished vintage studios and suites in a lovely, central Hyde Park location within walking distance of 57th St Beach, the University of Chicago and Museum of Science and Industry. All rooms include cable TV, and a phone with answering machine; suites feature a fully equipped kitchen. $162–202

The North Shore

See map on p.135 for hotel locations.
Hilton Garden Inn-Evanston 1818 Maple Avenue, at Clark St Evanston ☎ 847/475-6400, Ⓦwww .hiltongardeninn.com; Purple Line to Davis.

Pretty standard and pleasant modern business hotel, with complimentary wireless internet with a fitness room and a pool. Good public transportation access and a good bet if you are making a special trip to visit nearby Northwestern University. $159–209

Margarita European Inn 1566 Oak Ave, at Oak Park Ave, Evanston ⓣ847/869-2273, ⓦwww .margaritainn.com; **Purple Line to Davis.** Formerly used as housing for young working women in the early twentieth century, this stately brick and limestone hotel has 42 rooms, mini-suites and suites, some with shared bath. Wireless internet access available in the inn's common areas. Rates include continental breakfast. $79–169

Hotel Orrington 1710 Orrington Ave, at Church St, Evanston ⓣ847/866-8700, ⓦwww.hotel orrington.com; **Purple Line to Davis.** After a $34 million facelift, this recently reopened downtown Evanston hotel offers the most deluxe accommodations on the North Shore, with over 250 newly decorated, contemporary rooms and suites that boast plush bedding, in-room safe, "power shower" heads, and free high-speed internet access. The property also has a fitness centre and 24hr business centre. $149–249

Oak Park

See map on p.141 for hotel locations.
Carleton Hotel 1110 Pleasant St, at Harlem Ave ⓣ708/848-5000 or 1-888/227-5386, ⓦwww .carletonhotel.com; **Green Line to Oak Park.** Built in 1928, this charming boutique hotel in downtown Oak Park features about a hundred comfortable, spacious rooms and suites, most in the main hotel, with a couple dozen in an adjacent motor inn. Most rooms include kitchen area with microwave and refrigerator. $110–181

Longwell Hall Bed & Breakfast 301 N Scoville, at Chicago Ave ⓣ708/386-5043, ⓦwww .oakparknet.com; **Green Line to Oak Park.** English-style B&B around the corner from the Ernest Hemingway birthplace home and close to Frank Lloyd Wright homes in the historical district. It offers three modestly sized but comfortable rooms decked out with Laura Ashley wallpaper and antique furnishings. No smoking/pets. $85–100

Write Inn 211 N Oak Park Ave, at Lake St ⓣ708/383-4800, ⓦwww.writeinn.com; **Green Line to Oak Park.** Located in the heart of the Oak Park Historic District, with 66 renovated rooms and suites furnished with antiques and accessories from the 1920s, plus 45 short- and long-term rental apartments. Suites include mini-kitchens with fridge, sink and microwave. Check the website for online discounts. $95–171

Hostels and budget housing

Arlington House International Hostel 616 W Arlington Place, at N Geneva Terrace, Lincoln Park ⓣ773/929-5380 or 1-800/467-8355, ⓦwww.arlingtonhouse.com; **Red, Brown or Purple Line to Fullerton.** Lincoln Park's only hostel is basic and not much else – stay only if you can't afford anything else. Dorms have up to seven beds; private rooms are available. Within walking distance of the Lincoln Park Zoo and Conservatory and the neighbourhood's nightlife, and close to public transportation. Unlike many hostels, it's open 24hr, with no curfew. See map on p.90 for hotel location. $31–79

Chicago International Hostel 6318 N Winthrop Ave, at W Rosemont Ave, Edgewater ⓣ773/262-1011, ⓦwww.hostelworld.com; **Red Line to Granville or Loyola.** You'll almost always find a spot at this very basic 125-bed hostel near

▲ Harris Family Hostel

Loyola University just south of Rogers Park. Beds cost $20 per night, with dorms sleeping four to eight and sharing two unisex bathrooms. A few private doubles ($50) and triples ($71) – with bath – are also available, and if you stay ten days you get one night free. The hostel, recently renovated and under new management, has a kitchen, laundry, luggage storage and free parking. Accepts traveller's cheque, Visa and MasterCard, and requires a photo ID showing permanent residence outside Chicago. See map on p.135 for hotel location. $22–50

Hostelling International – Chicago (J. Ira and Nikki Harris Family Hostel) 24 E Congress Parkway, at S Wabash Ave, Loop ☎312/360-0300 or 1-800/909-4776, ⓦwww .hichicago.org. **Red Line to Harrison; Blue Line to LaSalle; Brown or Orange Line to Library-State/Van Buren.** Well run and meticulously clean, this modern, 500-bed hostel on the Loop's southern edge has dorms sleeping six to ten, most of which have adjoining bathrooms. Close to all El lines and within walking distance of Loop attractions, the lake, Grant Park, and Museum Campus. Facilities include a full-service kitchen, laundry room, luggage storage, internet access, Ping-Pong tables, and even a library. Open 24hr. Accepts cash, traveller's cheque, Visa, and MasterCard. $31–37

International House of Chicago 1414 E 59th St, at Blackstone, Hyde Park ☎773/753-2270, ⓦwww.ihouse.uchicago.edu; **Metra 59th St.** Simple housing for University of Chicago students that's open to the public. Right on campus and a block from the Metra at the University of Chicago/59th St train station, the 100-room building also has a little café, open on weekdays. The front desk is staffed 7am–11pm, after which check-in is not possible; there is, however, no curfew. Discounts are available for double rooms or on stays of a month or more. Accepts traveller's cheque and credit cards – you'll need the latter to make a reservation. See map on p.122 for hotel location. $60–70

12

Eating

A century and a half of immigration from as far afield as Poland and Peru has made for a rich culinary tradition that can make even a short trip to Chicago an epicurean delight. **Dining out** is a huge part of the city's culture – more relaxed and down-to-earth than in other major US cities, something reflected in the proliferation of reasonably priced restaurants. While you could easily drop several hundred dollars on a white-linen-style dinner, some of the things Chicago does best (notably pizza, steak, and hot dogs) can be had for less than $5. Sampling something from each part of the spectrum is ideal.

The former Chicago Stockyards supplied residents with beef, pork and lamb for over a century and its influence can still be felt in the presence of **hot-dog stands** like *The Wiener's Circle*, *Portillo's*, *Superdawg* and others (don't even try the sacrilege of putting ketchup on your hot dog here), as well as numerous **Italian-beef joints**. Not to mention, of course, a plethora of brawny **steakhouses**, several outstanding barbecue and ribs joints and a number of incredible burger places.

In a city where size matters and big is definitely better, local food portions are not just sizeable but extreme. Servers at many restaurants, especially Italian eateries, will make sure to ask you, "Did you want the *full* portion, or just the half?" When in doubt, go with the half – at worst you will still have room for dessert. Steaks are typically gargantuan, the **deep-dish pizzas** (see colour insert) can easily defeat even the most dedicated trenchermen and Italian beef sandwiches are piled high and slopping out all over the place: it's a rare Chicago diner who thinks they didn't get their money's worth.

While the cow may be king in the Midwest, **vegetarians** needn't feel excluded from the feeding frenzy. An eclectic crop of Italian and Asian restaurants along with all sorts of New American fusion cuisine and everything in between serve a medley of meat-free dishes. The much-vaunted *Green Zebra* is indicative of the trend towards inventive and flavoursome vegetarian-friendly delicacies served in a hip environment with no tie-dye and no nut-roast in sight. Close to the city centre nearly everything is available; for the best in **ethnic cuisines**, you will have to jump on a bus or train.

Relaxed weekend **brunches** are also something the city does well; the best places will have lines out the door and down the block, but there are any number of spots that will do in a pinch.

With the **Loop**'s residential allure rising, the paucity of restaurants and cafés in the area, beyond the prosaic chains, is set to change. Still, there are currently a clutch of stellar eating choices worth seeking out: the French haute cuisine at *Everest* or a classic Chicago breakfast at *Lou Mitchell's*.

However, for the most part, Chicagoans will eat dinner in local neighbourhoods rather than the Loop even if they are heading downtown for their post-dinner entertainment. Wandering away from the Loop will generally result in a more unique dining experience, and of course, it constitutes a bit more of an "adventure".

Most visitors stay in the **River North/Magnificent Mile** area, where a great number of the city's finest restaurants are located, like *Frontera Grill* (considered by many to be the best Mexican food in the US), the fashionable *Blue Water Grill*, and some of the best steaks in town at the *Chicago Chop House*. Just west of the Magnificent Mile's Water Tower is the packed restaurant row of Rush Street, locally known as the "Viagra Triangle" for its randy older crowd and unashamedly macho steakhouses. Just north, the appropriately named **Gold Coast** neighbourhood, Wells Street in **Old Town** and, a little further north, Halsted Street in **Lincoln Park**, cater to all tastes and tendencies with cuisine spanning everything from the sublime nouvelle American tasting menus served at *Charlie Trotter's* to cozy Italian trattorias and sleek sushi lounge bars. For further ethnic fare, quick jaunts to **Greektown**, around Halsted Street and Jackson Boulevard, and **Little Italy**'s Taylor Street are relatively easy and more than worthwhile. The restaurants tend to be more spread out in those neighbourhoods, so it's smart to check on a map before heading out. Further out, **Pilsen** on the southwest side has some excellent **Mexican food**. South and a little west of the Loop, **Chinatown** boasts a few no-frills but authentic restaurants that are the only reason some Chicagoans ever make the journey. Further south around 53rd or 57th Street, the **Hyde Park** area is your best bet for Southern soul food, or a hamburger in a collegiate setting.

Wrigleyville and **Lakeview** – particularly along eclectic Clark Street – have perhaps the most Chicago-style eateries, which is to say, artery-hardening combinations of sausages, ribs, and other anomalous greasebombs. North along the youthfully hip Southport Avenue, from Lincoln Avenue, stretching west along Roscoe to Damen, there has been a gastronomic explosion. Sleek restaurants nudge up against kitsch breakfast joints, delis, pizza chains, old-fashioned ice cream parlours, Irish-themed taverns and sophisticated wine bars. And, overlooking it all is a venerated Chicago institution: *Southport Lanes and Billiards* (see p.179), serving killer burgers. Further north, Viking delicacies like potato pancakes topped with lingonberries, pickled herrings and meat balls are on offer in the Swedish enclave of Andersonville. A bit to the west, six blocks along **W Devon Avenue** constitute "Little Bombay", where you will find the city's most authentic Indian cooking.

The listings in this chapter are arranged **geographically** and correspond more or less to the breakdowns in the Guide. Each neighbourhood is in turn split into two divisions: **Cafés and light meals**, which emphasizes spots for breakfast, lunch or a quick bite any other time; and **Restaurants**, for slightly more substantial dining, typically at dinner. However, there is certainly crossover between the two and many diner-type places, found in the first category, can be useful for inexpensive meals at dinnertime too. Likewise numerous upscale restaurants also serve lunch, often at a lower price than dinner menus. Note too that it's always good to have a **reservation** at the pricier establishments; if it's essential, we've said so in the review.

In each restaurant review we have given sample prices of typical dishes and also offered details on some of the culinary highlights at each eatery profiled in the listings.

Top Chicago restaurants by cuisine

A number of the restaurants in this chapter that are especially recommended come with the 🎋. This list will further help you locate a place to eat if you are looking for a particular type of cuisine.

American
Atwood Café, The Loop, see below
Charlie Trotter's, Lincoln Park, p.176
Handlebar, Wicker Park, p.181
Lux Bar, Gold Coast, p.173
MK, Near North, p.171
North Pond, Lincoln Park, p.176
Park Grill, The Loop, p.166
3rd Coast, Gold Coast, p.173

Bakeries and cafés
Bourgeois Pig, Lincoln Park, p.175
Earwax Café, Wicker Park, p.180
Intelligentsia, Lakeview, p.178
Letizia's Natural Bakery, Wicker Park, p.180
Twisted Sister Bakery, Old Town, p.174

Breakfast and brunch
Ann Sather, Lakeview, p.177
Bongo Room, Wicker Park, p.180
Orange, Lakeview, p.178

Chinese
Ben Pao, Near North, p.169
Red Light, West Side, p.183
Tamarind, South Loop, p.168

Delis and diners
Eppy's Deli, Near North, p.172
Jerry's Sandwiches, Wicker Park, p.181
Manny's Deli, South Loop, p.167
Tempo Café, Near North, p.171

French
Brasserie Jo, Near North, p.169
Everest, The Loop, p.166
Le Creperie, Lakeview, p.179

Fusion
Alinea, Lincoln Park, p.175
Le Colonial, Gold Coast, p.173
NoMI, Near North, p.172
Tru, Gold Coast, p.173

Greek
Athenian Room, Lincoln Park, p.175
Greek Islands, West Side, p.182
Rodity's, West Side, p.183

Indian/Pakistani
Hema's Kitchen, Lincoln Park, p.176
Khyber Pass, Oak Park, p.186
Sabri Nihari, Rogers Park, p.186

Italian
Café Spiaggia, Gold Coast, p.173
Francesca's On Taylor, West Side, p.182

The Loop

Cafés and light meals

Atwood Café in the *Burnham Hotel*, 1 W Washington St, at State ☎312/368-1900. Located in a legendary Chicago School building designed by Daniel Burnham (see p.53), the *Atwood Café* serves upscale comfort food in a warm and arty (if somewhat crowded) environment. Brioche French toast with fresh strawberries ($11) is a fixture at breakfast; at lunch, the house-made wild-mushroom veggie burger with fig-onion marmalade ($14) is the way to go. A typical dinner entree: seared scallops with pumpkin flan and Swiss chard ($27). Open for breakfast Mon–Fri 7–10am & Sat 8–10am; brunch Sun 8am–3pm; lunch Mon–Sat 11.30am–3.45pm; dinner Sun–Thurs 5–10pm, Fri & Sat 5–11pm.

Heaven on Seven 111 N Wabash St, 7th Floor, at Washington ☎312/263-6443. Chef/owner Jimmy Bannos has been serving up Cajun/ Southern Specialties like hoppin' john (black-eyed peas), gumbo, spicy corn bread, red beans and rice, and po' boy sandwiches ($10–13) in this seventh-floor memento-decked luncheonette for 28 years. There's another branch in Near North (see p.169). Mon–Fri 9am–4pm, Sat 10am–3pm.

Lou Mitchell's 565 W Jackson Blvd, at Clinton ☎312/939-3111. Started in 1923, this is Chicago's first diner, one block from Union Station. The menu has hardly changed, and the lines are long, but it's worth it to the businesspeople who pack in for the monumental omelettes, served with a mound of hash browns and thick, buttery

Osteria Via Stato, Near North, p.171
Rose Angelis, Lincoln Park, p.176
Trattoria No. 10, The Loop, p.166
Via Carducci, Lincoln Park, p.177
Vivere, The Loop, p.167

Japanese
Japonais, Near North, p.170
Kamehachi, Old Town, p.174

Mexican/Latin American
Frontera Grill and Topolobampo, Near North, p.169
Nacional 27, Near North, p.171
Nuevo Leon, Pilsen/West Side, p.183
Salpicón, Old Town, p.174
Twisted Lizard, Lincoln Park, p.177
Zapatista, South Loop/Near South Side, p.168

Middle Eastern
Old Jerusalem, Old Town, p.174
Sultan's Market, Lincoln Park/Wicker Park, p.177

Pizza
Bricks, Lincoln Park, p.176
Caffe Florian, Hyde Park, p.184
Calo Ristorante, Andersonville, p.178
Piece, Wicker Park, p.181
Pizzeria Uno, Near North, p.171

Pub food
Billy Goat Tavern, Near North, p.172
Twin Anchors, Old Town, p.175
Twisted Spoke, West Loop, p.184

Southern
Evanston Chicken Shack, Evanston, p.185
Ribs 'n' Bibs, Hyde Park, p.185
Stanley's Kitchen and Tap, Lincoln Park, p.177

Spanish
Café Iberico, Near North, p.169
Mercat a la Planxa, South Loop, p.168

Steak
Chicago Chop House, Near North, p.169
Kinzie Chop House, Near North, p.170
Pete Miller's Seafood & Prime Steak, Evanston, p.186

Southeast Asian
Arun's, North Side, p.185
Penny's Noodle Shop, Lakeview, p.179
Vong's Thai Kitchen, Near North, p.172

Vegetarian
Green Zebra, West Side, p.183
Karyn's Cooked, Near North, p.170
Victory's Banner, Lakeview, p.178

slabs of toast. Free Milk Duds and donut holes ease the wait. Inexpensive. Mon–Sat 5.30am–3pm, Sun 7am–3pm.
Potbelly Sandwich Works 190 N State St, at Lake ☎312/683-1234. For review see Lincoln Park branch on p.175.
Walnut Room 111 N State St, at Washington ☎312/781-3139. The crème of department store lunching, the *Walnut Room* has been ensconced on the seventh floor of the former Marshall Field's (now Macy's) for more than a century, and its Austrian chandeliers, marble fountain and coffered ceiling complement a snooty but not wallet-busting menu of sandwiches like the crab cake BLT ($12.95). The traditional meal remains Mrs. Hering's chicken pot pie ($10.95), concocted by the resident milliner in the late 1800s, followed by a slice of Frango mint chocolate ice cream pie. Mon–Sat 11am–7pm, Sun 1–6pm.

Restaurants

Aria in the *Fairmont Hotel*, **200 N Columbus Drive, at Lake ☎312/444-9494.** One of Chicago's globetrotting restaurants, *Aria* serves inventive Middle Eastern, Latin American, Asian, Indian and Mediterranean dishes (average entree $27) – as well as huge cuts of Midwest beef – in a modern but relaxed setting. Don't miss the delicious naan bread cooked in the centrepiece tandoori oven. Open for lunch daily 11.30am–2.30pm and for dinner Sun–Thurs 5–10pm, Fri & Sat until 11pm. Bar open daily 10.30am–1am.
Berghoff 17 W Adams St, at State ☎312/427-3170. This century-old, unbeatably nostalgic tavern survived Prohibition by selling food and root beer, closed a few years ago, then reopened essentially intact, with the founder's granddaughter at the helm. Opt

▲ Pizzeria in the Loop

for one of the "Berghoff Favorites" – heavy, satisfying German fare like sauerbraten or Wiener schnitzel ($18 at dinner, $15 at lunch) – washed down with a home-brewed beer. On the lower level, *Berghoff Cafe* is good for a lunch on the run, with inexpensive deli sandwiches, salad and pasta. Mon–Thurs 11am–9pm, Fri 11am–9.30pm, Sat 11.30am–10pm.

Everest 440 S LaSalle St, at W Van Buren ☎312/663-8920. Acclaimed chef-owner Jean Joho's dazzling French cuisine rivals the views from the 40th floor of the Chicago Stock Exchange building. The menu changes seasonally but you can expect to find dishes like pheasant wrapped and braised in Alsace-style cabbage and filet of venison with wild huckleberries and braised pear. Average bills per diner are in excess of $130. Far less wallet-draining is *Brasserie Jo,* Joho's casual alternative in River North (see p.169). Tues–Thurs 5.30–9.30pm, Fri & Sat 5.30–10pm.

Miller's Pub 134 S Wabash, at Monroe ☎312/263-4988. A Chicago institution, covered in autographed celebrity photos, *Miller's* serves some of the best ribs in town ($15–19), as well as excellent steaks and seafood ($10–30) and lighter, cheaper fare like omelettes and sandwiches ($7–12). Stop by for a drink at the very least for the welcoming atmosphere and priceless people-watching. Kitchen open daily 11am–2am; bar until 4am.

Nick's Fishmarket 1 Bank One Plaza, 51 S Clark at Monroe ☎312/621-0200. Good, if pricey, seafood, with appetizers like the zesty Maui Wowie salad, with bay shrimp,

hearts of palm, tomato, feta and avocado ($10), and traditional entrees ranging from simple roasted salmon to lobster thermidor ($31–58). *Nick's Grill* upstairs has a more casual, less expensive menu of sandwiches and salads. Mon–Fri 11.30am–2pm & 5.30–10pm, Sat 5.30–11pm.

Park Grill 11 N Michigan Ave, at Madison ☎312/521-7275. Like Millennium Park itself, this three-in-one eatery offers a little something for everyone: a year-round New American restaurant, a seasonal take-out café, and the vast al fresco *Plaza at Park Grill*, which occupies the city's ice rink in the summer. The café offers the best deals, with picnic fare like a barbecued half-chicken for $8 and gourmet salads and sandwiches for less, with the *Plaza* serving up grilled entrees in the $8–18 range, along with appetizers like crab cakes and duck tacos. The restaurant's the priciest (be sure to reserve), with mains from English pea ravioli to seared Ahi tuna averaging in the low to mid-$20s and a pre-theatre three-course prix-fixe for $35. Sun–Thurs 11am–9.30pm, Fri & Sat 11am–10.30pm.

Pizano's 61 E Madison, at Wabash ☎312/236-1777. You can satisfy your yen for deep-dish pizza at this unpretentious spot, founded in 1991 by Rudy Malnati Jr, the son of the founder of *Pizzeria Uno* in Near North (see p.171). Opt for Rudy's special, with sausage, mushroom, onion and green pepper – allow 30min' cooking time. Thin-crust pies are also available. The smaller original restaurant is a Near North gem (see p.171). Both Mon–Fri & Sun 11am–2am, Sat 11am–3am.

Russian Tea Time 77 E Adams, at Wabash ☎312/360-0000. Friendly pre-symphony spot near the Art Institute with an infectiously civilized old-world ambience. The vast menu (average dinner entree $18, average lunch entree $13) features Ukrainian borscht, *latkes* (potato pancakes), Uzbeki vegetarian stew, beef stroganoff, stuffed cabbage and other Eastern European classics. At high tea (daily 2.30–4.30pm), you'll get scones with cream and jam, a selection of savoury crepes and finger sandwiches, sweets including tortes, cakes and cookies, and a "fine pot of tea" for $22.95 a person. Sun–Thurs 11am–9pm, Fri–Sat until midnight.

Trattoria No. 10 10 N Dearborn St, at Madison ☎312/984-1718. This cosy underground retreat serves classic Italian fare. Begin with a salad of organic beets with fennel, arugula and baked marinated goat cheese ($9) or dive straight in with a plate of homemade ravioli filled with butternut squash, spicy sausage or lobster tail ($18–24), followed by an entree ($26–36) like veal scaloppini with pan-fried ricotta gnocchi, pancetta and leeks. Open for lunch Mon–Fri 11.30am–2pm and for dinner Mon–Thurs 5.30–9pm, Fri & Sat until 10pm.

Vivere 71 W Monroe, at Wabash ☏ **312/332-4040.** Perfect for a pre-theatre meal, *Vivere* is the best of the three family-owned restaurants in the Italian Village mini-complex, with unusual pastas ($17–23) like the aromatic, pheasant-filled agnolottini with butter and sage and entrees like salt shrimp with Sardinian-style couscous. Great wine list and desserts, too. Mon–Sat 5–10pm.

South Loop and Near South

Cafés and light meals

Eleven City Diner 1112 S Wabash Ave, at E 11th ☏ **312/212-1112.** Sun-splashed neighbourhood diner that's a mob scene for weekend brunch (try the challah French toast) but generally manageable at other times, with Jewish deli favourites like succulent pastrami sandwiches, latkes, knishes, matzoh-ball soup and brisket (after 4pm). Most sandwiches $12 and under. Breakfast served all day. Terrific milkshakes, too. Mon–Thurs 8am–10pm, Fri 8am–midnight, Sat 9am–midnight, Sun 9am–9pm.

Manny's Deli 1141 S Jefferson St, at W Roosevelt Rd ☏ **312/939-2855.** One of Chicago's only New York-style delis – and definitely one of the best in the city – with everything from matzoh-ball soup and giant corned-beef sandwiches ($10.95) to cheese blintzes and tongue sandwiches, served up cafeteria-style. Located next to the University of Illinois at Chicago, it draws a studenty crowd, along with some grizzled locals, including Barack Obama when he's in town. Mon–Sat 5am–8pm.

Orange 75 W Harrison ☏ **312/447-1000.** A happy, sunny place with potted orange trees and a citrus-soaked colour scheme, the second branch of this excellent breakfast café whips up a wonderful left-of-centre brunch. Steak and eggs Benedict ($13.95), "frushi" (sushi rolls filled with fruit instead of fish), French-toast kebabs soaked in coconut and skewered with fruit ($8.95), and gooey jelly-doughnut pancakes ($8.95) draw the salivating masses. *Orange* also serves lunch. Lines are long on the weekend, but there's orange-infused coffee while you wait. See p.180 for original Lakeview location. Mon–Fri 8am–2pm, Sat & Sun 8am–3pm.

Restaurants

The Bongo Room 1152 S Wabash Ave, at E 11th St ☏ **312/291-0100.** For review, see main location in Bucktown on p.178.

Chicago Firehouse Restaurant 1401 S Michigan Ave, at 14th St ☏ **312/786-1401.** What was formerly the wood-beamed, brickwalled courtyard of a 1905 firehouse now houses this upscale New American establishment, where the kitchen turns out standard steaks and chops ($34–46) as well as more modern fare like seared salmon with succotash ($26). The South Loop Peking Duck with caramelized pears, wilted spinach and sweet potatoes ($28) draws its inspiration from nearby Chinatown. Mon–Thurs 11.30am–10pm, Fri & Sat 10.30pm, Sun 4–9pm.

Edwardo's Natural Pizza 521 S Dearborn St, at Congress Pkwy ☏ **312/939-3366.** See Gold Coast location on p.173 for review.

Gioco 1312 S Wabash Ave, at 13th St ☏ **312/939-3870.** This stylish, white-tablecloth Italian spot has been bringing in a hip South Loop crowd by virtue of its simple but never-dull dishes like handmade spaghetti in a Tuscan-style meat ragu ($16) and truffle-scented scallops with white polenta and wild mushroom sauce ($24). Open for lunch Mon–Fri 11.30am–2pm, brunch Sun 9am–2pm, and dinner Sun–Thurs 5–10pm, Fri–Sat 5–11.30pm.

Hackney's 733 S Dearborn St, at W Harrison ☏ **312/461-1116.** This beloved suburban burger chain serves solid comfort food from one of the oldest buildings on Printers Row, its only Chicago location. Best known for the lean and wonderful Hackneyburger, served on dark rye ($8.45) and midriff-enlarging French-fried onion loaves ($6.95), *Hackney's* also has an excellent selection of tap beers. Mon–Fri 10.30am–11pm, Sat & Sun 8.30am–11.30pm.

Mercat a la Planxa 638 S Michigan Ave, at Balbo ☎312/765-0524. This South Loop newcomer has earned rave reviews with well-executed, generously proportioned Catalan specialties – from traditional tapas like garlic shrimp, ham croquettes and *patatas bravas* ($5–9) to fancier items like butter-poached lobster and seared foie gras (around $25). It's all served up in the eye-popping second-floor dining room or sidewalk café, pleasantly away from the bustle further north on Michigan. Lunch is a particularly good deal here, with heaped salads and crusty

▲ Mercat a la Planxa

sandwiches, most under $10. Mon–Thurs 6.30am–11pm, Fri & Sat until midnight, Sun until 10pm.

Penang 2201 S Wentworth Ave, at W 22nd Place ☎312/326-6888. More upscale and stylish than your average Chinatown place, *Penang*

specializes in Malay cuisine with a hint of Japanese. The menu has over 100 dishes on it – including chargrilled beef satay – and dozens of sushi offerings (though certainly not the best sushi you will ever taste). Inexpensive to moderate. Daily 11.30am–11pm.

Tamarind 614 S Wabash Ave, between Harrison and Balbo ☎312/379-0970. Bright, dependable pan-Asian restaurant with a particularly attractive lunch special: soup and salad with a Thai, Vietnamese or Chinese entrée for only $9. Service is friendly and efficient, and there's also a full sushi bar and a fine saki selection. Open daily 11am–11pm.

Three Happiness 209 W Cermak Rd ☎312/842-1964. Not to be confused with the *Three Happiness* on the main Wentworth strip. The spartan decor of this tiny namesake belies its highly praised Mandarin and Cantonese food. The dim sum dishes are worth a visit alone, filled with chicken or lotus seed or custard. The entrees, including stir-fried crab with a fiery chilli seafood sauce, and Mongolian beef are all inexpensive (average $8). Daily 9am–2am.

Zapatista 1307 S Wabash Ave, at 13th St ☎312/435-1307. With its vast sidewalk seating area, this trendy Mexican café – done up inside with rustic touches that befit its revolutionary namesake – is popular for its weekend brunch, starring $5 huevos rancheros, chimichangas, breakfast burritos and the inevitable pitchers of sangria. It's also a fine spot to fuel up before hitting the Museum Campus, with the $9.99 lunch special, or unwind afterward over house-made guacamole and sizzling fajitas. Dinner mains $10–16. Mon–Thurs 11.30am–10pm, Fri until 11pm, Sat 10am–11pm, Sun 10am–9pm.

River North

Cafés and light meals

Al's Number 1 Italian Beef 169 W Ontario St ☎312/943-3222. See West Side location on p.182 for review.

Ed Debevic's 640 N Wells St, at Ontario ☎312/664-1707. Sure, it's one of those wacky, 1950s-style diners where the waitstaff

sing, dance on the tables and serve up malts, burgers and fries. But the catch here is that the staff is also insulting, obnoxious and just plain rude. Not for masochists only – the food is actually quite tasty and cheap (around $9 for a burger and fries). Mon–Thurs 11am–9pm, Fri & Sat 11am–10pm. Breakfast served Sat & Sun 9–11am.

Heaven on Seven 600 N Michigan Ave
T 312/280-7774. Sun–Thurs 11am–10pm, Fri
& Sat 11am–11pm, plus weekend brunch
11am–2pm. Review in original Loop location
(see p.164).

Mr. Beef 666 N Orleans St, at Erie T 312/337-
8500. The little shack looks ready to fall over,
held together only by will and the love of the
diet-hating locals and celebrities. Jay Leno
froths over the giant Italian beef sandwiches
($5), dripping with juice and peppers. No
credit cards. Mon–Fri 8am–5pm, Sat
10.30am–2pm.

**Portillo's Hot Dogs 100 W Ontario St, at N
Clark St** T 312/587-8910. With more
than 28 locations in the Chicago area, this
flagship establishment, somewhere between
a fast-food place and a tacky novelty
restaurant, draws salivating locals, tourists,
taxi drivers and cops for unbeatable hot
dogs, served salad-style on steamed
poppy-seed buns ($2.25). The Italian beef,
thin-sliced meat piled into a hoagy and
slathered with gravy and peppers ($4.35), is
another tangy delight and there are even
some decent salads and veggie options.
Mon–Thurs 10.30am–11pm, Fri & Sat
10.30am–midnight, Sun 11am–11pm.

Restaurants

Ben Pao 52 W Illinois St, at N Dearborn
T 312/222-1888. Dark, lavish decor mixed
with a well-rounded Chinese menu (average
entree $16) that's got a little more pop to it
than you'd expect for a non-Chinatown
spot. The satays are particularly nutty and
the piquant Kung Pao chicken, seven-
flavour beef and cherry bomb shrimp all
pack a punch. There is also a great bar – try
the sake flights – and family-style meals for
groups of six or more ($18.95 per person at
lunch, $23.95 at dinner). Reservations
recommended. Mon–Thurs 11.30am–
9.30pm, Fri 11.30am–11pm, Sat 5–11pm,
Sun 5–9pm.

Brasserie Jo 59 W Hubbard St, at N Dearborn
T 312/595-0800. Celeb chef Jean Joho's
Alsatian brasserie is notable for its rather
striking giant clock, authentic zinc bar and
well-executed fish and steak dishes. The
menu here combines rustic French fare like
steak frites and onion tarts with fusion
dishes like shrimp and vegetables served
inside a filo-dough pouch; the average main
is about $20. There is an outstanding beer
selection and al fresco dining on the terrace

in summer. Wear a hat on Thursdays and
you'll get a free dessert; on Tuesday nights
(5–7pm) free tarte flambee (Alsatian pizza) is
offered at the bar. Sun–Thurs 5–10pm, Fri &
Sat 5–11pm.

**Café Iberico 739 N La Salle St, at W
Superior St** T 312/573-1510. In a town
packed with tapas bars, vast *Café Iberico*, a
perfect spot for large groups, still ranks
among the most popular – with lines out the
door on weekends and near-deafening
sound levels within, fuelled by huge jugs of
sangria and, on weekends, live Spanish
music. The tapas themselves, served up in
large portions, are fresh and surprisingly
cheap ($5–8 each). Stick to the classics –
spicy potatoes, Spanish tortilla, garlic shrimp,
chicken brochettes and the like – and you'll
do fine. Mon–Thurs 11am–11.30pm, Fri
11am–1.30am, Sat noon–1.30am, Sun
noon–11.30pm.

**Chicago Chop House 60 W Ontario St, between
N Dearborn and N Clark streets** T 312/787-
7100. Housed in an old brownstone, this
classic steakhouse with a piano bar is heavy
on Chicago memorabilia with wall-to-wall
photos of the city's mayors, mobsters and
meat merchants. Always packed, it remains
one of the best spots in town for prime cuts
of beef, lamb, steak or broiled fish (average
dinner main $30). Casual attire and attitude.
Mon–Thurs 11.30am–11pm, Fri 11.30am–
11.30pm, Sat 4–11.30pm, Sun 4–11pm.

Coco Pazzo 300 W Hubbard St, at N Franklin St
T 312/836-0900. Authentic Tuscan-style
roasted meats and delicious pasta dishes
served in an airy space with high ceilings,
wood floors and exposed beams. The rabbit-
ragout pasta ($17) is superb. The restaurant's
little sister, *Coco Pazzo Café* in Streeterville
(636 N St Clair St), offers much the same
quality at half the price, in a more informal
setting including a large outdoor terrace.
Open for lunch Mon–Fri 11.30am–2.30pm
and for dinner Mon–Thurs 5.30–10.30pm, Fri
& Sat 5.30–11.30pm, Sun 5–10pm.

**Frontera Grill and Topolobampo 445 N
Clark St, between W Hubbard and W
Illinois** T 312/661-1434. Run by Obama pal
Rick Bayless, these side-by-side Mexican
restaurants are deservedly regarded as the
best in the country. *Frontera Grill* (mains
around $15) is the more fun and casual of
the two but constantly packed; a limited
number of day-of reservations are available,
and groups of 5–10 can also reserve. The

169

appetizer platters are always a wonderful introduction, the guacamole a must and the *moles* sublime. The smarter, art-bedecked *Topolobampo* is almost impossible to get into with less than a couple of weeks' notice. Here, the five-course tasting menus ($85–90) are the best bets for first-timers. *Frontera*: lunch Tues–Fri 11.30am–2.30pm, brunch Sat 10.30am–2.30pm, dinner Tues 5.30–10pm, Wed–Thurs 5–10pm, Fri & Sat 5–11pm. *Topolobampo*: lunch Tues 11.45am–2pm, Wed–Fri 11.30am–2pm; dinner Tues–Thurs 5.30–9.30pm, Fri & Sat 5.30–10.30pm.

Green Door Tavern 678 N Orleans St, at Huron ⊤312/664-5496. A former speakeasy and grocery built just after the Chicago fire, this precariously tilted structure is now home to a friendly tavern which has Chicago memorabilia strewn across the bar. It's a comfortable place to linger and soak up the gritty 1920s aura. The tavern serves over a dozen varieties of burger (around $9), laden with all manner of toppings, and has at least ten beers on tap. Mon–Fri 11.30am–2am, Sat 11.30am–3am, Sun noon–9pm.

Hub 51 51 W Hubbard St, at Dearborn ⊤312/828-0051. Plate-eclipsing nachos and soft tacos, both made with organic chicken on homemade tortillas ($13), are the favourites at this Hubbard St newbie, a vast industrial space that somehow manages to be welcoming. Also on the menu: burgers with hand-cut fries and sushi rolls ($11–15), as well as an abundance of shareable appetizers. Live DJs on weekend nights. Mon–Wed 11.30am–midnight, Thurs & Fri until 2am, Sat until 3am, Sun 5pm–midnight (kitchen closes daily at midnight).

Japonais 600 W Chicago Ave, at N Larrabee St ⊤312/822-9600. French-inflected Japanese food served in designer industrial digs, with red and gold walls and a shimmering, glass-backed waterfall. The black-clad staff sashay through the aisles serving platters of nigiri, sashimi and *maki* ($3–17 each), and house specials including kobe beef rib-eye steak ($72) and maple-smoked duck ($28). For the best people-watching, have a martini in the lounge bar – all low sofas, ottomans and attitude – or outside on the patio in summer. Open for lunch Mon–Fri 11.30am–2.30pm and for dinner Mon–Sat 5–11pm, Sun 5–10pm.

Karyn's Cooked 738 N Wells St, at Superior ⊤312/587-1050. Upscale vegan fare served

in a comfortable, airy space, decked out with bamboo, on the edge of the River North Gallery District. The vegetable- and seitan-laden pizza ($9.50) is a good place to start, followed by the classic Buddha bowl ($10.95) – brown rice with grilled vegetables – or the tofu or seitan steak sandwich ($8.95). Wash it down with organic wine or beer or fresh-squeezed lemonade. Mon 11am–9pm, Tues–Sat 11am–10pm, Sun 10.30am–9pm. For the full "living foods" experience, try the original restaurant, *Karyn's Raw*, in Lincoln Park (see p.176).

Kinzie Chop House 400 N Wells St, at Kinzie ⊤312/822-0191. Business traffic from nearby Merchandise Mart keeps this steakhouse – hunkered right under the El – hopping, especially at lunch, when it's a cheaper but usually just as good, less-crowded alternative to the pricier steakhouses. There's also plenty of other dishes available, from peppercorn halibut to sesame-encrusted *ahi* to rock shrimp risotto. Steaks ranging from $25 to $40 will tip the budget, but most other dishes are, on average, $15. At lunchtime, they also serve burgers, sandwiches and salads (less than $10). Mon–Thurs 11am–10pm, Fri 11am–11pm, Sat 4–11pm, Sun 4–9pm.

Klay Oven 414 N Orleans St, at Kinzie ⊤312/527-3999. There are more menu items than you'll know what to do with at this popular Indian restaurant – but you can't go wrong with a reliable tandoori grill ($9 for half-chicken to $26 for rack of lamb or tiger prawns) or one of the vegetable dishes ($9) with homemade *paneer* (cheese cubes). The restaurant's signature oven cooks up eight varieties of bread and the lunch buffet, with more than 20 dishes on offer, is great value at $12. Open for lunch Mon–Fri 11.30am–2.30pm, Sat & Sun noon–3pm, and for dinner Sun–Thurs 5.30–10pm, Fri & Sat 5.30–10.30pm.

Le Lan 749 N Clark St, at W Superior St ⊤312/280-9100. A welcome antidote to the many raucous, club-like restaurants in the district, sedate *Le Lan* melds French and Vietnamese cuisines in a tasteful dining room accented with fresh bamboo, a jade tiled floor and an eye-catching dragon mural. The creative flourishes continue on the plate with dishes like a sweet-potato and honey-walnut salad ($9) and caramelized diver scallops with wild boar ribs ($28). Desserts like orange-ginger crème brûlée on a ginger snap cookie ($7) are not to be missed. Come on Tuesday for the $38 three-course prix-fixe, which is terrific value. Open for lunch Mon–Fri 11.30am–2pm and dinner Mon–Wed 5.30–10pm, Thurs–Sat 5.30–11pm.

MK 868 N Franklin St, at W Chestnut ☎312/482-9179. Trendy, upscale place named after founding chef Michael Kornick. They've perfected the concept of minimalist chic, offering New American cuisine that draws from local farms when possible, alongside a great wine list and an imaginative dessert selection (banana brioche bread-pudding with salted-peanut ice cream). Mains $27–52. Reservations recommended. Jackets recommended for men. Sun–Thurs 5.30–9.30pm, Fri & Sat 5.30–10.30pm.

Nacional 27 325 W Huron St, at N Orleans St ☎312/664-2727. This snazzy nuevo Latino restaurant named after the 27 nations of Latin America makes a valiant effort to include every one of them on the wide-ranging menu. Order a bunch of sides, like citrussy Mexican-style ceviche ($8–10), smoked chicken empanadas ($7.95) and barbecued lamb tacos ($3.95), then move on to fresh grilled fish, steak or Latin comfort foods like shrimp enchiladas ($22.95), washed down with a Brazilian *caipirinha* or Cuban *mojito*. On Wine-Down Wednesdays you can get a five-course meal with wine pairings for $45. Mon–Thurs 5.30–9.30pm, Fri & Sat 5.30–11pm. Bar open later.

Naha 500 N Clark St, at Illinois ☎312/321-6242. A trusted veteran of the River North dining scene, *Naha* specializes in inventive, Mediterranean-inspired preparations of regional, sustainable foods, all served up in an elegant, minimalist setting. Keep things simple at lunch with the Angus beef burger with hand-cut fries ($14), but try something wild for dinner, like "honey-lacquered" aged Moulard duck breast with huckleberries, celery root, broccoli rabe and port ($34). If you just want to sample, head to the lounge, which has a menu of small plates including spicy tuna, lamb kebabs and flatbreads, as well as an excellent platter of Spanish cured meats and cheeses, olives, peppers, dates and the like. Open for lunch Mon–Fri 11.30am–2pm and for dinner Mon–Thurs 5.30–9.30pm, Fri & Sat 5.30–10pm.

Osteria Via Stato 620 N State St, at E Ontario ☎312/642-8450. Stone walls and chunky wooden communal tables set the scene for the three-course prix-fixe dinner ($36.95), served in the traditional Italian style: antipasti, pasta and main course. The food is good, if not spectacular, but the location is convenient to the Mag Mile, and the ample sidewalk seating comfortable on a warm summer night. Desserts, notably silky *gelato* and an array of Italian cheeses are priced separately. Mon–Thurs 5–10pm, Fri & Sat 5–11pm, Sun 4–8.30pm, with adjoining wine bar open for lunch Mon–Sat 11.30am–4pm.

Pizano's 864 N State St, at Chestnut ☎312/751-1766. See Loop location, p.166, for review.

Pizzeria Uno 29 E Ohio, at Wabash ☎312/321-1000. The pizzeria that spawned an empire still serves delectable, fresh deep-dish pies from its original location. With only eighteen tables, it's far more intimate than its sprawling sibling, *Pizzeria Due*, a few blocks away. Avoid peak hours (weekend nights), when waits are interminable, and be sure to place your order with the host at the door to minimize lag time at your table – pizzas take about 45min to cook. Mon–sat 11.30am–1am Mon–Sat, Sun until midnight.

Tempo Café 6 E Chestnut St, at State ☎312/943-4373. This round-the-clock diner works for a quick, filling meal at any time of day but is especially good for breakfast – arrive before 9am to beat the lines – with massive three-egg omelettes ($8.25–10) stuffed with tasty fillings like apples and cheddar ("the Michigan") and served in the skillet with home fries and toast. Also popular for a late-night bite, as it's just a few blocks from the Rush Street bar scene. Cash only. Daily 24hr.

Vermilion 10 W Hubbard, at N State St ☎312/527-1060. Trendy Hubbard St spot featuring Latin-Indian cuisine in a sleek, loungey setting. Tapas dishes are great for a light meal; try the duck vindaloo arepa with pomegranate molasses ($12) or the blue-corn-crusted scallops ($12). Main dishes include lobster in curry-leaf gravy with coconut rice ($35) and chili-glazed, blackened tamarind ribs with sweet corn salsa and tortilla crisps ($24). For dessert, go with the Vermilion Hedonism, a molten chocolate cake with Indian spices and fruit sorbet ($10). Open for lunch Mon–Fri 11.30–2.30pm and for dinner Sun–Thurs 5–10pm, Fri & Sat 5–11pm.

Vong's Thai Kitchen 6 W Hubbard St, at State ☎312/644-8664. Globe-trotting celebrity chef Jean-Georges Vongerichten makes his presence felt in the Windy City with this inventive and affordable French-Thai spot. Sultry red walls set the mood for spicy cuisine, including pad Thai, crispy wide noodles and curries, all with your choice of meat or veggies ($9–15 at lunch, $14–20 at dinner). If you're not up for a full meal, order a "Black Plate" appetizer combo – shrimp and chicken satay, sushi rolls and salad ($14.95). Open for lunch Mon–Fri 11.30am–2pm, Sat noon–5pm; dinner Mon–Thurs 5.30–10pm, Fri 5.30–11pm, Sat 5–11pm, Sun 5–9pm.

The Magnificent Mile and Streeterville

Cafés and light meals

Eppy's Deli 224 E Ontario St, between N St Clair and N Fairbanks ☎312/943-7797. Small Jewish deli with a big personality just steps from the hyper-touristy Magnificent Mile. Among its charming quirks: the price of the soup (when you buy a sandwich) is geared to the air temperature, even in the dead of winter, and Larry, the owner, makes a point of writing snarky posters about the neigh-bouring sandwich chain *Subway*. Your best bet is the Reuben – juicy corned beef, Swiss, sauerkraut and Russian dressing on rye toast – which comes with two sides, a pickle and a fountain soda for $8.75. Daily 7am–8pm.

Fox & Obel 401 E Illinois, at N. McClurg Court ☎312/410-7301. The city's best gourmet market is an ideal spot to shop for a picnic lunch, but it also sports a fabulous indoor café that serves well-priced vittles all day long. Specialties include the Cobb omelette ($9) at breakfast, stuffed with scallions, tomatoes, bacon, avocado and blue cheese; the signature turkey club ($11) at lunch, featuring turkey, Black Forest ham, bacon, muenster cheese and basil-pesto mayonnaise on whole wheat; and the grilled flank steak with celery root and potato purée ($15) at dinner. Daily 6am–midnight.

Oak Street Beachstro 1001 N Lake Shore Drive ☎312/915-4100. Open-air restaurant on the sands of Oak Street Beach, serving typical American food (not bistro fare): sandwiches, salads, quesadillas and meaty entrees, all at prices about fifty percent higher than you'd pay inland (sandwiches $10–16, entrees $21–27). Still, the location can't be beat, and it's a great pit-stop if you're on a bicycle. Open May–Sept weather permitting Mon–Fri 11am–10.30pm, Sat & Sun 8am–10.30pm.

Restaurants

Billy Goat Tavern 430 N Michigan Ave, at E Kinzie St ☎312/222-1525. This dingy and beloved bar/grill lurking in the shadows underneath Michigan Ave was already famous when John Belushi immortalized the staff's ranting on *Saturday Night Live* in the 1970s. ("Cheezeborger, cheezeborger! No Pepsi – Coke! No fries – chips!") Though the tavern opened a second, sanitized location on Navy Pier (skip it), fame hasn't changed the original spot at all, which still serves dangerously greasy burgers ($3–5) and Schlitz beer on tap in a wood-panelled room with cracked linoleum flooring – either great atmosphere or none at all, depending on your view. *Tribune* scribes regularly perch on the grimy old stools. Cash only. Mon–Fri 7am–2am, Sat 10am–3am, Sun 11am–2am.

Kamehachi 240 E Ontario St, at N Fairbanks Ct ☎312/587-0600. See original Old Town location on p.174 for review.

Lawry's 100 E Ontario St, at Michigan Ave ☎312/787-5000. Yes, it's the same *Lawry's* that produces those bottles of seasoned salt available in supermarkets but the restaurant has the best prime rib in town – big juicy slabs ($31–49, depending on the cut and size), served from a rolling cart. Other than steak, the menu is rather limited: ribs, lobster tail, a fish of the day and a bountiful "spinning salad" but meat's the thing, anyway, and the restaurant is something of an institution, located in a grand old mansion with intimate alcoves and a regal spiral staircase. Open for lunch Mon–Fri 11.30am–2pm and for dinner Mon–Thurs 5–10.30pm, Fri & Sat 5–11pm, Sun 3–10pm.

NoMI in the *Park Hyatt*, 800 N Michigan Ave, at Chicago ☎312/239-4030. The 7th-floor views of Streeterville and the lake beyond (especially from the outdoor terrace) are reason enough to pay a visit if your budget allows. The menu jumps all over the place, with pretty standard breakfasts of eggs and waffles ($17); lunches of sandwiches, pasta and sushi ($27–34), and dinners featuring sushi along with French-inspired mains, like smoked prawn risotto ($36). Open daily for breakfast, lunch 11.30am–1.30pm and dinner 6–9pm.

Gold Coast

Cafés and light meals

Original Pancake House 22 E Bellevue Place, at N Rush ☎312/642-7917. Old-fashioned, ultra-casual breakfast joint with ample outdoor seating that's mobbed on the weekends (get here early or be prepared to wait). Egg dishes are hot and fresh, while the pancakes are fluffy – try the sticky apple-pancake house special – and the coffee surprisingly full-bodied for a diner. Almost everything's under $10. Other locations in Lincoln Park (see p.175) and Hyde Park (see p.184). Mon–Fri 7am–3pm, Sat–Sun 7am–5pm.

🏃 **3rd Coast** 1260 N Dearborn St, at Goethe. ☎312/649-0730. Tucked on the garden level of a Gold Coast apartment building, this neighbourhood favourite is known for its friendly service and its excellent and well-priced sandwiches ($6–10), salads and all-day breakfasts. Dinner entrees ($9.50–15) range from tacos to pasta to strip steak, but you're also free to linger over a cheese plate and a bottle of wine – and take what you don't finish back to your hotel. Daily 7am–midnight.

Restaurants

Café Spiaggia 980 N Michigan Ave, at E Oak St ☎312/280-2750. At this elegant but easygoing café you get the refined Italian cuisine of renowned sister restaurant *Spiaggia* (next door) without the stuffiness or the stratospheric prices. The decor is inspired by fifteenth-century Italy with marble floors, frescos and Venetian glass light fixtures. It's especially pleasant at lunch, when you can best enjoy lovely views over Michigan Ave and the lakefront from the floor-to-ceiling glass windows. Pastas are $16–18, mains around $25. Open for lunch daily 11.30am–2.30pm and for dinner Sun–Thurs 5.30–9pm, Fri & Sat 5.30–10pm.

Edwardo's Natural Pizza 1212 N Dearborn St, at Division St ☎312/337-4490. This friendly local chain's monumentally proportioned deep-dish pizza is something to behold, with its crispy crust and toppings made fresh ingredients like spicy, juicy sausage and crunchy vegetables with. Try the spinach-stuffed pie: the small ($17.25) can easily feed two. Other locations in the South Loop (see p.167), Lincoln Park (see p.176) and Hyde Park (see p.184). Sun–Thurs 11am–10pm, Fri & Sat 11am–11pm.

Le Colonial 937 N Rush St, at Walton ☎312/255-0088. The atmosphere merges French chic with Asian exoticism – all airy white space, swirling fans, palm trees and rattan furniture – while the menu gives gourmet zing to tasty Vietnamese dishes like wok-seared monkfish. There is also a lively bar and terrace upstairs and a sidewalk café open in summer. Lunch mains $17–25; dinner mains $18–31. Open for lunch daily 11.30am–2.30pm and for dinner Mon–Fri 5–11pm, Sat 5pm–midnight, Sun 5–10pm.

Lux Bar 18 E Bellevue Place, at N Rush ☎312/642-3400. This restaurant and bar successfully cultivates a casual neighbourhood ambience in a swanky space outfitted with marble, onyx, brass, mahogany and leather. The menu has a raft of shareable appetizers ($6–12) like quesadillas, crab cakes, potato skins and buttermilk-fried chicken sliders; burgers and sandwiches served with hand-cut fries ($9–15); fancier entrees such as filet mignon ($30); and all-day breakfasts ($9–14). In warm weather, ask to sit on the festive balcony. Mon–Fri 10.30am–2am, Sat 9am–3am, Sun 9am–2am.

🏃 **Tru** 676 N St Clair St, at E Huron St ☎312/202-0001. Consistently ranked as one of the top fine-dining options in this part of the country, *Tru* offers a three-course prix-fixe dinner for $95 and a nine-course seasonal prix-fixe "designed to create sensory overload" for $145, along with à la carte luxury items like whole-roasted foie gras ($145), back on the menu after being briefly outlawed by Mayor Daley. Chef Rick Tramonto delights in palate-tingling combinations such as salmon with Granny Smith apples or venison with cocoa, olives and

blood oranges. The impeccably white, minimalist decor is a serene backdrop for each global fusion dish's artful conception. Reserve well in advance; jackets required. Mon–Thurs 5.30–9.30pm, Fri & Sat 5–11pm.

Old Town

Cafés and light meals

Old Jerusalem 1411 N Wells St ☎312/944-0459. The hummus, served with piping-hot pita bread, is to die for at this cheap, bare-bones eatery, which also serves savoury renditions of the standard Middle Eastern offerings – tabouli, *baba ganoush* and, especially, falafel, served hot and crispy with garlicky tahini. Salads and appetizers are around $4, sandwiches $5–6, entrees $10–11. Sun–Thurs 11am–10.30pm, Fri & Sat 11am–11pm.

Twisted Sister Bakery 1543 N Wells St, at North Ave ☎312/932-1128. This cheerful, stylish new bakery has some tables but mostly caters to the takeout crowd by making a few tasty treats extremely well: thickly frosted cupcakes, creamy fruit tarts, and – best of all – crisp, buttery cookies ($13.99 per pound) in flavours like snickerdoodle, peanut butter, chocolate chip, molasses and corny lime. Also serves coffee to the local Intelligentsia. Mon–Fri 10am–10pm, Sat 9am–10pm, Sun 9am–9pm.

Restaurants

Adobo Grill 1610 N Wells St, at North Ave ☎312/266-7999. Next door to the *Second City* comedy club, in the Pipers Alley Building, this upscale Mexican place is known for excellent guacamole (mixed at your table to taste), strong margaritas and reasonably priced haute Mexican fare. Try such appetizers as the goat-cheese empanadas ($8.50) or tuna ceviche with mango and cilantro ($9.75); main courses include butternut squash and wild mushroom enchiladas ($13.95) and Mexican presentations of flank steak, pork chops and tilapia. Allot ample time if you're hoping to see a show, as the service is far from swift. There's another branch at 2005 W Division St in Wicker Park. Mon–Thurs

5.30–10pm, Fri 5.30–11.30pm, Sat noon–11.30pm, Sun noon–9.30pm.
Dinotto Ristorante 215 W North Ave, at Wells ☎312/202-0302. A good dinner spot across the street from Second City, the cosy and ever-thriving *Dinotto* does a brisk trade in traditional, no-frills Italian fare (average entree $16), including pasta tricolor *rotolo* in a creamy tomato sauce, steamed mussels, and chicken with gorgonzola. Service can be erratic, though. Mon–Thurs noon–11pm, Fri & Sat noon–midnight, Sun 5–10pm.
Kamehachi 1400 N Wells St, at Schiller ☎312/664-3663. Opened in 1967, *Kamehachi* was the first Japanese restaurant in Chicago and still offers supremely fresh, moderately priced sushi ($2–4 per piece, $5–12 per roll). The dragon roll, "Chicago crazy" roll (tuna, yellowtail, salmon and crab) and *gomae* (blanched spinach with peanut sauce) are all worth trying. There are two other restaurant locations, both in Near North (see p.172). Mon–Sat 11.30am–2am, Sun 4.30pm–midnight.
Salpicón 1252 N Wells St, at W Scott St ☎312/988-7715. Former *Frontera Grill/Topolobampo* chef Priscilla Satkoff serves up authentic, original Mexican haute cuisine in a colourful but mellow space just a few blocks from Second City. Entrees ($18–28) are simple and fresh: think charcoal-grilled fresh fish with salsa fresca and chicken *mole*. Cool, sweet desserts like *naranjas en dulce* (boiled orange quarters in a cinnamon-orange syrup) round out the experience. Open for dinner Sun–Thurs 5–10pm, Fri & Sat 5–11pm, and for brunch Sun 11am–2.30pm.
Topo Gigio Ristorante 1516 N Wells St, between W North Ave and W Burton Place ☎312/266-9355. Always crowded, welcoming Italian hotspot in Old Town, with relaxed garden seating in warm weather and superlative northern Italian fare year-round: chicken *cacciatore* and veal *saltimbocca* are among

the *secondi* ($14–28), while the exceptional pasta dishes ($14–20), from spaghetti with meatballs to tortellini *alla panna*, keep it pure and simple. Mon–Sat 11.30am–11pm, Sun 4–10pm.

Twin Anchors 1655 N Sedgwick St, at W Eugenie ☎312/266-1616. The long waits and loud, crowded dive-bar surroundings only seem to enhance the reputation of

this decades-old, nautical-themed institution, a speakeasy once upon a time. Succulent barbecue is the specialty – the meat slides off the bone of the baby-back ribs ($21) – but you can also get standard pub fare like burgers and sandwiches ($6.50–11). Mon–Thurs 5–11pm, Fri 5pm–midnight, Sat noon–midnight, Sun noon–10.30pm.

Lincoln Park

Cafés and light meals

Bourgeois Pig 738 W Fullerton Ave, at N Burling St ☎773/883-5282. The atmosphere is appropriately dark and literary at this DePaul-area café, with sandwiches (around $7.50) named after canonical works – try the healthy Sun Also Rises, smoked turkey and Swiss on sundried-tomato bread smothered with hummus and sprouts – as well as pastries, coffee and forty kinds of tea. Don't miss the black-and-white photos of Old Chicago upstairs. Mon–Fri 6.30am–11pm, Sat & Sun 8am–11pm.

Noble Tree Coffee 2444 N Clark St, at Arlington Place ☎773/248-1500. New independent coffeehouse with comfy chairs, antique fixtures, well-stocked bookshelves, art exhibits, fireplaces and free wi-fi spread over three storeys of a creaky-floored Lincoln Park townhouse. Top-notch local pies and strong coffee. Daily 7am–11pm.

Original Pancake House 2020 N Lincoln Park West, between Dickens and Armitage ☎773/929-8130. See Gold coast location on p.173 for review.

Potbelly Sandwich Works 2264 N Lincoln Ave, at W Webster Ave ☎773/528-1405. The original location of this popular sandwich chain – now with twenty branches throughout the Chicago area, including the Loop (see p.165) – still looks as it did in the days when it was an antique shop (selling potbelly stoves, naturally). The lines are always long, but they move fast, and the result is worth the wait. Try "The Wreck" (salami, roast beef, turkey and ham with Swiss cheese, on a warm roll), then watch as it's heaped with your choice of deli toppings, to get your $4 – yes, $4 – worth. Daily 11am–11pm.

Toast 746 W Webster Ave at N Burling St ☎773-935-5600. See Bucktown location on p.180 for review.

Restaurants

Alinea 1723 N Halsted ☎312/867-0110. At what is widely regarded as Chicago's best restaurant, housed in a discreet townhouse and helmed by chef-owner Grant Achatz, the attention to detail is impeccable, from the perfectly timed service to the elegant decor to sensational food that dabbles in what's become known as molecular gastronomy (think gels, emulsions and foams, with food pairings as seemingly bizarre as lobster and popcorn). There are two prix-fixe tasting menus: 13 courses for $145 and the epic 24-course "Tour" for $225, with wine pairings sending the bill still further into space. Allow plenty of time – the Tour can take up to five hours – and reserve well in advance. No jeans; jackets recommended for men. Wed–Fri 5.30–9.30pm, Sat & Sun 5–9.30pm.

Athenian Room 807 W Webster Ave, at N Halsted ☎773/348-5155. Students from nearby DePaul University flock to this Greek diner for the cheap, tasty gyros, Greek fries, and salads, though service hovers between casual and invisible. Entree prices range from $4.50 to $11. Daily 11am–10pm.

Boka 1729 N Halsted St, at W Willow ☎312/337-6070. A stylish choice close to the Steppenwolf Theatre, *Boka* presents creative New American fare in an eye-catching space with striking fabric "sculptures" draped across the ceiling. Expect appetizers like Maine diver scallops with pea wasabi sauce and entrees ($26–38) like braised beef cheeks with broccoli hash and cauliflower-Yukon potato mash. There's a see-and-be-seen patio open in summertime, and the pre-theatre three-course prix-fixe dinner for $35 per person (served until 6.15pm) is good value. Reservations recommended. Sun–Thurs 5–10pm, Fri & Sat 5–10.30pm.

Bricks 1909 N Lincoln Ave, at Wisconsin ☎773/255-0851. Snazzy subterranean pizzeria that eschews the familiar deep-dish route for perfectly executed thin-crust variations. Toppings run from the traditional (sausage and pepperoni) to the nouveau (pureed artichoke sauce and red peppers). Good prices ($10.50 for a small, $20 for a large) and a fine beer list to boot. Sun & Mon 5–10pm, Wed & Thurs 5pm–midnight, Fri & Sat 5pm–2am.

Café Luigi 2548 N Clark St, between W Wrightwood & W Deming Place ☎773/404-0200. New York-style pizza, done in the Second City fashion. Choose between thick and thin crust and then load on toppings from ham and green peppers to spinach and eggplant (about $3 a slice, or $13 for a fourteen-inch pie). Perhaps the most compelling things here are the pepperoni-stuffed breadsticks. Mon–Sat 11am–10pm, Sun 11.30am–9pm.

🏃 **Charlie Trotter's 816 W Armitage Ave, at N Halsted St** ☎773/248-6228. Superlative American and continental cuisine in a restored Lincoln Park brownstone from one of the country's most renowned chefs. The food isn't as experimental as you'll find at *Alinea*, but degustation menus still run $125–200 per person. Reservations required; jackets required for men. Two seatings per night: Tues–Thurs 6–6.30pm & 9–9.30pm, Fri & Sat 5.30–6.30pm & 8.30–9.30pm.

Chicago Pizza and Oven Grinder Co. 2121 N Clark St, at W Dickens Ave ☎773/248-2570. Local favourite specializing in grinders (Italian bread stuffed with Italian meats and cheeses, then baked) and pizza pot pie (a half- or full-pound bowlful of mushrooms, sausage, cheese and sauce, topped with bread dough and baked). Excellent salads and flatbreads, too. Waits can be long, giving you plenty of time to check out the site of the St Valentine's Day Massacre across the street (see p.97). Mon–Thurs 4–11pm, Fri 4pm–midnight, Sat noon–midnight, Sun noon–11pm.

Dee's Mandarin Restaurant 1114 W Armitage Ave, at N Seminary Ave ☎773/477-1500. Probably the best Chinese food outside Chinatown, this serene restaurant offers delectable sesame chicken ($11), wonderfully fresh garlic shrimp ($14) and refreshing Mai Tais. To the chagrin of Szechuan purists, sushi has recently been added to the menu. Live music on weekends; outdoor seating in summer. Sun–Thurs 4.30–10pm, Fri & Sat until 11pm.

Edwardo's Natural Pizza 2622 N Halsted St, between Schubert and Wrightwood ☎773/871-3400. See Gold Coast location on p.173 for review.

Geja's Café 340 W Armitage Ave, at N Orleans St ☎773/281-9101. Perfectly romantic and popular restaurant that serves up excellent fondue in a candlelit setting snugly decorated with oodles of dark wood (for extra privacy, ask for one of the curtained-off booths). Try the combination cheese and chocolate fondue special, with salad and coffee ($20 per person). Mon–Thurs 5–10.30pm, Fri 5pm–midnight, Sat 4.45pm–12.30am, Sun 4.30–10pm.

Hema's Kitchen 2411 N Clark St, at W Arlington Place ☎773/529-1705. For review see Rogers Park location on p.186.

Karyn's Raw 1901 N Halsted St, between Armitage and Willow ☎312/255-1590. For review see Near North location on p.170.

🏃 **North Pond 2610 N Cannon Drive, in Lincoln Park** ☎773/477-5845. One of the loveliest restaurant settings in the city, nestled beside a pond with skyline views. The changing menu deftly combines fresh organic ingredients in appetizers like a poached farm egg with polenta and glazed chanterelle mushrooms in a Parmesan emulsion ($12). Entrees ($32–38) range from grilled marinated goat leg medallions with butternut squash to grass-fed New York strip steak with beets; there's not much for vegetarians. The seasonal tasting menu is $85 per person. A great Chicago Sunday ritual is to linger over a two-course brunch with house-made pastries ($32 per person), then take a walk in the park. Reservations recommended. Open for lunch June–Oct only Tues–Fri 11.30am–1.30pm; dinner year-round Tues–Sun 5.30–10pm; brunch year-round Sun 11am–2pm

Rose Angelis 1314 W Wrightwood Ave, at N Lakewood ☎773/296-0081. Unpretentious, off-the-beaten-path Italian spot with tasty fresh pasta (spinach half-moons stuffed with ricotta and pesto or ravioloni filled with salmon), as well as grilled fish and meat, at reasonable prices – entrees average $15 at

Chicago food

It's taken nearly a century for Chicago to shed its image as a rough-and-tumble meatpacking town, with accordingly crude culinary tastes, but the city has finally gained gastronomic credibility. You can still get a plate-eclipsing porterhouse at one of its venerable steakhouses or a gut-busting deep-dish pizza, of course, but there's plenty more. Nowadays, Chicago's top-tier restaurants are as stylish and sophisticated as any in the country, while its plentiful tapas bars, cheap-but-terrific ethnic restaurants, old-school delicatessens and funky neighbourhood bistros round out the range of delectable options.

Pizza advert ▲

Pavement café ▼

Street stall snacks ▼

Classic Chicago

Even as tastes have shifted away from eating meat at every meal, carnivores will find a lot to love about Chicago. Among its best-known restaurants are classic **steakhouses** like *Lawry's* and *Chicago Chop House*, both of which serve up huge, tender slabs of beef with traditional sides like potatoes and creamed spinach. There's plenty to be found on the cheaper side of the spectrum, however. The **hot dog**, introduced in Chicago at the World's Fair of 1893, was an instant hit as an inexpensive, filling meal and quickly caught on in homes as well as at baseball parks around the country. In the Windy City, hot dogs are still served "Chicago style" at places like *Portillo's Hot Dogs* and *The Wiener's Circle*, with plenty of veggies (see box below) but no ketchup.

The city's historic obsession with red meat is further evident with the **Italian beef sandwich**, which became popular during the Depression. When beef was scarce, cooks in the West Side's Little Italy sliced the meat super-thin and served it on chewy rolls drenched with gravy. Today, *Mr. Beef* in River North is the most famous purveyor of this sloppy delight. Indeed, the only classic Chicago food *not* requiring the death of an animal is **deep-dish pizza**, invented

Top that

Possible **toppings** for the classic Chicago hot dog:

▶▶ mustard
▶▶ pickle spears
▶▶ chopped onion
▶▶ celery salt
▶▶ green relish

▶▶ tomato wedges
▶▶ sport peppers
(a type of pickled hot pepper)

in 1943 at *Pizzeria Uno* in River North. Two or three inches thick, the pies are loaded with cheese, veggies and, if desired, sausage or pepperoni, and topped with chunky tomato sauce.

Ethnic cuisine

Arriving during the late nineteenth and early twentieth centuries, European immigrants quickly made their impact on Chicago life. As these pockets of Polish, German, Swedish, Greek and Ukrainian settlers spread, throughout the city, so did their cooking traditions, resulting in a city rich with a variety of ethnic cuisines.

Wander along Milwaukee Street near Logan Square and you'll come across shops selling everything from Polish sausages to pierogi. *The Berghoff* in the Loop is an excellent place to sample waist-expanding German fare. Greektown is the obvious place to head for a hearty moussaka or Greek pastries, while Andersonville is the home of fine Swedish cuisine and baked goods – be sure to try pickled herring, and lutefisk; or try out one of the many branches of Ann Sather.

Chicago boasts some mind-blowing Mexican fare – head to the Pilsen neighbourhood for some of the best tacos and fajitas north of the border, or to the Maxwell Street Market on Sundays for savoury Mexican street food. And while visitors and Chicagoans alike frequent the dim sum restaurants of Chinatown, the more adventurous make the pilgrimage north to Rogers Park's "Little Bombay", where Chicago's sizeable South Asian population is thriving along Devon Avenue. Here, you'll find a plethora of inexpensive Indian, Bangladeshi and Pakistani restaurants, such as *Sabri Nihari*.

▲ Maxwell Street Market Mexican

▼ Swedish bakery cakes

Haute Chicago

Over the last two decades, Chicago's culinary establishment has worked hard to transcend its meat-and-potatoes roots, with the result being that the city now boasts some of the country's finest restaurants. The god of Chicago's epicurean innovation was **Charlie Trotter**, who in the late 1980s pioneered the use of the tasting menu to showcase wildly inventive fusion cuisine at his eponymous restaurant, located in a serene Lincoln Park townhouse.

Other celebrity chefs include the indefatigable **Rick Bayless**, who is famed for his TV show and numerous cookbooks and single-handedly subverted the notion that Mexican food is all chips and enchiladas with his superb Frontera Grill, now regarded as the best Mexican restaurant in the US. A taste of one of the restaurant's *chile braises* or moles should let you know why.

In 2005, provocative chef/owner **Grant Achatz** achieved national acclaim with his Lincoln Park restaurant *Alinea*, showcasing a futuristic form of fine dining that tantalizes, engages and sometimes perplexes the senses. The first course of an epic tasting menu of 13 or 24 creations could be anything from flavoured gas that you pump into your mouth with an atomizer to a grape wrapped in peanut butter served atop a device that resembles a steel torture implement.

In *Alinea's* wake, a number of restaurants have fused the tasting-menu concept with that of the tapas bar, allowing casual, social eaters to try some of the city's best food without blowing the bank. In the lounge of **Rick Tramonte**'s *Tru*, you can sample "small bites" off the tasting menu for a fraction of the usual cost.

Charlie Trotter in his kitchen ▲

Dinner at Tru ▼

Raspberry dessert ▼

dinner, $10 at lunch. It's best avoided during peak weekend evenings when the noise level detracts from the intimate setting. Open for lunch Tues–Fri 11am–2.30pm and for dinner Tues–Thurs 5–10pm, Fri & Sat 5–11pm, Sun 4.30–9pm.

Stanley's Kitchen and Tap 1970 N Lincoln Ave, at W Armitage Ave ☏312/642-0007. Loved and loathed in equal measure, *Stanley's* has made its name with its all-you-can-eat weekend comfort-food brunch ($12), served until 4pm. Not for the calorie-shy, the greasy fried chicken, macaroni and cheese, made-to-order omelettes, waffles and biscuits and gravy will keep you full for the day. Another artery-clogging bargain is the $10 Monday-night all-you-can-eat buffet. If you'd prefer to fill up on beer, there's plenty to choose from in the taproom. Mon–Fri 11am–2am, Sat 10am–3am, Sun 10am–2am.

Sultan's Market 2521 N Clark St, at W Deming Place ☏312/638-9151. Located amidst so-so sports bars, *Sultan's Market* is a breath of fresh Levant air. The excellent kefta kabob ($5), falafel sandwiches and Jerusalem salad ($3 each) are at the top of the heap here. And on your way out, don't forget to grab some Medjool dates or a piece of halvah. Mon–Thurs 10am–10pm, Fri & Sat 10am–midnight, Sun 10am–9pm.

🏃 **Taco and Burrito Palace #2 2459 N Halsted St, at Fullerton** ☏773/248-0740. This DePaul-area late-night Mexican joint doles out exceptional chimichangas, tacos, and burritos in humungous portions for around $5 apiece; full dinners cost under $10. The line snakes out the door late Friday and Saturday nights. Sun–Thurs 10am–3am, Fri & Sat 10am–5am.

Twisted Lizard 1964 N Sheffield Ave, at W Armitage Ave ☏773/929-1414. Given the small size of this restaurant's bar and the basement location, the usually long waits (worst on weekend nights) can seem even longer. Still, it's a good spot for no-frills filling and tasty Mexican standards – try the

queso fundido (baked cheese) – and pitchers of margaritas, in one of Lincoln Park's trendiest areas. Entrees $11–17. A patio is open for lunch daily in summer. At other times of year the hours are Sun–Thurs 4–10pm, Fri & Sat 11am–midnight.

Via Carducci 1419 W Fullerton Ave, at N Southport ☏773/665-1981. On the western fringes of Lincoln Park, this cosy neighbourhood trattoria serves monumental portions of hearty Southern Italian food. Order pasta classics like rigatoni primavera and spaghetti carbonara along with chicken Vesuvio and daily fish specials at dinner (mains $11–20). Lunch is a great deal, with pizzas and panini for around $8 and pastas and meat entrees around $10. Service can teeter on the lackadaisical but is always gracious. Mon–Thurs 11am–10pm, Fri 11am–11pm, Sat & Sun 4–11pm.

Vinci 1732 N Halsted St, at Willow ☏312/266-1199. Just up the street from Steppenwolf Theatre (the troupe of actors has their own table here), this warm and inviting place serves up sizeable and tasty portions of rustic Italian fare, from ricotta-and-spinach-filled ravioli with brown butter-sage sauce ($17.50) to marinated hen grilled under a hot brick ($18). Reservations recommended for pre-theatre meals, especially on weekends. Tues–Thurs 5.30–10pm, Fri & Sat 5.30–11pm, Sun 10.30am–2.30pm & 3.30–9.30pm.

🏃 **The Wiener's Circle 2622 N Clark St, at W Wrightwood Ave** ☏773/477-7444. Whether the staff is arguing amongst themselves or verbally assaulting you (in what appears to be good fun), you'll enjoy some of the best hot dogs in town, best eaten loaded up with all the pickles, peppers, onions and tomatoes you can get.The dialogue between the staff and drunken patrons can get a bit racy late at night, so be warned. Nothing at this traditional Chicago hot dog stand costs over $5. Mon–Thurs 10.30am–4.30am, Fri & Sat 10.30am–5.30am, Sun 10.30am–4am.

Lakeview and Andersonville

Cafés and light meals

Ann Sather 909 W Belmont Ave, at Sheffield ☏773/348-2378. With locations in Lakeview and Andersonville *Ann Sather* is a chain of

cosy Swedish diners that's become Chicago's most popular breakfast spot. The cinnamon rolls are legendary (2 for $3), while the Swedish pancakes with lingon-berries ($7.95) come a close second. Stick with the Swedish items on the increasingly American menu. Breakfast or lunch here will run from $7–11. Mon–Fri 7am–3pm, Sat & Sun 7am-4pm.

Intelligentsia 3123 N Broadway, at W Barry ☎773/348-4522. While its coffee – though good – may not be the *Starbucks*-killing super-brew that its proponents claim, there's no doubt that this is a choice spot to kill a few hours with a cup of joe, a pastry and a *Chicago Reader*. There is also an excellent tea selection from white to black to green to oolong. The hum of quiet conversation is never loud enough to break your concentration, though it does get very busy on weekends. A coffee and a pastry here shouldn't run more than $4–5. Mon–Fri 6am–10pm, Sat & Sun 7am–10pm.

M. Henry 5707 N Clark ☎773/561-1600. Great breakfast and lunch place located in Andersonville, serving traditional sandwich options: jerk chicken ($8.95), turkey ($9.25), and a Cajun spiced tilapia wrap ($9.50). The brunch and breakfast options are expansive and include the Dulce Banana Rumba ($8.75), which is thick brioche toast stacked with bananas and sprinkled with toasted pecans and raisins. The pancakes ($6.25) are heavenly, drizzled with a pomegranate bisque, while the wedges of vegetable quiche ($8.25), complete with roasted poblano peppers and shallots, are excellent. Worth the wait – there are very long lines at the weekend. Breakfast or lunch here will run anywhere from $7–10. Tues–Fri 7am–2.30pm, Sat & Sun 8am–3pm.

Orange 3231 N Clark St, between Aldine and Belmont ☎773/549-4400. See South Loop location on p.167 for review.

Southport Grocery 3552 N Southport Ave ☎773/665-0100. Chic café dining at this family-oriented deli/café, which combines quality ingredients to create such delicacies as the grilled brie sandwich ($8.50), a beet and fennel salad ($8) and a host of brunch items, like their bread pudding pancakes ($9). Wine pairing selections add extra finesse to the menu. There's outdoor seating in summer and a special menu for kids. Lunch or brunch here will cost $8–12. Mon–Fri 8am–7pm, Sat 8am–5pm, Sun 8am–3pm.

Swedish Bakery 5348 N Clark St, at W Summerdale ☎773/561-8919. This old-fashioned 1920s bakery serves delicious marzipan

cake and custard-cup sweet rolls, among other sugary offerings, and it's possible to pick up a few treats for around $4 or $5. Mon–Fri 6.30am–6.30pm, Sat 6.30am–5pm.

Victory's Banner 2100 W Roscoe St ☎773/665-0227. The Satisfaction Promise scrambled-egg dish here ($8.45) is one of the best egg creations you will taste – including spinach, thick slabs of feta, and sun-dried tomatoes, served with toasted hearth bread and potatoes. All the breakfast and brunch dishes are indulgent – even the French toast ($5.95) is bathed in cream; however the lunchtime sandwiches and wraps are healthily restrained – the café is run by a Buddhist. The mellow yellow decor and warm and fuzzy atmosphere make for a sedate Sunday antidote to a wild Saturday night. Expect to spend between $7–11. Wed–Mon 8am–3pm.

Restaurants

Café 28 1800–1806 W Irving Park Rd, ☎773/528-2883. For lovers of all things Latin, this upbeat Mexican café with a Cuban influence is a great neighbourhood joint. It has just enough polish and a sufficient injection of Latin spirit to woo the crowd of regulars who pack in for deliciously piquant dishes like grilled *chipotle* chicken ($13.50), almond-encrusted halibut ($19.50), jalapeño pork chops ($18.50), and Cuban *ropa viejo* ($13.50). Add the merriment of salsa music – of course – which is performed live on the weekend, and the potent *mojitos*, and it's an uplifting evening on every level. Also think about stopping by for weekend brunch, which features green tamales and eggs ($8.75) and banana and corn pancakes ($6.50) Dinner meals here cost between $13.50 and $22.50. Mon 5.30–9.30pm, Tues–Fri 11am–2.30pm & 5.30pm–10.30pm, Sat 10am–2pm & 5.30pm–10.30pm, Sun 9am–2pm & 5.30pm–9pm.

Calo Ristorante 5343 N Clark St ☎773/271-7725. With a dark interior that's quite charming and down-to-earth, *Calo* has been a staple of Andersonville dining for 45 years. In their large dining room, deep-dish pizza ($13–18) rules the day, along with grilled steak ($18.95) and shrimp and broccoli over pasta ($16.95). The other side of the restaurant has a cosy bar and if you want to order food and watch sport, it's a comfortable spot. A meal out here will run between $10–20. Mon–Thurs 11am–12.30am, Fri & Sat 11am–1.30am, Sun 2pm–11.30pm.

Le Crêperie 2845 N Clark St ☎773/528-9050. French bohème prevails at this unpretentious family bistro in an unlikely position close to the prosaic Clark and Diversey nexus. Sweet and savoury crêpe concoctions range from creamy chicken curry with mango chutney ($11) to seafood soaked in white wine ($12) or a decadent thickly loaded chocolate pancake topped with cream ($8). Appetizers such as tender *escargots* ($9) doused in garlic and French onion soup ($7) oozing cheese provide soothing winter comfort food. In summer, there's an outdoor patio garden. On Thursday nights, an accordion and trumpet duo meandering through the alluring, aged dining rooms with rickety wooden tables adds to the allure. Plan on spending around $10–15 for the various crêpes here. Tues–Fri 11.30am–11pm, Sat 11.30am–9.30pm, Sun 11am–9.30pm.

Magnolia 1224 W Wilson ☎773/728-8785. This smart, modern American bistro, with neutral decor, high ceilings, soft lighting and shiny wooden floors is one of Uptown's swankier eating places. Classic dishes are deliciously reinvented and, quite refreshingly, vegetables rank highly on each amply proportioned entree.. Braised lamb shanks over ratatouille ($24), seared scallops with goat cheese and artichoke ravioli ($25), and grilled sea bass over a roasted poblano pepper stuffed with leeks ($24) are typical. They also do a mean brunch on Sunday, which features eggs Benedict ($10) and a shrimp omelette ($11). Very convenient for a post-dinner visit to the *Green Mill* poetry slam on Sundays; see p.199. Main courses here range from $21 to $29 and brunch items range from $10 to $15. Tues–Thurs 5.30–10pm, Fri & Sat 5.30–11.30pm, Sun 10am–3pm & 5pm–9pm.

Penny's Noodle Shop 3400 N Sheffield Ave, at N Clark ☎773/281-8222. Cheap, quality and usually packed noodle joint that spans Asian cuisines with numerous curries ($5.50–$6.95), satays ($5.75), stir-fries ($6.95) and amazing spring rolls ($4.25). Relaxed ourdoor dining during the warmer months. Nothing at *Penny's* is more than $7.50, so it's a reliable place to have an affordable meal in these parts. BYOB. Open

Tues–Thurs & Sun 11am–10pm, Fri & Sat 11am–10.30pm.

Southport Lanes and Billiards 3325 Southport Ave ☎773/472-6600. This bowling alley that opened in 1922 still sets the pins by hand – the only one in the city to do so. A welcoming sports bar, with pool tables and steady contingent of Cubs fans, it's especially lively on game nights. The main reason to come is for the simply fantastic burgers ($7.95), served with curly fries. The mammoth chopped-chicken salad ($9.95) with bacon, Gorgonzola, olives and palm hearts is also fresh and tasty. Best bar food in town. Menu items here range in price from $6 to $10. Mon–Fri noon–2am, Sat noon–3am, Sun noon–1am.

Tango Sur 3763 N Southport Ave, at W Grace ☎773/477-5466. Small, family-run restaurant specializing in charred, Argentinian-style steaks ($23) and ribs along with *parrillada* (short ribs, beef, sweet breads and black sausage); not much in the way of sides, though the spinach mashed potatoes are a highlight. For the brave and the ravenous, and those who might not mind a long wait on a weekend evening. For dinner, plan on spending anywhere from $12 to $30 per person. BYOB. Mon–Thurs 5–10.30pm, Fri 5–11.30pm, Sat 3–11.30pm, Sun noon–11pm.

Taste of Lebanon 1509 W Foster Ave ☎773/334-1600. In the Swedish enclave of Andersonville, this hole-in-the-wall Lebanese joint may lack polish but it's a local institution, serving ludicrously cheap but authentic Middle Eastern staples. Nutty falafel ($4.50) is stuffed inside fluffy pita, then drizzled with tahini sauce. The chicken shawarma wraps with a spicy cinnamon sauce ($5.50) are arguably the best in the city, and the stuffed grape leaves ($2.95) are refreshingly minty and vegetarian-friendly. Don't leave without trying the baklava ($2.25). Across the street, stop by at the family-run Middle Eastern bakery which sells excellent spinach pies, cheese, hummus and *baba ganoush* at ridiculously low prices – a great place to prepare for a festival picnic. For lunch or dinner here, plan to spend between $5 and $9. Mon–Sat 11am–8pm.

Uncommon Ground 3800 N Clark St ☎773/929-3680. Close to Wrigley Field, this accessible, artsy café-bar-restaurant with a welcoming vibe serves an excellent-global fusion brunch. The Montana omelette ($12) with

▲ Hot Chocolate treat

bacon, potatoes and sour cream is a perfect pre-Cubs filler. The lunchtime and dinner offerings include the sunshine salad ($7); (organic greens, avocado, seeded flatbread and sunflower seeds), pistachio-crusted tilapia ($21) and crispy halibut fish tacos ($13). With art exhibitions, live music, reading material and outdoor seating in summer, it's worth lingering for a while. Don't miss a thick, soothing, hot chocolate ($2.75) by the fireside in winter. Lunch here will run between $7 to $11 and dinner mains run $11 to $23. Sun–Thurs 9am–11pm, Fri & Sat 9am–midnight.

Bucktown and Wicker Park

Cafés and light meals

Bongo Room 1470 N Milwaukee Ave, between Evergreen Ave and Honore St ☏773/489-0690. This hip brunch spot located right above Wicker Park's left ventricle combines ambient music and a lounge-bar vibe – stroller yuppies start lining up early – with long waits and a slightly overpriced menu, but the food is worth it. Some notable attractions here include their vegetarian croissant ($7.50) and the ultra-decadent cherries jubilee French toast ($9.25), topped with cinnamon-brandy crème anglaise. Another location has opened in the South Loop (see p.167). $4.95–10.75. Mon–Fri 7.30am–2.30pm, Sat & Sun 9am–2.30pm.

Earwax Café 1561 N Milwaukee Ave, at North Ave ☏773/772-4019. Excellent coffeehouse that serves plenty of satisfying vegetarian fare. Has a fun, hip and quirky atmosphere pitched at the area's hipster residents. The menu pitches back and forth between the fine seitan reuben ($7.50) slathered in vegan thousand island dressing and the meat lover's blue cheese steak sandwich ($8.95). $4.95–8.95. Daily 9am–11pm.

Letizia's Natural Bakery 2144 W Division St, at Hoyne Ave ☏773/342-1011. Delicious panini made with *focaccia* bread and laden with melted mozzarella, pasta, pizza, coffee and pastries are on offer at this tiny café, with an outdoor patio – all food is made on site and without bleached flour by Letizia herself, who hails from Rome. On the lunch side, the "La Dolce Vita" panini ($6) features

prosciutto, basil and tomato. *Letizia's* also has a rotating list of soups and slices of cheesecake ($4). Sun–Wed 6am–11pm, Thurs–Sat 6am–5pm.

Margie's Candies 1960 N Western Ave, at W Armitage Ave ☏773/384-1035. Famous neighbourhood ice-cream parlour (it opened in 1921) that serves a cavity-inducing array of home-made candies and deliciously creamy shakes and malts. The turtle sundae ($4.95) is a good bet and the list of toppings is exhaustive. There's a second branch at 1813 W Montrose (☏773/348-0400). Deserts here will set you back anywhere from $2.50 to $7.95. Daily 9am–midnight.

Toast Two 2046 N Damen Ave, at W Armitage Ave ☏773/772-5600. Delicious omelettes, a French Toast Orgy (French-toast slabs stuffed with fruit or mascarpone cheese and filled with granola, fresh fruit and honey, $10) and eggy breakfast staples are served in a small dining room with an outdoor patio which is very popular with Bucktown's yuppified, beautiful young things. The huge sandwiches here include steak and Gorgonzola ($11) and a more modest grilled cheese and tomato ($6), and are worth building up an appetite for. And you will – long waits of up to an hour are common at the weekend. There's a smaller branch at 746 W Webster (☏773/935-5600). Breakfast and lunch options here will set you back between $6 to $11. Mon–Fri 7am–3pm, Sat & Sun 8am–4pm.

Vienna Beef Factory Store & Deli 2501 N Damen Ave, between Fullerton and Diversey avenues ☏773/235-6652. Sit elbow to elbow with the factory workers having their breakfast or lunch, munching on steaming hot dogs right off the assembly line. Many other fine Vienna meat products are available, including corned beef, pastrami and Polish sausages. You can buy dogs by the case at the company store. Lunch here (or an early morning breakfast bite) ranges from $2 to $6. Mon–Fri 6am–4pm, Sat 10am–3pm.

Restaurants

Café Absinthe 1954 W North Ave, at N Milwaukee Ave ☎773/278-4488. You pay for the atmosphere at this trendy North Avenue restaurant – a dark, curtained haunt for beautiful people where you enter through a back alley to the sound of moody jazz. The wine list is extensive, and the nouveau American cuisine includes entrees like cured duck leg ($21) and their highly lauded black wing ostrich filet ($10). Dinner entrees $21–28. Mon–Thurs 5.30–10pm, Fri & Sat 5.30pm–11pm, Sun 5.30pm–9pm.

Adobo Grill 2005 W Division St in Wicker Park ☎773/252-9990. See Old Town location on p.174 for review.

Handlebar 2311 W North Ave, between Claremont and Oakley ☎ 773/384-9546. Located away from the main triangle of Wicker Park activity, *Handlebar* is a place that draws in bike messengers, vegetarians and beer lovers. The apple-wood smoked tofu ($11.25) is pretty damn tasty, and sides like garlic mashed potatoes and fried plantains ($2.50) round things out here. Don't forget their generous beer list, which features regional favourites like the Great Lakes Edmund Fitzgerald Porter and the appropriately named Delirium Tremens. Visitors should plan on spending anywhere from $5 to $12 on a visit here. Mon–Thurs 10am–midnight, Fri & Sat 10am–2am, Sun 10am–11pm.

Hot Chocolate 1747 N Damen Ave ☎773/489-1747. Mindy Segal, former pastry chef at the venerable *MK* (see p.171), has launched her own chocolate haven to seduce Bucktown's arbiters of chic. The front drips down the exterior glass windows like melted chocolate and everything from the walls, industrial piping, chairs, bar and even the gracious staff are clad in tones of chocolate and caramel. The major draw here, not surprisingly, are the worthily praised desserts, which includes a posh take on a Snickers,

hot chocolate tasters, vanilla-layered strawberry and rhubarb cake and caramelized bananas with banana coffee cake and banana ice cream (all $11). As of late, the restaurant has bolstered their non-chocolate-infused items and dinner selections include Berkshire pork loin with homemade sauerkraut ($27) and artisanal cheese selections ($12). At peak hours, the long waiting times can be frustrating. For dessert only, plan on spending around $12 to $15; on the dinner side, entrees run $16 to $30. Open for dinner and dessert Tues & Wed 5.30–10pm, Thurs 5.30–11pm, Fri & sat 5.30pm–midnight, Sun 5.30pm–10pm. Lunch is served Wed–Fri 11.30am–2pm, and they have a brunch Sat & Sun 10am–2pm.

Jerry's Sandwiches 1938 W Division St ☎773/235-1006. With a gas-fired fireplace that can make the Chicago winters a bit less daunting, *Jerry's* is known around town for its prodigious sandwich menu. Of course, there are a few standouts, most notably the "Sissy M" (roast chicken, grilled onions, feta, olive relish and lemon mayo; $9.45) and the "Alice W" (roast salmon, avocado, cucumber, feta, wasabi mayo; $11.20). The "Milton F" option allows visitors to make up their own concoction. Brunch at *Jerry's* rounds up items such as French toast on challah bread ($8.95) and fried green tomatoes and scrambled eggs ($8.95). All told, you'll probably spend between $7 and $12 here for a meal. Sun–Wed 11am–10pm, Thurs–Sat 11am–2am.

Le Bouchon 1958 N Damen Ave, at W Armitage Ave ☎773/862-6600. Tiny and romantic French bistro, with inexpensive appetizers like *escargots* and steamed mussels ($8) and entrees like braised Moroccan-style lamb shank ($22.50) or sautéed rabbit in a white-wine sauce ($18.50). Later on in the evening, Bucktown's bohemians take over from an older early-evening crowd. The tables can be too close together for some tastes. Entrees here range from $18 to $23. Mon–Thurs 5.30pm–11pm, Fri & Sat 5pm–midnight

Piece 1927 W North Ave ☎ 773/772-4422. Raucous and fun, *Piece* distinguishes itself by way of its pizza and its on-premises brewery. Pizza is served "New Haven"-style (sparsely distributed toppings, with an emphasis on the sauce and crust), which represents a stark change from the overstuffed "Chicago-style" pizza. The beer selections include the salaciously named "Full Frontal Pale Ale" and "Dysfunctionale", which is also a pale ale. The place is not for those who are looking for a quiet evening out, as karaoke, DJs, and televised sport rule the roost (all of which can be quite enjoyable). Pizzas run from $10 to $15. Mon–Fri 11.30am–2am, Sat 11am–3am, Sun 11am–2am.

Spring 2039 W North Ave, at N Damen Ave ☎773/395-7100. New American food with an Asian twist (and even some Middle Eastern accents) in one of Chicago's top restaurants. Decor is clean and peaceful, like a rock-garden-turned-restaurant, and the menu features interesting flavour minglings like Maine sea scallops with oxtail and grilled Hawaiian prawns with pork belly dumplings. Main courses at dinner range from $22 to $36. Tues–Thurs 5.30–9.30pm, Fri & Sat 5.30pm–10.30pm, Sun 5.30pm–9pm.

The West Side

Cafés and light meals

Al's Number 1 Italian Beef 1079 W Taylor St, at Aberdeen St ☎312/226-4017. Takeout joint that was once the king of Italian beef before numerous copycats began arriving – and still turns out a tasty sandwich ($5.50), especially the "dipped" varieties. You would be hard pressed to spend a grand total of more than $8–10 at *Al's*. There's another one in River North (see p.168). Daily 11am–1am.

Café Jumping Bean 1439 W 18th St, at S Loomis St ☎312/455-0019. Popular Pilsen hangout for local artists. The funky decor – the furniture and walls covered in bright, expressionistic swatches of colour – that mixes a coffeehouse groove with Latino café fare. Try one of the hot foccaccia sandwiches ($4.25–5.10). Mon–Fri 6am–10pm, Sat & Sun 6am–8pm.

Mario's Italian Lemonade 1068 W Taylor Street near S Carpenter St; no phone. Hundreds of people flock to *Mario's* every summer (they open around May 1 and close in early Sept) for the shaved Italian ice, lemonade and other sundry items such as *lupini* (Italian nuts) and various candies. A large sized "ice" (which contains your choice of various fruits and flavours) costs around $3, and if you want you can get a whole bucket for your friends for $12. Everything here is very affordable, and it's a nice way to spend a hot summer night. Daily 11am–midnight.

Restaurants

Blackbird 619 W Randolph St, at S Jefferson St ☎312/715-0708. Marvellous and innovative New American cuisine in a super-trendy setting, though often overcrowded and pricey. Appetizers include sauteed skate wing with sarsaparilla ($12) and crispy confit of suckling pig ($13). Reworked American classic entrees are a delight for ardent carnivores with roasted walleye with cocoa beans ($32) and braised skirt steak with spaghetti squash ($35). Save room for the heavenly desserts – kalamata olive cake with honeycrisp apples ($10) and pear cider doughnuts ($10). Dinner mains $25–35. Mon–Thurs 5.30pm–10.30pm, Fri & Sat 5.30–11.30pm.

Francesca's on Taylor 1400 W Taylor St, at S Loomis St ☎312/829-2828. Among the best Italian places in Little Italy and also the city, *Francesca's* serves up authentic food like spinach-filled pasta ($14.95), penne with Italian sausage ($13.95) and a heavenly carpaccio ($8.95) in a lively and fun atmosphere. Happily, unlike the other *Francesca* restaurants in Chicago, this one takes reservations. Dinner entrees $13.95–26.95. Mon 5–9pm, Tues–Thurs 5pm–10pm, Fri–Sat 5pm–11pm, Sun 4pm-9pm.

Greek Islands 200 S Halsted St, at W Adams St ☎312/782-9855. Greek and Middle Eastern food, a cut above most other restaurants in the area, serving faultless classics – the seafood dishes are fresh and creatively executed – in a huge, colourful dining room with an open kitchen. The service is very attentive and it's open. Make sure and try dishes like the *keftedakia* (meatballs in a tangy tomato sauce; $5.50) or *garides* (baked shrimp, feta and tomato sauce served over rice; $14.95). Crowded all

▲ Patio at Greek Islands

week long and justifiably so. Dinner mains run between $12.95 and $17.95. Sun–Thu 11am–midnight, Fri & Sat 11am–1am.

Green Zebra 1460 W Chicago Ave ☎312/243-7100. Vegetarian food reaches its apogee at this new boutique restaurant with industrial-chic decor. Small taster portions of ambitious dishes such as a chanterelle mushroom popover ($14), and a carmelized onion tart with mustard greens and caraway ($12) are aimed at providing "high touch" cuisine in a "high tech" world. For die-hard carnivores there's usually at least one meat and fish option. Penance food this definitely isn't, with desserts that include honey crisp apple beignets ($8) and vegan chocolate cake ($8). Mon–Thurs 5.30–10pm, Fri & Sat 5–11pm, Sun 5–9pm.

La Vita 1359 W Taylor St ☎312/494-1414. *La Vita* is a bit of an overlooked gem in Little Italy and its ambience is such that it's rather perfect for a quiet gathering of friends or an amorous outing. The wine list is generous and the solid entrees include mushroom-stuffed ravioli ($16) and chicken marsala ($18). Dinner entrees range from $13 to $24. Mon–Thurs 11am–10pm, Fri 11am–11pm, Sat 5pm–11pm, Sun 4pm–10pm.

Marche 833 W Randolph St, at Green ☎312/226-8399. One of the highlights of the West Randolph restaurant row, this French bistro packs them in every night with its ballyhooed cuisine – including the Norwegian salmon with spring onions ($20.95) and the braised rabbit ($23.95) – and energetic nightclub-style atmosphere, popular with the glittery, fashionable crowd. Dinner main courses $16.95–24.95.

Sun–Thu 5.30–10pm, Fri & Sat 5.30pm–midnight.

Nuevo Leon 1515 W 18th St, at Ashland Ave ☎312/421-1517. Excellent, traditional Mexican food – among the best in Chicago – served since 1962 in a colourful family-style restaurant in the Pilsen neighbourhood, especially lively after Sunday-morning mass. The shrimp fajitas ($11.50) stand out, as does the guacamole ($7). Combine a trip out here with a visit to the nearby National Museum of Mexican Art (see p.120) and bring your own alcohol; they'll supply a bucket and ice. Dinner will run between $10 and $16. Daily 7am–midnight.

Parthenon 314 S Halsted St, at W Jackson Blvd ☎312/726-2407. Longstanding Greektown standby that continues to draw the faithful with its consistent and affordable food. The *taramasalata* (fish roe with sour cream; $5.50) and *tzatziki* (yogurt with cucumber and garlic; $5.50) are highly recommended. There's nothing modest about the *Parthenon* – you can feast on a whole roasted suckling pig that could feed a dozen people if your hunger demands it. For the less famished, there are tasty gyros and kebab platters ($11.50). It claims to have invented flaming *saganaki* (fried cheese doused with Metaxa brandy; $5.50); it's worth trying as much for the serving spectacle as for the deliciously rich taste. Main dishes $11.50–24.95. Daily 11am–midnight.

Red Light 820 W Randolph St, at S Green St ☎312/733-8880. Dark, upscale West Side pan-Asian restaurant, popular with a young, sleek crowd that comes to munch on the chicken vindaloo ($19) and the octopus and avocado kimchi salad ($10). Dinner mains $19–31. Sun–Thurs 5.30–10pm, Fri & Sat 5.30pm–midnight.

Rodity's 222 S Halsted St, at W Adams St ☎312/454-0800. Friendly mom-and-pop place serving first-rate Greek chicken ($12.95), *avgolemono* (egg-lemon; $3) soup, and *saganaki* ($6). It's a bit more relaxed than the other Greek restaurants in the area, so the attentive waitstaff won't rush you either. Main courses $11.95–21.50. Sun–Thurs 11am–midnight, Fri & Sat 11am–1am.

Sushi Wabi 842 W Randolph ☎312/563-1224. For its über-fresh taste and hip but unpretentious ambience, *Wabi* is the best sushi restaurant in town, successfully embodying its eponymous ethos of "refined simplicity". Kaleidoscopic *maki*, *nigiri* and sashimi are served on chunky wooden blocks in a spartan setting of exposed rafters and brick walls, simple banquette seating and low lighting. The dragon roll with tempura shrimp, *unagi* (eel) and avocado ($14), the Ecuador roll with *magur* (tuna; $17), and *hamachi* (yellowtail; $8.50), are as appealing to the eye as they are to the taste. For appetizers, try the *hotategai* (sea scallops in an apple and plum sauce; $9.50) or *gomae* (spinach with sesame peanut sauce; $5.25). There is a tiny bar area, serving a wide selection of sake and syrupy sweet plum wine. Reservations advised. Sushi and the usual accompaniments will run between $11 and $19. Wed–Sat 5pm–midnight, Sun–Tues 5–11pm.

Twisted Spoke 501 N Ogden Ave, at W Grand Ave ☎312/666-1500. Out-of-the-way restaurant/bar with rooftop dining and somewhat affected biker atmosphere. You can't go wrong with the half-pound Fatboy burger ($8.75) and the margaritas. If you find yourself here around midnight (a dicey proposition at best), you'll experience "Smut and Eggs", with porn projected from TV screens. Prices run between $7 and $11. Mon–Fri 11am–2am, Sat 9am–3am, Sun 9am-2am.

South Side and Hyde Park

Cafés and light meals

Caffè Florian 1450 E 57th St, at S Blackstone Ave ☎773/752-4100. Reliable coffee joint, also serving pizza and sandwiches heavy on the vegetarian side of things, where University of Chicago students and locals deconstruct radical issues. The spinach pizza ($7.50–11.50) is a good bet, as is the chicken curry wrap ($7.75) Dinner or lunch here will run between $7 and $11). Open Mon–Thurs 11am–10pm, Fri 11am–11pm, Sat 10am–11pm, Sun 10am-10pm.

Medici on 57th 1327 E 57th St, at S Kenwood Ave ☎773/667-7394. Typical college hangout, with stained-glass windows downstairs, two levels of graffiti-covered tables, fine pizza, juicy burgers and their highly-lauded "Eggs Espresso" (three eggs prepared via their espresso machine; $3.95); . "The Med"'s high point is Sunday brunch, particularly the fresh-squeezed orange juice. Dining at the *Medici* will cost between $5 and $9. Mon–Thurs 11am–11pm, Fri 11am–midnight, Sat 7am–12am, Sun 7am–midnight.

Negro League Café 301 E 43rd St ☎773/536-7000. A tribute to athletes who played in the Negro leagues prior to desegregation in the 1940s, the walls are covered in baseball memorabilia including a "Wall of Fame". The food is also worth the trek, with an innovative, less hearty twist on classic soul food dishes. Try the chicken wingettes with a spicy peach glaze ($5.99) for appetizer, followed by the soul food plate, which brings together baked chicken, collard greens, macaroni and cheese and candied yams ($9). There's also an uplifting gospel brunch on Sundays. Dinner mains from $9 to $18. Tues–Thurs 11am–11pm, Fri & Sat 11am–2am, Sun 1–8pm.

Original Pancake House 1517 E Hyde Park Blvd ☎773/288-2322. See Gold Coast location on p.173 for review.

Restaurants

Dixie Kitchen & Bait Shop 5225 S Harper Ave, at 53rd St ☎773/363-4943. Delicious Southern cooking at good prices, served in a room with playful 1930s decor. The menu ranges from delicious Southern BBQ sandwiches ($8.69) to hot Cajun and Creole gumbos ($11.95) and jambalaya ($8.95). The fried-green-tomato appetizer ($5.99) is a must and the service simply wonderful. Expect to pay between $7.99 and $12.9. Sun–Thurs 11am–10pm, Fri & Sat 11am–11pm.

Edwardo's Natural Pizza 1321 E 57th St in Hyde Park ☎773/241-7960. See Gold Coast location on p.173 for review.

La Petite Folie 1504 E 55th St, at Lake Park Blvd ☎773/493-1394. Hyde Park's only upscale French restaurant – in terms of the menu and decor, not the price – is tucked away in a tiny mall beside Walgreen's. This smart but cosy bistro with pristine white tablecloths and warm baguettes and butter as a preamble serves classic French cuisine; roulade of sole, veal tenderloin and a tasty foie gras variation – perhaps the cheapest you will find anywhere. The prix-fixe menu (three courses, around $28, served 5–6pm) is often the best deal. Main courses $17–28. Tues–Fri 11.30am–2pm & 5–10pm, Sat & Sun 5–10pm.

Mellow Yellow 1508 E 53rd St ☎773/667-2000. A 1970s retro classic with a well-honed menu of spit-roasted chicken ($5.99), burgers ($6.99–8.99), savoury crêpes ($6.45–7.95), six different kinds of chilli ($5.99) – a resounding winner at the Taste of Chicago summer food festival (see p.247) – and old-school desserts like apple pie ($3.99) and bread pudding ($4.99). The time-warp decor with lava lamps and leafy foliage, and its laid-back vibe has made it a Hyde Park landmark for almost thirty years. A meal here will run between $5 and $10. Mon–Thurs 6am–9pm, Fri & Sat 6am–11pm, Sun 6am–10pm.

Pearl's Place 3901 S Michigan ☎773/285-1700. Despite the rather soulless facade and unfortunate location next to a motel, *Pearl's* Southern soul food with a Creole twist is as soulful as it comes. Main dishes such as juicy fried chicken ($8.95), collard greens with smoky pork bits ($3.95) and potato pie ($3.95) with a melt in your mouth crust are as comforting for the stomach as they are for the wallet. Great for the area's post-church Sunday brunch, although be prepared to wait in line, a long time. Meals run $8–11. Mon–Thurs 8am–8pm, Fri & Sat 8am–9pm, Sun 8am–7pm.

Piccolo Mondo 1642 E 56th, at S Hyde Park Blvd ☎773/643-1106. While it doesn't offer much in the way of decor, *Piccolo Mondo*'s basic Italian fare is quite good and specialities include mostaccioli pasta with salmon ($17.95) and chicken vesuvio ($14.95). Dinner entrees $11.95–17.95. Mon–Thurs 11.30am–8.30pm, Fri & Sat 11.30am–9.30pm, Sun 11.30am–8.30pm.

Ribs 'n' Bibs 5300 S Dorchester Ave, at E 53rd St ☎773/493-0400. For no-frills takeout ribs, this Hyde Park institution is the place to go. Go for the Jr. Ranch Hand ($10.85), half a slab of their dripping-with-sauce ribs and fries. Wear an old shirt, as this food splatters. Taking in the ribs (or anything else) here will run you anywhere from $5 to $11. Sun–Thurs 11am–midnight, Fri & Sat 11am–1am.

Rogers Park and the North Shore

Restaurants

Arun's 4156 N Kedzie Ave, at W Warner Ave ☎773/539-1909. Chef-owner Arun Sampanthavivat leads diners on an odyssey through the world of Thai cuisine at this elegant spot, widely regarded as one of the country's finest Thai restaurants. The two-level space is full of intimate dining nooks decked out with art by the chef's brother. For the full experience, splash out for the $85 "chef's design menu". Following a discussion of your spice tolerance and gastro-aversions, you'll be served six appetizers, four entrees, and a dessert duo finale. Reservations are a must. Tues–Sat 5–10pm, Sun 5–9pm.

Dave's Italian Kitchen 1635 Chicago Ave, between Davis and Church, Evanston ☎847/864-6000. With a neon sign that lets visitors know they're in the right spot, *Dave's* serves up Italian food in the tried and true American fashion: on red-and-white-checked tablecloths, amid hundreds of old wine bottles. The lasagna "con amore" ($10), with spinach, pesto, mozzarella, ricotta and marinara sauce, is certainly worth a try. Sun–Thurs 4–10pm, Fri & Sat 4–11pm.

Evanston Chicken Shack 1925 Ridge Ave, at Garnett Place, Evanston ☎847/328-9360. Chicago proper has the much heralded *Harold's Chicken Shack*, while Evanston has its own chicken shack of some repute. Those unacquainted with the world of fried chicken and its various accompaniments might do well to start things off with a rib-tip and chicken combo ($6.80), and then move on into the more advanced territory of okra and their "red beans'n'rice" ($1.84 each). Mon–Sat 10am–12.45am.

Hema's Kitchen 2439 W Devon Ave, at N Artesian ☎773/338-1627. Good-value Indian/

Pakistani dishes from the traditional recipe collection of chef-owner Hema Potla, a native of Hyderabad. The *buna gosht* (lamb sautéed with peppers and curry leaves) and *sag murg* (chicken with peppers and spices) are two of her scrumptious specials ($12–13). Lots of vegetarian options too. Bring your own booze. *Hema's* popularity has extended to a second location in Lincoln Park (see p.176). Daily 11am–11pm.

Pete Miller's Seafood & Prime Steak 1557 Sherman Ave, between Grove and Orrington, Evanston ☎847/328-0399. *Pete Miller's* aims to recreate the type of clubby, post-WWII dinner club that warms the heart of every red-blooded American and hits the bull's eye. The steak (around $40) is consistently good, though the casual visitor may really just appreciate the laid-back atmosphere, enhanced by nightly live jazz, and the persuasive drink menu. Mon–Thurs 4.30pm–1am, Fri & Sat 4.30pm–2am, Sun 4.30pm–midnight.

▲ Curry on W Devon Ave

Sabri Nihari 2502 W Devon Ave, at N Campbell ☎773/743-6200. Family-friendly establishment serving the most authentic Pakistani food you're liable to get in the Windy City. The speciality is the namesake *sabri nihari*, a kind of beef stew, but other dishes more than measure up, among them the subtly spiced frontier chicken and the charcoal-grilled chaplee kabab. Average entree: $7.50. No alcohol. Daily noon–midnight.

Oak Park

Cafés and light meals

Great Harvest Bread Co. 736 Lake St, at Oak Park Ave ☎708/848-5700. Conveniently located chain bakery that specializes in made-to-order sandwiches on thick slices of fresh bread, along with good chocolate-chip cookies. Mon–Fri 6.30am–7pm, Sat 7am–5pm, Sun 8am–3pm.

Restaurants

Geppetto's Pasta and Pizza 113 N Oak Park Ave ☎708/386-9200. Archetypal small-town restaurant with decent thin-crust and deep-dish pizzas, soups, deli sandwiches and pasta dishes, as well as a well-stocked salad bar. Service can be painfully slow, though. Sun–Thurs 11am–11pm, Fri & Sat 11am–midnight.

Khyber Pass 1031 Lake St, at Forest ☎708/445-9032. Standard white-tablecloth Indian restaurant with polite service and particularly tasty chicken tikka masala, samosas and naan. If you're a big eater, the $10 all-you-can-eat lunch buffet is good value. Belly dancers on Saturday nights. Daily 11.30am–3.30pm & 5–10pm.

Drinking

C hicago has been defined by its boisterous **drinking scene** since at least the early 1900s, when Schlitz, a major local brewery, owned more land than anyone else in town, save another pillar of the community, the Catholic Church. Muckraking journalist George Turner estimated in 1907 that in some "wards" (neighbourhoods) there was roughly one bar per 150 residents.

The city's hard-drinking reputation was cemented during the Prohibition era of the 1920s and 1930s, when the need for beer and bathtub gin consumed Chicago in the gangland violence that has become one of the city's most notorious historical associations. Today, drinking in Chicago remains a serious pursuit; you'll find more **sports bars** here than in New York and Los Angeles combined. Only slightly less ubiquitous are the city's popular **beer gardens** – casual outdoor patios that teem in summer with people who've made up ingenious excuses to get out of work early. Many of the new lounge bars also function as restaurants – the food certainly transcends the standard greasy bar fodder; see "Eating", Chapter 14, for bars we recommend more for their food.

Chicago's bar scene tends to be quiet early on in the week, picking up on Wednesday and through the weekend. Weekend brunches at some establishments turn into rather Bacchanalian affairs. Late-night drinking is also a hallmark of the city's bar scene: the average 2am weekday **closing time** extends to 5am on Saturdays in some places. Bars are packed right up to closing time, and late-night bars often have lines at 2am that are longer than the ones you'll see earlier in the night.

Remember to carry **photo ID** or your passport with you; many bars won't let you in without it. You have to be 21 to drink in Illinois and the law is rigorously adhered to in all bars – if you look under 35 years old you will almost certainly be carded. **Smoking** is not allowed in Chicago bars.

Drink prices are fairly reasonable compared to other major US cities, except in the most upscale bars. **Beer** is usually cheap, between $3.50 and $6 a pint, and many bars have happy hours (roughly 4–8pm) featuring drink specials, usually half-price drafts of domestic beers, or a bucket of six bottles for the price of five. Local favourites include **Old Style**, a mass-produced lager brewed in Milwaukee, and the many varieties of **Goose Island**, a robust Chicago beer from a brewery that runs a few of its own bars in the city (see p.191).

Mixed drinks and **wine** are more expensive, typically from $5 to $10, depending on the fanciness of the establishment. A few odd cocktail combinations have persisted here, like the brutal but effective **Car Bombs** – a shot of whiskey dropped into a full pint of Guinness and downed in one swoop.

Drinking by neighbourhood

While every neighbourhood has its own cluster of bars, with distinct flavours and themes, **Near North** has more per square mile than anywhere else in Chicago, with most of them concentrated around the raucous and tourist-heavy intersection of **Rush** and **Division** streets.

River North has some fancy places for cocktails, as does the Mag Mile, where luxury hotel chains have poured tons of money into their sumptuous lounges. The *Drake Hotel* exudes turn-of-the-century grandeur, while the *W* hotels draw the urban sophisticates with their self-consciously sleek and sexy vibe. Conservative, collegiate **Lincoln Park** is known for its dozens of sports bars – with a recent leaning towards cultivating a less macho veneer – but also has a number of quality lounges and pubs. Despite the clutch of Cubs bars around Wrigley Field, nearby **Lakeview** has perhaps the best variety, ranging from the ubiquitous Irish theme pub to alternative scene bars, poised wine bars and gregarious singles' hunting grounds. The bohemian denizens of **Bucktown**, **Wicker Park** and **Ukrainian Village** frequent an eclectic mix of bars ranging from grungy saloons with beer-soaked floors to sleek lounges with exotic fish tanks.

The **Loop** mostly caters to an after-work office crowd and theatregoers, though there are a couple of excellent taverns in the increasingly gentrified **South Loop**.

There isn't much in the way of destination drinking on the **South Side**, with the exception of **Hyde Park** and the traditionally Irish neighbourhood of **Beverly/Morgan Park**, at Western and 103rd Street, which hosts the nation's largest neighbourhood St Patrick's Day parade (see p.245).

The Loop

Berghoff 17 W Adams St, at State ☎312/427-3170. Though known primarily for its food, this German-American institution also serves its own much-vaunted beer and root beer – as well as $3 bar snacks like mini-bratwursts and potato pancakes – in its atmospheric bar. Get a full stein of *Berghoff's* seasonal brew for $2 on Mondays and Tuesdays.

Cardozo's Pub 170 W Washington ☎312/236-1573. Hard-edged subterranean pub close to City Hall, where political movers and shakers head for an industrial-strength lunchtime drink, sustenance and TV time-out. With a raw ambience, it makes for interesting people-watching and eavesdropping.

Cavanaugh's 53 W Jackson Blvd ☎312/939-3125. A resolutely locals watering hole where men in suits exchange lively banter with the genial barstaff, located inside the landmark Monadnock Building – look for the green-and-white awning down the side alley. The cozy, wood-panelled interior, with its brass fixtures and green leather bar and stools, is a welcoming retreat from the frenzy of the Loop.

Monk's Pub 205 W Lake St, at Wells St ☎312/357-6665. Unassuming neighbourhood dive bar with a good line-up of beers

▲ Berghoff bar

and a wide selection of pub fare, including great half-pounder burgers with a multitude of toppings and chilli, the house special. Packed between noon and 1pm with business people engaged in animated chatter or gripped by the CNBC ticker on the TV screen.

Whiskey Blue in the *W* hotel, 172 W Adams St, at Wells St ☎312/782-4933. One of the few spots in the Loop for upscale drinking, with most cocktails well over $10. The leggy waitresses are a trademark of *W* hotel bars, while the lounge decor and low lighting is sleek and sexy.

South Loop and Near South

Alcock's Bar 411 S Wells St, at W Congress Parkway ☎312/922-1778. This bar overflows with Bears fans whenever the team plays at home, even offering express bus service to the game. Otherwise it's a mellow joint popular with Board of Trade workers, with rock 'n' roll blaring from the jukebox and bottled beers, as well as pizzas, pasta, sandwiches and hot dogs at lunch.

River North

The Bar at the Peninsula Chicago 108 E Superior St, at N Michigan Ave ☎312/337-2888. Reminiscent of a gentlemen's club, with leather armchairs and a signature "Gentleman's Retreat Tea" – a selection of appetizers, a glass of bourbon and a cigar – this plush lounge attracts a well-heeled, debonair crowd. There is an extensive array of high-priced cocktails and cigars, not to mention a stunning view of the city.

Basil's in the *Talbott Hotel*, 20 E Delaware ☎1-800/525-2688. This lordly English country-manor-style bar is a dandy spot to sip a single malt whiskey, a Cognac or an *añejo* tequila amidst deep mahogany furniture, shiny brass fixtures and foxhunting paintings.

Blue Frog 676 N LaSalle St, at W Erie St ☎312/943-8900. This almost-hidden dive bar is mellow and popular for its shelves of near-complete board games, from Operation to Battleship to Kerplunk. There are over twenty kinds of bottled beers and an outdoor deck in summer. A refreshingly fun alternative to all the chains in the area.

Brehon Pub 731 N Wells St, at W Superior St ☎312/642-1071. The family-owned *Brehon* (Gaelic for lawyer) has been a neighbourhood

fixture for over twenty years, and flaunts its connection to the motherland with a green facade, copious shamrocks, Irish flags and more than a whiff of genuine Irish hospitality. There are twelve beers on tap and a service-able menu of pub food, plus a pool table, dartboard and a jukebox. On St Patrick's Day, just about every pub-crawl gang makes a pit stop here.

Celtic Crossings 751 N Clark St, at W Chicago Ave ☎312/337-1005. One of Chicago's more authentic Irish pubs. With no TVs, it's best suited for a pint and good conversation. Choose from a dozen beers on tap, mostly imports, including Murphy's, Newcastle Brown and Guinness. The Irish owners keep it real, the crowd is mature, the vibe unpretentious. Irish bands often play on Saturday nights and Sunday afternoons.

Clark Street Ale House 742 N Clark St, between Chicago Ave and Superior St ☎312/642-9253. Relax at the handsome cherry-wood bar with one of the vast selection of domestic beers (almost one hundred including 25 draft beers, a couple of good house brews and local specialties), dozens of Scotches and cigars. There's also a pleasant outdoor garden in summer. Lively atmosphere, popular with the after-work crowd and graduate students.

Cru Café & Wine Bar 25 E Delaware St between State and Wabash ☎312/337-4078. Just south of the Rush Street drinking corridor, there's great people-watching at this wine bar replete with chandeliers, fireplace and a poised vibe. Order one of the hundreds of wines or a glass of port, munch on a meat and cheese platter or slurp a few oysters and relax in the muted candlelight to an ambient house soundtrack. On the downside, the service can be erratic.

Motel Bar 600 W Chicago Ave, at Larrabee St ☎312/822-2900. Smack up against the Chicago River, the *Motel Bar* replicates with retro zeal the 1970s motel-lobby experience with orange booths, brown sofas and a menu with old-school classics like mac-n-cheese and meatloaf. The bar hews to the classics as well, mixing up good, strong Tom Collins, Harvey Wallbangers and Cosmopolitans. There's outdoor seating, too.

Narcisse 710 N Clark, at Superior ☎312/787-2675. Appropriately named, this ultra-swanky lounge, dripping with chandeliers, velvet, marble and serious attitude draws the A-list celebrities and local wannabes dressed to the nines, with its decadent vibe and suave milieu. If money is no object, the high-class menu, including oysters, caviar, lamb carpaccio and filet mignon, is hard to fault and best enjoyed with one of their fine signature champagne cocktails.

O'Callaghan's 29 W Hubbard St, at N Dearborn ℡312/670-4371. Down-to-earth after-work and after-hours bar with a long, hand-carved bar from Ireland. It attracts a mixed crowd, including journalists from the nearby *Tribune* office on Michigan Ave. The drinks are nothing special but the welcoming staff and late-night bar menu of burgers and simple appetizers keeps regulars coming back for more.

The Redhead Piano Bar 16 W Ontario St, at N State St ℡312/640-1000. Known for its cabaret acts, this suave bar also serves excellent martinis – thirty types in all – as well as an extensive list of Scotches, tequilas and ports. The crowd is on the older side for River North nightlife (30s–50s), and the dress code (no T-shirts or gym shoes) is strictly enforced.

Rockit Bar and Grill 22 W Hubbard, at Dearborn ℡312/645-6000. It's saloon chic at this bar and grill that references Wild West culture with antler chandeliers, brown leather chairs and distressed wooden tables placed strategically across its two levels. The rugged vibe extends to the menu with the specialty Kobe Rockit burger, thick slabs of crab cake and calamari. On the second level, plasma TVs and pool tables draw the tie-shedding, post-work crowds.

10pin Bowling Lounge 330 N State St, at Kinzie ℡312/644-0300. Nightclub-style bowling alley where the lights are low, the jukebox loud and the lanes topped by oversize screens playing music videos. The martini menu includes twenty varieties, such as the signature 10pintini with raspberry vodka and pomegranate juice, and the kitchen doles out American comfort food like mini burgers, pizzas, s'mores and fries ($5–10). Shoe rental $3.95 ($4.95 for "cool shoes"); bowling $4.95 per person per game before 5pm, $6.95 after; discounts Sun–Tues.

Whiskey Sky in the *W* hotel, 644 N Lake Shore Drive, at E Erie St ℡312/255-4463. The views of Lake Michigan from this 33rd-floor lounge are great but the place is so popular that you have to put your name on the guest list

in advance if you hope even to drink here on a Friday or Saturday night. A haven for models, sports figures and business types, who don't baulk at the $11 martinis.

Gold Coast

Butch McGuire's 20 W Division St, at N Dearborn St ℡312/337-9080. An institution on the singles scene since the 1960s, *Butch McGuire's* is the most popular of all the Division St bars, which means that on weekend nights it heaves with prowling singles and has all the sophistication of a frat house. Between Thanksgiving and Christmas, the holiday tinsel, stuffed animals and motorized trains add to the suffocation. Open till 5am on Saturday nights. Full menu with standard pub fare.

Coq d'Or in the *Drake Hotel*, 140 E Walton St, at N Michigan Ave ℡312/787-2200. Sophisticated, leather-booth-lined piano bar that's popular with suits at lunch and a genteel, martini crowd after work. The menu includes choice burgers and what may be the finest club sandwich in the city.

The Leg Room 7 W Division St, at N State St ℡312/337-2583. Sandwiched in between the crowded Division St drinkeries, this velvety little lounge with ice-cold martinis and perfectly tacky leopard-print decor is popular with college students, who come to get hammered and dance to DJ-spun disco grooves.

Mother's 26 W Division St ℡312/642-7251. Immortalized in the 1980s movie *About Last Night*, *Mother's* provides the quintessential Division St experience – a frenzied singles scene where the young and the raucous writhe on the dancefloor to a cacophonous medley of tunes.

P.J. Clarke's 1204 N State Parkway, at E Division St ℡312/664-1650. The two-storey sibling of the famed Manhattan restaurant serves legendary burgers on red-check tablecloths but is, in essence, a classic neighbourhood drinking den (especially on the ground floor), with an oak-and-brass bar and an older clientele than the one you'll see around the corner on Division St. The atmosphere is fun and friendly, and there's an impressive selection of imported beer and Scotch as well.

Signature Room 875 N Michigan Ave, at E Chestnut St ℡312/787-7230. An unashamedly touristy, but quintessential Chicago ritual.

Take the elevator to the 96th floor of the John Hancock Building, order a cocktail, relax and take in the breathtaking views of the city. Especially beautiful on a snowy winter's day when the lake is frozen over. The decor is shabby, the service frustratingly slow, but the experience unforgettable.

Whiskey Bar in the *Sutton Place Hotel*, **1015 N Rush St, between Oak St and Belleville Place** ☏ **312/475-0300**. Refurbished in 2007, the local branch of this chainlet of style bars run by Rande Gerber, Cindy Crawford's husband, now has a Latin decor but the see-and-be-seen sidewalk café remains, as do the beautiful bartenders. Food is provided by *Mexx Kitchen*, serving upscale (and overpriced) versions of ceviche, guacamole and seared fish.

Zebra Lounge 1220 N State Parkway, just north of Division St ☏ **312/642-5140.** Kitsch decor and eccentric personalities mix and mingle at this black-and-white, closet-sized piano bar which has been drawing lounge singers, middle-aged swingers, transvestites and young preppies since the 1930s. It's rollicking until the early hours and the keyboard player only enhances its appeal.

▲ Zebra Lounge

Old Town and Lincoln Park

Black Duck 1800 N Halsted, at Willow ☏ **312/664-1801.** Conveniently located for a pre- or post-Steppenwolf Theatre drink, the smart-casual, dimly lit *Black Duck* draws a post-work yuppie crowd during the week, and a sportier element on the weekends. There's a full menu of American food

(sandwiches, steaks and chops), but martinis are the real specialty.

Delilah's 2771 N Lincoln Ave, at W Diversey Parkway ☏ **773/472-2771**. A resounding locals' favourite, *Delilah's* feels out of place in sedate Lincoln Park, with all-black decor, punk rock on the jukebox, a pinball machine and cult-movie screenings. A huge whiskey and beer selection, nightly drink specials, DJs spinning everything from classic punk to R&B, and pool tables add to its appeal.

Glascott's 2158 N Halsted St, at W Dickens Ave ☏ **773/281-1205**. Also known as *Glascott's Groggery*, this friendly neighbourhood pub has been around since 1937, run by a family that's been in the business since the 1800s. Popular with baseball-cap-wearing, bar-hopping types, it shows all the local Cubs' games on TV and offers food from the *Athenian Room* next door (p.175).

Goose Island Brew Pub 1800 N Clybourn Ave, near N Sheffield Ave ☏ **312/915-0071**. Helping to refine the Midwestern palate for hand-crafted beer, *Goose Island* has had a brewery and pub in this huge, brick warehouse space since 1988. There are now more than ten home brews on tap every day in the pub, and you can tour the brewery on Sundays at 3pm and 4.30pm; the $5 fee includes a beer tasting. They also have a pub in Wrigleyville (see p.192).

John Barleycorn Memorial Pub 658 W Belden Ave, at N Lincoln Ave ☏ **773/348-8899.** One of the city's most popular bars and beer gardens, this former speakeasy draws on a nautical theme to attract a mix of students from nearby DePaul University, young couples, families and beer lovers (more than thirty brews to choose from). Though it can get crowded on weekends, it's not uncomfortably so. There's another location in Wrigleyville (see p.193).

Liar's Club 1665 W Fullerton Ave, at N Clybourn Ave ☏ **773/665-1110**. Located in an industrial no-man's-land, the dark and decaying *Liar's Club* is a singles bar verging on a dance club, bathed in red lights, with everyone grooving to the Ramones or drum 'n' bass with a total lack of pretension. For a more chilled ambience, there are pool tables and sofas on the second floor. The drinks are cheap and the weekend cover charge is just $5, but be prepared to wait a while to get in.

McGee's 950 W Webster Ave, at N Sheffield Ave ☏ **773/549-8200**. Beneath the El tracks, this

Irish sports bar has dozens of TV screens, 28 beers on tap and excellent pub food, including $1 hamburgers on Monday nights. The crowd is split between DePaul students and twenty-something urban sophisticates.

Old Town Ale House 219 W North Ave, at N Wieland St ☎312/944-7020. A favourite with artists, photographers and literary types since it opened in 1958, this dimly lit dive, with its antique decor and lending library, has character to spare; check out the mural behind the bar that honors *Second City* alumni including John Belushi and Bill Murray. Some *Second City* members have even tied the knot here, while others hung out, played pinball and drank copiously. Open until 4am during the week and 5am at the weekend.

Red Lion Pub 2446 N Lincoln Ave, at W Montana St ☎773/348-2695; Brown or Purple Line to Fullerton. A friendly English pub where you'd be comfortable dropping by solo. Claiming to be haunted, it has a host of dedicated regulars (many UK expats) and features a series of weekly readings (usually in the fantasy vein). English pub grub includes sausage rolls, beans on toast and Welsh rarebit.

Webster's Wine Bar 1480 W Webster Ave, at N Clybourn Ave ☎773/868-0608. In a surprising location, this candlelit bar with a European ambience is a relaxing spot for a glass of wine – choose from the monumental list (35 wines available by the glass, over 400 served by the bottle), which includes excellent themed two-ounce sample servings if you are struggling to commit. The knowledgeable and friendly staff is always willing and able to help you choose. It's a very popular spot with young couples who pair off in the dim lighting among the book-lined walls. There are some better-than-average appetizers, like the exceptional pear and brie quesadilla, salads, sandwiches and cheese platters.

Lakeview, Wrigleyville and Andersonville

Carol's Pub 4659 N Clark St, near W Leland Ave ☎773/334-2402. A taste of the American South in Chicago, *Carol's* is well known for its focus on loud country music. They do feature live local bands from time to time, and the cover charge is usually around $5. Another draw is their late license, which means they don't close until

5am on Saturday nights, and 4am the rest of the week.

Cubby Bear 1059 W Addison St, at N Clark St ☎773/327-1662. Opened in 1953, the spacious, crowded, and loud *Cubby Bear* would be just another sports bar if it weren't for Wrigley Field across the street. When the Cubs are in town, the twelve 32" TVs and two large projectors turn on and the crowds squeeze in to down the beer and liquor specials of the day soaked up with greasy wings, dripping Italian beef sandwiches and succulent burgers.

Cullen's Bar & Grill 3741 N Southport Ave, at W Waveland Ave ☎773/975-0600. Unlike most Irish pubs in Chicago, *Cullen's* has an air of authenticity, as the bartenders here can actually pour a Guinness properly. This boisterous joint draws young groups of Lakeview professionals with its welcoming staff, above-average pub food (try the delectable shepherd's pie), and live Celtic music several nights a week. There's also outdoor seating in warm weather.

Duke of Perth 2913 N Clark St, at W Oakdale Ave ☎773/477-1741. The city's only Scottish pub, with more than seventy kinds of single-malt Scotch whiskey, all-you-can-eat fish 'n' chips on Wednesday and Friday ($9.50) and a full line-up of Scotch delicacies like leek pie and Scotch eggs. On Mondays, all entrees are two for one. The staff is enthusiastic and the atmosphere is relaxed and unassuming. During summertime, the beer garden is a perfect retreat.

Goose Island Brew Pub 3535 N Clark St, near Addison St ☎773/832-9040. For review, see Lincoln Park location on p.191.

Hopleaf Bar 5148 N Clark St ☎773/334-9851. If you are looking for a spot in Uptown or Andersonville, be sure to stop by this stellar bar, sporting one of the most extensive beer selections in Chicago (over 200 to choose from, half of which are Belgian). The decor, with European vintage posters, also takes its inspiration from the country with one of the finest beer cultures and even the food pays homage with wonderful steamed mussels served with fries, duck, and gooey Gruyère cheese and ham sandwiches. With no TV, conversation reigns and there's even a good selection of magazines for those drinking alone.

The Irish Oak 3511 N Clark St ☎773/935-6669. This Irish pub – the entire establishment was designed and made in Ireland and shipped over – with around a decade under its belt has quickly become a local favourite. Located near Wrigley Field, it's a pleasant alternative to the raucous sports bars on game days, and features live music on Thursday, Friday and Saturday, plus great shepherd's pie, 25¢ wings on Mondays, and all-you-can-eat fish 'n' chips ($10.75) on Friday.

Jake's Pub 2932 N Clark St near W Oakdale Ave ☎773/248-3318. Amidst an environment of tired and corny sports bars stands *Jake's Pub*. It falls squarely into the dive bar category, and it makes no apologies. A beer and shot type of place and it's cash only. Dog-lovers bring their animals and the jukebox ranges from the Clash to Ol' Blue Eyes.

John Barleycorn Memorial Pub 3454 N Clark St, ☎773/549-6000. For review, see Lincoln Park location on p.191.

Redmond's 3358 N Sheffield Ave, at W Roscoe St ☎773/404-2151. A world apart from the traditional sports bar, this upscale, uplifting place with welcoming staff offers a full menu of comfort food dishes, including ribs, mac and cheese and Guinness stew, as well as plush booths and thirty-odd beers. Sample them in the outdoor patio area.

Resi's Bierstube 2034 W Irving Park, at N Lincoln and N Damen Aves ☎773/472-1749. Located beyond Lakeview's northern reaches, *Resi's* is worth the trek if you're looking to immerse yourself in some hearty German ambience – this bar is hard to beat. Choose from more than thirty Bavarian beers on tap, 150 bottles of imported beer, and fifteen *Weiss* (wheat beers). There's also a veritable smorgasbord of bratwurst, knackwurst, schnitzel and wieners to be enjoyed while surrounded by Oktoberfest posters and souvenirs or you can sit in the pleasant beer garden out back.

Sheffield's Wine and Beer Garden 3258 N Sheffield Ave, at W Belmont Ave ☎773/281-4989. When the weather's warm, lines wrap around the entrance of this leafy outdoor beer garden for the fine assortment of wines and beers (twenty drafts, plus bottles). The indoor bar is intimate with lots of nooks and crannies in which to hide away.

Simon's Tavern 5210 N Clark St, at W Foster Ave ☎773/878-0894. This former speakeasy, now an aged Swedish bar (dig the Viking-style decorations and hunting paraphernalia), has a beautiful, long wooden bar and good Andersonville neighbourhood cred. The

friendly staff, full of historical info, tend to a crowd that's a mix of Swedes, gays and lesbians, and people who come for a slice of chilled-out, Chicago-style conversation and excellent deals on cocktails.

Will's Northwoods Inn 3030 N Racine St, near W Nelson St ☎773/528-4400. While you may not make it up to Wisconsin during your visit to Chicago, you can visit Will's. It's a bar that celebrates all things Wisconsin and, as such, there's a good mix of taxidermy and related Wisconsin sports memorabilia on the walls. Cheese curds, brats and hefty cheeseburgers are staple food items here.

▲ Duke of Perth

Bucktown, Wicker Park, and Ukrainian Village

California Clipper 1002 N California Ave, at W Augusta Blvd ☎773/384-2547. This former speakeasy, near Humboldt Park, has plenty of retro appeal with vintage booths, Art Deco bar and low lighting. Frequent free live music at the weekends, and the last Monday of every month is bingo night. Open until 2am during the week, until 3am on Saturday.

Club Lucky 1824 W Wabansia Ave, at N Honore St ☎773/227-2300. Retro Rat Pack-styled hangout, where the drinks are strong and the moderately priced food is straightforward and satisfying.

Gold Star Bar 1755 W Division St, at N Wood St ☎773/227-8700. All-business, old-fashioned Ukrainian Village bar where the focus is on drinking cheap beer ($2 bottles of Budweiser) in strictly blue-collar surroundings with a great classic and alt-rock jukebox.

Hideout 1354 W Wabansia Ave, at W Willow St ☎773/227-4433. Tucked away among the warehouses between Old Town and Bucktown, *Hideout* is a sedate bar that just happens to be the centre of Chicago's alternative country-music scene. A refreshing change to the crop of rather self-conscious bars, it attracts an eclectic, straight-talking, plain drinking (mostly beer) crowd for the almost nightly shows, which include everything from Charles Darwin impersonators to soul legend Mavis Staples.

Map Room 1949 N Hoyne Ave, at W Armitage Ave ☎773/252-7636. One of Bucktown's best bars, the *Map Room* offers a wide selection of beers (over one hundred varieties) in a travel-themed setting – bookshelves lined with *National Geographic*, guidebooks and seemingly random (yet appropriate) gazetteers. Crowded every night (there's usually some drink special on tap), the friendly, family-owned bar has live music on the weekend and a popular "international night" on Tuesday – a buffet focussing on a single country's cuisine; a couple of beers earns you a free plate. It's also one of the few bars in the area to have football on the television direct from the UK or Europe. In the mornings it functions more as a coffee shop, a laid-back place to read and soak up the local vibe over coffee and bagels.

Marie's Rip-Tide Lounge 1745 W Armitage Ave, at N Hermitage Ave ☎773/278-7317. A small, late-night tavern, which peaks after midnight, between Lincoln Park and Bucktown, serving a mixed crowd – everyone from yuppies to blue-collar types to artist-wannabes and determined bar-crawlers who've been tossed out of every other tavern in the neighbourhood. The staff – especially the adorably testy and cantankerous Marie herself, who has been part of the local scene since the 1960s – is part of its appeal. Check out the one-of-a-kind skeet shooting game that hangs precariously over the bar.

Nick's Beergarden 1516 N Milwaukee Ave, at W North Ave ☎773/252-1155. Right under the El tracks, the rather slovenly *Nick's* succeeds largely because it's one of the few late-night bars in Wicker Park (open till 4am Sun–Fri, 5am on Sat). Still, it's a congenial place with a beer garden (open May–Nov) and live music (usually blues) on weekends. Most people don't start arriving until midnight, when the unusually large space fills up fast.

Northside Bar & Grill 1635 N Damen Ave, at W Wabansia Ave ☎773/384-3555. While bars come and go in trendy Wicker Park and Bucktown, the gregarious and unbuttoned *Northside* has carved a lasting place for itself with its huge, mouth-watering burgers, which get devoured by the largely beer-drinking crowds of pretty young people who fill the year-round outdoor patio.

Quencher's 2401 N Western Ave, at W Fullerton Ave ☎773/276-9730. This hip microbrewery in the northern reaches of Bucktown has been around since 1979, long before the trend hit the mainstream. There's an astonishing array of more than 200 beers and a newly added food menu which includes a notable chilli and an intriguing pizza covered with tater tots. Live music every night.

Rainbo Club 1150 N Damen Ave, at W Division St ☎773/489-5999. An old neighbourhood standby that's become chic by virtue of its trendy Ukrainian Village location. Graced by artists past and present – including Nelson Algren – there is an authentically retro feel to the place (pinball machine and photo booth), complemented by both the above-average music that spans all genres and the inexpensive beers that satisfy all tastes. Lounging in the comfy booths, the crowd ranges from glam twenty-somethings to boho students and hipster moms.

Subterranean 2011 W North Ave, at N Damen Ave ☎773/278-6600. One of the best bars around the six-corner intersection of N Milwaukee, W North and N Damen aves, this nineteenth-century brothel and gambling house (thus the chandelier and ornate woodwork) is now a three-floor cabaret, lounge and dance club. The first floor, *The Lounge*, achieves a sexy, red-light-district vibe, while the two-floor *Cabaret* upstairs is a cool live-music venue featuring everything from reggae and hip-hop to house, Motown and open music mics. There are drinks specials each night, and generally there's a minimal cover charge as well when a DJ or live band is in the house.

The West Side

Betty's Blue Star Lounge 1600 W Grand Ave, at N Ashland Ave ☎312/243-8778. A barebones, late-night bar (until 4am during the week, 5am on Sat) and live music venue that brings in a hip but relaxed crowd for the cheap beers and the soulful ambience. Live music tends to focus on hip-hop and house, courtesy of local DJs and musicians, and weekends bring a carnival dance party vibe with hard-core revellers showing up and picking up the pace around midnight.

Jaks Tap 901 W Jackson Blvd, at S Peoria St ☎312/666-1700. Forty draft beers (Bellhaven to Warsteiner) and an extensive brewpub menu are the highlights of this University of Illinois-Chicago area bar. Exposed brick walls and lots of gleaming wood add to the atmosphere. The bar food is a cut above average, drawing local workers at lunchtime. Decent pizzas will satisfy the late-night munchies. After some pizza, pick up a cue stick and take advantage of the pool tables.

Matchbox 770 N Milwaukee Ave, at N Ogden Ave ☎312/666-9292. Be prepared to get up close and personal with some of Chicago's most idiosyncratic locals at this slender bar – one of the smallest and most intriguing places in the city. The very tight space, excellent martinis and friendly atmosphere make for a fun, communal experience.

Plush 1104 W Madison ☎312/491-9800. An unpretentious lounge bar with a playfully decadent vibe, complete with velvet sofas and decorated in lavish tones of gold and crimson. Middle Eastern overtures include fragrant hookahs and belly-dancing nights on Tuesdays. Martinis and Champagne are the libations of choice. There is also a dinner menu featuring global-fusion dishes.

Tasting Room 1415 W Randolph St, at N Ogden Ave ☎312/942-1212. A two-storey, tastefully decorated wine bar, complete with sofas and armchairs, that's more about the wine than the ambience, the *Tasting Room* employs several sommeliers to help visitors with their choices which can be paired with tasty appetizers (from cheese selections, including global cheese tasters to pizzas, to meat and seafood plates). Don't miss the great views of the skyline from the second floor. The wine is also available for purchase in the Randolph Wine Cellars, attached to the bar. All in all, the place has a surprisingly non-pretentious vibe and it's well worth a visit.

South Side and Hyde Park

The Cove Lounge 1750 E 55th St, at S Everett Ave ☎773/684-1013. A Hyde Park hole-in-the-wall that caters mainly to a handful of regulars, except on Thursday nights when crowds of UC students take full advantage of the $6 pitchers. A vaguely nautical-meets-sports-bar boosts the place's generally pedestrian interior.

Jimmy's Woodlawn Tap 1172 E 55th St, at S Woodlawn Ave ☎773/643-5516. Referred to strictly as "*Jimmy's*" after the bar's late owner, this dimly lit bar is an oasis for locals and students alike, who love its tweedy airs and cheap drinks and burgers. The interior is sparse on decor (save a clutch of University of Chicago items), but the conversation topics here range from Sartre to the White Sox.

Keegan's Pub 10618 S Western Ave, at W 106th St ☎773/233-6829. Wood-panelled walls, flags, portraits of Irish writers, finely poured Guinness, a fireplace and fervour for the White Sox are the name of the game at this classic neighbourhood joint in Beverly, the South Side Irish enclave. It's a friendly enough drinking den even if the staff is not overly excited to wait on a new face and certainly the best bet for a drink if you are heading to a Sox game.

Rogers Park and North Shore

Moody's Pub 5910 N Broadway, at W Rosedale Ave ☎773/275-2696. Far up north lies this little gem, an intimate dim-lit bar with a medieval aura, hidden behind chunky wooden doors. It oozes charm and serves a prime selection of beer and refreshing summertime cocktails. In winter, punters hang out by the fireplace munching burgers (highly recommended) and slurping hot chocolate, while in summer the languorous beer garden has been known to suck people in for entire afternoons.

Rhythm Room 1715 Maple Ave, at Church St, Evanston ☎847/491-9723. Swanky jazz bar inside the Century Theatres building is a choice spot to kill time before or after a movie. High ceilings, floor-to-ceiling windows, overstuffed leather chairs and couches, oversize martinis, decent appetizers, a pool table and free wi-fi complete the picture.

14

Nightlife and entertainment

Chicago has one of the best **music scenes** in the US, often reflecting the changing musical landscape of the country as a whole. From the early days of jazz and blues to the rise of mainstream alternative rock, Chicago has made its mark, albeit in its characteristically down-to-earth way.

Although Louis Armstrong and scores of other top musicians brought jazz from New Orleans in the early 1920s, Chicago's musical identity is rooted in the **blues**; indeed, Chicago is considered the capital of modern electric blues. During the genre's heyday in the mid-twentieth century, blues clubs lined the streets of Chicago's South Side around the influential Chess Records studio (see p.268), where blues legends Muddy Waters, Willie Dixon, Junior Wells and Koko Taylor all recorded. Economic forces have more or less pushed – or pulled – blues clubs from the South Side to the city's North Side and on an average weeknight you'll find five or six different blues acts performing in Near North and Lincoln Park alone. One would think **jazz** would be bigger in Chicago than it is; what it lacks in size, though, it more than makes up for in quality, with serious crooners like six-time Grammy nominee Kurt Elling and Patricia Barber performing locally on a regular basis. Of course, don't forget newer arrivals on the scene like saxman Frank Catalano, who holds court at *Andy's* and the *Green Mill*. Indeed, finding live jazz on any night of the week won't be hard – a visit to premier jazz club *Green Mill* (see p.199) deserves at least a night.

Besides blues and jazz, Chicago has a burgeoning **alternative rock** scene that started in the late 1980s with quality (albeit obscure) acts such as Eleventh Dream Day and came of age in the early 1990s, with breakthroughs by the Smashing Pumpkins and Liz Phair. More recently, much critical acclaim has been won by Wilco, champions of the now-established **alternative country** (or "alt country") scene which popped up in the late 1990s. As far as dance music goes, **house** and **techno** basically started in Chicago in the mid-1980s, and that's what you'll hear in many of the dance clubs, which thump till the wee hours, mostly on Thursday through Sunday nights. Indeed, the legacy of Chicago house DJs like Frankie Knuckles and Marshall Jefferson is so strong that in 2005, Mayor Richard M. Daley declared August 10 "House Unity Day" to commemorate the birthplace of the genre. In the past few years, the city's **hip-hop** scene has gained serious cred too and taken a foothold in the city's dance clubs, thanks to smash albums from Grammy-winning producer and performer Kanye West and veteran local rapper Common. The venues in Chicago are another distinction: the city has some of the country's best **rock**

halls, many of them former movie palaces and theatres converted into concert spaces. Just about every major American band, it seems, includes the city on their itineraries, and you'll be able to hear them here for not much more than $30 a ticket, much less for more obscure or indie groups.

As for a sampling of where to go: **Near North, Lincoln Park** and **Lakeview** have the highest concentration of blues and dance clubs; **Bucktown** and **Wicker Park** cater to alternative and indie rockers, while rock 'n' roll can be heard just about anywhere there's a stage and a tap. Ethnic and world music get their due at venues like *HotHouse* and *Old Town School of Folk Music*, as do gospel, hip-hop, reggae, samba and country.

For **current music listings**, pick up the excellent free weekly *Chicago Reader* – copies come out Thursday afternoon in street boxes and bookstores all over town and are usually all gone by Saturday. Other good free sources include the weekly *New City* and the gay and lesbian *Windy City Times*. Full listings also appear in the Friday issues of the *Chicago Sun-Times* and the *Chicago Tribune*, and *Chicago* magazine has useful arts and restaurant listings. The Gramaphone Ltd **record store**, at 2843 N Clark St (℡773/472-3683), is the best place for details on one-off **dance** nights.

Major concert venues

Allstate Arena 6920 N Mannheim Rd, Rosemont ℡847/635-6601; **Blue Line to River Rd, transfer to Regional Transportation Authority (RTA) bus #221 or #222. $11–20 parking for concerts.** Soulless, out-of-the-way stadium northwest of Chicago in Rosemont, pulling in big-name concerts, with seating for 18,000-plus.

Jay Pritzker Pavilion Randolph St and Michigan Ave, in Millennium Park ℡312/742-1168; **Green, Brown, Orange, or Purple Line to Randolph.** Intricate, Frank Gehry-designed outdoor stage and lawn that plays host to free seasonal concerts, including the Grant Park Music Festival and September's World Music Festival. For details, see p.248.

Petrillo Music Shell Columbus Drive and Jackson Blvd, in Grant Park; Red Line to Jackson. Multi-purpose outdoor stage and lawn in the Loop, often used for free summer concerts – notably the Chicago Blues Festival (see p.247). If you want to see the performers, get a seat near the stage; otherwise just camp out on the lawn with a blanket.

Ravinia Festival Ravinia Park Rd, Highland Park ℡847/266-5100; **reachable via Metra train (Union Pacific North Line).** A Chicago gem, this performance complex is located on the North Shore about 25 miles north of the Loop. Just a fifteen-minute ride on the Metra commuter train (board at the Ogilvie Transportation Center and get off at the Ravinia Park stop), the pavilion makes for the most intimate outdoor music venue in summer, featuring top acts of nearly every musical genre, with numerous performances by the Chicago Symphony Orchestra. Bring a picnic and sit on the lawn or buy a ticket for a seat in the pavilion (there are also concerts in the two small theatres). Ticket prices vary, though they are usually not less than $15. **United Center** 1901 W Madison St, West Side ☎ 312/455-4500; #20 Madison bus. Home to the Chicago Bulls and Blackhawks, this stadium on the sketchy side of the neighbourhood also draws superstar music acts. With a 20,000-plus capacity, it's not the most intimate place to hear music by any stretch, but if you want to see the top performers, you'll go.

Blues

Some sixty **blues clubs** are scattered throughout the city, most of them of the somewhat cramped yet cosy variety and adorned with all manner of blues memorabilia. Chicago blues was born and nurtured on the South Side (see Contexts, p.267), and for true aficionados, a visit to one of the few remaining clubs there is almost mandatory – though take care, as the area can be dodgy, especially after dark. That said, excellent blues can also be heard in any number of clubs right in the heart of the city, and many bars and clubs include live blues acts in their line-ups. Names to watch out for include Son Seals, Vance Kelly, Melvin Taylor and Buddy Guy – any one of these bluesmen can put on a powerhouse show.

Cover charges range from next to nothing to about $25, depending, usually, on the club's proximity to the tourist circuit; some require a two-drink minimum. If you happen to be around in the summer, there are plenty of outdoor music concerts to be had, including June's massive Chicago Blues Festival (see p.247). The city also runs neighbourhood blues and gospel **tours** from time to time; see p.29 for details.

Blue Chicago 536 N Clark St, at W Ohio St ☎ 312/661-0100 and 736 N Clark St, at Superior St ☎ 312/642-6261, ⓦ www.bluechicago.com; **Red Line to Grand.** Touristy blues joints featuring mostly female vocalists – they won't disappoint if you're looking for a blues scene close to the Near North hotels – there's almost always one loud, audience-involved rendition of *Sweet Home Chicago*. The $8 cover charge ($10 on Fri & Sat) gets you into both clubs, the smaller of which (no. 536) is not much bigger than a closet.
B.L.U.E.S. 2519 N Halsted St, Lincoln Park ☎ 773/528-1012; Brown or Red Line to Fullerton. Open since the 1970s, this intimate club has hosted all the greats, and has live blues every night of the week. They sometimes have deals with *Kingston Mines* across the street (see opposite). The cover on weekends is around $10, less on weekdays.
🎺 **Buddy Guy's Legends** 754 S Wabash Ave, South Loop ☎ 312/427-0333; Red Line to Harrison. This large club, owned by the veteran guitarist and vocalist, has great acoustics and atmosphere and live blues every night (Guy himself has an extended stint each Jan). The roster features new talent and established greats, and though

▲ Buddy Guy's Legends

somewhat touristy it's worth dropping by, if only because it's a classic. Monday nights are jam nights. Covers range from $8 to $12 during the week, $15 to $25 on weekends.
Checkerboard Lounge 5201 S Harper Court ☎ 773/684-1472; #6 to 53rd Street. Long a fixture in the city's South Side, the *Checkerboard Lounge* moved over to Hyde Park a few years back. The setting isn't the greatest (the decor leaves much to be desired), but local favourites like Vance Kelly do offer up some tasty licks. Cover ranges

from $10–15; and make sure to call before to confirm the line-up.

House of Blues 330 N Dearborn St, Near North ☏312/527-2583, ☺www.hob.com; Red Line to Grand. Despite its name, this swish concert venue puts on all kinds of music, including blues, but with a schedule of mostly touring acts, you won't find much local flavour here. The acoustics are phenomenal and the waitstaff attentive, though, and the popular Sunday Gospel Brunch ($45.50) alone merits a visit. Concert tickets start around $20.

Kingston Mines 2548 N Halsted St, Lincoln Park ☏773/472-2031; Brown or Red Line to Fuller ton. Opened in 1968, this Chicago blues staple is one of the city's oldest blues clubs, appropriately dark, loud, and smoke-filled. It's packed every night and consistently delivers some of the finest blues around. Bands alternate on two stages, keeping up a constant stream of music throughout the evening; big names perform till 5am on Saturdays. Cover $12–15.

Rosa's Lounge 3420 W Armitage Ave, West Side ☏773/342-0452. Run by an Italian mother-and-son duo, *Rosa's* is a soulful, welcoming, and excellent blues club, with a solid calendar of shows (Tues–Sat). The only drawback is the location: it's about thirty blocks west of downtown, so you'll need a taxi. Covers vary ($5–15).

Underground Wonder Bar 10 E Walton St, Near North ☏312/266-7761; Red Line to Chicago. Cramped subterranean bar (not for light-weights or wallflowers) with live music 365 days a year, ranging from blues and jazz to reggae, performed well into the wee small hours (until 4am during the week and 5am on Sat). A bit dark and louche, in a good way. Impromptu celebrity appearances have been known to happen, but it's more likely you will catch a performance from owner Lonie Walker and the Big Ass Company Band. If it's your birthday, beware. Cover charges ($5–10) apply.

Jazz

Jazz clubs are by no means as abundant in Chicago as they are in New York and a good portion of the jazz that Chicago hears happens in bars not entirely devoted to the genre. On the other hand, the two clubs especially recommended below easily hold their own against the country's best.

Andy's 11 E Hubbard St, Near North ☏312/642-6805; Red Line to Grand. A casual fixture on Chicago's jazz scene, popular for its lunchtime concerts and Monday-night improv jam sessions. While many Chicago bars offer occasional "jazz" trios and such, *Andy's* is devoted entirely to jazz – tradi-tional, mainstream and bebop. The crowd is a mix of drinkers, jazz lovers and diners here for the menu of pizza, ribs, steaks and seafood. Mon–Fri 7pm–midnight, Sat till 1am. Cover $10–15.

Chicago Cultural Center 78 E Washington St, the Loop ☏312/346-3278; Red Line to Washington. Home to the city's main visitor centre (see p.37), this splendid old building also has gallery spaces where classical and jazz groups host weekly free lunchtime and evening concerts. The crowd is a real mix – suits on lunchbreak, travellers and music lovers in the know.

Green Dolphin Street 2200 N Ashland Ave, Lincoln Park ☏773/395-0066, ☺www.jazzitup .com; #74 bus or Red Line to Fullerton. This sophisticated and casually elegant restaurant and jazz bar attracts a mixed crowd. The music, depending on the night, could be anything from Afro-Cuban to big band. Kick back with a cigar from the floor-to-ceiling humidor or tuck into the eclectic menu.

Green Mill 4802 N Broadway, Uptown ☏773/878-5552, ☺www.greenmilljazz .com; Red Line to Lawrence. This former speakeasy and Al Capone haunt is pure Jazz Age Chicago and should not be missed. Though far from downtown, it's the most revered jazz club in the city, both for its acts, which range from bebop to progressive jazz as well as a notable weekly poetry slam, as well as its atmosphere – the beautiful interior still retains its period charm. Open till 4am. Cover varies, usually around $8.

Jazz Showcase 806 S Plymouth Court, South Loop ☏312/360-0234, ☺www .jazzshowcase.com; Red Line to Grand. If you're looking for top talent and are willing to pay a hefty cover, then the late Chicago music

▲ Andy's

mogul Joe Segal's place might be for you. Since 1947, it's been the venue of choice for mainstream jazz artists, from the Count Basie band to Hargrove and Brubeck. Shows at 8pm & 10pm Mon–Sat and 4pm, 8pm & 10pm on Sun. Students get a discount. $20–25, cash only.

Velvet Lounge 67 E Cermak Rd, Near South ☏ 312/791-9050, ⓦ www.velvetlounge.net. This relaxed tavern run by Chicago jazz institution Fred Anderson has live jazz five nights a week, and is a good place to catch the more exploratory side of recent Chi-town jazz. The mix of ensembles is impressive and reflects Chicago's continuing importance as a hub of jazz innovation.

Rock

One look at the music listings in *The Reader* will reveal dozens of **rock bands** performing any night of the week, mostly on the city's North Side in Lincoln Park, Lakeview and Wicker Park. Catching a show in one of the rock halls is a quintessential Chicago experience, especially at venues like *Metro*, *The Riviera* or *The Vic*. For smaller shows in more down-to-earth surroundings, Wicker Park's *Double Door* and *The Empty Bottle* in the Ukrainian Village offer some of the best in the city.

The bigger venues

The Aragon Ballroom 1106 W Lawrence Ave, at N Broadway, Uptown ☏ 773/561-9500, ⓦ www .aragon.com; Red Line to Lawrence. The acoustics may be wanting at this 4500-seat behemoth, but the ornate decor and size keep it on Chicago's short list of top concert venues.

The Congress Theatre 2135 N Milwaukee Ave, Bucktown ☏ 773/252-4000, ⓦ www .congresschicago.com; Blue Line to Western. This former movie palace with Gothic trimmings now attracts mainly indie and punk acts, popular DJs and a smattering of up-and-coming rock acts. Cover charges vary.

Metro 3730 N Clark St, Lakeview ☏ 773/549-0203, ⓦ www.metrochicago .com; Red Line to Addison. This club's excellent acoustics and reputation as a top venue for national and local indie acts pull in Chicago's party crowds. The *Smart Bar*, in the same building, is a dance club (see p.203).

Park West 322 W Armitage Ave, at N Clark St, Lincoln Park ☏ 773/929-5959, ⓦ www .parkwestchicago.com; Brown Line to Armitage. Spacious standby that tends to host mellow solo artists and troubadours, plus the sensitive folks who follow them. The acoustics here are some of the best in the city.

The Riviera Theatre 4746 N Racine Ave, Uptown ☏ 773/275-6800, ⓦ www.rivieratheatre.com; Red Line to Lawrence. Part of this area's music triumvirate (joining *Aragon* and *Green Mill*), the ageing but characterful *Riviera* hosts major rock acts like Les Claypool and The Pretenders. Definitely a mixed crowd here as well, as you'll get everything from emo types to hard-core hipsters. It's also got a swanky interior, complete with elaborate ceiling carvings and fancy box seats.

The Vic 3145 N Sheffield Ave, Lakeview ☏ 773/472-0449, ⓦ www.victheatre.com; Brown or Red Line to Belmont. Huge former vaudeville theatre that now sees a steady flow of popular rock, folk and comedy acts. A great place to catch a show – the acoustics are good and there's ample space to stand (on the floor) or sit (in the balcony). The only drawback is its tendency to be louder and sweatier than most other venues. Also hosts "Brew & View", movie screenings accompanied by beer and pizza, when there's not a concert on.

The smaller clubs

Cubby Bear 1059 W Addison St, at N Clark St, Wrigleyville ☎773/327-1662, ⓦwww .cubbybear.com; Red Line to Addison. Busy by day with crowds from neighbouring Wrigley Field, this boisterous sports bar features alternative rock bands after dark (Wed–Sat), though music takes a backseat to the sports scene. Cover $5–7.

The Double Door 1572 N Milwaukee Ave, Wicker Park ☎773/489-3160, ⓦwww.doubledoor.com; Blue Line to Damen. This club has been on top of the alternative music scene since it opened in 1994; its stage has been graced by a who's who of rock acts, from Smashing Pumpkins and Veruca Salt to Liz Phair and even the Rolling Stones. There's usually some indie band playing on most nights; the crowd is very Wicker Park (unshaven, consignment-store dress, messy hair), and there are pool tables downstairs if the music gets too loud. Covers vary, though it's usually half what the big North Side music venues charge.

Elbo Room 2871 N Lincoln Ave, Lakeview ☎773/549-5549, ⓦwww.elboroomchicago.com; Brown Line to Diversey. Known around Chicago as the place where band Liquid Soul got their start, this easygoing venue has lost a bit of its edge over the years, though it still puts on music most nights of the week, from ska and alternative rock to funk and acid jazz.

The Empty Bottle 1035 N Western Ave, at W Cortez St, Ukrainian Village ☎773/276-3600, ⓦwww.emptybottle.com; Blue Line to Division. A hole-in-the-wall club that showcases some top talent, ranging from up-and-coming indie bands to avant-garde jazz and progressive country. Truly loud (earplugs sold at the bar), though rarely overfilled and always enjoyable, with a crowd (hip college kids, urban yuppies, slacker twentysomethings, etc) as varied as the music.

Schubas Tavern 3159 N Southport Ave, Lakeview ☎773/525-2508, ⓦwww .schubas.com; Brown Line to Belmont. A small mainstay of the neighbourhood, booking an impressive roster of rock, alternative country, and roots revival bands. The intimate setting and wide range of up-and-coming acts make this a great place to see a show. The bar in front is very popular between sets and on weekends; the side room, *Harmony Grill*, serves up tasty American fare. Fri till 2am, Sat till 3am. Cover varies.

Folk, country and world music

Chicago's **world music** scene is surprisingly healthy, with Irish and rootsy folk music leading the list. Almost any of the neighbourhood taverns will have Irish or Celtic music on weekends, especially on Sundays, while a smaller number put on some form of **country** or **folk music**. The *Old Town School of Folk Music* (see p.103), northwest of Lakeview is perhaps the city's best venue for world music – their diverse concert offerings range from Afrobeat and Latin dance to local hip-hop and Caribbean jazz.

While we've listed some excellent venues below, it's worth noting that some of them will require a bit of transit time on a bus or train.

Abbey Pub 3420 W Grace St, at N Elston Ave, Old Irving Park ☎773/478-4408, ⓦwww .abbeypub.com; Blue Line to Addison. One of Chicago's unsung supporters of aspiring musicians and new music, with live performances every night (Irish music on Sun). The only drawback is its location in Old Irving Park, northwest of Lakeview. Covers vary.

Equator Club 4715 N Broadway, Uptown ☎773/728-2411; Red Line to Lawrence. Former speakeasy owned by Al Capone; now features live African and Caribbean music, sometimes by internationally recognized recording artists.

Exodus II 3477 N Clark St, Wrigleyville ☎773/348-3998; Red Line to Addison. Across the street from the *Wild Hare* (see p.202), this smaller, lesser-known reggae venue is less crowded and also a bit seedier, but if reggae's your thing, chances are you'll overlook the drawbacks. Rarely a cover.

FitzGerald's 6615 W Roosevelt Rd, Berwyn ☎708/788-2118, Ⓦwww .fitzgeraldsnightclub.com; Blue Line to Harlem. Excellent venue for alternative country, Cajun and zydeco but it's way out in the western suburb of Berwyn and hard to reach without a car. The club has live music every night, and despite the location, it's – along with right alongside the *Abbey, Schubas*, and the *Double Door* – among the cream of Chicago's small-scale music venues.

Hideout 1354 W Wabansia Ave ☎773/227-4433, Ⓦwww.hideoutchicago .com; Red Line to North/Clybourn. This small, eclectic roots and country-music bar is located two blocks north of North Avenue, in a no-man's-land east of Bucktown and Wicker Park; best to call for directions. The music might as well be right in your lap and the crowd relishes the club's low profile. Fri till 2am, Sat till 3am.

Kitty O'Shea's 720 S Michigan Ave, South Loop ☎312/294-6860; Brown Line to Harrison. Inside the *Hilton Chicago and Towers*, this great Irish pub offers Irish music most nights, starting at 9.30pm. The crowd is a mix of hotel guests and conventioneers, as well as a few discerning locals. Daily 11am–2am.

Martyr's 3855 N Lincoln Ave ☎773/404-9494, Ⓦwww.martyrslive.com; Brown Line to Irving Park. Restaurant and bar offering an eclectic roster of live entertainment by touring artists, with traditional Irish music on Monday and open-mic rockabilly on the first Thursday of each month.

Old Town School of Folk Music 4544 N Lincoln Ave, Lincoln Square ☎773/728-6000, Ⓦwww .oldtownschool.org; Brown Line to Western. Fabulous school and concert space in Lincoln Square (east of Uptown) for one of the city's enduring folk music traditions. Folk isn't all you'll hear, though; you might catch a concert of merengue or Western swing, or performances of African dance. Concerts start around 7pm, and tickets range from $5 to $25. Its curriculum of music classes (everything from fiddle to African drums) is the best in the city.

Wild Hare and Singing Armadillo Frog Sanctuary 3530 N Clark St, Wrigleyville ☎773/327-4273, Ⓦwww.wildharereggae.com; Red Line to Addison. Chicago's premier venue for reggae. There's no cover before 9pm, and the whole place feels like a Jamaican dancehall and gets packed and sweaty.

Dance clubs

Chicago's **club life** is ever-changing, with new venues popping up all the time, especially in the old warehouses west of the Loop. In fact, the city owes its thriving club scene to the birth of house music here during the early 1980s. Many of those warehouses have since evolved into extravagant dance clubs, with velvet couches, VIP rooms, mega-dancefloors and expensive lighting and sound systems. You don't have to haunt the clubs to hear top DJs, though – many of the late-night bars and lounges downtown have resident DJs spinning on weekend nights. These days, the "hot" club of the moment seems almost arbitrary – rather confusing given that they all offer, more or less, the same thing. In general, the larger and more ostentatious the club, the younger the crowd; the smaller, lesser known clubs tend to attract a late 20s and early 30s crowd with their more intimate settings.

Cover charges range from $5 to $25, and dress is typically upscale. Do not wear jeans or athletic shoes, or you're likely to be turned away at the door. Also, be prepared for long waits to get in ($10–20 will usually persuade a bouncer to let you in immediately, however, though that's no guarantee).

The clubs listed below have proven their staying power and are also among the best; if in doubt, or looking for the new hot thing, consult any number of the listings papers mentioned at the beginning of the chapter.

Betty's Blue Star Lounge 1600 W Grand Ave, at N Ashland Ave, West Side ☎312/243-1699, ⊛www.bettysbluestarlounge.com. Casual bar/club that transforms into a raging after-hours hot spot for a twenty- and thirty-something crowd. Up-and-coming and established DJs spin funk, dub, classic house and hip-hop every night of the week, and cheap drinks pull in both clubbers and some serious drinkers. Sun–Fri 7am–4am, Sat 11am–5am. Take a cab there and back.

Crobar 1543 N Kingsbury St, west of Old Town ☎312/266-1900, ⊛www.crobar.com; Red Line to North/Clybourn. Hyper-trendy warehouse club near the river, spinning old-school house, techno and hip-hop from standout resident DJs like Felix da Housecat. More exclusive than the other big-name clubs – without ostentatious dress you may be turned away at the door. Thurs, Fri & Sun 10pm–4am, Sat till 5am.

Excalibur 632 N Dearborn St, Near North ☎312/266-1944; Red Line to Grand. An institution in the city, and quite touristy because of it – not to mention for its location – blasting rock, techno and R'n'B on several floors; Thursdays are dedicated to Latin music. Important architectural tidbit: This building was the first home for what later became the Chicago History Museum.

Funky Buddha Lounge 728 W Grand Ave, West Side ☎312/666-1695, ⊛www.funkybuddha.com; Blue Line to Grand. Small and fashionably plush dance lounge, open every night. A favourite of younger clubgoers for having a thoroughly mixed crowd and the city's top DJs.

Le Passage 937 N Rush, Gold Coast ☎312/255-0022, ⊛www.lepassage.tv; Red Line to Chicago. Hidden in an alley off Rush St is the entrance to this chic French-Moroccan restaurant/lounge, with a touch of South Beach and New York. It's popular with an after-work, thirty-something crowd, and, oddly, people do come here to eat, but the house music and dance scene is the main draw. The location's convenient if you're staying downtown, the crowd is upscale (as is the dress) and covers can be hefty ($20).

Rednofive 440 N Halsted St, near Grand Ave, West Side ☎312/733-6699, ⊛www.rednofive.com; Blue Line to Grand. Dark, underground space that heads up Chicago's A-list clubs with its cutting-edge DJ styles.

Reserve 858 W Lake St, West Side ☎312/455-1111, ⊛www.reserve-chicago.com. At this swank, Asian-inspired club (think candles, brushed copper and dark wood furniture), the city's most fabulous late-night crowd – mostly moneyed thirty-somethings – lounges to European "mash" music and indulges in pricey bottle service. Call ahead to get on the guest list. Weekend cover men $20, women $10. Tues–Fri 6pm–2am, Sat 7pm–3am.

Smart Bar underneath *Metro*, 3730 N Clark St, Wrigleyville ☎773/549-0203, ⊛www.smartbarchicago.com; Red Line to Addison. Great techno and old-school house on the weekend (with occasional appearances by legendary DJ Derrick Carter) in the neighbourhood's post-industrial surrounds. Weekdays see a mix of punk, Goth and Eighties nights. Open late – till 5am on Fri and Sat, and especially crowded when shows at the *Metro* (see p.200) let out. Cover after 11pm (around $5).

Sonotheque 1444 W Chicago Ave ☎312/226-7600, ⊛sonotheque.net. Designed to offer an acoustically perfect listening experience, this minimalist, linear lounge emphasizes sophisticated international DJs spinning an eclectic mix of down-tempo sounds and attracts a likewise upscale crowd. Occasional cover $2–10 for guest-DJ sets. Sun–Fri 7pm–2am, Sat 7pm–3am.

Sound-Bar 226 W Ontario St ☎312/787-4480, ⊛www.sound-bar.com; Brown Line to Chicago. The neighbourhood's newest mega-club boasts a sleek decor of stainless steel and smoked glass and a 4000-square-foot dancefloor filled with club kids grooving to sets by acclaimed resident DJs Chris Eterno, John Curley and others. Sunday is gay night. No cover before 11pm with RSVP, $10–20 after. Thurs & Fri 9pm–4am, Sat 9pm–5am.

(14)

NIGHTLIFE AND ENTERTAINMENT | Dance clubs

15

Performing arts and film

Chicago theatre is downright phenomenal, comprised of a unique blend of traditional "Broadway" plays and offbeat works by one of its soulful theatre companies, the Steppenwolf or the Goodman.

The **classical music** is equally stellar: the Lyric Opera of Chicago is internationally renowned and the Chicago Symphony Orchestra is one of the best in the country, performing hundreds of shows a year. A few smaller groups also routinely put on free concerts around the city. Two **dance companies**, the classically inclined Joffrey Ballet and the more avant-garde Hubbard Street Dance Chicago are regarded as US emissaries to the world dance community, yet manage to remain quite visible throughout the city. Second City, with all its lore, has brought the spotlight to Chicago's **improvisational comedy scene**, and should not be missed on even a short stay in town. And if none of this appeals, there is also a strong **film** presence in Chicago, with ample opportunity to catch even the most obscure indie film or documentary. For **information** on how to find out what's on, see box opposite.

Theatre

Typically of Chicago, its inhabitants have developed theatre in their own style – daring and in-your-face – with two major theatre companies leading the charge: the basement-born **Steppenwolf Theatre** in Old Town and the slightly more refined **Goodman Theatre** in the Loop. In recent decades, Chicago actors and writers, following in the footsteps of noted actors and Steppenwolf alumni John Malkovich, Joan Allen and Gary Sinise, saw the local stage as a springboard to the bigger and better, which is to say New York's Broadway – the pinnacle of American theatre. But on the heels of much success and many a Tony Award, the trend is changing and Chicago has become a stage where actors strive to remain. Garage theatres and local one-room venues have grown in number and, as such, they've become a wonderful complement to the city's revived **Theatre District** in the Loop along Randolph Street. Here in the Loop, gloriously restored old vaudeville theatres and movie palaces like the **Oriental Theatre**, the **Cadillac Palace**, and the **Chicago Theatre** host touring productions of Broadway shows as well as pre-Broadway launches of productions, making the city one of the finest theatre destinations in the country.

For current **information** on plays and **tickets**, check with the **League of Chicago Theatres** (228 S Wabash Ave, Suite #200 ☎312/554-9800, ⓦwww.chicagoplays.com), a local alliance of most Chicago theatres, formed to promote the scene, with all the current information on what's running where. **Hot Tix** (ⓦwww.hottix.org), the service for last-minute, half-priced theatre and dance tickets, has **booths** at 72 E Randolph St, the Chicago Water Works Visitor Center (see p.37) and 163 E Pearson St.

The *Chicago Reader* (ⓦwww.chireader.com), available at cafés, bars and newsstands throughout the city, is always great for **listings and showtimes**, as are the *Chicago Sun-Times* (ⓦwww.suntimes.com) and the *Chicago Tribune* (ⓦwww.chicagotribune.com). Alternatively, ⓦwww.broadwayinchicago.com is the website for three big-name, downtown theatres – the Cadillac Palace, Oriental Theatre and the LaSalle Bank Theatre (formerly the Shubert Theatre). Two radio stations, WBEZ 91.5 FM (ⓦwww.wbez.org) and WFMT 98.7 FM (ⓦwww.networkchicago.com/wfmt), are other sources of events happening around the city.

Away from the Loop, a number of mid-sized venues like **Victory Gardens** and **The Royal George** put on a mix of dramas, musicals and comedies – most of them locally produced – and smaller companies like **Black Ensemble Theatre** and **Red Orchid** ply their trade. The lists below represent only select venues and companies as the full list is far too long to include; consider them as a jumping-off point.

Theatre District auditoriums

Cadillac Palace Theatre 151 W Randolph St, at N LaSalle St ☎312/977-1700, ⓦwww.broadwayinchicago.com; **Brown, Blue, Green, Orange or Purple Line to Clark.** The facade has a boring high-rise look about it but step inside and you'll see a space somewhat reminiscent of a French chateau, dripping with crystal chandeliers, huge mirrors and gold add-ons. This huge (2300 seats) theatre was built in 1926 – it succeeded and suffered over the years but thanks to recent renovations it's now back on the national circuit for touring Broadway plays and musicals.

The Chicago Theatre 175 N State St, at E Lake St ☎312/902-1500, ⓦwww.thechicagotheatre.com; **Brown, Green, Orange, Purple or Red Line to State/Lake.** Built in 1921 in the French Baroque style, the *Chicago* was created with grand intentions, faced economic pressures and nearly succumbed to the wrecking ball. But in 1986 the theatre was restored and reopened with a gala performance by Frank Sinatra and now welcomes touring Broadway shows and big-name musicians.

LaSalle Bank Theatre 22 W Monroe St, at S State St ☎312/977-1700, ⓦwww.broadwayinchicago.com; **Blue or Red Line to Monroe.** Restored in late 2005, the former Shubert Theatre is one of Chicago's classier, elder Loop venues. Originally a vaudeville show house, the space is a prime destination for big-name, big-budget Broadway shows.

Oriental Theatre, Ford Center for the Performing Arts 24 W Randolph St, at N Dearborn St ☎312/977-1700, ⓦwww.broadwayinchicago.com; **Brown, Green, Orange, Purple or Red Line to State/Lake.** Opened in 1927, the *Oriental*, with its ornate and bizarre interior – impressive domed ceiling, swank chandeliers, and an abundance of sculpted seahorses, goddesses and elephants – was built to resemble an Asian temple. It reopened in 1996 after a massive restoration project.

Mainstream companies

Chicago Shakespeare Theater 800 E Grand Ave, at Navy Pier, Streeterville ☎312/595-5600, ⓦwww.chicagoshakes.com. Spanking new Navy Pier stage that hosts the city's only all-Shakespeare company, in an intimate, courtyard-style theatre, where the actors perform on a catwalk-like stage that juts out into the audience. Constantly sold out, this company puts on consistently professional, if occasionally staid, productions of the Bard's plays.

Goodman Theatre 170 N Dearborn St, at E
Randolph St, the Loop ☎312/443-3800,
ⓦwww.goodman-theatre.org; Brown, Green,
Orange, Purple or Red Line to State/Lake.
Even though they're the city's oldest and
perhaps most respected company, the
Goodman puts on contemporary interpretations of classics, from Shakespeare to
O'Neill, in a recently built, state-of-the-art
theatre complex. The *Goodman* has two
stages: the 856-seat Albert Ivar Goodman
Theatre and the Owen Bruner Goodman
Theatre, a moveable courtyard theatre with
roughly 400 seats. Ask about "Tix-At-Six"
for half-priced tickets that go on sale at
6pm the day of performance (tickets go
fast, so it's best to show up by 5.30pm).
For further ticket information, call or stop
by the box office.
Lookingglass Theatre Company 821 N
Michigan Ave, Near North ☎312/337-0665,
ⓦwww.lookingglasstheatre.org. This edgy
group, headquartered in the Chicago
Water Works Visitors Center, boasts past
productions that include the original
staging of *Metamorphoses*, Mary Zimmerman's 2002 Tony Award-winning play
performed in and around an onstage pool
of water.
Steppenwolf Theatre 1650 N Halsted St, at W
Willow St, Old Town ☎312/335-1650, ⓦwww
.steppenwolf.org; Red Line to North/Clybourn.
The cornerstone of the Chicago theatre
scene; for history, see box below.

Off-Loop theatres

Apollo Theater 2540 N Lincoln Ave, at W Wrightwood Ave, Lincoln Park ☎773/935-6100,
ⓦwww.apollochicago.com; Brown, Purple or
Red Line to Fullerton. This 440-seat space in
Lincoln Park hosts children's productions on
the weekends and has been home to wildly
popular open runs of female-friendly shows
like Eve Ensler's *Vagina Monologues* and,
more recently, the *Million Dollar Quartet* (a
tribute to a legendary and impromptu
meeting between Elvis Presley and some
other celebrated 1950s rock legends).
Athenaeum Theatre 2936 N Southport Ave, at W
Oakdale Ave, Lakeview ☎773/935-6860, ⓦwww
.athenaeumtheatre.com; Brown Line to Wellington.
This old performance complex, built in 1911,
is one of the more widely used theatre and
performance venues on the North Side –
there's always something happening on either
the main stage or the smaller studios.
Bailiwick Arts Center 1229 W Belmont Ave, at N
Racine Ave, Lakeview ☎773/883-1090, ⓦwww
.bailiwick.org; Brown, Purple or Red Line to
Belmont. Chicago's leading gay and lesbian
theatre centre, which frequently offers
concurrent performances.
Black Ensemble Theater 4520 N Beacon St, at W
Sunnyside Ave, Uptown ☎773/769-4451, ⓦwww
.blackensenbletheater.org; Brown Line to
Montrose. A wonderful success story, this
small and perennially popular company is
basically a front for founder, director, producer

The Steppenwolf Theatre

The **Steppenwolf** is Chicago's most innovative company; it's a brand still seen today
in the work of long-time members like **John Malkovich** and **Gary Sinise**, who
occasionally return to grace the group's stage. Three actors (Sinise, Jeff Perry, and
"Oz" star Terry Kinney) founded the company in a church basement in the far north
suburb of Highland Park in 1974. In the decades since, it has grown to three stages
in a sleek, modern edifice in Old Town, and a 34-actor company which now includes
familiar names like Joan Allen, Kevin Anderson, John Mahoney, Laurie Metcalf and
Martha Plimpton. Their emotionally raw 1982 production of Sam Shepard's *True
West*, directed by Sinise and starring Malkovich and Metcalf, was an unparalleled
success, running for four months before transferring to New York (the first of many
Steppenwolf productions to do so) and is regarded as seminal by many in the theatre
world. Subsequent high points include 1986's live stage extravaganza of Tom Waits'
concept album, *Frank's Wild Years*, at the Briar Street Theatre, and the Tony Award-
winning adaptation of *The Grapes of Wrath* in 1990. More recently, the theatre has
seen the world premiere of ensemble member Tracy Letts' Pulitzer Prize finalist *Man
from Nebraska* in 2003, and welcomed Malkovich back in 2005 for the premiere of
Stephen Jeffreys' *Lost Land*.

and actress Jackie Taylor's long-running theatrical homages to legends like Ella Fitzgerald, Jackie Wilson and Etta James. **Briar Street Theatre 3133 N Halsted St, at W Fletcher St, Lakeview ☎773/348-4000, ⒲www .blueman.com; Brown, Purple or Red Line to Belmont.** This no-frills Boystown theatre is the current home of the long-running Blue Man Group show, a bizarre, multi-sensory production starring three famously bald, blue-headed men. Pop Dadaism for the masses. **Chicago Dramatists 1105 W Chicago Ave, at N Milwaukee Ave, West Town ☎312/633-0630, ⒲www.chicagodramatists.org; bus #66.** A small, bare-bones space that presents dramatic works by up-and-coming local playwrights. Always top quality (and affordable). **Court Theatre 5535 S Ellis Ave, at E 55th St, South Side ☎773/753-4472, ⒲www.court theatre.org.** On the South Side's University of Chicago campus, the Court produces historically classic comedies and dramas, each deftly written. It will often host two shows simultaneously on its separate stages. Tickets range from $24 to $34, though half-price tickets are available two hours before the show.

Drury Lane Theatre Water Tower Place 175 E Chestnut St, Near North ☎312/642-2000, ⒲www.drurylanewatertower.com. This former movie theatre was renovated and reopened in the summer of 2005 as a 575-seater which stages Chicago and American premieres of new musicals and plays, as well as Broadway crowd-pleasers like *The Full Monty* and classics like *Grand Hotel*. Tickets are $50–60.

ETA Creative Arts Foundation 7558 S Chicago Ave, at E 75th St, South Side ☎773/752–3955, ⒲www.etacreativeartsfoundation.org. The leading African-American arts organization on the South Side that's been putting on successful, often family-oriented, plays for some thirty years now.

Mercury Theatre 3745 N Southport Ave, at W Grace St, Lakeview ☎773/325-1700; Brown Line to Southport. Smallish live-theatre venue (300 seats), two doors north of the *Music Box Theatre*. Open only since 1996, it's quickly become one of the city's small-stage favourites, often hosting plays of the family-friendly variety for months at a time.

Royal George Theatre 1641 N Halsted St, at W Willow St, Old Town ☎312/988-9000, ⒲www .theroyalgeorgetheatre.com; Red Line to North/ Clybourn. Right across Halsted from the

Steppenwolf (see opposite), this is a modest, two-stage theatre that hosts both long-running comedy shows and touring dramas. **Theater on the Lake 2400 N Lake Shore Drive, at W Fullerton Parkway ☎312/742-7994, ⒲www.chicagoparkdistrict.com.** Waterside venue where local theatre groups like Steppenwolf and Second City put on sampler shows for a couple weeks at a time during the summer. **TimeLine Theatre 615 W Wellington Ave, at N Broadway St, Lakeview ☎312/409-8463, ⒲www.timelinetheatre.com; bus #22.** Currently in a small space tucked away on a quiet residential street, this spunky little group produces works by Gore Vidal and other contemporary works like *The History Boys*. **Victory Gardens Theater 2433 N Lincoln Ave Lincoln Park ☎773/871-3000, ⒲www.victory gardens.org; Brown, Purple or Red Line to Fullerton.** This Tony-winning company has produced a considerable number of premieres (more than any other in Chicago), and is known for helping nurture new and less experienced talent, especially of the local variety. The group recently moved to the historic *Biograph Theatre* at 2433 N Lincoln Ave and their recent works have featured new and emerging playwrights from Serbia, West Africa and, of course, Chicago. They also offer a special performance for families every Saturday.

Fringe theatre and itinerant companies

About Face Theatre 1222 W Wilson Ave ☎773/784-8565, ⒲www.aboutfacetheatre.org. This groundbreaking company addresses issues of gender and sexuality in smart, visually stunning productions. Recent hits include the Chicago premiere of *Take Me Out*, the world premiere of the musical *Winesburg, Ohio*, and the original production of the multiple-Tony-winning *I Am My Own Wife*. **Redmoon Theater 1463 W Hubbard St, West Side ☎312/850-8440, ⒲www.redmoon .org.** Experimental company specializing in "theatrical spectacles" that fall somewhere between *outré* performance art, puppet shows and surrealist theatre. **Stage Left Theatre 3408 N Sheffield Ave ☎773/883-8830, ⒲www.stagelefttheatre.com.** Founded in 1982, this collective of actors, directors, writers and designers produces mostly new plays that raise debate about political and social issues, from 9/11 to apartheid and the death penalty.

PERFORMING ARTS AND FILM | Theatre

Comedy

Comedy on stage in Chicago is almost entirely made up. That is, there's an improvisational comedy troupe – based on a model invented by the legendary **Second City** theatre back in the late 1950s – on seemingly every block and in every little theatre space (most of them are itinerant) ready to take audience suggestions and spin them into a (possibly) funny routine; check the *Reader* for weekly listings. One of the few exceptions is the venerable **Zanies**, a straight-up standup–comic joint in Old Town.

ComedySportz Theatre 2851 N Halsted St, at W Wolfram St, Lakeview ☏773/549-8080, ⓦwww .comedysportzchicago.com; Brown or Purple Line to Diversey. A wholly Chicago creation, this blend of sports and comedy – two teams of comics battle against each other in song and scenes – is a fun, audience-driven experience, which you'll find outright weird or just plain funny. "Competitions" happen Thurs–Sat, beginning at 8pm; $17.

ImprovOlympic 3541 N Clark St, at W Addison St, Wrigleyville ☏773/880-0199, ⓦwww .improvolympic.com; Red Line to Addison. A couple of former *Second City* folks founded this improv landmark back in the early 1980s. Their particular style of improv – called "The Harold" – takes one audience suggestion and spins it into a piece of instant comic theatre lasting a half-hour or more. Alumni include Mike Myers, Andy Dick and Tina Fey.

Neo-Futurarium 5153 N Ashland Ave, at W Foster Ave ☏773/275-5255, ⓦwww .neofuturists.org; bus #22. Up on the far North Side resides this strange little place, where is performed the long-running *Too Much Light Makes the Baby Go Blind*, a blitzkrieg of thirty mini-plays in sixty minutes. The $8–13 admission is determined at the door by a pair of dice.

The Playground 3209 N Halsted St, at W Henderson Ave, Lakeview ☏773/871-3793, ⓦwww.the-playground.com; Brown Line to Addison. Solo, skit, team and improv comedy shows run every Thursday through Sunday night.

Second City 1616 N Wells St, at W North Ave, Old Town ☏312/337-3992, ⓦwww .secondcity.com; bus #22. For over four decades, *Second City* has been a breeding ground for the nation's top comics, launching dozens of fledgling comics to stardom. The troupe performs a nightly series of sketches mixed with improvisation – never less than hilarious. There's also a smaller stage – *Second City e.t.c.* (1608 N Wells St) – producing similar material in the same building. Cover charge and two-drink minimum. See box on p.91 for more.

Zanies 1548 N Wells St, at W North Ave, Old Town ☏312/337-4027, ⓦwww.zanies.com; bus #22. Pretty much the only place to see standup comedy in the city, *Zanies* packs them into its somewhat rough-at-the-edges club with two or three shows a night. Often the comics are less than stellar, but you can occasionally catch big names slumming. Cover charge and two-drink minimum.

Classical music and opera

Chicago's classical music scene is a straightforward affair – there's the internationally acclaimed **Chicago Symphony Orchestra** (CSO) and then all other groups a tier or two lower. The city is also home to several top-notch summer music **festivals** at Ravinia and in Grant Park (see p.67).

The Chicago Symphony Orchestra

The CSO Symphony Center, 220 S Michigan Ave ☏312/294-3000, ⓦwww.cso.org. Performs at about ten times a month Sept-June when they're not touring domestically or internationally, which they do several times per year, generally for one or two weeks at a time. After having George Solti at the helm for many years, since 2006 the one hundred-plus members of the CSO have followed the lead of Bernard Haitink, who is well known for his previous work with the Concertgebouw Orchestra and the London Philharmonic Orchestra. Tickets for the CSO can be pricey, between $25 and $200, the cheapest seats far away in the gallery. Alternatively, CSO offers "RUSH" seating, general admission for any available seat just before the performance. Seats are not confirmed, so you may be asked to move to a free seat elsewhere if the original ticketholder should arrive late. Inquire about this last-resort option with the ticket agent in the lobby just before showtime.

Smaller orchestras and chamber groups

The Chicago Chamber Musicians 2 Prudential Plaza, 180 N Stetson St ☎312/819-5800, ⓦ www.chicagochambermusic.org. This cadre of devout musicians put on some fifty concerts a year, many of which are held at DePaul University's Concert Hall, 800 W Belden Ave (☎773/325-7260), in Lincoln Park. They are best known (and loved) around town for their "First Monday" series – free lunchtime performances underneath the Cultural Center's Tiffany dome on the first Monday of every month.

Chicago Chamber Orchestra ☎312/922-5570, ⓦ www.chicagochamberorchestra.org). Founded in 1952, the 35-member orchestra also perform at the Cultural Center, with monthly shows encompassing works from the Baroque to the present.

Chicago Sinfonietta ☎312/236-3681, ⓦwww .chicagosinfonietta.org. This Evanston orchestra under the leadership of Mahler Award-winner and Emmy nominee Paul

Freeman, has a multicultural feel to the music they produce, and tends to fuse classical with modern – everything from solos to orchestra-backed marimba performances. They hold a good number of their concerts at Symphony Center.

The Chicago Youth Symphony Orchestras ☎312/939-2207, ⓦwww.cyso.org. A full (110-piece) orchestra comprising elite high-school musicians from the Chicagoland area; they perform a fall and a winter show each year, usually held at Symphony Center.

Music of the Baroque ☎312/551-1414, ⓦwww .baroque.org. The Midwest's largest group (60 musicians) playing sixteenth- and seventeenth-century music, perform in St. Michael's Church, St Paul's Church, First United Methodist, as well as a bunch of suburban venues, weekdays throughout the year – single event tickets are available.

Opera

Lyric Opera of Chicago Civic Opera House, 20 N Wacker Drive ☎312/332-2244, ⓦwww .lyricopera.org. Nearly as acclaimed as the CSO, the Lyric is tops for opera in Chicago and is, indeed, one of the finest opera companies in the world, having welcomed performers ranging from Maria Callas and Pavarotti to dancer Rudolf Nureyev in the magnificent – and recently restored Art Deco building. Its season is from mid-September to early February, and most performances are sold out. If you want even a chance at a pricey ($30–165) ticket, you'll have to put yourself on the Lyric Opera mailing list and they'll send out a "Priority

Other classical groups

Beyond the CSO, there are a number of classical music groups in Chicago performing nearly every day of the week, at the Symphony Center during the summer and when the CSO is off touring. **Chicago Chamber musicians** (see above) present intimate monthly concerts of classic works by composers like Haydn and Brahms; **Music of the Baroque** (☎312/551-1414, ⓦ www.baroque.org) focusses on earlier works for chorus and orchestra. Also, smaller **free concerts** are frequent at the *Chicago Cultural Center* (see p.45); Newberry Library, 60 E Walton (☎312/255-3700, ⓦwww.newberry.org); The 4th Presbyterian Church of Chicago, across from the *John Hancock Center* (☎312/787-4570, ⓦwww.fourthchurch.org); Old St Pat's Church, 700 W Adams (☎312/648-1021, ⓦwww.oldstpats.org); Holy Name Cathedral, 735 N State St (☎ 312/787-8040, ⓦwww.holynamecathedral.org); *The Museum of Contemporary Art*, 220 E Chicago Ave (☎ 312/280-2660, ⓦwww .mcachicago.org); and a few other venues. Check the *Reader* or call venues for complete event listings.

Individual Ticket brochure" in late July – this will have instructions about purchasing tickets and current availability. Student tickets can be had for $20 for select performances, so check out their website for all the particulars. **Chicago Opera Theater** ☎312/704-8414, ⓦwww.chicagooperatheater.org. If you can't land a ticket to the Lyric, this is a viable, slightly less costly ($15–115) alternative, with lower-budget productions of lesser-known classics and contemporary works at the *Harris Theater for Music and Dance* in Millennium Park.

Cinema

Chicago is definitely on the shortlist of US cities with a lively film scene, which means several things: there are growing lists of decent – and public – **film festivals**, a bunch of cool venues to see classics, indies, foreign flicks and documentaries, as well as a respectable number of mainstream cinemas citywide, each pumping out the Hollywood hits. Venues range from mega-sized Omnimax theatres to music auditoriums that double as film houses to standard three- or four-screen first-run complexes.

For **information**, the free *Reader* (ⓦwww.chireader.com/movie) always has up-to-date lists of showtimes, as does *New City* (ⓦwww.newcitychicago .com/chicago/film). **Moviefone** (☎312/444-3456) is a great way to find shows and showtimes at any cinema in Chicago, though you'll need either the zip code or the venue's approximate area of town.

Film festivals

Black Harvest International Festival of Video and Film (Aug ⓦwww.artic.edu /webspaces/siskelfilmcenter). A long-running and fascinating annual collection of new African and African-American works rarely (if ever) screened anywhere else in the country. Held at the *Gene Siskel Film Center* (see opposite).

Chicago Outdoor Film Festival (mid-July to Aug ☎312/744-3315). Free movie festival on Tuesday nights at Butler Field in Grant Park (Monroe St and Lake Shore Drive), where you can sit on a blanket with a picnic and watch classic flicks like *Vertigo* and *Mr. Smith Goes to Washington*.

Chicago Underground Film Festival (late Oct ⓦwww.cuff.org). A little more unbuttoned than most, this fest was born out of frustration with the relative inaccessibility and mainstreaming tendencies of other fests. Two students started it in 1993 and it's been a hit ever since, showing indie, experimental and documentary films.

Chicago International Film Festival (Oct ☎312/683-0121, ⓦwww.chicagofilm festival.org). Held over a couple of weeks throughout the city, this is now the oldest competitive film festival in North America (1964), and, though it doesn't have the reputation of say, the Sundance Film Festival, it is a highly respected event in the US motion picture world. Categories range from feature films, to first- and second-time directors, documentaries, short films, student and animated films.

Chicago International Children's Film Festival (Oct–Nov ☎773/281-9075, ⓦwww .cicff.org). The oldest and largest of its kind in the country, this showcases hundreds of feature and short films for (and often made by) children all over the world and also includes hands-on film workshops for kids. Held over two weeks in October and/or November at *Facets Cinémathèque* (see opposite).

Reeling: the Chicago International Gay and Lesbian Film Festival (late Aug to early Sept). See p.223.

Generally, the price of admission is about $9, though many of the smaller and second-run houses show films for half as much.

First-run cinemas

600 North Michigan Avenue Near North ☎312/255-9340; **Red Line to Grand.** Nothing special, but this nine-screener upstairs from *Eddie Bauer* shows a decent mix of mainstream and semi-arty films.

Landmark Century Centre Cinema 2828 N Clark St, at W Diversey Parkway, Lakeview ☎773/248-7744; **bus #22.** On the top two floors of this vertical shopping mall, showing independent and foreign-language films – one of the city's better-run cinemas.

Music Box **3733 N Southport Ave, at W Waveland Ave, Lakeview** ☎773/871-6604, ⓦwww.musicboxtheatre.com; **Brown Line to Southport.** The owners of this grand old neighbourhood cinema bill it as a "year-round film festival", and, while it's not quite that, it is a good place to watch interesting flicks – cult, classic, indie, horror, whatever. Funky interior and live organ music between films.

Pipers Alley 1608 N Wells St, at W North Ave, Old Town ☎312/337-0436; **bus #22.** Three-screen complex in Old Town, which always has a good pick of artsy movies that verge on mainstream.

River East 21 322 E Illinois St, at N Fairbanks Court, Streeterville ☎847/765-7262; **bus #65.** Recently opened Streeterville complex with a whopping 21 screens – good for watching blockbusters, since they're generally playing on three to four screens here.

Second-run and indie flicks

Brew & View at The Vic Theatre 3145 N Sheffield Ave, at W Belmont Ave, Lakeview ☎773/929-6713, ⓦwww.brewview.com; **Brown, Purple or Red Line to Belmont.** The name says it all: the

place to come to watch flicks and drink beer ($3 per pitcher, Mon–Thurs). Second-run movies, classics and audiences that tend to sing and quote along. Admission is only $5; must be 18 to enter, 21 to drink.

Facets Cinémathèque 1517 W Fullerton Ave, at N Greenview Ave, Lincoln Park ☎773/281-4114, ⓦwww.facets.org; **Brown, Purple or Red Line to Fullerton.** Daily screenings of cutting-edge films and, in their attached rental store, an enormous (and nationally renowned) cache of cult, experimental and hard-to-find videos. Also hosts several annual film festivals.

Gene Siskel Film Center 164 N State St, at Randolph St, the Loop ☎312/846-2600, ⓦwww.artic.edu/webspaces/siskelfilmcenter; **Brown, Green, Orange, Purple or Red Line to State/Lake.** Splashy, sleek, new two-screen complex (named after the beloved, late *Chicago Tribune* film critic), part of the School of the Art Institute of Chicago, with classics, revivals, indie premieres, festivals etc.

Three Penny Theater 2424 N Lincoln Ave, at W Fullerton Ave, Lincoln Park ☎773/525-3449, ⓦwww.3penny cinema.com; **Brown, Purple or Red Line to Fullerton.** Aged but cheap little cinema with two screens, showing second-run films, right across from the *Biograph Theatre*. See Victory Gardens, p.97.

Univ. of Chicago DOC Films 1212 E 59th St, at S Woodlawn Ave, Hyde Park ☎773/702-8575, ⓦwww.docfilms.uchicago.edu. On the University of Chicago campus, this appropriately brainy movie-house has daily screenings of just about any type. The longest continuously running student film-society in the nation, it was founded in the 1930s as an informal film society.

Dance

Two companies, the **Joffrey Ballet** and **Hubbard Street Dance Chicago**, are Chicago's real gift to the world dance community, although there are a number of smaller dance companies that inevitably are a part of the local dance scene.

For current what's-on information, the **Chicago Dance and Music Alliance** (☎312/987-1123, ⓦwww.chicagoperformances.org) is a great source. The Alliance website is loaded with numbers and venue information.

Companies

Ballet Chicago Studio Company ☎312/251-8838, ⊛www.balletchicago.org. Roving like the Joffrey but not nearly as renowned a classical ballet troupe, Ballet Chicago does have a school, and has been performing – and training – since it opened doors in 1997. Geared toward the style of George Balanchine, famed twentieth-century choreographer.

Chicago Moving Company ☎773/880-5402, ⊛www.chicagomovingcompany.org. Modern dance under the guidance of Nana Shineflug, an artist and performer who is of great acclaim in Chicago. Concerts and classes since 1972.

Hubbard Street Dance Chicago 1147 W Jackson Blvd ☎312/850-9744, ⊛www.hubbardstreetdance.com. More contemporary than Joffrey Ballet but equally talented, continually turning out some of the nation's best dance, with its characteristic blend of jazz, modern, ballet and theatre-dance. Prices for their performances range between $25 and $86.

Joffrey Ballet 70 E Lake St ☎312/739-0120, ⊛www.joffrey.com. The city's prime classically oriented dance company, one of the country's best. Transplanted from New York in 1995, the group uses Chicago as a home base, performing at the *Auditorium Theatre* (see opposite), with tickets between $35 and $75 per seat.

Mordine and Company Dance Theater ☎312/654-9540, ⊛www.mordine.org. One of the nation's longer-running contemporary dance companies (1968), right behind the Joffrey Ballet and alongside the River North Dance Company. They were for many years headquartered at the *Dance Center of Columbia College*.

Muntu Dance Theatre ☎773/602-1135, ⊛www.muntu.com. Dance troupe that performs all sorts of African tribal dances, with a contemporary take on everything. They usually perform only a few shows a year, sometimes at the *Museum of Contemporary Art* or Hyde Park's *DuSable Museum*, among others.

River North Dance Company ☎312/944-2888, ⊛www.rivernorthchicago.com. Created by four standout Chicago dancers in the late 1980s, River North (performing mostly at the *Athenaeum Theatre*; see opposite) comprises a mainly Midwestern cast and devotes itself to jazz and contemporary dance.

Venues

Athenaeum Theatre 2936 N Southport Ave, at W Oakdale Ave, Lakeview ☎773/935-6860 or 312/902-1500. See p.206 for details.

Auditorium Theatre 50 E Congress Parkway, at S State St, the Loop ☎312/922-2110 or 902-1500, ⊛www.auditoriumtheatre.org; Red Line to Harrison. Beautiful Sullivan-designed theatre with exceptional acoustics, which hosts the Joffrey Ballet as well as touring music acts, Broadway shows and the occasional solo act, like Tom Waits.

▲ Auditorium Theatre

Chicago Cultural Center 78 E Washington Blvd, at N Michigan Ave, the Loop ☎312/744-6630; Brown, Green, Orange or Purple Line to Randolph. The loft-like Sidney R. Yates Gallery on the fourth floor of the *Cultural Center* has frequent free dance performances, among them the "About Dance" programme, which combines discussions about dance with performances by groups like Dance Africa Chicago.

Dance Center of Columbia College 1306 S Michigan Ave, at E 13th St, South Loop ☎312/344-8300, ⊛www.dancecenter.org; Red Line to Roosevelt. Theatre in a Columbia College building a few blocks from the main campus, with contemporary dance concerts from troupes like Bebe Miller Company, Merce Cunningham Dance Company and experimental group The Seldoms, plus classes in the other six studios.

Harold Washington Library 400 S State St, at E Congress Parkway, the Loop ☎312/747-4300; Red Line to Roosevelt. The Library often hosts dance and music performances from mostly local artists – recent acts have included the Chicago-based Nucleus Dance Collective and The Chicago Jazz Orchestra – in its lower-level auditorium.

Joan W. and Irving B. Harris Theater for Music and Dance 205 E Randolph Drive, the Loop ☎312/334-7777, ⊛www.harristheaterchicago .org; Brown, Purple, Orange or Green Line to Randolph. Boasting prime acoustics and excellent sightlines, this dazzling, 1525-seat gem in Millennium Park hosts performances of ballet, contemporary dance by Hubbard Street Dance Chicago and classical, chamber, opera and folk music.

Museum of Contemporary Art Theatre 220 E Chicago Ave, at N DeWitt Place, Streeterville ☎312/397-4010, ⊛www.mcachicago.org; Red Line to Chicago. The *MCA's* street-level theatre often hosts dance performances by local troupes, like tap troupe Chicago Human Rhythm Project.

Ruth Page Center for Arts 1016 N Dearborn St, at W Oak St, Gold Coast ☎312/337-6543, ⊛www.ruthpage.org; Red Line to Clark/Division. Designed to accommodate dance and theatre groups in search of a permanent home, it hosts the performances of the various groups in residence there at any one time; recent groups have included River North Dance Company, Luna Negra Dance Theatre and Mordine & Company Dance Theater (see opposite).

Galleries

While it may not have the diversity and edge of New York or Los Angeles, Chicago's **art scene** has come a long way since the early 1970s, when any visitor to the city would have had great difficulty in finding an art community of any description. The gritty warehouse district of **River North** was first to fill the void, as artists and dealers turned raw spaces into loft studios and galleries. After a fire tore through the area in 1989, some artists and owners chose to relocate rather than rebuild, but many remained, and have been joined in the years since by new ventures. Today River North still boasts the greatest concentration of galleries in the city, easily reached by taking the Blue Line to Chicago.

For more experimental work – especially mixed-media and installation art – head to the **West Loop**. Galleries are a bit more far flung than they are in River North but are well worth the extra schlepping involved; the densest clusters are around the intersection of Peoria and Washington streets (closest public transport: #8–Halsted bus to Randolph Street) and on Fulton Market between Peoria and Racine. Come during October's Around the Coyote Art Festival – which moved from **Wicker Park** to the West Loop in 2008 – to witness the district in full flower (see p.249).

To the southwest, the Mexican enclave of **Pilsen** has earned a reputation as a haven for up-and-coming artists, thanks to its relatively cheap rents. Galleries tend to come and go, though, so be sure to snag a copy of the free *Chicago Gallery News*, available from most hotels and galleries, before you head out. On the opposite end of the spectrum, the **Magnificent Mile** harbours a couple of dozen fine-art galleries, most geared to high-end collectors; the handful of galleries in the Hancock Center are worth a peek if you're in the area. Other art spaces are scattered throughout the city and suburbs, especially **Evanston** and **Oak Park**.

Most galleries host receptions for new shows on Friday evenings (5–9pm), and there are plenty of Chicago glitterati on hand for great people-watching. Two **mass openings** are worth noting: the first Friday after Labor Day in September kicks off the **fall gallery season**, while on the first or second Friday in January, all of the galleries have coinciding openings. Again, consult *Chicago Gallery News* for locations and times, or visit the publication's frequently updated website, ⓦ www.chicagogallerynews.com.

River North Gallery District

Addington Gallery **704 N Wells St, between Superior and Huron; Tues–Sat 11am–6pm** ☏ 312/664-3406, ⓦ www.addingtongallery.com. Specializing in painting with a focus on the physicality of the process and materials, Addington represents about twenty-eight artists, mostly Americans.

Jean Albano Gallery 215 W Superior St, between Franklin and Wells; Tues–Fri 10am–5pm, Sat 11am–5pm ☎312/440-0770, ⊛www.jean albanogallery.com. Conceptual and flamboyant contemporary painting, sculpture, photography and mixed media, including the works of abstractionist Valerie Beller of Chicago and Argentine native Luciana Abnit, whose desolate images and enigmatic landscapes expose themes of human absence.

Andrew Bae Gallery 300 W Superior St, at Franklin; Tues–Sat 10am–6pm ☎312/335-8601, ⊛www.andrewbaegallery.com. The focus here is on contemporary Asian art, with a stirring and serene collection of prints, sculpture and decorative arts by emerging artists from Japan and South Korea. The imagery, often naturalistic, tends to be simple, but the themes are complex and often metaphysical.

Roy Boyd Gallery 739 N Wells St, between Superior and Chicago; Tues–Sat 10am–5.30pm ☎312/642-1606, ⊛www.royboydgallery.com. In this location since 1985, Roy Boyd represents mostly abstract painters, with some sculptors thrown in, including a good number of Art Institute graduates.

Carl Hammer Gallery 740 N Wells St, between Superior and Chicago; Tues–Fri 11am–6pm, Sat 11am–5pm ☎312/266-8512, ⊛www.hammergallery.com. The bilevel *Hammer Gallery* was a pioneer in championing the work of "outsider", or self-taught, artists, like Chicago native Henry Darger, in the late 1970s and still represents a handful of outsiders, along with other boundary-pushing contemporary artists from the US and abroad.

Marx-Saunders Gallery 230 W Superior St, between Wells and Franklin; Tues–Fri 10am–5.30pm, Sat 11am–5pm ☎312/573-1400, ⊛www.marxsaunders.com. Internationally recognized gallery of glass art, featuring everything from classically inspired vases in eye-popping colours to sculptural confections both primitive and delicate.

Ann Nathan Gallery 212 W Superior St, between Wells and Franklin; Tues–Fri 10am–5.30pm, Sat 11am–5pm ☎312/664-6622, ⊛www.annnathangallery.com. An eclectic assortment of paintings, sculpture and ornate furniture by famous and up-and-coming regional and national artists.

▲ Chicago gallery

Printworks Gallery 311 W Superior St, between Franklin and Orleans; Tues–Sat 11am–5pm ☎312/644-9407, ⊛www.printworkschicago.com. Established in 1980, this excellent gallery specializes in works on paper by established and emerging artists. There is an "Affordable Art" section that shows paintings priced at $300 and under. Usually closed for two weeks in the summer; call ahead.

Zg Gallery 300 W Superior St, at Franklin; Tues–Sat 10am–5.30pm ☎312/654-9900, ⊛www.zggallery.com. Contemporary art in a variety of media, much of it in a playful, imaginative vein.

Zolla/Lieberman Gallery 325 W Huron St, at Orleans; Tues–Fri 10am–5.30pm, Sat 11am–5.30pm ☎312/787-3300, ⊛www.zollaliebermangallery.com. A River North fixture since 1976, this is one of the largest galleries in the district. Deals mostly in contemporary painting but the most famous artist in the stable is a Montana-based sculptor, Deborah Butterfield, who makes large equine figures out of cast bronze.

The West Loop

FLATFILEgalleries **217 N Carpenter St, at Lake; Tues–Sat 11am–6pm** ☎312/491-1190, ⊛www.flatfilegalleries.com. Originally a photography gallery, *Flatfile* has grown to encompass contemporary painting and sculpture as well. The large space showcases five artists' work at a time, and you can peruse more than 1000 photos and work on paper, stored in flat files, as long as you don white gloves.

Rhona Hoffman Gallery **118 N Peoria St, at Randolph; Tues–Fri 10am–5.30pm, Sat 11am–5.30pm** ☎312/455-1990, ⊛www.rhoffman gallery.com. One of the first galleries to move to the area, featuring an eclectic, visually arresting rotation of contemporary art, both by now deceased masters (Sol Lewitt, Leon Golub) and relative newcomers like photographer Tania Bruguera of Cuba.

Intuit: The Center for Intuitive and Outsider Art **756 N Milwaukee Ave, at Ogden; Tues, Wed, Fri & Sat 11am–5pm, Thurs 11am–7.30pm** ☎312/243-9088, ⊛www.art.org. Off-the-beaten-path art centre promoting outsider art, aka art brut, folk art, self-taught art or visionary art through exhibitions, educational programmes and the biannual magazine *The Outsider*. The centre's one permanent exhibit is a reconstruction of artist Henry Darger's studio apartment in Lincoln Park, crammed full of the comic books, children's books, newspapers and other material that inspired forty years' worth of "Vivian Girls" stories. Another gallery has rotating shows of outsider art – usually fascinating stuff.

McCormick Gallery **835 W Washington Blvd, between Peoria and Green; Tues–Sat 10am–5.30pm** ☎312/226-6800, ⊛www.thomas mccormick.com. The *McCormick Gallery* has a twofold mission: representing the estates of several famous twentieth-century modern artists – among them Melville Price, Mary Abbott and Perle Fine – and showing work by contemporary painters and sculptors, including Bill Barrett.

G.R. N'Namdi Gallery **110 N Peoria St, at Randolph; Tues–Fri 11am–6pm, Sat 11am–5pm** ☎312/563-9240, ⊛www.grnnamdi.com. The oldest and largest African-American-owned gallery in the world, *G.R. N'Namdi* was founded in Detroit in 1981. Now it has three locations (Chicago, Detroit and New York) and a stable of more than sixty artists, many of them abstract painters.

Andrew Rafacz Gallery **835 W Washington Blvd, between Green and Peoria; Tues–Fri 11am–6pm, Sat 11am–5pm** ☎312/404-9188, ⊛www .andrewrafacz.com. Formerly called *Bucket Rider*, the gallery represents emerging and mid-career artists, including graffiti and installation artists. Much of the work has a pop-psychedelic feel.

Pilsen

Chicago Arts District **1945 S Halsted St; opening hours are individual to each studio** ☎312/738-8000, ext 112, ⊛www.chicagoartsdistrict.org. This thriving and diverse artists' community, just southwest of the Loop, covers twelve blocks around the intersection of 18th St and S Halsted St. Once down-at-the-heel, the area is now largely made up of bright and airy lofts, housing about 100 artists' studios and 25 galleries. Many are open on the second Friday of every month, from 6 to 10pm, and feature some of Chicago's most daring and thought-provoking artworks (call ☎312/377-4444 or visit CAD's website for more information).

The Magnificent Mile

Valerie Carberry Gallery **in the John Hancock Center, 875 N Michigan Ave, Suite 2510; Mon–Fri 10am–5pm, Sat 11am–5pm** ☎312/397-9990, ⊛www.valeriecarberry.com. Carberry's focus is on American art produced between 1915 and 1965, though she also represents four contemporary painters – three of them women – and does a brisk trade in the secondary art market selling work by the likes of Milton Avery, Laszlo Moholy-Nagy, John Marin, Robert Motherwell and Jackson Pollock.

Richard Gray Gallery in the John Hancock Center, 875 N Michigan Ave, Suite 2503; Mon–Fri 10am–5.30pm ☎312/642-8877, ⓦwww .richardgraygallery.com. One of the forerunners of Chicago's buoyant gallery scene, this compelling gallery specializes in the finest modern art. Impressive exhibitions feature such contemporary masters as Jackson Pollock, Georgia O'Keeffe, Roy Lichtenstein, Mark Rothko and Willem de Kooning.

Wicker Park

Around the Coyote Gallery 1935 1/2 W North Ave; Tues–Fri 10am–6pm, Sat noon–6pm ☎773/342-6777, ⓦwww.aroundthecoyote.org. The twenty-year-old nonprofit dedicated to boosting the visibility of working Chicago artists opened this 2400-square-foot gallery in 2004. It hosts monthly exhibitions of work by emerging artists, play readings and other cultural events but is no longer the hub of the Around the Coyote art festival, now held in the West Loop.

Evanston

Maple Avenue Gallery 1745 Maple Ave; Tues & Wed 10.30am–6pm, Thurs, Fri & Sat 10.30am– 8pm, Sun noon–5pm ☎847/869-0680, ⓦwww .mapleavenuegallery.com. In downtown Evanston, this sleek industrial space, whose artworks range in price from $600 to over $6000, features around thirty local and international artists at any one time, across a variety of different media including paintings, original prints, mixed media and sculpture. Of particular interest are the works of Jim Martin, Lily Balasanavo and Carol Sams.

Gay and lesbian Chicago

As the metropolis of the Midwest, Chicago has long been a cultural and social magnet for small-town **gays and lesbians**, who make up a sizeable minority here and are fairly visible, not just at the **Pride Festival** or **Northalsted Market Days**, two of the city's most popular summer events. This visibility has had a small political impact: in 2001, Illinois' first openly lesbian mayor, Joanne Trapani, was elected in suburban Oak Park, while the Chicago city council in 2002 passed an ordinance outlawing discrimination against transgendered people. Cultivating a spirit of inclusiveness, Chicago's Mayor Daley, never one to shy away from polemics, said he would have "no problem" issuing gay marriage licenses.

Gay life in Chicago revolves around the North Side area known as **Boystown**, a part of the Lakeview neighbourhood that stretches east from Halsted Street to the lake and north from Belmont Avenue to Grace Street. **Halsted** in particular has been the long-standing centre of gay life and most of the action in Boystown focusses on the street's gay bars and gay-friendly restaurants around Roscoe Street.

Increasingly, however, the more affordable and less congested Swedish enclave of **Andersonville** (see p.104) to the north has been steadily attracting gays and lesbians away from Lakeview for several years. It boasts a host of increasingly stylish restaurants, bars and shops, focussed around N Clark and Foster and catering to the gay community and a hip crew of straight denizens. And even further to the north, still-developing **Edgewater** and **Rogers Park** seem destined to be the next pockets in Chicago's already robust gay, lesbian, bisexual and transgender scene.

You can get a feel for Chicago's gay scene by picking up a copy of the *Chicago Free Press* (Ⓦ www.chicagofreepress.com) or *Windy City Times* (Ⓦ www.outlines chicaco.com), both **weeklies** with extensive gay and lesbian news and local event listings. For nightlife info, try *Gay Chicago* or *Boi Chicago*, weekly rags that detail just where the boys (and, occasionally, girls) will be partying next. All are free and can be picked up at corner boxes or in bars. **Lesbians** should check out the Chicago-specific Ⓦ www.dykediva.com, a fun, helpful site that lists upcoming lesbian parties, readings, concerts and seminars. For a list of other gay resources and organizations in Chicago, see p.223.

Accommodation

While few properties in the area cater exclusively to gay men and lesbians, you'll feel right at home in just about every hotel in and around Boystown.

Prices range from $85–250, based on the cheapest double-room rate available during high season.

The Ardmore House 1248 W Ardmore Ave, Edgewater/Andersonville ☎773/728-5414, ⓦwww.ardmorehousebb.com; Red Line to Thorndale. Cosy, exclusively gay B&B in a comfortably furnished, restored Victorian on a quiet residential street close to the lake and a gay beach (Hollywood Beach). Three rooms share two full baths, plus an outdoor hot tub with secluded sundeck. Other amenities include internet access, satellite TV and a nightly social hour, as well as continental breakfast on weekdays and full hot breakfast on weekends. Reservations required; two-night minimum stay on weekends. $77–160

Best Western Hawthorne Terrace 3434 N Broadway, Wrigleyville ☎773/244-3434 or 1-888/860-3400, ⓦwww.hawthorneterrace.com; Red Line to Belmont. Close to Wrigley Field, this boutique hotel with vintage charm draws a pretty even mix of gay and straight guests. Most spacious rooms are equipped with internet and satellite facilities, refrigerators and microwaves. There is a patio terrace and parking. Complimentary breakfast is included. $125–199

Hotel Burnham 1 W Washington St, the Loop ☎312/782-1111 or 1-866/690-1986, ⓦwww.burnhamhotel.com; Red or Blue Line to Washington; Brown, Green, Orange or Purple Line to State/Lake. This gorgeous boutique hotel oozes turn-of-the-century grandeur and is very gay-friendly – mention the "pride rate" for a significant discount. Marble, mosaics, crystal and mahogany at every turn complement original features from 1895. A pet-friendly hotel, so even your pooch can bask in the luxury. Check the website for fantastic discounts. For more details, see p.150. $199–509

City Suites 933 W Belmont Ave ☎773/404-3400 or 1-800/248-9108, ⓦwww.cityinns.com; Brown, Purple or Red Line to Belmont. Within easy reach of Boystown, although the price you'll pay is the grinding noise from passing trains and traffic. A friendly boutique hotel whose rooms, while nothing special, are reasonably well equipped with data ports and refrigerators. The Art Deco lobby has been given a welcome facelift and a decent continental breakfast is included in the price. Eclectic mix of gay men, artists and performers. For more details, see p.158. $155–218

Days Inn Lincoln Park-North 644 W Diversey Parkway, Lincoln Park ☎773/525-7010, ⓦwww.lpdaysinn.com; Brown or Purple Line to Diversey. Gay-friendly hotel of particular appeal for its good location just a ten-minute walk from Boystown. What it lacks in character and charm it makes up for in convenience, service and value. For more details, see p.158. $121–219

Flemish House of Chicago 68 E Cedar St, Gold Coast ☎312/664-9981, ⓦwww.chicagobandb.com; Red Line to Clark/Division. Gay-owned and friendly, but mostly straight clientele at these B&B apartments in a beautifully renovated 1892 row house. Six guest rooms done in attractive English Arts and Crafts style, each with full kitchen, bath, TV and phone. Rates include self-serve continental breakfast. No smoking or children; two-night minimum stay. $155–215

The Gold Coast Guest House 113 W Elm St, Gold Coast ☎312/337-0361, ⓦwww.bbchicago.com; Red Line to Clark/Division. Relaxed, gay-friendly B&B with easy access to Mag Mile shopping and dining. For more details, see p.157. $129–229

Majestic 528 W Brompton Ave, Boystown ☎773/404-3499 or 1-800/727-5108, ⓦwww.cityinns.com; Red Line to Addison. Quiet, elegant inn near the lake on a residential Boystown street. For more details, see p.158. $122–257

Villa Toscana 3447 N Halsted St, Boystown ☎773/404-2643 or 1-800/404-2643, ⓦwww.thevillatoscana.com; Red Line to Belmont. Six clean, smallish rooms in a gay-owned Victorian B&B, with a mostly gay male clientele. The house, in the heart of Boystown, set back from the street with a private sundeck, has three rooms with private bath; others are shared. No smoking or pets. Basic amenities include phone, cable TV and self-serve continental breakfast. Reserve at least a month ahead. $109–149

Cafés and restaurants

While many Chicago **restaurants** attract a sizeable gay following (Randolph Street's *Blackbird* (see p.182) and *Marche* (see p.183). The places listed below have become fixtures on the city's gay and lesbian scene.

Angelina 3561 N Broadway, Boystown
☎773/935-5933; Red Line to Addison.
Romantic, low-lit atmosphere and reasonable prices make this cozy Italian date-spot a neighbourhood favourite. Well-balanced menu features goat cheese and beet salad ($10), duck risotto with caramelized onion ($18), spicy Italian sausage with pine nuts ($17) and hot chocolate bread pudding topped with vanilla-bean ice cream ($9). Dinner mains here run between $15 and $23. Sun–Thurs 5–10pm, Fri & Sat 5–11pm.

Ann Sather 909 W Belmont Ave, Lakeview
☎773/348-2378; Red Line to Belmont. Local Swedish chain, which has developed into something of a gay institution, bearing the hallmark of its proprietor, gay activist and city council member Tom Tunney. For more details see p.177. Breakfast or lunch here will run from $7 to $11. Mon–Fri 7am–3pm, Sat & Sun 7am–4pm.

Arco de Cuchilleros 3445 N Halsted St, at W Cornelia, Boystown ☎773/296-6046. Excellent tapas bar on the north end of Boystown, bustling with a predominantly gay clientele, which provides dozens of tasty possibilities in a no-frills but comfortable setting. Tapas faves here include the batter-dipped chicken with black peppercorn and brandy sauce ($8.95) and the shrimp sautéed with garlic and cayenne ($8.95) Stay a while with a pitcher of delectable sangría. Moderate. Each tapas order runs from $6.25 to $8.95 and main courses run from $10.50 to $17.25. Tues–Thurs 5–11pm, Fri & Sat 5–midnight Sun 4–10pm.

Caribou Coffee Company 3300 N Broadway, Boystown ☎773/477-3695; Red Line to Belmont. Not your typical chain coffee shop. Affectionately nicknamed "Cariboy", this comfortable, cruisy café is packed most nights and weekend afternoons with gay men reading, lounging in easy chairs, and watching the scenery go by. Coffee and other treats $2–5. Sun–Thurs 6am–10.30pm, Fri & Sat 7am–11pm.

Cornelia 738 W Cornelia, Boystown
☎773/248-8333; Red Line to Addison. This rustically elegant restaurant with crisp white tablecloths, black-and-white photographs of gay icons and a centrepiece piano serves a broad menu of bistro fare ranging from shiitake pancakes ($7) to fried calamari ($8) and predictable classics such as pork chops ($14) and salmon with spinach ($16). When it's good, it's fantastic, but consistency is not *Cornelia's* strong point. There is outdoor seating in summer and great service. Dinner mains here will run between $14 and $25. Daily 5.30pm–1am.

Firefly 3335 N Halsted St, Boystown
☎773/525-2505; Red Line to Belmont. This recent arrival, just down the block from the boy bars, is a loungey, late-night space offering creative French bistro fare at reasonable prices. Don't miss the creamy parmesan deviled eggs ($6) or the pan-seared tilapia with basil mashed potatoes ($18). *Firefly* goes above and beyond with its extensive martini list, which includes the Lentini (mandarin vodka, midori and sour mix). Dinner mains here run from $12 to $21. Mon & Wed–Sat 5.30pm–1.30am, Sun 5.30–12.30pm.

Jin Ju 5203 N Clark, at Foster Ave, Andersonville ☎773/334-6377; Red Line to Berwyn. A local favourite, this approachable Korean restaurant caters to the western palate and the budget-minded with reworked traditional dishes such as *te gim* (tempura; $11), *bi bim bop* (rice with beef, vegetable and egg; $13) and spicy ribs ($18). The decor is stylishly understated with soft lighting and a hip clientele. The drinks are one of the major draws, with the signature *sojutini* (Korean grain liquor made from sweet potato). Main dishes run from $13 to $18. Sun & Tues 5–9.30pm, Wed & Thurs 5–10pm, Fri & Sat 5–11pm.

Joy's Noodles 3257 N Broadway, Boystown
☎773/327-8330; Red Line to Belmont. Good, super-cheap pan-Asian plates bring dedicated patrons out in full force at this very casual neighbourhood BYOB joint. Delicious *lard na* (fried rice noodles with chicken and broccoli; $7.50), chicken satay ($6.50), baby egg-rolls ($4) and more. The service is friendly, the atmosphere inviting

and there is an outdoor garden in summer. Dinner or lunch out at *Joy's* will run between $6 to $10. Sun–Thurs 11am–10pm, Fri & Sat 11am–11pm.

Kit Kat Lounge and Supper Club 3700 N Halsted St, Boystown ☎773/525-1111; Red Line to Addison. At this cool South Beach-inspired lounge club, the decor of exposed brick contrasts with bright white *Miami Vice* booths and leopard-skin prints. The menu features upscale comfort food with a smattering of exotic, coconut-infused delicacies. The food isn't terribly special, but they do have inventive names, a la the "Gone With the Wind" (grill seared blackened pork chop with bacon collard greens and cornbread; $19). Camp entertainment comes in the form of drag queens who strut through the narrow room, mimicking gay icons from the 1940s and 1950s. Dinner mains here run from $16 to $25. Tues–Sun 5.30pm–2am.

Tomboy 5402 N Clark St, Andersonville ☎773/907-0636; Red Line to Berwyn. Lesbian-owned standby with a hip gay and lesbian crowd and comfortably chic exposed-brick decor. Each dish is perfectly executed and artfully presented. The signature dish is a seared yellow-fin tuna steak with *wasabi* ($16), while more Mediterranean flavours include a goat-cheese-stuffed chicken breast ($15), gazpacho soup ($6) and filet mignon ($25). Desserts are worth saving room for; try the much-vaunted bread

pudding. BYOB (corkage $5) in addition to a fully stocked bar. Dinner mains here run from $15 to $28. Tues–Thurs 5pm–10pm, Fri & Sat 5pm–11pm.

Tweet 5020 N Sheridan Rd, at W Argyle Ave, Andersonville ☎773/728-5576; Red Line to Argyle. The quirky and perky *Tweet* is a relative newcomer with a small but perfectly formed menu of breakfast favourites including organic buckwheat pancakes ($6.50), country ham ($4) and aebleskiver ($7; Danish beignets served with powdered sugar and syrup). Breakfast runs from $7 to $10. Wed–Mon 9am–3pm.

Yoshi's Café 3257 N Halsted St, Boystown ☎773/248-6160; Red Line to Belmont. If you can get past the generic, upscale diner decor, you're in for a treat. The French cuisine, infused with Japanese flavours and textures, results in delicious concoctions like chicken and mushroom spring roll with cucumber salad ($9) or grilled sea scallops with green-tea pasta in pesto sauce ($17). The desserts, including *crème brûlée* ($8) and chocolate mousse layered with berries and crunchy caramelized *mille feuilles* ($9) are delicious. Outdoor seating in summer provides great people-watching. Brunch is served on Sundays with doughy *brioche* and fresh carrot juice. The service is sleek and the wine list comprehensive. Dinner mains $13–21. Tues–Thurs 5–10.30pm, Fri & Sat 5–11pm, Sun 11am–2.30pm & 5–9.30pm.

Bars and clubs

Most gay and lesbian **bars** in Chicago do not charge a cover; those that do are noted below. The minimum drinking age is 21 and strictly enforced – always carry a **photo ID**. Many of the places listed are frequented by a mixed crowd and you'll find that even bars and clubs that tend to be exclusively gay will still be welcoming to a straight clientele.

Atmosphere 5355 N Clark St, Andersonville ☎773/784-1100; Red Line to Berwyn. This far North Side neighbourhood bar, with exposed brick walls and metal decor, attracts a crowd of mostly men, both straight and gay, and some lesbians. There's a small dancefloor if the DJ's music so moves you – 80s on Wednesdays and pop and house on Saturdays. The requisite lure of drink specials features $2 Bud on Fridays and $12 pitchers of Stoli on Wednesdays.

Baton Show Lounge 436 N Clark St, Near North ☎312/644-5269; Red Line to Grand. You won't believe your eyes when you see the drag queens at this famed River North club, which draws more straight men, tourists and bachelorette parties than gay men. Showtimes Wed–Sun 8.30pm, 10.30pm, and 12.30am. $10–14 cover with two-drink minimum.

Berlin 954 W Belmont Ave, Lakeview ☎773/348-4975; Red Line to Belmont. Legendary dance spot where a pumped, mixed crowd grooves to some of Chicago's hottest DJs. The boys come out for "Testosterone Tuesdays", while ladies gather for "Women Obsession Wednesdays", every week except the last of the month. The last Sunday of every month is a Prince Night – where the artist's tunes are played and the crowd is decked out in the requisite flamboyant attire. Cover $3–5.

Big Chicks 5024 N Sheridan Rd, Andersonville ☎773/728-5511; Red Line to Argyle. A fixture on the scene, this laid-back Far North favourite features a dancefloor, pool table and despite its name, an eclectic, mostly gay male crowd. With the owner's eclectic artwork covering the walls, erotic outpourings on the TV monitors, and DJs on the weekends, this is a night of fun and fetish, guaranteed. Free Sunday-afternoon barbecues in summer pack the place. Free parking in the alley behind the bar.

Charlie's 3726 N Broadway, Lakeview ☎773/871-8887; Red Line to Addison. Sporting brassy buckles and lashings of leather fringing, Midwestern cowboys strut their stuff on the large dancefloor which takes up most of the small space at this popular late-night country bar. Free line-dance lessons Mondays and Wednesdays at 7.30pm and Saturdays at 9pm. There's karaoke on Tuesdays and, after 2am on Friday and Saturday nights, the DJ spins house music until the wee hours. Small cover on weekends. Mon & Tues till 2am, Wed–Fri till 4am, Sat till 5am.

Circuit Nightclub 3641 N Halsted St, Lakeview ☎773/325-2233; Red Line to Addison. After a makeover in 2004, this cavernous nightclub is the place to be for circuit boys and club kids on Saturday nights, when the glowsticks come out and the techno starts pumping. The front room or "Rehab Lounge" hosts disco bingo on Mondays and karaoke on Tuesdays, while the amped-up, camped-up, back room is dedicated to unbridled grooving with a spicy Thursday Latin night, plus a wild ladies dance party on Fridays. Cover $5–15. Sun–Wed till 2am, Thurs & Fri till 4am, Sat till 5am.

The Closet 3325 N Broadway, Lakeview ☎773/477-8533; Red Line to Belmont. Tiny, aptly named late-night lesbian hangout with a small bar and an even smaller dancefloor. It's also very popular with the boys, who flood the place on weekends when the 2am Halsted bars let out. Sun–Fri 2pm–4am, Sat noon–5am.

Crobar Nightclub 1543 N Kingsbury St, Lincoln Park ☎312/337-5001; Red Line to North/Clybourn. Following massive renovations, *Crobar* returned in 2003 with a disco-industrial look and continues to be the pinnacle of Chicago's adrenaline-fuelled, and liquor-infused, hard-core dance club scene. Put on your tightest, most glittery clubwear for Sunday "Anthem" Club (gay, lesbian and everything else), a hugely popular night of progressive dance music for muscle boys and glam girls in this enormous dance complex. Cover $10–30.

Gentry of Chicago 440 N State St, Near North ☎312/836-0933; Red Line to Grand. This intimate cabaret, popular with showtune lovers and piano barflies, features live entertainment every day of the week and draws a mostly male crowd of suits from the neighbourhood. The main room features a martini bar and lures a more mature crowd, while the lower level has video projections and a more youthful vibe. Sunday nights are open mic. Two-drink minimum cover.

Roscoe's 3356 N Halsted St, Lakeview ☎773/281-3355; Red Line to Belmont. Boystown's best hangout for younger guys, this comfortable video bar and club has five rooms befitting different moods, a pool table, fireplace, and a large dancefloor, which packs in the leather-clad cheek by jowl. The outdoor patio, open in summer, serves light meals, and is prime cruising territory in summer. Theme nights include karaoke Mondays and game show Wednesdays. $5 cover on Saturdays.

Sidetrack 3349 N Halsted St, Lakeview ☎773/477-9189; Red Line to Belmont. This sleek, friendly video bar draws a thirty-something male crowd and sprawls over four connected rooms, including the airy "glass bar", with lofty ceilings, a rooftop deck and a wall of windows looking out onto Halsted. Great frozen drinks, including a potent, purple Ketel One Crush, which fatally slides down as easy as lemonade. Music is generally pop divas – Madonna, Britney, Kylie and Cristina. Theme nights are huge, particularly Sunday showtunes and Thursday comedy clips.

Spin 800 W Belmont Ave, Lakeview ☎773/327-7711; Red Line to Belmont. A tattooed and pierced mixed crowd call this bar and dance club home. Dollar drinks draw a big crowd on

Fireball early Feb (☎773/244-6000, ⊛www.heartsfoundation.com). Three days of nonstop dancing at clubs around the city. Proceeds benefit the Hearts Foundation, which supports local HIV/AIDS service organizations.

International Mr Leather weekend before Memorial Day (⊛www.imrl.com). A fabulous extravaganza – whether you are gay or straight – of fetish, fun and S&M at this quite surreal event – usually hosted in the most unexpected of locations (in 2009, it was held at the relatively staid *Chicago Hilton & Towers*). Leather-loving men (and women) come from all over the world to mingle, buy the latest leather, props, toys and reading and video material, as well as to check out the competition to crown the hottest leather man of all.

Chicago Pride Festival late June (☎773/348-8243, ⊛www.chicagopride.com). The Gay Pride month-long series of events celebrating Chicago's gay community culminates with the Gay Pride Parade as 250 colourful floats, pop music, food and frivolity gather along Halsted St and Broadway on the last Sunday in June. Throughout June, look out for theatre, panel discussions, athletic events and religious services.

Northalsted Market Days early Aug (☎773/883-0500, ⊛www.northalsted.com). This two-day street fair is one of the largest in the Midwest and offers some great people-watching. Staged in Boystown, it draws more than 250,000 people with live music played on three stages, hundreds of vendors and food from dozens of local restaurants.

Windy City Rodeo third weekend in Aug (☎312/409-3835, ⊛www.ilgra.com). At this annual gay fundraising event, whip-cracking cowboys and cowgirls from across the US compete in roping, bull riding and racing, sandwiched between bar crawls, music, dancing and victory galas.

Reeling: the Chicago International Gay and Lesbian Film Festival early November (☎773/293-1447, ⊛www.reelingfilmfestival.org). Established festival, running for two weeks at venues around the city showing a quality mix of shorts, documentaries and feature-length movies with both entertaining and avant garde themes and production.

Wednesdays ($5 cover), as does the Friday shower contest. Small cover on Saturdays.
Star Gaze 5419 N Clark St, Andersonville ☎773/561-7363; Red Line to Berwyn. Chicago's main lesbian hangout, this dance club and restaurant draws an all-ages mixed crowd, including some straight men. There's an inviting outdoor beer garden, plus pool tables, darts and a limited menu of bar food, salads and pastas. Fridays feature salsa music, with $2 drinks on Thursdays and karaoke on Sundays. Closed Mon.

T's Bar & Restaurant 5025 N Clark St, Andersonville ☎773/784-6000; Red Line to Lawrence. This casual, colourful Andersonville spot hosts a laid-back mixed crowd and offers bar-food staples such as cheesy fries and chicken tenders up front. There are couches and a pool table in the back, where on Wednesday nights there's open mic; popular with the lesbian crowd. All-you-can eat fish and chips ($12) on Tuesdays and nightly drink specials on other days.

Gay organizations and resources

About Face Theatre ☎773/784-8565, ⊛www.aboutfacetheatre.com. Well-respected and exploratory theatre company that analyzes issues of gender and sexuality both on stage and in workshops at area schools. Previous productions have included *Monsieur Proust*, the work of Tony Award-winner Mary Zimmerman, produced in association with the Steppenwolf Theatre; see p.206.
Brown Elephant 3651 N Halsted ☎773/549-5943; Red Line to Sheridan. All proceeds

from this Wrigleyville resale shop go towards the Howard Brown Health Center which specializes in HIV- and AIDS-related treatments and counselling. An Aladdin's cave of everything from books and CDs to jewellery and clothes, computer accessories and knick-knacks. Daily noon–6pm.

Chicago Area Gay & Lesbian Chamber of Commerce 1210 W Rosedale ☎773/303-0167, ⓦwww.glchamber.org; Red Line to Thorndale. Helpful community organization offering info packets for visitors and listings of shopping resources, jobs and more.

Gerber/Hart Library 1127 W Granville Ave ☎773/381-8030, ⓦwww.gerberhart.org; Red Line to Granville. North of the city, in Edgewater, this circulating library holds more than 13,000 books and an extensive archive of periodicals, videos and artefacts relating to gay, lesbian, bisexual and transgender individuals. Run by volunteers, the Gerber is very active in the gay community with outreach programmes and a strong Gay Pride event presence.

Illinois Gender Advocates 47 W Division St Suite 391 ☎312/409-5489, ⓦwww.itstimeil.org; Red Line to Clark/Division. A political advocacy group for the transgender community, organizing demonstrations and vigils, publishing newsletters and more.

Illinois HIV and STD HELPLine ☎773/929-4357. Provides crisis counselling and information on gay-related health issues. Mon–Fri

▲ Gerber/Hart Library

9am–9pm, Sat & Sun 10am–6pm. National AIDS hotline: ☎1-800/342-2437.

Unabridged Books 3251 N Broadway ☎773/883-9119; Red Line to Belmont. Long-standing, friendly, independent Boystown bookstore with extensive gay and lesbian sections, from literature to erotica, as well as a great travel section and a treasure-trove of sale shelves. Mon–Fri 10am–9pm, Sat & Sun 10am–7pm.

Women & Children First 5233 N Clark St ☎773/769-9299, ⓦwww.womenandchildren first.com; Red Line to Berwyn. One of the nation's largest feminist bookstores, this Andersonville favourite stocks over 30,000 women's interest books, children's books and gay and lesbian titles. Frequent readings and discussion groups too. Mon & Tues 11am–7pm, Wed–Fri 11am–9pm, Sat 10am–7pm, Sun 11am–6pm.

18

Shopping

Shopping is one of Chicago's strong suits, on a level with blues music and modern architecture. Along with a smattering of multi-storeyed and comprehensive department stores in the Loop and Near North, Chicago ranks right up there near New York among US cities in terms of variety and experience; in addition, the spacious stores and down-to-earth service make shopping here relatively hassle-free. You'll be able to shop even in the dead of winter, thanks to the abundance of huge indoor malls, though eventually you'll come into contact with the freezing temperatures outdoors, which is not the most delightful proposition.

As for shopping **categories**, the city is especially strong on **malls** you'd actually be interested in visiting, esoteric **music** shops and **vintage and thrift stores**. This doesn't mean that trendy **boutiques** and the most modern fashions aren't accounted for as well; in truth, whatever you're looking for should be relatively easy to find.

Shopping by neighbourhood

Shopping is concentrated in a few key areas of the city, all of them reachable by the El – we've indicated stops with each neighborhood overview below.

The Loop

As you might expect in the business district, some major department stores, like Macy's, line **State Street**, while **Wabash Avenue** has the pick of most everything else – camera shops, T-shirt stores and several branches of Chicago's celebrated popcorn store, Garrett's.

You'll have no trouble getting here as all El trains stop in the Loop, before spinning out into the city's more distant neighbourhoods.

The Magnificent Mile and Near North

The **Magnificent Mile**, or North Michigan Ave, Chicago's most famous shopping destination, draws throngs of shoppers for its malls and stores of all

breeds, from big-name designers (Gucci, Armani) to commercial shopping (Niketown, The Gap, Bloomingdale's, Saks Fifth Avenue). Pick one of the malls or an end of the street, and work your way in the opposite direction.

To reach N Michigan Avenue on the El, take the Red Line to Chicago or Grand.

Gold Coast and Old Town

Boutique shopping at its priciest happens along **Oak Street**, adjacent to the north end of Mag Mile. It's never very crowded and for those with some extra coin to throw around, it's the best place to do so – home to lots of ultra-fashionable designers. As for Old Town, the little strip of **Wells**

Street between Division and North Avenue has a fair number of lesser-known boutiques.

Gold Coast is reachable on the Red Line (get off at Clark/Division and head east toward State Street), while the Brown Line stops at Sedgwick in Old Town.

Lincoln Park

The centre of the Lincoln Park shopping scene is the intersection of **Armitage Avenue and Halsted Street** and for most Chicagoans, it's the best place to shop: away from the throngs on Michigan Avenue, reachable by the El or by car (with much easier parking on the side streets), and with plenty of restaurants, cafés and bars to take a break from it all. The shops on Armitage tend to be of the local variety, many of which are recent arrivals. Halsted Street receives plenty of spillover.

You can reach Lincoln Park on the El by taking the Brown Line to Armitage. The #73 Armitage bus runs to Bucktown and Wicker Park from here.

Lakeview

One thing to remember with Lakeview shopping: take the El, or hop a cab; if you're driving, most shops do not have their own parking and you're likely to search for a spot on the street for quite some time. **Belmont Avenue**, loaded with alternative and retro shops, is your best bet. **Clark Street**, which crosses through many neighbourhoods, in fact hits its most interesting stride at its intersection with Belmont, though that's not to say that the rest of Clark isn't worth exploring.

Take the Red Line to Belmont to reach Lakeview.

Bucktown and Wicker Park

The shopping in these parts happens on two main strips, **Milwaukee and Damen avenues**. South of the "six corners" intersection of North, Milwaukee and Damen avenues, Milwaukee Avenue more or less defines Wicker Park retro chic, with all sorts of oddball stores. Prices jump up as you head over to Damen Avenue and then north of the six corners. Here boutiques are geared more toward the yuppie than the starving artist, as the area grows a bit more in tune with its Lincoln Park neighbour.

To get to Bucktown and Wicker Park on the El, take the Blue Line to Damen. You can also hop to Lincoln Park from here on the #73 bus, which travels along Armitage Avenue.

Arts, crafts and antiques

Broadway Antique Market 6130 N Broadway, Edgewater (north of Uptown) ☎773/743-5444. In this 20,000-square-foot, two-storey space, more than 75 antique dealers peddle everything from vintage advertising signage to metalware, fine art, pottery, art glass, furniture and lighting.

Findables 1643 N Milwaukee Ave, Wicker Park ☎773/235-9740. This aptly named all-in-one gift boutique stocks a wide array of jewellery, china, candles, ornaments, picture frames and the like.

Fourth World Artisans 3727 N Southport Ave, Lakeview ☎773/404-5200. Handcrafted folk art, clothing, textiles, musical instruments and jewellery from Africa, India, Australia

▲ Broadway Antique Market

and the Americas are featured in this gift shop on the Southport strip.

Gallery 37 Store 66 E Randolph St (inside Gallery 37 Center for the Arts), the Loop ⊤312/744-7274. Works by emerging and apprentice artists on view at the Loop's Gallery 37 – part of the School of the Art Institute of Chicago (see p.50) – can be bought in the gallery's store, be it lawn ornaments, mosaics, jewellery or furniture. Closed Sun.

Pagoda Red 1714 N Damen Ave, Bucktown ⊤773/235-1188. Huge showrooms on two floors carrying high-quality eighteenth- and nineteenth-century Chinese art (pottery, rugs, furniture etc) – a nice change from the funky, casual secondhand stores in the neighbourhood.

Poster Plus 200 S Michigan Ave, the Loop ⊤312/461-9277. Three storeys of fine art and vintage posters, as well as art-themed trinkets and custom framing. A great place to pick up any number of posters related to all things Chicago, including architecture, festivals and reproduction prints.

Primitive Art Works 130 N Jefferson St, River North ⊤312/575-9700. Intriguing River North gallery featuring four floors of ethnic artefacts – jewellery, furniture, textiles, etc – that makes for a fascinating hour's worth of browsing. The staff's enthusiasm for the place is infectious.

Tabula Tua 1015 W Armitage Ave, Lincoln Park ⊤773/525-3500. This small kitchenware store has unusual platters and place settings, engraved cheese spreaders and other gift-worthy items.

Books

General bookstores

Barnes & Noble 1441 W Webster Ave, Lincoln Park ⊤773/871-3610; **1130 N State St, Gold Coast** ⊤312/280-8155. Either of these huge outlets will have any recent or noteworthy title you'd ever want, except perhaps for academic textbooks or highly specialized works. Occasional author readings and children's storytelling; call for complete schedule.

Borders 150 N State St, the Loop ⊤312/606-0750; **830 N Michigan Ave, Near North** ⊤312/573-0564; **2817 N Clark St, Lakeview** ⊤773/935-3909. Massive, well-stocked book and music store. The N Michigan Ave branch is the biggest and best of the city's chain bookstores, centrally located right on the Mag Mile, with a café, frequent readings and signings and and loads of room to sit and browse.

Europa Books 832 N State St, Near North ⊤312/335-9677. This quaint neighbourhood bookstore packs a lot into little space, including an excellent selection of foreign-language books, newspapers and magazines.

Rare, used and specialty books

Abraham Lincoln Book Shop 357 W Chicago Ave, River North ⊤312/944-3085. You'll find more than eight thousand new, used and

antiquarian books on the shelves, covering the Civil War and other US military history, plus a host of collectibles and, of course, tomes on Lincoln himself.

Afrocentric Bookstore 4655 S King Drive ⊤773/924-3966. The city's best selection of African-American-related books, along with plenty of magazines, calendars and greeting cards. The store also hosts occasional readings.

Chicago Rare Book Center 703 Washington St, Evanston ⊤847/328-2132. Specializes in hard-to-find children's literature, jazz and blues, modern literature, art, Chicago and the Midwest.

Myopic Books 1564 N Milwaukee Ave, Wicker Park ⊤773/862-4882. Artsy and academic Wicker Park book haven selling both new and used rare titles.

O'Gara & Wilson 1448 E 57th St, Hyde Park ⊤773/363-0993. Great little bookstore that has sold new and used books (both popular and obscure) since the late 1930s.

Powell's Bookstores 2850 N Lincoln Ave, Lincoln Park ⊤773/248-1444; **828 S Wabash Ave, South Loop** ⊤312/341-0748; **1501 E 57th St, Hyde Park** ⊤773/955-7780. If you go to just one used bookstore in Chicago, make this your stop. Their stock frequently includes high-end photographic volumes at deep discounts, works on medieval literature, philosophy and stand-out offerings in the area of Chicago history. Just about everything is covered in their stores, save popular fiction.

Prairie Avenue Book Shop 418 S Wabash Ave, the Loop ☎312/922-8311. Serene and spacious place where you can browse the phenomenal architecture selection (12,000+ titles) to your heart's content. There is a tremendous selection of titles in related fields, including urban planning, interior design and graphic design. The store also hosts frequent readings and signings.

Seminary Co-op Books 5757 S University Plaza, Hyde Park ☎773/752-4381. Cavernous basement bookstore with a devout following, where row upon row of shelves is crammed with academic titles. They also have a sister store, 57th Street Books, a few blocks away at 1301 E 57th St.

Unabridged Books 3251 N Broadway, Lakeview ☎773/883-9119. This Boystown favourite carries much gay and lesbian literature and a good all-around selection of fiction and non-fiction titles, children's literature and travel guides. Great sale section at the back.

Clothes and fashion

Chain stores

Anthropologie 1120 N State St, Gold Coast ☎312/255-1848; 1780 Green Bay Rd, Highland Park ☎847/681-0200. Major fashion chain that blends in well with the neighbourhood. Expensive women's clothing and home furnishings with a romantic/bohemian slant.

Banana Republic 744 N Michigan Ave, Near North ☎312/642-0020; 2104 N Halsted St, Lincoln Park ☎773/832-1172. The ubiquitous chain's flagship store is on Michigan Ave, whose casual men's and women's clothes are snapped up by huge swathes of the country's 20–40 age group.

Burberry 633 N Michigan Ave, Near North ☎312/787-2500. Michigan Ave branch of the British stalwart clothier, known for its distinctive plaid; once conservative, the label is now popular with trendy urban types.

The Gap 555 N Michigan Ave, Near North ☎312/494-8580. Affordable men's and women's basics (jeans, T-shirts, etc) that coordinate with just about anything.

Designer stores

Boss Hugo Boss 520 N Michigan Ave, Near North ☎312/660-0056. Tailored men's and women's clothing, sportswear and accessories in an elegant Shops at North Bridge outlet.

Cynthia Rowley 810 W Armitage Ave, Lincoln Park ☎773/528-6160. This Chicagoan's designs cater to pretty young things, with a good selection of flirty dresses and dainty separates.

Giorgio Armani 800 N Michigan Ave, Near North ☎312/751-2244. The last word in classically styled luxury Italian fashion.

Gucci 900 N Michigan Ave, Near North ☎312/664-5504. Designer Tom Ford's empire of style; it doesn't get more expensive than this.

Ralph Lauren 750 N Michigan Ave, Near North ☎312/280-1655. All-American high-end fashion label.

Boutiques

apartment number 9 1804 N Damen Ave, Bucktown ☎773/395-2999. Expensive men's boutique with an eye for of-the-moment labels and hot new designers.

Betsey Johnson 2120 N Halsted St, Lincoln Park ☎773/871-3961. Very distinctive, brightly coloured and funky clothing from this New York designer; somewhat over the top for conservative Chicago.

Celeste Turner 857 W Armitage Ave, Lincoln Park ☎773/549-3390. Armitage Ave staple, with cool dresses and tops, but a bit pricey – T-shirts might set you back $80, a sweater $180.

Jake 939 Rush St, Gold Coast ☎312/664-5533; 3740 Southport Ave, Lakeview ☎773/929-5253. High-end denim, tees and casual wear for men and women from exclusive lines like Nudie, Trovata and Yanuk, plus local designers Kent Nielsen and Cecilie Broch.

Jane Hamill 1117 W Armitage Ave, Lincoln Park ☎773/665-1102. Stylish dresses, shoes and jewellery from local designer Hamill. A good shop to find a sun dress.

Krista K 3458 N Southport Ave, Lakeview ☎773/248-1967. Upscale women's apparel

– including stylish maternity wear – with a mix of local designers and trendy labels like Seven for All Mankind and True Religion.

Out of the West 1021 W Armitage Ave, Lincoln Park ☎ 773/404-9378. Cowboy-themed clothing and accessories, including boots, Lucky Jeans, Aztec-inspired turquoise jewellery, buckles, picture frames, lamps and much more.

p.45 1643 N Damen Ave, Bucktown ☎ 773/862-4523. Hip boutique that doubles as an art gallery for designers. Spacious, with an attentive staff and a chic selection of both casual and dressy styles.

Shopgirl 1206 W Webster Ave, Lincoln Park ☎ 773/935-7467. Tiny, expensive boutique away from the Armitage strip that does well nonetheless by carrying some trendy labels including Three Dots, Trina Turk and Shoshanna.

Sugar Magnolia 34 E Oak St, Gold Coast ☎ 312/944-0885. Distinctive upscale Chicago boutique that's managed to hold its own against Oak Street's ultra high-end competition. Stocks new and established designers.

Trousseau 3543 N Southport Ave, Lakeview ☎ 773/472-2727. Tops in women's lingerie, from brightly coloured pyjamas to lacy French bras.

Vive la femme 2048 N Damen Ave, Bucktown ☎ 773/772-7429. One of the city's only boutiques for stylish, full-figured women (sizes 12–28).

Vintage, secondhand and thrift

Brown Elephant Resale Store 3651 N Halsted St, Lakeview ☎ 773/549-5943. Secondhand clothing – and actually much more, including records, books and furniture – with proceeds going to the Howard Brown Memorial Clinic.

Daisy Shop 67 E Oak St, 6th Floor, Gold Coast ☎ 312/943-8880. Those willing to settle for gently worn couture will find a good selection from top designers at reduced – but still steep – prices.

Hollywood Mirror 812 W Belmont Ave, Lakeview ☎ 773/404-4510. Sells more junky trinkets than you'd ever wish upon anyone but it's a stimulating place nonetheless. While they do sell an assortment of vintage clothing, just as much of a draw here is the kitschy ambience, helped along by the disco ball and lights, and loud punk music.

Lenny & Me 1463 N Milwaukee Ave, Bucktown ☎ 773/489-5576. Friendly consignment

store that has a great assortment of women's clothing, though mostly for petite frames.

McShane's Exchange 1141 W Webster Ave, Lincoln Park ☎ 773/525-0211. This high-end women's consignment store can be a treasure-trove of bargains, with everything from fur coats to Chanel suits at a fraction of retail price.

Recycle 1474 N Milwaukee Ave, Wicker Park ☎ 773/645-1900. Designer-conscious consignment store, with men's and women's jeans, shirts and more.

Strange Cargo 3448 N Clark St, Wrigleyville ☎ 773/327-8090. Vintage clothing, jokey T-shirts, used Levis, wigs, costumes, wacky postcards and all sorts of random kitsch adorn the shelves at this local favourite.

Una Mae's Freak Boutique 1528 N Milwaukee Ave, Wicker Park ☎ 773/276-7002. Affordable vintage clothes, perfumed candles and an odd array of knick-knacks make this a quintessential Wicker Park locale.

Discount clothing

Filene's Basement 830 N Michigan Ave, Near North ☎ 312/482-8918. One of those stores where you can find everything, from soap trays to brand-name clothes, all at discounted prices

Marshall's 600 N Michigan Ave, Near North ☎ 312/280-7506. Though you'll have to plough through racks and racks of clothing – from discount to designer labels – you'll usually find a bargain or two.

Nordstrom Rack 24 N State St, the Loop ☎ 312/377-5500. Great deals on high-end men's and women's clothing, home accessories and particularly shoes.

TJ Maxx 11 N State St, the Loop ☎ 312/553-0515. Large store that takes in discounted and discontinued items from major department stores, applying deep discounts along the way. Men's and women's clothing are good bets here, along with a flotsam-jetsam approach to housewares and a variety of odds and ends.

Shoes

City Soles/Niche 2001 W North Ave, Bucktown ☎ 773/489-2001. Shoes with attitude – imports from Spain, Italy and elsewhere. Also carries bags and other accessories.

DSW Shoe Warehouse 3131 N Clark St, Lakeview ☎ 773/975-7182. Thirty-five thousand pairs of name-brand and designer men's and women's shoes, from sandals and slippers to athletic and dress footwear. Socks and handbags too.

Hanig's Footwear 660 N Michigan Ave, Near North ⊤312/642-5330; **also Hanig's Birkenstock Shop, 847 W Armitage Ave, Lincoln Park** ⊤773/929-5568. Carries major brands of walking shoes like Ecco, Mephisto and Dansko. The Lincoln Park branch has one of the largest selections of sandals in the city.

John Fluevog Shoes 1539 N Milwaukee Ave, Wicker Park ⊤773/772-1983. Flamboyantly trendy shoes from this Canadian label.

Johnston & Murphy 625 N Michigan Ave, Near North ⊤312/751-1630. Staple for quality, conservative dress shoes.

Lori's Designer Shoes 824 W Armitage Ave, Lincoln Park ⊤773/281-5655. The quintessential women's shoe store and one of the best in Chicago; styles run the gamut and there's also a good selection of one-of-a-kind bags and purses.

New Balance Chicago 2369 N Clark St, Lincoln Park ⊤773/348-1787. Small neighbourhood store selling one of the top brands in running shoes.

Niketown 669 N Michigan Ave, Near North ⊤312/642-6363. This giant Nike retail outlet is a tourist attraction in itself, thanks in part to the video theatre and miniature basketball court.

Cosmetics and fragrances

Aroma Workshop 2050 N Halsted St, Lincoln Park ⊤773/871-1985. A great place for candles, though you'll find scented oils, incense and the like here as well; there's also a mixing bar where you can create your own scents.

Fresh 2040 N Halsted St, Lincoln Park ⊤773/404-9776. One of the hottest stores in Chicago, with knowledgeable staff and an extensive – though slightly expensive – selection of candles, soaps, lotions and other beauty products.

MAC 40 E Oak St, Gold Coast ⊤312/951-7310. Trendy make-up brand that caters to a

youngish crowd, known for its glamour-heavy look.

Merz Apothecary 4716 N Lincoln Ave (at the intersection of Lincoln, Western and Lawrence), Lincoln Square ⊤773/989-0900. Opened in 1875, this pharmacy is loaded with bath, body and natural-health products, including some rare European items.

Powder Room 705 W Armitage Ave, Lincoln Park ⊤773/640-1194. Recently arrived boutique cosmetics shop carries hard-to-find lines like Little Shop of Beauty, Jelly Pong Pong, SugarBaby and a couple of dozen others, all in a cute Lincoln Park storefront.

Department stores and malls

Department stores

Barney's New York 25 E Oak St, Gold Coast ⊤312/587-1700. Boutique department store carrying a highly edited selection of all the major designers. A more congenial and less-crowded version of its New York counterpart.

Bloomingdale's 900 N Michigan Ave, Near North ⊤312/440-4460. Flagship Midwest store of the famous New York retailer. You could easily spend half a day in here and skip the rest of the Mile; part of the 900 N Michigan Ave mall, it's in close proximity to restaurants and plenty of other shops.

H&M 840 N Michigan Ave, Near North ⊤312/640-0060; **22 N State St, the Loop**

⊤312/263-4436. Swedish department store concept offering trendy but affordable European fashions for men, women and children.

Lord & Taylor 835 N Michigan Ave, Near North ⊤312/787-7400. Whether this conservative department store succeeds in revamping its slightly dated image remains to be seen, though its sales are usually worth a look. Located in the same mall as the larger Macy's.

Macy's 111 N State St, the Loop ⊤312/781-1000; **835 N Michigan Ave, Near North** ⊤312/335-7700. The famous New York-based retailer has finally arrived in Chicago, with its main store located right here in the former Marshall Field's Department Store building. There are the usual suspects: high-end quality garments, designer scarves, impeccable customer service, and a rather grand setting for a day of shopping. Check out the blue Tiffany dome (see p.56) and the *Walnut Room* restaurant, a Field's (and now, Macy's) institution. The smaller N Michigan branch still carries most designers.

Neiman Marcus 737 N Michigan Ave, Near North ☎312/642-5900. This high-end, designer-oriented store comes with more attitude than the others, but at least there's usually plenty of room to shop.

Nordstrom 55 E Grand Ave ☎312/464-1515. Huge high-end retail chain with an excellent shoe department. Known for top customer service.

Saks Fifth Avenue 700 N Michigan Ave, Near North ☎312/944-6500. Similar to Neiman Marcus in its clothing lines and high price point, but known for its customer service and sales. Tends to be among the most crowded of the city's department stores. The first-floor make-up department is especially popular.

Sears 2 N State St, the Loop ☎312/373-6000. After several years' absence, the department store giant has returned to downtown with its affordable but rather staid merchandise.

Malls

900 North Michigan 900 N Michigan Ave, Near North ☎312/915-3900. Northernmost of the Michigan Ave malls and its most upscale, with six levels that are home to Bloomingdale's, Gucci, J. Crew and some seventy other stores. *The Oak Tree* restaurant (level 5) is a pleasant breakfast and lunch spot with great Mag Mile views.

Chicago Place 700 N Michigan Ave, Near North ☎312/642-4811. Eight-storey space that includes Saks Fifth Avenue, Joy of Ireland and fifty other stores, plus the largest food court on the Mag Mile.

The Shops at North Bridge 520 N Michigan Ave, Near North ☎312/327-2300. Airy, four-storey Mag Mile complex dominated by Nordstrom's, with a clutch of children's stores, shoe stores and an upscale food court.

Water Tower Place 835 N Michigan Ave, Near North ☎312/440-3166. Chicago's first and most famous vertical mall – seven stories and over one hundred big-name storeys, including Macy's and Lord & Taylor, plus a massive mezzanine-level gourmet food court.

Food and drink

Breadsmith (Wells Street Bread Co) 1710 N Wells St, Old Town ☎312/642-5858. This small, fabulous bread shop is a superior alternative to the numerous chain coffee and breakfast joints in the area.

Fox & Obel Food Market 401 E Illinois St, Near North ☎312/410-7301. You don't need to be a gourmand to appreciate the superb selection of cheeses, fresh fish, meats, deli items and baked goods on offer at this gourmet food emporium; there's a café here, too (see p.172).

🏃 **Garrett Popcorn Shop 26 W Randolph St, the Loop** ☎312/201-0511; **4 E Madison St, the Loop** ☎ 312/263-1108. Lines routinely stretch out the door at this venerated Chicago institution, whose caramel-and-cheese flavoured popcorns are out of this world. Other popular varieties include cashew, pecan or macadamia caramel crisp.

House of Glunz 1206 N Wells St, Old Town ☎312/642-3000. Small family-run wine shop,

purported to be the oldest wine shop in the nation. Great place to pick up some unique, inexpensive wines.

Lutz Continental Café & Pastry Shop 2458 W Montrose Ave, Lincoln Square ☎773/478-7785. Half-century-old German-style bakery where you can soak up the old-world ambience in the café at the back or take home delectable strudels, cakes, pastries and marzipan from the glass cases up front.

Vosges Haut-Chocolat 520 N Michigan Ave (in the Westfield North Bridge Center), Near North ☎312/644-9450; **951 W Armitage, Lincoln Park** ☎773/296-9866. Gourmet chocolate boutique renowned for truffles made with unique flavours and spices like ancho chile powder, absinthe and balsamic vinegar.

Wikstrom's Gourmet 5217 N Clark St, Andersonville ☎773/275-6100. Assorted food from all over Scandinavia: Gothenburg sausage, Kavli flatbread, Danish pumpernickel bread, Swedish lingonberries and the like.

Museum and gallery shops

ArchiCenter Shop 224 S Michigan Ave ☎312/922-3432; 875 N Michigan Ave (ground floor of the John Hancock Center), Near North ☎312/751-1380. The Chicago Architecture Foundation's retail arm, with a good selection of architecture-related books and knick-knacks.

The Art Institute of Chicago Museum Shop 111 S Michigan Ave, at W Adams St, the Loop ☎312/443-3534. Art books, reproductions and a host of museum-related gift items.

Bariff Shop for Judaica Spertus Museum, 610 S Michigan Ave, South Loop ☎312/322-1740. A small shop devoted entirely to Judaica, with art, ceremonial pieces, books and more.

MCA Store 220 E Chicago Ave, Streeterville ☎312/280-2660. Within the Museum of Contemporary Art, this small store carries art-related posters, gift cards, books and home accessories.

Music shops

Blue Chicago Store 534 N Clark St, Near North ☎312/661-1003. The blues club's own store, packed with CDs, shirts, posters and assorted paraphernalia, including the club's signature art by John Carroll Doyle. For club review, see p.198.

Dave's Records 2604 N Clark St, Lincoln Park ☎773/929-6325. Vinyl-only store with largish selection: some 50,000 new and used LPs, 45s and 12-inch dance music and hip-hop.

Dr Wax 5226 S Harper Ave, Hyde Park ☎773/493-8696. This outfit carries new and used CDs, LPs and tapes but its strongest suit is its extensive secondhand CD bins.

Dusty Groove America 1120 N Ashland Ave, Wicker Park ☎773/342-5800. Small space that packs a mighty wallop with rare and hard to find imports that on any given day could include Estonian punk compilations from the 1970s, obscure Latin jazz reissues and Ennio Morricone soundtracks. CDs dominate here but they also carry new and used LPs.

Gramaphone 2843 N Clark St, Lincoln Park ☎773/472-3683. Packed to the gills with an outstanding selection of house, dance and techno discs, from mainstream to underground, from Chicago and everywhere else. DJs spin in the back and you can listen to any CD before you buy.

Jazz Record Mart 25 E Illinois St, the Loop ☎312/222-1467, ⌨www.jazzrecordmart.com. Billing itself as "The World's Largest Jazz and Blues Shop", with the floor space and stock to back up the claim. In addition to aisles of new jazz and blues CDs, they also carry plenty of used vinyl, plus books and videos. There is also the occasional in-store performance (check website for schedule). A must-stop for blues and jazz lovers.

▲ Jazz Record Mart

Reckless Records 1532 N Milwaukee Ave, Wicker Park ☎773/235-3727; 3161 N Broadway, Lakeview ☎773/404-5080. Chicago branches of the London-based used-music chain, with an extensive selection of CDs, DVDs and vinyl (especially indie, punk and imported electronica) at fair prices.

Rock Records 175 W Washington St, the Loop ☎312/346-3489. More than 20,000 music titles fill the bins at this superstore, with everything from classical to rap and hard rock. Posters, concert tees and thousands of DVDs too.

Symphony Store 220 S Michigan Ave, the Loop ☎312/294-3345. One of the city's top spots to visit if you're looking for a classical music title. A wide array of recordings in stock.

Sporting goods shops

Active Endeavors 853 W Armitage Ave, Lincoln Park ☎773/281-8100. A Lincoln Park mainstay and part of the Armitage Ave shopping route, this small, popular retailer sells outdoor gear and clothes.

Erehwon Mountain Outfitter 1000 W North Ave ☎312/337-6400. Probably Chicago's best selection of outdoor adventure clothes and gear.

Londo Mondo 1100 N Dearborn St, Gold Coast ☎312/751-2794; 2148 N Halsted St, Lincoln Park ☎773/327-2218; 444 W Jackson Blvd, the Loop ☎312/648-9188. Excellent selection of designer swimwear, workout clothing and inline skates for active folks.

The North Face 875 N Michigan Ave, Near North ☎312/337-7200. Functional and stylish outdoor clothing and equipment, geared toward affluent adventure enthusiasts.

Orvis 142 E Ontario St, at N Michigan Ave, Near North ☎312/440-0662. Mag Mile version of this dependable New England retailer, with fly-fishing gear and ruggedly fashionable outdoor wear.

Running Away 1753 N Damen Ave, Bucktown ☎773/395-2929. Very cool boutique runner's shop, with a yoga studio downstairs.

Specialty shops

All She Wrote 825 W Armitage Ave, Lincoln Park ☎773/529-0100. Warm, family-run stationery store with unique and cool gifts and decorations.

The Alley 854 W Belmont Ave, Lakeview ☎773/348-5000. A temple to all things Goth, this landmark of alternative and fetish Chicago is worth a look if you're in the area. Entrance is in the alley.

Central Camera 230 S Wabash Ave, the Loop ☎312/427-5580. Century-old camera shop with knowledgeable staff. Student discounts available.

Chicago Tribune Gift Store 435 N Michigan Ave, Near North ☎312/222-3080. Hats, shirts and other souvenirs plastered with the *Tribune* logo.

City of Chicago Store 163 E Pearson St (across from the Water Tower), Near North ☎312/742-8811. As the name might suggest, Chicago souvenirs of all kinds. The real find here is the truly unique selection of old CTA signs and transit maps.

Iwan Ries & Co 19 S Wabash Ave ☎312/372-1306. This second-floor cigar shop has been a Chicago family business for nearly 150 years. Over one hundred different cigar brands and at least 13,000 pipes on hand.

Paper Source 232 W Chicago Ave, Near North ☎312/337-0798; 919 W Armitage Ave, Lincoln Park ☎773/525-7300. Wonderful paper boutique with a world of stationery, journals, cards, photo albums and wrapping paper.

Scrapbook Source 557 W North Ave, Old Town ☎312/440-9720. From stickers and glitter to albums, paper, cutting tools and stamps, this store offers a complete selection of scrapbooking supplies, plus table workspace for use by customers.

Spacetime Tanks 2526 N Lincoln Ave, Lincoln Park ☎773/472-2700. If your idea of relaxation means floating in vats of water in complete darkness, this "float center" is for you. Four isolation tanks, each renting at $40/hr. Closes at 9pm every night except Sunday (6pm).

Uncle Fun 1338 W Belmont Ave, Lakeview ☎773/477-8223. Wall-to-wall jokes and novelty toys – whoopee cushions, fake body parts and more.

Waxman Candles 3044 N Lincoln Ave, Lakeview ☎773/929-3000. Scented and unscented columns, tapers, globes and drip and non-drip candles are handmade at this funky, eclectic storefront, which also stocks cool candlesticks and candleholders large and small.

19

Sports and outdoor activities

I n Chicago, professional sports attachments seem to permeate all levels of society and you'll find that just about everyone has a handle on local teams, including the Cubs (Major League Baseball), the Bears (National Football League), and the Bulls (National Basketball Association). Supporting the local pro teams is a huge part of the Chicago mindset; walk the streets and you won't go far without passing some Chicago sports paraphernalia plastered across store windows or inside a crowded sports bar.

Attending a **professional sports event**, be it a baseball, football, basketball or hockey game, should be a priority for any visitor, if only to get a bit of insight into this aspect of the American psyche. At the top of the list is a Cubs game at Wrigley Field, where you can experience Chicago at its proudest while soaking up the atmosphere of one of the great standing shrines to old-school sports stadiums.

Locals are just as enthusiastic about **participatory activities** and the city has been blessed with miles of lakefront parkland, fantastic for jogging, cycling, in-line skating, swimming, volleyball, fishing, boating, golfing or simply lazing on a beach. Most of the action happens throughout Lincoln Park, the wide swath of green scenery and lakefront property that stretches six miles north of downtown.

Spectator sports

"Going to the game" in Chicago is a year-round pastime, since there's always a sport in season: football in the autumn and winter; ice hockey and basketball in the autumn, winter and spring; and baseball and soccer in the spring, summer and autumn. When it's too cold for most locals to be active themselves – be it

Getting tickets

You can buy **tickets** to most professional sporting events in Chicago through Ticket-master (☎312/559-1212 or 559-1950, 🅦www.ticketmaster.com); it's also possible to buy them at one of several Ticketmaster outlets throughout the city (including the Hot Tix booths at 72 E Randolph St and 163 E Pearson St).

Another option is to buy directly from the individual team's box office, especially at the last minute. If all else fails, you can try ticket brokers, although they usually charge higher prices. Try either Gold Coast Tickets (☎1-800/889-9100, 🅦www.goldcoasttickets.com) or Stubhub! (☎1-866/788-2482, 🅦www.stubhub.com).

playing softball or tennis or jogging by the lake – you'll often find them packed into sports bars in a sort of hibernation until warm weather comes and everyone floods outside again.

Baseball

Chicago boasts one of America's most beloved ballparks, **Wrigley Field** at 1060 W Addison St, at Clark St (see p.100), and one of the country's usually mediocre baseball teams, the **Chicago Cubs** (☎773/404-2827, Ⓦwww.cubs.com). Although the Cubs haven't won a World Series since 1908, the team's fans are famously loyal. Seeing a game there is a must even for non-baseball devotees. For a true Wrigley experience, sit in the general admission outfield bleachers, home to the rowdiest of fans, known as the "bleacher bums", who follow their own set of rules for each game, such as always throwing back a home-run ball hit by the opposing team.

While the popular Cubs have remained consistent under-achievers, their South Side rivals, the less celebrated **Chicago White Sox** (☎312/674-1000, Ⓦwww.chisox.com) have fared far better, winning the 2005 world series, their first since 1917. They now play at the more modern but sterile U.S. Cellular Field at 35th Street and Dan Ryan Expressway – the previous stadium, Comiskey Park (see p.123), which was demolished in 1991, used to be right next to where the new one is.

The regular baseball season runs between April and September, with the play-offs in October. Ticket prices for Cubs games are $12–250; $10–57 for Sox games.

For those looking to experience minor league baseball in the Chicago area, the Schaumburg Flyers play May through September at Alexian Field. The games have a bit more family atmosphere, and the tickets tend to be around $10–14. It's outside of the city, but visitors can pick up a Metra train out there from the Oglivie Transportation Center west of the Loop. More

▲ Wrigley Field

information on the Flyers can be found at Ⓦwww.flyersbaseball.com

Basketball

Neither the **Chicago Bulls** (☎312/455-4000, Ⓦwww.nba.com/bulls) nor the city of Chicago had any real idea what impact one acquisition – **Michael Jordan** in the 1984 draft – would have on their next fifteen years. Jordan went on to become quite simply the best player in the history of professional basketball, almost single-handedly changing the fortunes of the Bulls and the game as a whole. He led the team to win six NBA titles in the 1990s, and his gravity-defying heroics still inspire the next generation of basketball hopefuls. His retirement from the Bulls in 1999 left the team reeling and the squad is just starting to recover, thanks to an influx of young players.

The basketball season begins in the autumn and play-off games stretch into the summer. Tickets for Bulls games, played in the **United Center** at 1901 W Madison St, start at $10 for the upper level, with courtside seats costing $600.

Football

Known as the "Monsters of the Midway", football's **Chicago Bears** (☎ 312/295-6600, ⓦ www.chicago bears.com) have been playing at **Soldier Field** at 425 E McFetridge Drive since the 1970s (before they played primarily at Wrigley Field). The stadium recently underwent a massive $600 million renovation (see p.71), which basically constructed a new, modern stadium within the historic colonnades and exterior walls of the old site, resulting in a hodgepodge of architectural styles that has justly gained it the nickname "the mistake by the lake".

Despite years of down seasons, the Bears still pack the stadiums come autumn and tickets are highly coveted. As with other Chicago professional sports teams, fans are extremely loyal (verging on the obsessive) and routinely fill the seats despite the sub-zero temperatures at the lakefront stadium. Founded in 1919 as the Decatur Staleys by legendary coach George Halas, the team was the nation's first pro football squad and became the Chicago Bears in 1922. The 1985 team, under the lead of coach "Iron Mike" Ditka lost one game all season, won the Super Bowl and ranks as one of the great teams of all time.

The football season opens in the first week of September and runs through December, with the play-offs happening in January Tickets for Bears games are $50–330.

Ice hockey

In this rough-and-tumble city, professional hockey has a major following. In the **Chicago Blackhawks**' heyday in the early '90s, with star players Jeremy Roenick, Chris Chelios and Ed Belfour, their games earned a reputation as one of the loudest sporting events in the country and when the October to April season rolls around (play-offs until early June), tickets (☎ 312/455-7000, ⓦ www.chiblackhawks.com) are

generally hard to get. The Blackhawks play at the United Center (see p.117) and tickets for games start at $10, with rinkside seats going for $250.

Alternatively, you can catch a minor league game at **Allstate Arena** at Mannheim Road and Lunt Avenue, in Rosemont, with the **Chicago Wolves** (☎ 847/724-4625, ⓦ www .chicagowolves.com) and while the play won't be as spectacular as you'd see at a Blackhawks game, it's another entertaining way to get a taste of Chicago's intense sports scene.

Soccer

Ironically, one of Chicago's most successful professional sports teams in recent years is also one of its most underappreciated: the **Chicago Fire** (☎ 1-888/657-3473, ⓦ www.chicago -fire.com), of Major League Soccer. Since joining the league in 1998, the squad, with an international roster of players from Mexico, Jamaica, Africa, Eastern Europe and the US, has advanced to three MLS Cup finals, winning one of them.

The Fire play at the brand-new $70 million, 20,000-seat Toyota Park soccer stadium in southeast suburban Bridgeview at 71st and Harlem. The stadium is accessible via buses that leave the Midway station on the CTA's Orange Line. Tickets for Fire games range from $15–75.

Horse racing

One of the country's best tracks for thoroughbred horse racing is located northwest of Chicago in Arlington Heights – a half-hour's ride on Metra commuter rail. **Arlington Park Race Course**, 2200 Euclid Ave (☎ 847/385-7500), is open May through September (Wed–Sun), with gates opening at 11am and post time (first race) usually at 1pm. The highlight of the season is the running of the high-stakes **Arlington Million**, a 1.25-mile turf race that draws top steeds from around the world for a seven-figure purse.

SPORTS AND ACTIVITIES | Spectator sports

Besides the usual races, the track also hosts "Party in the Park" on Friday afternoons, pulling in the after-work crowds with cheap drinks and live music on the front lawn; the first race doesn't start till 3pm.

To get there, board the Union Pacific Northwest line at Ogilvie Transportation Center and get off at the Arlington Park stop (round-trip $8.60). The train drops you right at the park.

Outdoor activities

Chicagoans tend to hibernate during the winter, taking shelter from the cold, wind and snow that hit the city between November and March (and sometimes later). But when the weather finally shifts in the spring, locals break outside and take advantage of the warmth with countless outdoor activities, from jogging, biking or playing volleyball along the lake to tennis, golf, softball, sailing and birdwatching. Most of the action centres in Lincoln Park (see p.93), whose bike paths and green space are particularly inviting to the city's young, physically fit crowd.

Bicycling

With hundreds of miles of **bike trails** and a paved path along the lakefront, Chicago is a cyclist's dream. This main path alone spans 15 miles, from the far northern neighbourhood of Rogers Park to the University of Chicago in Hyde Park on the South Side – passing by the heart of downtown – and it makes for one of the best outdoor experiences in the city. The path is easily accessible, too, with entrances at every underpass along Lake Shore Drive. The city's streets are also handy for cycling, with 120 miles of bike lanes on stretches of Halsted Street, Wells Street, Lincoln Avenue and Damen Avenue, among others. The North Shore area of Chicago is a popular destination for cyclists too; the nine-mile asphalt and crushed-stone **Green Bay Trail** from Wilmette to Highland Park is a particular favourite. The City of Chicago publishes a **free map** with bike lanes and paths and recommended routes through the city and suburbs. Call ☏312/742-2453 for a free copy.

Bike Chicago Navy Pier ☏312/755-0488, North Ave Beach ☏773/327-2706, ⓦwww.bike chicago.com. This outfit has more or less cornered the bike rental market in Chicago, and with two key (and relatively accessible)

rental outlets, it should be your first call for bikes and in-line skates. Prices start around $10 per hour or $25 per day. All rentals include locks and maps.

Chicagoland Bicycle Federation ☏312/427-3325, ⓦwww.chibikefed.org. Organization that promotes cycling in the city, hosts cycling tours and events and offers services like bike registration and safe bicycling tips.

Chicago Cycling Club ☏773/509-8093, ⓦwww .chicagocyclingclub.org. Local social club that organizes rides every Saturday and Sunday between April and October, most leaving at 8.30am from the clock tower in Lincoln Park (at Waveland Avenue and the lakefront path, just south of the golf course). Rides range from 15 to 100 miles and are open to riders of all experience levels.

On the Route Bicycles 3144 N Lincoln Ave ☏773/477-5066, ⓦwww.ontheroute.com. Full-service bike shop that also rents road bikes, mountain bikes and city bikes; the latter rent for around $35 per day (24hr), $20 per half-day.

Birdwatching

Chicago's best place for **birdwatching** is the **Magic Hedge**, an area of trees and shrubs east of Lake Shore Drive at Montrose Point (look out for the sign on Montrose Harbor Drive). Jutting out into Lake Michigan, this grassy area is right in a major migration path and can be visited year-round. Sightings of more than three hundred species of birds have been recorded on this sandy hill.

The best time to visit is during spring and fall migrations but on any given day you're likely to spot up to fifty-odd species, including warblers, swallows and falcons; especially eye-catching are the thousands of purple martins that flock here in early August.

Boating

As the city sits right on an enormous lake, the popularity and accessibility of boating is no surprise (see "Fishing", opposite, as well). The **Chicago Sailing Club**, 2712 N Campbell Ave (☎773/871-7245, Ⓦwww.chicagosailingclub.com), organizes sailing lessons, rentals and charters from dock B at the north end of Belmont Harbor, at Belmont and the lake. Rentals are available to the public, with J22 boats from $45 to $65/hour, and J30 boats from $80 to $100/hour. The club also offers windsurfing lessons and equipment rentals, often from Montrose Beach, just north of the harbour. To get to Belmont Harbor, take Lake Shore Drive north of Belmont to Recreation Drive, then turn right and follow the road back to the harbour.

Between May and September, there's a paddleboat rental service on Lincoln Park's South Pond, outside *Café Brauer*, 2021 N Stockton Drive ($12 per 30min or $16 per hr). Boat rental is available from 10am to dusk.

The Chicago Area Sea Kayaking Association Ⓦwww.caska.org. This web-based organization offers evening paddles on Lake Michigan and is a good source for current information on kayaking around Chicago.

The Lincoln Park Boat Club ☎773-549-2628, Ⓦwww.lpbc.net/Paddling. Social club that offers paddling and rowing classes, just south of W Fullerton Ave, at the Lincoln Park Lagoon.

Bowling and billiards

Bowling fans will find plenty of alleys in Chicago – including two new spaces that give the pastime a trendy spin. All but two of the following alleys offer both bowling and billiards facilities.

10Pin 330 N State St, in Marina City, River North ☎312/644-0300, Ⓦwww.10pinchicaog.com. Trendy downtown bowling lounge with 24 lanes and a 128-foot HDTV video wall, plus a casual menu of gourmet pizzas and comfort food (before 5pm $4.95 per person per game; after 5pm $6.95 per person). Sun–Thurs 11am–midnight, Fri 11am–2am, Sat 11am–3am.

Diversey River Bowl 2211 W Diversey Parkway ☎773/227-5800, Ⓦwww.drbowl.com. A cheesy yet fun place to bowl amid flashing strobe lights, smoke machines and loud Eighties music. Lane prices vary by the day: Mon–Thurs $19 per hr, Fri & Sat $32 per hr, Sun $26 per hr. Shoes $3. Daily noon–2am, Sat till 3am.

Lucky Strike 322 E Illinois St, Streeterville ☎312/245-8331, Ⓦwww.bowlluckystrike.com. Hollywood-based nightspot drawing a club-ready crowd with 18 lanes, 11 pool tables, three separate bar areas, and American fare like burgers and buffalo wings. Bowling $4.95–6.95 per person per game; pool $10–14 per hour. Daily 11am–2am.

Seven Ten Lounge 2747 N Lincoln Ave in Lincoln Park ☎773/549-2695. This Art Deco alley, with eight lanes and six pool tables, has two bars as well as decent finger food. The lanes may not be the best in the city, but the ambience makes up for it. Lanes cost $20/hour and shoes $2, while pool tables are $12 per hour. Mon–Wed 5pm–midnight, Thurs & Fri 5pm–2am, Sat noon–3am Sun noon–midnight.

Southport Lanes & Billiards 3325 N Southport Ave, Lakeview ☎773/472-6600. Really a bar with four bowling lanes and a few pool tables but the vintage setting – complete with human pinsetters – makes this a fun place to bowl. You'll need to call ahead to reserve a lane, as the place is extremely popular. Rates are a little cheaper than elsewhere ($15 per hr, $3 for shoes). During the week, lanes are less busy, opening at 6pm and closing when demand falls off or when the bar closes, usually around 1am. On weekends lanes open in the early afternoon and stay open later (but are often occupied by private parties and groups). As for pool, there are six regulation-size tables ($6 per hr during the week, going up to $12 per hr on peak nights).

Chicago's beaches

In summer, the city's beaches are swamped with locals trying to escape the intense heat and humidity. While none are secluded or private in any way – Lake Shore Drive is buzzing nearby – they are a pleasant place to take a break and catch some rays.

The city's main beaches are listed below; several other popular beaches are located further north in Rogers Park and on the North Shore (see p.134 for more information).

All of the beaches listed below are free and usually open from 9am to 9.30pm between May and September; you'll find public restrooms in the vicinity.

The main beaches

Foster Avenue Beach Sedate, clean beach near the northern tip of Lincoln Park. The beach house has concessions and outdoor showers.

Fullerton Avenue Beach Just east of Lake Shore Drive, this concrete stretch is popular thanks to the adjacent *Theater on the Lake*, which occasionally hosts evening shows on summer weekends (see p.207).

Montrose Beach Wide, sandy beach with volleyball courts; less crowded than the North Avenue and Oak Street beaches. You'll find Lincoln Park's bait shop here, as well a fishing pier (see "Fishing", below).

North Avenue Beach Just east of Lake Shore Drive, the city's most popular beach has volleyball nets, a Bike Chicago outlet (see p.237) and a boat-shaped beach house with concessions and volleyball equipment rental, along with *Castaway's Bar & Grill*.

Oak Street Beach A place to see and be seen, this busy, fashion-conscious patch of sand just east of Michigan Avenue is decked out with volleyball courts and a bistro, with skyscrapers as a backdrop.

Waveland Bowl 3700 N Western Ave, one block north of W Addison St, Roscoe Village ☏773/472-5902, ⓦ www.wavelandbowl.com. The rare bowling alley that's open 24 hour, 7 days a week – it's often full with leagues until around 9.30pm. Open since 1959, the recently refurbished alley has three regulation-size pool tables, an arcade and a little theatre showing Disney flicks for kids. Prices depend on when you play, but expect to pay between $10 and $25 per hour for bowling, with games being more expensive after 5pm and on weekends. Prices for pool table rental also vary, though you'll generally pay $8–20 per hour.

Fishing

Few people come to Chicago with **fishing** in mind but the city has several places where anyone can put a line in the water. Chicago is, after all, on a lake well endowed with fish (especially coho and king salmon), and though angling trips and charter service are by no means plentiful, they do exist.

Most charter boats launch from north or south of the city, though a few service downtown fishermen (see p.240). Check the **Chicago Sport-fishing Association**'s website (ⓦ www.great-lakes.org/il/fishchicago) for a list of charter boat operators. Prices usually start from $400 per six people for four hours.

If fishing from a boat doesn't appeal, there are a number of places where you can fish from shore. Popular fishing spots include Lincoln Park's **South Lagoon**, the pier at **Montrose Harbor** and just about anywhere there's a cement embankment along the lake. Fly fishermen often head to the pier at the south end of the North Pond to practice their casting – it's surrounded by floating rings that serve as targets.

The Park Bait Shop, at Montrose Avenue and Harbor Drive (☏773/271-2838), can set you up with bait (minnows and worms).

19

SPORTS AND ACTIVITIES | Activities

239

Captain Al's Charter Service 400 E Randolph Drive ☎312/565-0104, ⓦwww.captainalscharters.com
Captain Bob's Lake Michigan Charters ☎1-888/929-3474, ⓦwww.confusioncharters.com
Spendthrift Charters ☎1-800/726-7309, ⓦwww.spendthriftcharters.com

Golf

There are dozens of excellent **golf courses** within the greater Chicago area, as well as a few courses close to downtown.

Diversey Driving Range & Mini-Golf 141 W Diversey Parkway ☎312/742-7929, ⓦwww .diverseydrivingrange.com; Brown/Purple Line to Diversey. A terrific alternative to Waveland, this driving range is open daily 9am–8pm, year-round (they have 25 heated mats) and rents clubs; a bucket of sixty balls costs $8, with the last bucket sold around 7.15pm. And don't forget the 18-hole miniature golf course, which costs $7 for a round.

Harborside International Golf Center 111th St and Bishop Ford Expressway ☎312/782-7837. One of the best courses in the area – a links-style eighteen-hole course far down on the South Side. The only drawback is that you'll need your own transport to reach the course. Tee-time must be booked in advance and greens fees start around $82 for eighteen holes. It's much cheaper ($57) if you show up after 3.30pm.

Jackson Park Golf Course 63rd Street and Lake Shore Drive ☎773/667-0524. An eighteen-hole course on the South Side that's open year-round, from dawn to dusk. Greens fees start around $20.

Sydney R. Marovitz Golf Course 3600 Recreation Drive ☎773/667-0524. Also known as "Waveland", this popular nine-hole course is right on the lakefront near downtown and best suited for casual players who want to squeeze a few holes into their day (you'll need to book in advance, though). Rounds start around $15.

Jogging

Jogging remains one of the city's favourite athletic pastimes, thanks in large part to the extensive park system and the lakefront trail, where the majority of the city's runners tend to congregate; jog either on the paved bike path or the dirt path – scenic routes either way. You can join the trail at most avenues and gauge your run using the mile markers along the way. Aside from the lakeshore path, the city's parks offer miles of gravel-lined and paved jogging and walking trails; call the Chicago Park District at ☎312/742-7529 for more information.

The **Chicago Area Runners Association** (☎312/666-9836, ⓦwww .cararuns.org) organizes runs that meet at the north end of Diversey Harbor (membership not necessary). They can also provide information on upcoming races, as well as training for the **Chicago Marathon**, the city's biggest running event (☎312/904-9800, ⓦwww.chicagomarathon.com), which occurs on the first or second Sunday in October.

Kids' Chicago

C hicago has come a long way in terms of providing services to younger residents and visitors over the past decade or so, and alongside mainstays like Navy Pier (a very kid-friendly destination), visitors will find other tiny nooks and crannies throughout the city that offer things such as children's menus, toys and interactive activities to keep them occupied and enjoying the trip.

Major **museums** with special activities for children include the Chicago History Museum (see p. 93), the Field Museum (see p. 68) and, of course, the Chicago Children's Museum at Navy Pier (see below). In many ways, Lincoln Park can be thought of as extended child-friendly environment, as visitors can wander along the lake from the North Avenue Beach over to the Farm-In-the-Zoo (see p.242) over at the Lincoln Park Zoo (see p.94). After a break, families will want to continue walking north to the Peggy Notebaert Nature Museum (see p.242). More ideas for family fun can be found in Chapter 19, Sports and outdoor activities, as well as Chapter 21, Festivals.

Conservatories, museums and zoos

Brookfield Zoo 8400 31st St, Brookfield, ☏708/688-8000, Ⓦwww.czs.org; Metra train from Chicago's Union Station to Hollywood. Like most zoos, Brookfield Zoo is very child-friendly, and adults can get in on the act as well. In terms of the main attraction (animals, of course), the Zoo has has a "Bear Grotto" (complete with Alaskan brown bears), a tropical jungle with anteaters and gorillas (in different enclosures, obviously), and a "Pachyderm House" with elephants, rhinos and even tapirs. Special activities for children include brightly coloured playground equipment, dolphin shows, hands-on feeding opportunities and the Hamill Family Play Zoo, where young people can pretend to be a zoo director or animal keeper. General admission is $12, seniors and children aged 3–11 $8. "All-in-One" tickets include general admission and entrance to the dolphin shows and other activities; $24, seniors and children aged 3–11 $18. late

May–late Oct 9.30am–6pm, late Oct–late May 10am–5pm.

Chicago Children's Museum at Navy Pier Navy Pier, Near North/Streeterville ☏312/527-1000, Ⓦwww.chicagochildrensmuseum.org; Bus #29, #65 or #124. Art, nature and playfulness all intersect at the Chicago Children's Museum. Located on Navy Pier, the museum brings together an urban garden (The BIG Backyard, complete with oversized toadstools and enormous insects), a hands-on dinosaur dig and an Indoor treehouse. The museum is also well-known for its seasonal exhibits like "Snow Much Fun!", which features an indoor skating rink (no skates required, just socks) and a place to build an "ice" fort out of a variety of materials. Admission Is $9 for adults and children, $8 for seniors; free to under-15s on the first Monday of every month, free to all Thurs 5–8pm. Sun–Wed & Fri 10am–5pm, Thurs & Sat 10am–8pm.

▲ Children's Museum at Navy Pier

Farm-in-the-Zoo 2001 N Clark Street near Armitage Avenue, Lincoln Park ☎312/742-2000, ⓦ www.lpzoo.org/animals/FARM/index .php; Bus #151. Located within the Lincoln Park Zoo (see p.94) this rather unique part of the complex allows visitors to peer into the world of a small demonstration farm right in the middle of Chicago. Guests can get up close and personal with pigs, ponies and goats on the grounds. In the main barn, children can learn about honeybees through an oversized piece of honeycomb (in the summer, real live bees are added to the mix) and look into an oversized egg. During the summer months, visitors can also take in a cow-milking demonstration and even feed the cows as well. Admission is free. Daily April–Oct 9am–6.30pm, Nov–March 10am–5pm

Garfield Park Conservatory 300 N Central Ave, West Side ☎312/746-5100, ⓦ www.garfield -conservatory.org; Green Line to Conservatory- Central Park Drive station. A true Victorian-era masterpiece, the Garfield Park Conservatory was built and designed by master landscape architect Jens Jensen between 1906 and 1907. All told, the exhibition areas and the various outbuildings occupy over 4.5 acres, inside and out. Children of all ages will enjoy the thematic exhibits, which as of late, have included the colourful and dramatic glass sculptures of Dale Chihuly nestled among the plantings and the Zimbabwean stone sculpture of Chapungu. The real highlight for children here is the Elizabeth Morse Genius Children's Garden. Here children can take a ride down a twirling "stem" that also happens to be a slide, meander through the Discovery Area and its hands-on exhibits, and a seven-foot-tall seed just waiting to be climbed on. Before heading out to the Conservatory, check on the website for special programming. Admission is free. Daily 9am–5pm, until 8pm on Wed.

Kraft Education Center Art Institute of Chicago, 111 S Michigan Ave, the Loop ☎312/443-3657, ⓦ www.artic.edu/aic/kids/; Brown, Green, Purple, Pink or Orange Line to Adams station. The Art Institute of Chicago has had some form of children's gallery since 1926, and their Kraft Education Center is the contemporary incarnation of this type of work. Here, children can play with African masks, feel their way through the "Touch Gallery", which features portrait sculptures from different time periods, and even sign up for one of their "Mini Masters" classes for 3–5 year olds. Visitors must pay the usual entrance fee for the Art Institute (see p.48) but children under 12 are always free. The Center keeps the same hours as the Art Institute: Mon–Wed & Fri 10.30am–5pm, Thurs 10.30am–8pm, Sat & Sun 10am–5pm.

Lincoln Park Conservatory 2391 Stockton Drive near W Fullerton Parkway, Lincoln Park ☎312/3747-7736; Bus #151 (Sheridan). Built in the last decade of the nineteenth century, the Lincoln Park Conservatory contains a tropical palm room, ancient ferns and exotic plants from Indonesia, Central America and Africa. It's located an orchid's throw away from the Lincoln Park Zoo, and on a typically cold Chicago day it's the perfect respite from a walk through the zoo. Children will appreciate the informative placards and there's usually something in one of the exhibits that's quite delightful, such as a model train display or a series of sound installations. Admission is free. Daily 9am–5pm.

Peggy Notebaert Nature Museum 2430 N Cannon Drive near Fullerton Parkway, Lincoln Park ☎773/755-5100, ⓦ www.chias .org/ Bus #151. Opened in 1999, the museum was developed in order to offer the general public "more than dioramas and taxidermied animals". They have succeeded with their museum space, and the setting In the back of the building (right on a genuine restored wetland) Is a nice place to have a picnic lunch. Inside, visitors can make their way through a 2700-square-foot greenhouse filled with butterflies (over 75 species

In total), learn about the mysterious and sometimes quixotic world of the Chicago River and walk through three recreated environments, Including a savanna and a dune. Admission is $9, $7 for students & seniors, $6 for children aged 3–12, free for children under-3s. Mon–Fri 9am–4.30pm, Sat & Sun 10am–5pm.

Theatre

Chicago Children's Theatre Little Theatre, The Museum of Science and Industry, Hyde Park ☎773/225-0180 or 1-866/811-4111, ⓦwww.chicagochildrenstheatre.org; Bus #6 or Metra train to 55/56/57 Street station. The Chicago Children's Theatre Is known for its work with other collaborative theatre groups, so at any given production you might encounter giant puppets, dancing paper cut-out figures or creative musical ensembles providing a lively accompaniment. They also provide special shows for younger children (aged 3–6), so parents will feel a bit more comfortable when making plans for a theatre-based excursion. Tickets for adults are $28, $18 for children 12 and younger.

Emerald City Theatre Apollo Theater building, 2540 N Lincoln Ave, Lincoln Park ☎773/935-6100, ⓦwww.emeraldcitytheatre.com; Brown, Purple or Red Line to Fullerton. The Emerald City Theatre is known for its work with some of the children's classic theatre repertoire, such as Hansel & Gretel, Doctor Dolittle, and Cinderella. The theatre is also quite accommodating when working with large groups who wish to plan a special outing. Tickets are $15 for adults, $12 for children 12 and younger.

Noble Horse Theatre 1410 N Orleans St, Old Town ☎312/266-7878, ⓦwww.noblehorsechicago.com; Brown Line to Sedgwick. A team of horses performing a version of the Nutcracker isn't something that most people would expect amidst Old Town's quaint old brownstones. The performances rotate around, depending on the time of year, but the *Noble Horse* offers seasonal favourites like the Nutcracker, along with a rather rousing version of the "Legend of Sleepy Hollow" (possibly a bit scary for young children). Their staple performance is "Quadrille", which takes visitors back to the time of Napoleonic Europe. Also, the *Noble Horse* offers carriage rides around the city, which start at $35 per half-hour. Ticket prices range from $18–28 for adults, and $14–18 for children 12 and younger.

Festivals and events

D
uring the freezing winter, Chicagoans tend to hibernate, with just a handful of events able to lure locals out into the cold. But after St Patrick's Day, the Windy City comes alive with **festivals and events**. The biggest festivals take place downtown, in either Grant Park or Millennium Park, and feature the time-honoured combo of music, food and lots of beer. But nearly every neighbourhood throws an annual party as well, and these smaller gatherings, with local arts, crafts and music, can provide a provocative glimpse into Chicago's tightknit communities. For information on events sponsored or endorsed by the city, contact the Chicago Convention and Tourism Bureau or the Mayor's Office of Special Events (see box below). The website Ⓦchicago.eventguide.com also maintains a substantial list of festivals and events. Dates tend to change from year to year; call the numbers listed and check the local press for exact dates and times.

For a list of national public holidays, see Basics, p.36. Additional festivals are listed in "Gay and lesbian Chicago", p.206, and "Performing arts and film", p.210. Grant Park's summer festivals are discussed in the box on p.67 in Chapter 2.

January

Chicago Boat, RV, & Outdoors Show mid-Jan ☎312/946-6200, Ⓦwww.chicagoboatshow.com. Boat-lovers' extravaganza at McCormick Place, where you can check out more than 600 boats, 300 RVs and hundreds of booths catering to outdoor enthusiasts from all over the Midwest.
Chicago Cubs Convention mid-Jan ☎773/404-CUBS, Ⓦchicago.cubs.mlb.com. Cubs fans pay upwards of $100 to attend this popular weekend at the *Hilton Chicago* to meet, get autographs from and pose for photos with their favourite players.

Proceeds benefit Cubs Care, the team's charity organization. Tickets sell out months in advance, so book early or be prepared to pay scalper rates.
Chicago Sketch Comedy Festival 10 days in mid-Jan ☎773/327-5252, Ⓦwww.chicagosketchfest .net. Founded in 2002, the festival showcases Second City-style sketch comedy – short, scripted comedic skits – by gathering more than a hundred national and international groups to perform. All shows are at the Theatre Building Chicago, 1225 W Belmont Ave, in Lincoln Park.

Official event information

Chicago Convention and Tourism Bureau ☎1-877/244-2246 or 1-866/710-0294 (TTY), Ⓦwww.explorechicago.org
Mayor's Office of Special Events ☎312/744-3315, Ⓦwww.cityofchicago .org/specialevents

February

Chicago White Sox Soxfest early Feb ☎312/565-0769, ⓦchicago.whitesox.mlb.com. Fans of the South Side sluggers get their fix of player autographs and photos at this weekend event at the *Hyatt Regency Chicago*.

Chinese New Year Parade 1st Sun after Chinese New Year (early Feb) ☎312/326-5320, ⓦwww.chicagochinatown.org. Painted horses, traditional lion dancers and a 100-foot-long dragon snake along S Wentworth Ave from Cermak to 24th St. The parade also features Miss Chinatown and her court, plus a flurry of fireworks at the neighbourhood's biggest celebration of the year.

Chicago Auto Show mid-Feb ☎630/424-6030, ⓦwww.chicagoautoshow.com. The nation's largest auto show, a ten-day event at McCormick Place where the world's top automakers show off nearly 1000 different vehicles, from tame trucks to futuristic concept cars.

Snow Days Chicago mid-Feb ⓦwww.explorechicago.org. Free five-day winter festival in the Spirit of Music Garden in Grant Park, featuring a snow sculpting competition, dog sled demonstrations, food and beverage tents and children's activities.

March

St Patrick's Day Parade Sat before St Patrick's Day ☎312/942-9188, ⓦwww.chicagostpatsparade.com. One of the city's most raucous celebrations, with the Chicago River dyed an emerald green for the occasion. Parade starts at Balbo and goes north on Columbus past Buckingham Fountain to Monroe St.

South Side Irish St Patrick's Day Parade St Patrick's Day ☎773/393-8687, ⓦwww.southsideirishparade.org. Less touristy and more authentic than the downtown event, this is the nation's largest neighbourhood parade, drawing up to 300,000 revellers as it meanders through Irish communities Beverly and Morgan Park on Western from 103rd to 115th sts.

Chicago Flower & Garden Show second week in March ☎773/435-1250, ⓦwww.chicagoflower.com. Lush gardens, hands-on demonstrations and hundreds of product and educational booths highlight this weeklong event for green thumbs at Navy Pier. $12 for weekday tickets, $14 weekends.

Greek Independence Day Parade late March or early April ☎773/775-4949, ⓦwww.chicagogreekparade.com. A Chicago tradition for more than forty years, with one hundred-plus Greek-American religious and civic organizations marching in honour of Greece's independence from the Ottoman Empire, declared on March 25, 1821. The parade runs through Greektown along Halsted St between Randolph and Van Buren sts.

April

Festival Día de los Niños last Sat in April ☎773/553-3687, ⓦwww.chicagodiadelosninos.com. Commemorating Children's Day, which is celebrated throughout Mexico and Latin America on April 30, the parade kicks off at noon at Blue Island Ave and 18th St and proceeds west to Harrison Park, where there's dancing, food, music and art activities for kids.

Smelt Fishing varies ⓦwww.ifishillinois.org. For a couple of weeks each spring between March and May, thousands of finger-sized smelt (salmon-like fish, tasty when pan-fried), swarm along the lakeshore to spawn around 2–3am. Anyone with a net is welcome to join in the fun.

May

Kids & Kites Festival first Sat in May
☎773/467-1428, ⓦwww.chicagokite.com.
Kids can make and fly their own kites, buy
kites and watch professional flyers strut
their stuff with stunt kites at this family-
friendly event at Montrose Harbor in
Lincoln Park.

Polish Constitution Day Parade first Sat in May
☎773/745-7799, ⓦwww.may3parade.org.
Polish folk dancers, marching bands and
local Polish organizations march on
Columbus Drive in Grant Park in this, the
nation's largest parade commemorating
Poland's constitution, signed May 3, 1791.

Cinco de Mayo Festival first week in May
☎312/744-3315, ⓦwww.el5demayo.org. Five-
day party celebrating Mexico's 1862 victory
over the French, with live music, food
vendors, a soccer tournament and a parade
that winds through Pilsen along Marshall
Blvd, between Cermak Rd and 26th St.

Art Chicago early May ☎312/527-3701,
ⓦwww.artchicago.com. Hundreds of international galleries show and sell work at this
contemporary art show at the Merchandise
Mart, which also features lectures, panel
discussions and special exhibitions like
"New Insight", which gives exposure to top
graduate students at the best masters of
fine arts programmes in the US, including
the School of the Art Institute.

**Great Chicago Places & Spaces Festival mid-
May** ☎312/744-3315, ⓦwww.greatchicago
places.us. The Mayor's Office of Special
Events teams up with the Chicago Architecture Foundation to offer more than 100 free
tours of the city on a Saturday in mid-May.

Asian American Festival late May ☎847/878-
1900, ⓦwww.aacchicago.org. From Thai food
to Indian stand-up comedy, this five-day
event at Daley Center Plaza celebrates
Asian culture with food vendors, activities
and live entertainment.

Memorial Day Parade Sat before Memorial Day
☎312/744-3315, ⓦwww.chicagoparades.us.
One of the nation's largest Memorial Day
parades, with more than 10,000 participants
and close to 300 marching units, veterans'
groups and bands making their way from
Balbo to Monroe along Columbus Drive.

June

Ravinia Festival early June to early Sept
☎847/266-5100, ⓦwww.ravinia.org. Pack a
picnic basket and head north to suburban
Highland Park, where for $10–15 you can
snag a place on the lawn and listen to a
classical concert by the Chicago
Symphony Orchestra – the festival's
resident group – or a variety of touring
acts. Lawn tickets to pop shows like Sheryl
Crow or Hootie and the Blowfish run $15–
25 and tend to sell out in advance, so be
sure to call before setting out. Pavilion
seats are available, too, but they cost a
pretty penny.

Printers Row Book Fair first weekend in June
☎312/222-3986, ⓦwww.printersrowbookfair
.org. Booksellers from around the country
peddle their wares – new, used and
antiquarian – under five tented blocks in the
historic Printers Row district on Dearborn St
between Congress Parkway and Polk St.

**Chicago Gospel Music Festival first weekend
in June** ☎312/744-3315, ⓦchicagofests.com
/gospel_festival. Fifty free concerts in
Millennium Park draw enthusiastic crowds
of gospel music fans, some of whom sing
a few bars themselves at the open-mic
sessions in the Youth Tent.

57th Street Art Fair first full weekend in June
☎773/493-3247, ⓦwww.57thstreetartfair.org.
Hyde Park fair with more than 300 artists
displaying and selling their work in painting,
photography, jewellery, sculpture and other
media.

Ribfest Chicago first weekend in June
☎773/525-3609, ⓦwww.northcenterchamber
.com. Weekend-long neighbourhood street
party on Lincoln Ave between Irving Park Rd
and Warner Ave, with two live music stages,
kids activities, crafts vendors, an amateur
cook-off and ribs aplenty.

**Andersonville Midsommarfest second weekend in
June** ☎773/665-4682, ⓦwww.andersonville.org.
Everybody's a little Swedish on this weekend,
as the city's Scandinavian enclave puts on a
fun two-day party with live music, dancing,
street vendors and a pet parade, all along
Clark St from Foster to Balmoral aves.

Chicago Blues Festival second weekend in June
☎ 312/744-3315, 🌐 www.chicagobluesfestival
.org. Without a doubt the best blues festival
in the world, it's also Chicago's largest music
festival. Over three days, more than seventy
performers play on six stages in Grant Park
to the rapture of more than 600,000 fans.
Past performers include B.B. King, Buddy
Guy, Bonnie Raitt and Ray Charles.

Old Town Art Fair second weekend in June
☎ 312/337-1938, 🌐 www.oldtowntriangle.com.
Crowded but fun weekend in one of the
city's prettiest neighbourhoods, with
hundreds of booths hawking art, plus food
and drink. Several lovely residential gardens
are opened to the public, too.

Wells Street Art Festival second weekend in June
☎ 773/868-3010, 🌐 www.chicagoevents.com.
Fine-art fair/street party for North Side
yuppies, with 250 exhibitors competing for
attention. There's a live music stage, food
vendors, and children's theatre, all on Wells
St between North Ave and Division St. Daily
10am–10pm.

Taste of Chicago late June to early July
☎ 312/744-3315, 🌐 www.tasteofchicago.us.
More than three million people throng Grant
Park to enjoy free concerts and scarf down
300 menu items from 70 local restaurants,
including deep-dish pizza, cheesecake and
hot dogs as well as high-end gourmet fare,
at this massive ten-day festival.

July

**Independence Eve Fireworks Spectacular 3rd
July** ☎ 312/744-3315. Free pyrotechnic
display over Grant Park the night before
the Fourth of July, with 5000 explosives
going off in the sky as the Grant Park
Symphony Orchestra saws away at
patriotic favourites in the Petrillo Music
Shell. About a million spectators attend – it
takes place during the Taste of Chicago,
which is already crammed – so arrive early
to get a spot on the grass.

Rock Around the Block second weekend in July
☎ 773/665-4682, 🌐 www.starevents.com.
Lakeview traffic comes to a standstill as this
local music festival takes over the intersection of Lincoln, Belmont and Ashland aves,
with thirty bands jamming continuously on
three stages.

Chicago Yacht Club Race to Mackinac mid-July
☎ 312/861-7777, 🌐 racetomac.nemexinc.com.
This prestigious, invitation-only race from
Chicago's Monroe Harbor to Mackinac
Island, Michigan – A 300-mile span –
celebrated its 100th anniversary in 2008.
Watch the boats parade past Navy Pier with
their ceremonial flags raised before the race.

**Old St. Pat's World's Largest Block Party 3rd
weekend in July** 🌐 worldslargestblockparty.com.
Touted as one of the city's best places to
meet your mate, this church fundraiser draws
20,000 randy singles for food, drink and live
music in the West Loop to raise money for its
namesake church at 711 W Monroe St.
Tickets are $35 per person in advance, $40
at the door, and include five drinks.

Sheffield Garden Walk 3rd weekend in July
☎ 773/929-9255, 🌐 www.sheffieldfestivals.org.
Lincoln Park neighbours open their private
gardens to the public (more than 100 on
view), while attendees stroll through the
neighbourhood, guzzle beer and listen to
the decent live music at St. Vincent DePaul
Church, 1010 W Webster Ave, at Sheffield.

Venetian Night late July/early Aug ☎ 312/744-
3315, 🌐 www.venetiannightchicago.us. Half a
million onlookers lounge along the lake at
dusk as more than 35 elaborately decorated
and illuminated boats promenade from the
Shedd Aquarium to the Chicago Yacht Club,
with further entertainment provided by the
Grant Park Symphony Orchestra and a
post-parade fireworks display.

August

Retro on Roscoe 1st weekend in Aug
☎ 773/665-4682, 🌐 www.starevents.com. Yet
another neighbourhood street party, this
one in fun, funky Roscoe Village (Roscoe St
and Damen Ave), featuring an antique show,

chili cook-off, cooking demonstrations, food
and craft vendors and a full line-up of bands
playing tunes from the 1970s, 80s and 90s.

Bud Billiken Parade & Picnic second Sat in Aug
☎ 773/536-3710, 🌐 www.budbillikenparade.com.

The largest African-American parade in the US, named after a mythical guardian of children. Drill teams, dancers and local school kids march along King Drive from 39th to 51st streets, then live it up at a music festival and barbecue in Washington Park.

Chicago Air & Water Show second weekend in Aug ☏312/744-3315, ⊛www.chicagoairand watershow.us. Sleek military aircraft zoom over the lake performing aerobatic stunts for onlookers; prime views can be had along the lakefront between Oak St and Fullerton Ave. Skip the water show, unless you don't mind fighting the crowds for a glimpse of the lacklustre "Ski Show Team".

Chicago Carifete mid-Aug ⊛www.chicago carifete.com. Exuberant Caribbean celebration in Hyde Park reaches its peak with a costume parade on the Midway Plaisance, where scantily clad dancers shake their collective bootie to local DJs' reggae and calypso beats. Food and craft stalls, too.

¡VIVA! Chicago Latin Music Festival late Aug ☏312/744-3315, ⊛www.vivachicago.us. Big-name merengue, salsa, reggaeton, norteña and mariachi bands jam in Grant Park at this two-day event, alongside local merchants selling traditional food, clothing and jewellery.

Chicago Triathlon last weekend in Aug ☏773/404-2281, ⊛www.chicagotriathlon.com. Eleven thousand well-muscled men and women swim, bike, and run for glory along Lake Michigan in one of the world's largest triathlons. Participants choose between two courses – Sprint (.75km swim, 22km bike, 5km run) or International (1.5km swim, 40km bike, 10km run).

Taste of Greece 3rd or 4th weekend in Aug ☏847/509-8050. This is when all the souvlaki, moussaka and other goodies are taken out of the restaurants onto stalls that run for several blocks of S Halsted St. Great food but a surprising lack of music and other elements of Hellenic culture.

▲ Taste of Greece Festival

September

Chicago Jazz Festival Labor Day weekend ☏312/744-3315, ⊛www.chicagojazzfestival.us. A mellow holiday-weekend crowd enjoys free jazz on three stages in Grant Park; there's an arts and crafts fair and wine garden, too.

German-American Festival first weekend in Sept ☏630/653-3018, ⊛www.germanday.com. Following the annual Von Steuben Parade, the old German neighbourhood of Lincoln Square throws a party with live oompah music and dancing, and more beer and bratwurst than you can shake a stick at.

Berghoff Oktoberfest mid-Sept ☏312/427-3170, ⊛www.berghoff.com. This three-day beer bash on Adams St in front of the legendary German restaurant packs the streets with after-work revellers enjoying live music and gorging on knockwurst, potato salad and, of course, homemade pilsner.

Chicago Celtic Festival mid-Sept ☏312/744-3315, ⊛www.celticfestchicago.us. Free art fair and music festival in Grant Park, with several stages of live music, dance and storytelling, plus vendors hawking handmade clothing and jewellery, and plenty of Guinness.

World Music Festival late Sept ☏312/744-3315. Musicians from as far as Niger, Turkey and Brazil perform at venues all over the city.

October

Chicago Country Music Festival **first weekend in Oct** ☎ 312/744-3315, ⊛ www.chicagocountrymusicfestival.us. Big names often turn out for this free, foot-stomping two-day festival, now held in Soldier Field Parkland, just outside the stadium. With line dancing, dance lessons, and music on two stages.

Columbus Day Parade **second Mon in Oct** ☎ 708/450-9050, ⊛ www.jccia.com. Chicago's Italian-American community stages this massive televised parade up Columbus Drive from Balbo to Monroe in celebration of the explorer's "discovery" of America in 1492. Marching bands, floats, beauty queens and more.

Around the Coyote Arts Festival **mid-Oct** ☎ 773/342-6777, ⊛ www.aroundthecoyote.org. More than 100 artists display and sell their works for a weekend in the West Loop, in what's become the city's hottest art fest. A full schedule of artists' talks, live music, literary readings and theatre performances round out the event.

Chicagoween **all month** ☎ 312/744-3315, ⊛ www.chicagoween.us. Daley Plaza is ground zero for a month full of family-friendly Halloween events from pumpkin-carving and storytelling to haunted houses and even the Haunted "L" – a spooky tour of the Loop with costumed storytellers.

Chicago Marathon **second Sun in Oct** ☎ 312/904-9800 or 1-888/243-3344, ⊛ www.chicagomarathon.com. The fastest marathon in the world (thanks to the flat terrain), this event draws some of the world's best runners and almost 40,000 others. A party atmosphere prevails, with thousands of spectators along the race route – especially around mile seven at Broadway and Belmont Ave, where a cheering station of drag queens makes even the most tired runner smile.

North Halsted Halloween Parade **31 Oct** ☎ 773/868-3010, ⊛ www.chicagoevents.com. You'll see some of the city's most outlandish costumes in this Boystown parade, which proceeds up Halsted from Belmont to Addison, and ends with live entertainment and a fierce costume contest.

Chicago Humanities Festival **Oct through mid-Nov** ☎ 312/661-1028, ⊛ www.chfestival.org. This six-week festival brings some of the world's hottest thinkers and artists to Chicago for topical panel discussions, readings, concerts and performances.

November

Dance Chicago **all month** ☎ 773/935-6860, ⊛ www.dancechicago.com. Dance festival showcasing more than 120 local and international jazz, ballet, tap, hip-hop, flamenco and modern dance troupes, performing at the Athenaeum Theatre in Lakeview.

Lincoln Park ZooLights **late Nov to early Jan** ☎ 312/742-2165, ⊛ www.lpzoo.com. Ice carving, train rides, hot chocolate and a classic Santa in the lion house keep things hopping at Chicago's beloved free zoo, which is open late and illuminated with more than two million lights during the holidays.

Magnificent Mile Lights Festival **Sat before Thanksgiving** ☎ 312/409-5560, ⊛ www.themagnificentmile.com. Kick off the holiday season with a full day of children's music performances (at 401 N Michigan Ave) leading up to the lighting of more than one million lights strung from Oak St to Wacker Drive, followed by a fireworks show at the river.

Thanksgiving Parade **last Thurs in Nov** ⊛ www.chicagofestivals.org. More than 400,000 spectators brave the cold to watch marching bands, entertainers and giant helium balloons make their way up State Street on Thanksgiving morning (8.30–11am).

Holiday Tree Lighting Ceremony **day after Thanksgiving.** At Daley Plaza at 4pm, the mayor flips a switch and *voila* – the city's holiday tree (actually made of many smaller fir trees) lights up.

Christkindlmarket **late Nov to late Dec** ☎ 312/744-3315, ⊛ www.christkindlmarket.com. Dozens of festively decorated timber booths at Daley Plaza sell handcrafted ornaments, and holiday trinkets, along with German fare like bratwurst, sauerkraut and hot, spiced red wine.

December

Winter WonderFest mid-Dec to early Jan
☎312/595-7437, Ⓦ www.navypier.com. Family
festival at Navy Pier with hundreds of
decorated trees and plenty of entertainment,
including puppet shows, storytellers, a
skating rink and Santa himself.

New Year's Eve Fireworks 31 Dec ☎312/595-
7437. A family-friendly New Year's Eve party
where hip-hop dancers, live music and taiko
drumming culminates with an 8.15pm
fireworks display outside on Dock St. Stick
around till midnight for another lakefront
fireworks show.

Contexts

Contexts

A history of Chicago

From its beginnings as a collection of houses and a very tiny military fort through its emergence as a provincial industrial town to becoming one of the world's great cities, Chicago's growth can be seen as a microcosm of the US. And while the nation's self-styled "Second City" is inherently American, the history of the major metropolis of the Midwest is truly unique.

1673–1833: the early years

The first Europeans to arrive officially in Chicago were explorers from New France (now Quebec). The cartographer **Louis Joliet** and missionary **Jacques Marquette** had been sent on an empire-building expedition by Louis XIV, the so-called Sun King, whose plan was to shore up his country's holdings in the New World by connecting New France and New Orleans with fresh territory. Marquette and Joliet, guided by friendly local **Powatomi Indians**, arrived in what's now Chicago in the autumn of 1673.

At this time, the shores of Lake Michigan were a fur-trapping hub, having been settled by **Native Americans** for almost seven hundred years. It's also likely that other European settlers had passed through earlier and a year after Marquette's and Joliet's arrival the explorers encountered a fellow French-Canadian, **Pierre Moreau**, nicknamed "The Mole", a trapper who'd already also established a thriving, illicit trade in alcohol to the Indians. The word *checagou* derives from Joliet's attempts to phonetically transcribe the local Native American name: it's been variously glossed as "great and powerful", "striped skunk" and "wild onion" (after the plants that grew in abundance locally), although its true meaning has never been confirmed.

Claiming the area for France, Joliet and his party soon moved on, leaving a small settlement of three hundred or so. France hoped this town might become a gleaming metropolis, its answer to the powerful and thriving British settlements of New York and Boston. Sadly, it was a case of bad luck and bad timing: the royal coffers were running on empty, and there was little money left to spend on a town few in France would ever see. Soon the settlement was abandoned and *Checagou* slipped into obscurity. For the next few years, the territory flip-flopped between the colonial powers, eventually landing in American hands after the War of Independence.

Given Chicago's history of often contentious race relations, the fact that the city's acknowledged founder, **Jean-Baptiste Point du Sable**, was a person of colour is wryly ironic. A Haitian-born fur trapper, who after arriving in 1779 amassed a sizeable fortune, he married a Powatomi Indian girl and built an estate where the *Chicago Sun-Times* building now stands. Du Sable's settlement was strategically important and by 1803 – recognizing the continuing colonial threat from a disgruntled Britain – the American government had established a garrison here, known as **Fort Dearborn**. Indeed, open war with Britain broke out nine years later, and Fort Dearborn was the site of a major atrocity, when British-backed Indians torched the building and ambushed the evacuees from the fort, slaughtering two-thirds of them.

After America won the war, Fort Dearborn was soon rebuilt. By the time of Chicago's incorporation as a town in 1833, there were 350 residents living in the area now bounded by Kinzie, Desplaines, Madison and State streets. That same year, the town's first newspaper, *The Chicago Democrat*, went to press. The stop-and-start phase of Chicago's settlement was over and for the next seventy years it would grow at breakneck speed to become one of the largest, most prosperous cities in America and a symbol of nineteenth-century economic success.

1834–70: emerging as a city

In fact, the first sign of Chicago's healthy future had come when the **Erie Canal** opened in 1825: by linking New York City's Hudson River with the hamlet of Buffalo, which sat on the eastern reaches of Lake Erie, the canal opened up the entire state of Illinois to commerce. Some savvy Chicagoans spotted how Buffalo exploded, virtually overnight, into a thriving transport hub and were soon snapping up swathes of local land for next to nothing.

In the industrialized nineteenth century, Chicago had an advantage that no man could manufacture: its location. Of course, the land they were sitting on wasn't terribly helpful, as it consisted largely of marshy muck. Those Buffalo-watchers recognized this, and so invested heavily in infrastructure like waterways and railroads; unusually, they also spent money on better sewers and drains. Indeed, Chicago city planners have always thought big and by treating their nascent town like a city, locals were well prepared to seize economic opportunities when they appeared.

The first of those was the construction of the **Illinois and Michigan Canal**, begun in 1836. This waterway would connect the Illinois River to the Mississippi and so to the thriving shipping hub of New Orleans; a year later, swollen by the influx of thousands of construction workers, Chicago was large enough to incorporate as a city. Then it hit a snag, a nationwide depression that lasted for three years and was precipitated by President Andrew Jackson's ham-fisted meddling in the rickety national banking system.

After this, construction of the canal slowly resumed, while simultaneously local leaders turned their attention to Chicago's own water system. Since the city was built on marshy, swampy land, no cellars or drains had been possible at first, so now the streets were clogged with sewage. In 1859, an ingenious engineer, who'd recently arrived from New York State, devised a strange but simple solution – **raise the buildings**. Each structure was ratcheted off the ground to a height of four to seven feet, and drainage systems were then installed in the newly created first floor.

The engineer responsible was **George Pullman**, who'd later make his name as a railroad magnate; like Pullman, it's to the railroads that Chicago owes almost everything.

The arrival of the railways

As the railroads laid down tracks to and from the city, Chicago became the **terminus for cross-country travel**: few rail companies operated networks both east and west of the Mississippi River, and so all cargo, both freight and human, had to be unloaded there. This was the first key impact of the railroad: travellers would often stay (and spend) for several days before continuing their journey, while cargo hauling created hundreds of new jobs. In fact, during this time, the population of Chicago more than tripled – from 30,000 in 1850 to 112,000 ten years later.

▲ The El

If this first effect funnelled America through Chicago, the second scattered Chicago across America. The rest of the US became a **market for goods** from merchants based in the city: soon, Chicago was the hub of America's **grain and lumber trades**. Businessmen here were best placed to reach any corner of the country and many became phenomenally wealthy. They then pumped money back into the city, building fabulous mansions and endowing institutions.

Third came the definitive **defeat of St Louis**, Chicago's snazzy southern rival three hundred miles away in Missouri. St Louis was already a thriving city in the early 1830s when Chicago was little more than a hamlet, linked by the Mississippi River to New Orleans and warm enough that its waterways wouldn't ice up in winter. But St Louis relied on the steamboat, which was easily eclipsed by Chicago's cheaper, more efficient railroad network. St Louis struggled on until the Civil War, which was the final, lethal blow: its Confederate economy depended on trade with the South, while Union Chicago was quick to provide the massive northern army with provisions, especially meat.

Chicago's **meatpacking plants** were perhaps the most visible by-product of its pole position in the railroad race – at one point it was even nicknamed "Porkopolis" (though Illinois poet Carl Sandburg's "Hog Butcher to the World" would be the nickname that stuck). Since meat could be quickly transported cross-country from Chicago, it was a natural base during the Civil War and by 1862 had become the largest meatpacking city in the world. The legendary **Union Stockyards** opened on the South Side in 1865; indeed, the stockyards were so large – ten miles of feed trough on one hundred acres of land – that they became a tourist attraction. Chicago's pragmatic leaders turned butchery into business. There was a disassembly line, where hog slaughter was so efficient that, unlike individual butchers who threw away almost half a carcass (like cartilage and bones), almost nothing was wasted: aside from meat, the plants turned out bouillon, brushes and even instrument strings. One local bigwig butcher used to boast that he made use of every part of a pig but the squeal.

The railroads didn't just move food and goods, they also moved people. The train made travel speedy and convenient as never before, in essence creating a **commuter class**. Soon the city's middle class was moving out of downtown and into larger houses and bigger yards further afield – in fact, Naperville, to the west of the city, was the world's first "railroad suburb".

Finally, the spaghetti junction of railroad lines meeting in Chicago spurred reform in one offbeat area: **time**. As late as 1883, there was no standard time in America – it could be 2.30pm in New York City, while a few hundred miles away it was 2.46pm in Washington, DC. Until the industrial age, variable timekeeping like this had caused few problems, but with the railroads came timetables and so confusion. Often, companies synchronized the clocks along their own lines but this might bear little resemblance to local time; it also meant that many stations had several clocks, featuring the time according to each railroad company *plus* the local time. It's not surprising that Chicago, where fifteen railroad lines met, was one of the key drivers behind New York-based Charles Dowd's reforms of 1869, where he suggested the creation of four time zones, much like those we use today. This came to pass on November 18, 1883 at twelve noon, when the standard time zone system was created, courtesy of strong lobbying by the major railroads.

Destruction and rebirth: 1871–95

Chicago's **transformation** into a modern city was spurred on by a terrible citywide **fire**, which would turn it from a city of wood to a city of steel and give the world the skyscraper. Subsequent progress was speedy, culminating with a high point in the **World's Columbian Exposition of 1893**.

The Great Fire of 1871

As Chicago's economic prosperity reached its peak, the most defining event in city history occurred – one which, at first, would seem to have doomed its progress but instead made sure the already burgeoning city would rebuild in spectacular fashion: **the Great Fire of 1871**.

Urban conflagrations weren't unusual in those days – most major American conurbations, Chicago included, had already suffered at least one. In fact, a blaze on October 7, 1871 (only the day before the Great Fire itself), which had already destroyed twenty acres west of downtown.

The subsequent fire started at around 9pm on October 8 in a barn owned by Patrick and Catherine O'Leary, situated at what's now the intersection of Jefferson and Taylor streets. The classic story tells how a kicking cow knocked over a nightlight and so started the blaze but the truth is probably more prosaic. Local cow-championing researchers have uncovered the existence of Daniel "Pegleg" Sullivan, whose mother's cow was also billeted in the same barn. Most historians now agree it's more likely that Sullivan, having stopped by to feed the animal – perhaps in a drunken state – accidentally started the blaze and blamed the cow to save his skin.

Two factors hindered firefighters' immediate response: firstly, they were all exhausted after spending the previous night dousing the massive West Side blaze; secondly, an inept watchman misjudged the fire's location and sent the alert to the wrong crew. By the time they arrived, the flames were too strong to put out. For two days, until rain came in the early hours of October 10, Chicago burned at the rate of 65 acres each hour. Losses were staggering: exact statistics vary but around 18,000 buildings were destroyed, damage was estimated at $200 million and 90,000 people were left homeless. Mercifully, only 250 or so people died, thanks in part to the lake, into which many waded for safety away from the flames.

Only the **Water Tower** and the **Pumping Station**, gaudy neo-Gothic hulks of stone lurking at the upper end of Pine Street (now N Michigan Avenue; see p.80) didn't burn. An architectural shame, perhaps, but at least the city's drinking-water supply wasn't affected.

The city at its apogee

Chicago's survival, however, despite the devastation across downtown, was due to more than clean(ish) drinking water. The only reason the city could bounce back as quickly as it did was that the fire had left Chicago's three major industries – the lumberyards, the stockyards, and the railroads – untouched. Since Chicago was then at the heart of the country's economy, as well as its geography, businessmen across America turned their attention to rebuilding the city.

Hence, only two years later, downtown had been completely rebuilt. The creative opportunities afforded by Chicago's blank canvas also attracted men like Louis Sullivan and Frank Lloyd Wright (see *Chicago Architecture* colour section), whose architectural impact lingers even today. In the years following the fire, Chicago's buildings grew larger and more impressive until, in 1885, the **world's first skyscraper** was constructed downtown. Chicago seemed unstoppable, but the city was starting to show symptoms of urban unrest and dissent.

The most famous – and telling – incident was the **Haymarket Riots** of 1886. Union leaders, always powerful in Chicago's massive factories and yards, had begun a movement for shorter working hours and a citywide strike was announced for May 1. Three days later, at a protest meeting over worker treatment, a bomb was detonated as police tried to clear the demonstrators. Officer Mathias J. Degan died instantly, while seven other policemen lingered on for several days before also expiring. The citywide witch-hunt resulted in the trial of eight so-called "Haymarket Martyrs": seven were condemned to death and the eighth sentenced to fifteen years in prison. In the end, though, only four were executed; one committed suicide while two more saw their sentence commuted to life in prison. Although seven years later in 1893, Governor Altgeld would pardon and release the three remaining men, the Haymarket riots highlighted for the first time the worker-owner friction that would reach paralyzing levels in the twentieth century.

If 1893 was the year when Chicago made a headline-grabbing debut on the world's stage, it was also a difficult time for local industry: the country was in a depression and job losses in Chicago were significant. It was the year the paternalistic millionaire **George Pullman** – who'd masterminded the elevation of the city forty years earlier – also went from hero to villain in the eyes of the local working class. Pullman was a railroad millionaire, although he didn't own an inch of track: instead, inspired by the gruelling trip he'd made from New York to Chicago, he turned his ingenuity to sleeping cars. Pullman's prototypes were well enough received but it was his flair for publicity, rather than his engineering know-how, that saw him through: after Lincoln's assassination, he offered his namesake car to bring Lincoln's body home to Illinois and travel through towns across America on its way.

Soon, Pullman cars were a common sight in every station and Pullman himself was a multimillionaire, employing thousands of people at his factory in Chicago. The railroads weren't immune to industrial unrest like the Haymarket Riots; in fact, an **1877 national strike** had driven home to Pullman the problems of keeping his workforce happy, or rather, docile. His answer was to build a town for them to live in and so control every aspect of his employees' lives: buying up chunks of land far on the South Side, he started construction in 1879 and had quickly built a model community (albeit one where rents were 20 percent higher than elsewhere). The town prospered until 1893 when Pullman, his profits slashed by the Depression, fired thousands of workers and cut wages by 25 percent but wouldn't lower rents. Things came to a head on June 26, 1894, when union leaders called for a boycott of the sleeping cars across the network; although Pullman's strong-arming saw him eventually emerge victorious, it was at a high price – from then until his death three years later, he was vilified by his employees.

1893: The World's Columbian Exposition

Despite such economic unrest, 1890s Chicago considered itself a grand city, with a rightful claim to be a thriving rival to New York itself. But while New York had the prestigious Columbia University, the original **University of Chicago** had gone bust several years earlier. William Rainey Harper then masterminded the creation of a new university, located in the newly annexed area of Hyde Park on the South Side. The university would symbolize Chicago's egalitarian, pragmatic attitude by admitting both women and men from the outset, working on a quarters system to allow flexibility for its staff and overseeing an active university press to disseminate its ideals. Harper turned to **John D. Rockefeller**, nineteenth-century America's answer to Midas and a staunch Baptist to boot (the university was initially conceived as a Baptist bastion), for funds; Rockefeller pledged $600,000, contingent on the city raising $400,000. Since local Baptists couldn't cough up enough cash, the religious mission of the university was revised and Marshall Field – who until then had never been known as a philanthropist – stepped in with additional funding. The university, designed in a neo-Gothic style, opened in 1892. Sadly, the genial Harper would only live to see his dream realized for another fourteen years before dying at a young age in 1906.

But establishing the university was only a national coup; city bigwigs wanted to hog the world spotlight and turned to the idea of a Great Exhibition. The last fair had been in Paris in 1889, the centenary of the French Revolution; it was decided to hold a fair in America to acknowledge the 400th anniversary of Columbus's arrival. The catfight between New York and Chicago was fierce – in fact, it's where the nickname "Windy City" came from, when a Manhattan journalist derided the braggadocio of Chicago's committee. But the wind blew Chicago's way, and Congress finally voted in its favour: the city would host the **World's Columbian Exposition**, albeit a year late in 1893.

Daniel Burnham and Louis Sullivan, both beloved local architects (see box, p.53), were appointed to oversee the fair, alongside legendary planner **Frederick Law Olmstead**, the creator of New York's Central Park. The site they chose, **Jackson Park**, was a swampy marshland close to the new university in the Hyde Park district. What's more, the 1892–93 winter was severe, even by Chicago standards, and hampered progress; so it wasn't until the fair actually opened on May 1, 1893, that anyone knew whether all construction would be completed in time.

The fair was an unqualified triumph and capped Chicago's century: known as the "White City" thanks to its burnished, floodlit white buildings, the fair covered six hundred acres, attracted more than 27.5 million visitors (almost half

The birth of modern shopping

Chicago may be lauded for launching the skyscraper but it's rarely credited for its other contribution to modern life: the **department store**. Admittedly, the first such shop, Bon Marché, was actually in Paris (it's still there) but even if the French conceived the department store, it was immediately adopted and raised to adulthood by Chicago's shopkeepers along the "Ladies' Half Mile" of State Street.

The first retail genius was Potter Palmer, who invented the idea of the refund – in fact, for several years, the jaw-dropping practice of accepting returns, no questions asked, was known as the **"Palmer System"**. He focussed on female customers, greeting them at the door by name and escorting them round his store, and his refund system encouraged women to make impulse purchases for the first time. But it was Palmer's protégé Marshall Field who turned shopping into an art form. Field and his partner, Levi Leiter, bought a controlling stake in Palmer's store in 1865; sixteen years later, he renamed it and ran it solo. Trim, elegant, and highly private, Field held fast to his rigid maxims: "The customer is always right" and "Give the lady what she wants". At its peak in 1900, **Marshall Field's** was serving 250,000 customers a day and employed 8000 people. Among the store's various innovations were bringing goods down from high shelves and putting them on counters so customers could touch and feel them; placing a perfume hall by the doors so that passers-by would be drawn in by the heady smells; opening a bargain basement; and offering annual sales and gift certificates.

At the same time as Field was wowing downtown, local entrepreneur Aaron Montgomery Ward was servicing rural shoppers. Having worked at Field's store for two years before becoming a travelling salesman, Ward took what he learned from both jobs and produced a revolutionary new product in 1872: **the mail-order catalogue**. Mail-order shopping made merchandise, from basic to deluxe, accessible to everyone. Ward opened up an entirely new market for consumer goods, much of it in rural, hard-to-reach places. Ward's business was a nineteenth-century equivalent of Wal-Mart and Amazon.com combined, buying goods in such vast quantities that he was able to undercut rural merchants by up to 75 percent. Soon, he had a rival in Richard Sears and Alvah Roebuck, who modelled their business after his – and eventually bested him thanks to Sears' instinct for snappy advertising. Both eventually opened brick-and-mortar stores and though Sears is now a household name, sadly Montgomery Ward's went into Chapter 11 bankruptcy in 2000 and has closed its final few doors.

These shopping pashas have left their mark across the city: Marshall Field has his namesake museum (see p.68), the Merchandise Mart (see p.85) and even the University of Chicago (see p.127); Palmer's wife Bertha donated her extraordinary Impressionist collection to the Art Institute (see p.50); while Palmer has the greatest memorial of all – an entire neighbourhood. By putting up his first magnificent mansion in what's now the Gold Coast (see p.87), he encouraged his cronies to follow suit and almost single-handedly created the wealthy enclave.

of the number of people then living in America), and featured 250,000 exhibits from 46 nations. Some of the most popular included the Electricity Building, which showcased the various uses of the new electricity including Elisha Gray's telautograph, a prototype fax machine that was designed to send writing or drawings by telegraph. The Streets of Cairo display was also popular, featuring raunchy belly dancers – although the legendary minx known as Little Egypt didn't, as is popularly supposed, make her debut at the fair; she actually surfaced for the first time two years later in Coney Island, New York. But it was **George Ferris's wheel** that grabbed the most headlines.

Burnham had challenged engineers across America to come up with a worthy retort to the Eiffel Tower of 1889: he received submissions including a replica of Dante's Hell (probably not a crowd-pleaser) and man-made mountains. But it was Ferris's idea to take the observatory from the Eiffel Tower and pivot it that won Burnham over. Ferris put up his 250-foot-high wheel in less than five months, using his own money: it was a smart investment, as 1.4 million riders paid 50¢ apiece to ride for two revolutions in one of its 36 cabins.

The fair's only surviving building is now the Museum of Science and Industry (see p.126), as Burnham's **Palace of Fine Arts**, constructed in temporary materials, was painstakingly disassembled to its stone skeleton and then rebuilt in stone.

1895–1920: race and reforms

The years up to World War I would transform Chicago yet again as the city experienced tremendous growth from persons immigrating from Europe and, later, African-Americans moving from the American South. Chicago's always depended on **immigration**, like the labourers who came to work on the first canal and turned it from a town into a city. But the new arrivals from Europe and the Deep South both enriched and complicated city life in new ways.

Some 2.5 million Europeans arrived in Chicago in the forty years from 1880. The largest communities were **Polish**, **Italian** and **Russian Jewish**, each contributing in a different way to the new cosmopolitan make-up of Chicago. The Poles – stirred by Polish-language newspapers exhorting them to *Swój do Swego* (Support Your Own) – created a self-sufficient, self-contained community that floated on the surface of existing society rather than integrating. The Italians also resisted integration, partly because many men had come alone and planned to return to Italy having earned extra money for their families. Many of the Italians were from rural areas and so avoided working in factories, instead preferring lower-paid outdoor jobs like construction and railroad maintenance. The Russians established Maxwell Street Market (see p.118) and many worked as peddlers or shopkeepers, so coming into contact with many other immigrant and established groups, therefore integrating most quickly of all.

African-American immigration during the nineteenth century to Chicago was also significant and unsurprising: Chicago was one of the main stops on the Underground Railroad and had always had a liberal attitude to race relations (for example, D.W. Griffith's hit film *Birth of a Nation* [1915], which glorified the KKK, was banned from the city's cinemas). More than such social concerns, though, there were pressing economic reasons: during World War I, European immigration all but ceased and local white labourers saw their chance to agitate for higher wages. In response, business leaders turned to cheaper black labour. Again, the railroad was also partly responsible: many Pullman porters on the trains were African-American and they would take copies of *The Chicago Defender*, the city's black newspaper, along with them to distribute during their travels. The net result was that Chicago's African-American population more than doubled from 44,000 in 1910 to 109,000 ten years later.

There was little integration, though: most blacks were confined to a narrow and terribly overcrowded strip along S State Street, part of which was an entertainment district known as **The Stroll**. Despite the segregation, racial violence wasn't commonplace: the one major exception was the 1919 Race Riots, sparked by the death of a black teenager, Eugene Williams. On July 27, Williams had been out swimming with friends in the lake when they drifted past a "whites only" beach. Struck on the forehead by a rock thrown by a white sunbather, he fell unconscious and drowned. When his friends called in the local

By 1910, almost one in two people in the United States lived in a town with more than 2500 inhabitants and, with such mass urbanization, problems like crime and disease were rife. Chicago was no exception and local architect **Daniel Burnham** began investigating ways of imposing the moral order of a village onto growing cities. The far-reaching ideology he helped develop became known as the **City Beautiful movement**.

Inspired by the harmony of Europe's new Beaux Arts style, key features of the City Beautiful movement included wide, tree-lined avenues, monumental buildings, ample greenspace and frequent plazas or fountains. There were even proscriptions on lampposts, which had to be attractive as well as functional, and straight roads, which had to be broken up by winding streets whenever possible.

Burnham outlined his blueprint for the perfect city at the **World's Columbian Exposition** in 1893, whose construction he oversaw: the fair's structures were uniform and its parks enormous. A city built on these principles, he argued, would be crime-free, due to a combination of civic duty and plenty of police. Burnham's plans weren't popular with everyone but he began hawking his ideas to cities around the country. Returning to his hometown, he worked with the Commercial Club of Chicago to publish this ambitious plan for the city in 1909 – the first regional urban plans ever published in America, stretching out sixty miles from the lakefront past Chicago's current suburbs. Ultimately, the Chicago Plan Commission only approved two of his ideas: the straightening of the river and, more importantly, the concept of a **public lakefront park**, which, more than any of his buildings, is perhaps Burnham's greatest legacy to the city. In recent years, Burnham's plans regarding an outer railroad loop and other ideas from the original scheme have been revived, giving the work new resonance.

police and pointed out the man responsible, the officer refused to arrest him. Six days of riots ensued, only calmed when the state governor sent 5000 troops to the city. It's worth noting that there are varying accounts of the Williams story with unreliable, contradictory facts, and that the recession of 1919 and the resultant unemployment was as much a reason for the violence as his death.

Around this time of massive immigration, the **Progressive Movement** was sweeping the country. This new political sense focussed on social justice and the harms of industrialization. Predictably, gritty Chicago was a prime focus – see Upton Sinclair's fictionalized account of the stockyards *The Jungle*, for example. Groundbreaking social worker Jane Addams established Hull-House (see p.119) after a trip to London's Toynbee Hall, which was designed to provide social services to the working-class poor. From its founding in 1889, Hull-House mushroomed into a massive complex that even included a library and a gym. For her efforts, Addams was eventually awarded the Nobel Peace Prize in 1931. It was also in the early part of the century that Daniel Burnham conceived of and began to implement his City Beautiful plan, which was as much about civic pride as it was architecture (see box above).

Chicago's Roaring Twenties

Despite the city's best efforts to paper over its associations with organized crime, Chicago will always be known as the home of **Al Capone**. It's ironic that the era of molls, mobsters and murderous ambushes was brought about by zealous reformism like the Progressive Movement. National temperance advocates had

▲ Al Capone

jostled for a ban on alcohol for several years and many prominent women's groups, such as the Women's Christian Temperance Union (headquartered in nearby Evanston), focussed on its harmful effects on the modern family (in other words, the number of abusive alcoholic husbands it produced). Although Chicago's voters came out 6:1 against **Prohibition**, it was introduced nation-wide on January 16, 1920.

Predictably, banning alcohol only glamourized it further, especially among the upper classes, for whom serving a cocktail before dinner became a subversive sign of power and wealth. Chicago's illicit alcohol industry was controlled by individual gangs, each of whom supplied different districts of the city. The so-called **Beer War**, much like many gang murders today, broke out when one man decided to take over the whole city.

That man, born Alphonse Caponi in New York but better known as Al Capone, arrived in Chicago in 1919, running **speakeasies** before widening his ambitions to take control of the booze supply on the city's South Side.

He was never averse to offing troublesome competitors and ten years after his arrival, Capone made his final, decisive move. On the morning of February 14, 1929, his henchmen (dressed as local cops) gathered seven members of the rival Bugs Moran gang, lined the men up against a wall in a garage, and shot them at point-blank range. The so-called **St Valentine's Day Massacre** cemented Capone's legend, as well as scaring off Bugs, who'd overslept and therefore escaped execution. Moran ceded his North Side territory to Capone, who finally controlled the whole city. He wouldn't enjoy his spoils for long because in 1931 Capone was sent to Alcatraz prison by his nemesis, **Eliot Ness**, whose band of determined and bribe-resistant investigators earned the nickname "The Untouchables". The gangster was actually convicted of tax evasion, and served a short sentence before retreating to his mansion in Miami where he expired in 1947 of an advanced case of syphilis. Despite his relatively brief hold over the city's newspaper headlines, it would take six decades before another individual would replace Capone in the minds of outsiders. That person happened to be basketball superstar Michael Jordan, much to the relief of city boosters.

1930–55: The World's Fair, the war and waning fortunes

By 1933, when it was clear that Prohibition was all but useless, the laws were repealed. Chicago, now known more for robberies than railroads, decided to up its image by launching a new **World's Fair**, this time in celebration of the city's own centenary and called "A Century of Progress". But despite the massive attending numbers (39 million visitors over two years) and the fact that it even operated at a slight profit, the 1933 fair had none of the cultural impact its predecessor had enjoyed. Tellingly, there's little evidence left that it ever took place and its architectural impact was minimal. Some reserved particularly harsh criticism for the fair's architecture, including one-time Chicagoan Frank Lloyd Wright, who declared that the buildings were in fact, "a sham".

There is plenty of evidence of the other major event in Chicago from this era – although the only local reminder is a small plaque on the campus of the University of Chicago. Underneath the squash courts there, on a cold December morning in 1942, visiting Italian professor **Enrico Fermi** and his team achieved the first controlled release of nuclear energy. Fermi had been brought to Chicago to undertake such secret experiments only ten months before; at 3.25pm on December 2, he achieved his goal of a **controlled nuclear chain reaction**. His work paved the way both for fossil fuel-free power stations and the wrenching devastation of the atom bomb, which was dropped on Japan three years later and finally ended World War II.

The years after the war were difficult for Chicago, as race relations grew contentious like elsewhere in America. Many white locals and later, African-Americans and other ethnic groups fled to the new suburbs, leaving downtown to its own devices. Less than sixty years since its first, world-busting fair, Chicago was on a downward slide until the election of a man who looms large in the good, the bad and the ugly of American political life: Richard J. Daley.

The Boss and his wake

Richard J. Daley (aka The Boss) served five consecutive terms as mayor of Chicago, establishing a political dynasty and ruling the city as *de facto* king in a way that few other mayors anywhere in America have ever managed. He secured such governmental *carte blanche* through Chicago's unique local political structure: as a staunchly Democratic city, the local party (Cook County Democratic Party, or CCDP) effectively selects then elects the mayor uncontested. Daley had worked to fill the CCDP (nicknamed, somewhat ominously, "The Machine") with his supporters over several years and by rewarding them handsomely – as was expected – after his election, his path to power remained clear.

Born in 1902, Daley was a hardworking but otherwise unremarkable young man; his eventual ascension was never prefigured in his early years. Pragmatic and no-nonsense, Daley's politics were a comfortable fit for this blue-collar, industralized town: he was socially conservative, but financially liberal. He's most infamous for his gross mishandling of the protests around the **1968 Democratic Convention** (see box, below).

Despite this debacle, Daley made many valuable contributions to the city: he was a great builder, if not a sensitive handler of his staff or opponents. He poured money into the Loop and managed to keep Chicago solvent in the 1970s, when cities like New York, Detroit, Cleveland and Philadelphia were hobbled by their financial troubles. Daley's most visionary act was the attention he lavished on hitherto forgotten Douglas Aircraft field; the city had purchased it in 1946 but left it languishing until Daley realized that a great city like Chicago needed a world-class airport. He thus became the driving force behind the development of **O'Hare Airport**, as the field had been renamed, the largest airport in

The riots of the 1968 Democratic Convention

In August of 1968, when the leaders of the National Democratic Party gathered in Chicago to formally select their candidate for the upcoming presidential election, the country was in the throes of the Vietnam War and reeling from the assassination of Martin Luther King Jr, as well as resulting outbreaks of violence across the country.

Several months ahead of the convention, young antiwar activists formulated plans and applied for permits to hold an antiwar protest march during the convention. All permit requests were denied except one that enabled the group to rally at the Grant Park bandshell. Here, the countercultural **Youth International Party** (called "Yippies"), led by social activist **Abbie Hoffman**, held a "Festival of Life" concert and rally that drew about 5000 protestors. Afterwards, when a group of antiwar demonstrators started to protest outside the convention, local police steamed into the crowd and brutalized them in an incident that came to be known as the **Battle of Chicago**. Over the next five days, protestors clashed with thousands of police, Army troops and National Guardsmen in Lincoln Park and in Grant Park along Michigan Avenue. Television cameras were there to record much of the bloody action so it's not surprising that the media were seen by the police as the enemy – several reporters and photographers were among the victims of violence, which sent more than 100 each of protestors and police to the hospital. When eight demonstrators – including Hoffman – were arraigned in federal court the following year, the circus-like trial mesmerized the media and demonized Daley; it took nearly four years but the **Chicago Eight** were each found not guilty of conspiracy to induce a riot.

the United States when it opened and decades later still one of the busiest in the world. Incidentally, its call letters – ORD – derive from its original name, Orchard Airport, when it was under ownership by Douglas.

Both supporters and opponents of Daley were shocked when he died in office in 1976 and this political hiccough was compounded when his spunky protégée **Jane Byrne** ran for mayor against an incompetent incumbent in 1979. She in turn was desperately ill-suited to the job. A great headline-grabber (Byrne moved into the deprived Cabrini Green projects for a short but highly publicized period), who'd pledged to fight the grinding wheels of the Machine, she was instead crushed by it and booted out of office by another Democrat, **Harold Washington**, in 1983.

The city's first black mayor was an unwilling victor – he'd never really wanted to run and had already incurred the wrath of the CCDP during his campaign. He won largely because the two other candidates – Byrne and **Richard M. Daley**, the former mayor's son – split the white vote. Nearly three-quarters of African-Americans in Chicago voted during his election and one precinct on the South Side even called the Board of Elections in mid-afternoon and asked if they should close, since everyone registered in that ward had already voted. Sadly, Washington was a lame-duck mayor during his first term because the CCDP opposed everything he supported and vice versa. After he won for a second time, Washington was slowly achieving a constructive political consensus when, like Daley, he unexpectedly died in office of a heart attack in 1987.

Chicago today

Ever since Washington, it's been Richard M. Daley all the way. Unlike his father, he's a CEO-style mayor, delegating duties and running the city like a corporation. It's a smart move in a place that has always been driven by commerce and, as a city, has always been run by big business. City Hall seems as **corrupt** as ever, with recent years seeing countless scandals ranging from ghost payrolling and bribery to corruption in the city's contractor hiring processes, but nothing has come close to toppling the younger Daley. In part, this is because, scandals aside, the city has thrived under his rule. Daley has done much to improve Chicago, from implementing countless civic and educational programmes to improve residents' quality of life, through the addition of miles of bike paths and parks, to the creation of **Millennium Park**. Indeed, in 2005, Daley was named "the nation's best big-city mayor" by *Time Magazine*.

In the 1990 census, locals were dismayed that Los Angeles's population finally eclipsed Chicago's and seized second place to New York; in fact, with its Second City moniker stolen, in some ways the city is still searching for a new identity. As part of that new identity, Chicago must embrace its role as a truly multicultural city: recent census figures indicate that since 2000, 80 percent of the Chicago area's population growth can be accounted for by the **growing Hispanic population**.

Ironically, the one factor that originally proved such a boon to the burgeoning Chicago – its location in the centre of the North American continent – is an albatross for any city that has international ambitions. Decisions in the early 2000s by corporate giants like **Boeing** and **OfficeMax** to move to or retain their headquarters here thus have to be considered a coup, as the city tries to chart its course in twenty-first-century America.

▲ Barack Obama

In any case, the city's continued evolution under "Da Mayor" has meant strong economic growth, although that is now being tested by the global recession, just as everywhere else. The Windy City has also become more attractive to tourists than ever. In 2004, Chicago drew a record 34 million visitors and was also the nation's number-one destination for business travellers. In 2008, the election of long-time Hyde Park resident Senator **Barack Obama** to the office of President of the United States further cemented Chicago's image in the mind of people from Shanghai to southern Illinois and promised to keep the city squarely in the eye of tourists and entrepreneurs.

Chicago blues

Chicago has been nearly as central to the evolution of modern **blues** as New York was to the evolution of modern jazz. While far from the only area where country blues musicians started to plug in, it was where more decided to do so than anywhere else. Throughout the first half of the 1900s, blacks poured into Chicago from the South, bringing with them the music of their birthplaces, yet also needing to adapt to the ways of the big city. It took a while before loud, stinging electric guitar leads, harmonicas and a hard-hitting rhythm section became the law of the land. Once this format had established supremacy in the 1950s, though, it pretty much stuck, characterizing not just Chicago blues but most electric blues worldwide.

Early Chicago blues

Between 1900 and 1960, the black population of Chicago increased from about 30,000 to over 800,000. Many of them came from the South, especially Mississippi; by 1930, Chicago had more Mississippi-born residents than any other town outside the state. Displaced Southerners wanted to hear the kind of blues music they had grown up with and gravitated towards performers from the lands they had left. At the same time, relocated Southern musicians were adapting their styles to the Northern way of life, playing louder and at a more energetic pace. Chicago blues became more urban throughout the 1930s and early 1940s via fuller ensembles, a more pronounced beat and some early ventures into amplification.

The most important figure of early Chicago blues was not a performer, but producer/A&R director **Lester Melrose**. Melrose built a stable of Chicago's leading talent under one umbrella, arranging for two major labels, **Columbia** and **Victor**, to record **Big Bill Broonzy**, **Memphis Minnie**, **Tampa Red**, **Washboard Sam**, **Big Joe Williams**, **Arthur "Big Boy" Crudup**, **John Lee "Sonny Boy" Williamson** and **Bukka White**. Much of the music was in fact released on the **Bluebird label**, a subsidiary of Victor, and thus referred to as "the Bluebird beat". By using this pool of musicians to back up each other in the studio, Melrose created a "house sound" of sorts, a concept that in the decades to come would be widely applied both within and outside of the blues field. He aimed for a band sound, using not only guitar but also piano and often a bass and washboard or drums for a rhythm section.

Modern listeners may find the Melrose/Bluebird beat stuff tame even in comparison with the early Chess sides of a few years later, yet they were directly influential upon the performers that would up the wattage. Big Bill Broonzy, who linked folk and blues styles, was a key inspiration on Muddy Waters, who would record a tribute album to Broonzy in the 1960s. John Lee "Sonny Boy" Williamson was crucial in making the harmonica a viable lead instrument in blues. A Southern musician, Rice Miller, would call himself Sonny Boy Williamson after Williamson was murdered in 1948; causing never-ending confusion among record-buyers, Miller recorded his own influential body of work for Chess in the 1950s and 1960s as "Sonny Boy Williamson", and blues reference books have to resort to calling John Lee Williamson "Sonny Boy Williamson I", and Rice Miller "Sonny Boy Williamson II". **Big Maceo** was the king of the early Chicago blues piano players with his forcefully direct style, often accompanied by guitarist Tampa Red; his trademark tune was *Worried Life Blues*, a core nugget of the fatalistic blues repertoire.

Muddy Waters and Chess Records

Lester Melrose seemed to have locked up the Chicago blues market, but after World War II changes in the music business and society made the Bluebird beat sound passé. Independent companies were spurting up to challenge the Columbia/Victor dominance, and a more amplified, rhythm-and-blues-oriented sound was ascendant. One of these labels was **Chess Records**, and after some false starts it would become a major power in the R&B market with the electric Chicago sound, particularly with transplanted Mississippian **Muddy Waters**.

Waters was well known as a young blues player in Mississippi, where he was recorded for the Library of Congress by folklorist Alan Lomax in the early 1940s. His decision to move to Chicago in 1943 was typical of the circumstances that led many to pack up their bags – a dispute with the boss over his sharecropping wages led him to try his luck up north, where discrimination was not so rife and economic opportunity better. Muddy at first found work as a truck driver, but his heart was in playing the blues, as he moonlighted at rent parties and clubs. Like musicians all over the country, he was finding that amplification and a band were needed to make himself heard in urban crowds. Waters didn't dilute his Mississippi Delta blues slide and moaning vocals; he just fleshed them out and made them louder. In a way this was a throwback to a sound that predated the Lester Melrose stable, but it had a clear bite and power that was modern and more forceful.

Waters made his first recordings (unissued at the time) for Melrose but found a more sympathetic outlet when he began recording for Aristocrat, a label run by brothers **Phil and Leonard Chess**, which was making some tentative forays into the blues market. His 1948 single *I Can't Be Satisfied/I Feel Like Going Home* wasn't much different from what he had sung in the Delta; in fact he had cut both songs under different titles for his Library of Congress sessions. Now he had the urban market, however, and the single became an R&B hit, to be followed by other classics like *Long Distance Call* and *Rollin' Stone*. Despite his success, his studio sound lagged behind the advances he had made as a live performer, heading a full band. Still, reluctant to tinker with the winning format of *I Can't Be Satisfied*, the Chess brothers – who had changed the name of their label to Chess by 1950 – recorded Muddy almost as a solo artist, with only a string bass to accompany him. Waters was on the verge of leaving Chess when Leonard Chess relented and starting using a full band, with guitars, harmonica, piano, bass and drums in the early 1950s.

If for nothing more than his records, Muddy Waters would be a blues giant – *Hoochie Coochie Man*, *I Just Want to Make Love to You*, *Mannish Boy*, *Got My Mojo Working* and *Trouble No More* are classic staples of rock and blues set-lists, and his B-sides and outtakes were scarcely less accomplished. In addition to being an excellent guitarist, he was more importantly a singer whose confidence suffered no fools, putting over both boasting and sorrowful lyrics with a last-word bearing, absent of any meekness or resignation. Waters also had an eye for assembling the best Chicago blues talent, and several of his sidemen would become stars or respected solo artists, including guitarist **Jimmy Rogers**, pianist **Otis Spann**, and a slew of **harmonica players**: Little Walter, Junior Wells, James Cotton and Walter Horton.

More classic Chess blues

Chess is most associated with the sound of what in-the-know blues hounds call the **four big Ws**: Muddy Waters, Little Walter, Howlin' Wolf and Sonny Boy Williamson. It had a harsh (in the good sense of the word) sheen with upfront electric guitar leads and searing harmonica, propelled by a granite-hard, propulsive rhythm section. Like Sam Phillips at Sun Records, Chess added an otherworldly echo (with primitive tape delay) that, along with their skill at recording the instruments at slightly over-amplified levels, added to the room-filling depth of the recordings.

Little Walter made his initial impression as harmonica player in Muddy Waters' band in the early 1950s and started a solo career after his instrumental, *Juke*, tore up the R&B charts in 1952. What Jimi Hendrix was to rock guitar, Little Walter was to blues harmonica, redefining the parameters of the instrument in a way that permanently changed how it was played, and has not been matched to this day. Walter used his harp like a horn, swooping and improvising jazzy phrases, amplifying it so that it could compete on equal terms with electric guitars and boldly using the more complex chromatic harp to get tones and shadings that were impossible to coax out of standard models. On top of this he was a good singer with an arsenal of great material: the instantly memorable *My Babe* was his biggest hit, while *Mean Old World*, *Mellow Down Easy* and *Off the Wall* weren't far behind. Although he was still a young man, he went into a dreadful artistic and health tailspin in the 1960s, culminating in death resulting from a street fight in 1968, aged only 37.

Howlin' Wolf was engaged in an ongoing battle with Muddy Waters for supremacy in the Windy City blues scene and while he never dislodged Waters' unofficial crown, his raspy, haunted voice projected more charisma than any other classic Chicago blues stars did. Wolf was already well on his way to prominence with his recordings at Sun Studios in Memphis in the early 1950s but after his move north his music grew in frightening intensity and hard-rocking drama. *Smokestack Lightning*, *The Red Rooster* (aka *Little Red Rooster*), *Spoonful*, *Wang Dang Doodle* and *I Ain't Superstitious* are delightfully bone-rattling performances, removed from the reckless thrust of rock 'n' roll by only a thin margin, which accounted for the entry of many of his songs into the sets of famous 1960s rock groups like the Rolling Stones and Cream.

Sonny Boy Williamson, aka Rice Miller, had already recorded and performed in Arkansas and Mississippi for a while before hooking up with Chess. In a brazen act of nerve he appropriated the name of the first, late John Lee "Sonny Boy" Williamson. Unlike just about everybody else who tried similar tricks throughout the music biz, he got away with it, not least because his talent was equal to or greater than that of the original Sonny Boy. Less experimental and more country in his harmonica playing than Little Walter, Williamson was still a wizard at making wordless witty comments with his riffs. Already in his middle age when he began his stint at Chess, he was a humorous yet wizened songwriter and vocalist, contributing his own stack of blues standards with tunes like *One Way Out*, *Don't Start Me to Talkin'*, *Eyesight to the Blind* and *Nine Below Zero*.

The four Ws only represented a fraction of the company's blues output, however. Chess had some less adventurous piano-based blues hits with **Eddie Boyd** and **Willie Mabon** and odd records with **J.B. Lenoir**, whose voice was so high-pitched that many mistook him for a woman and who exhibited unusual sociopolitical consciousness on numbers like *Eisenhower Blues* and *Korea Blues*. Part of the company's success was based on the presence of session musicians and songwriters that never became widely known to the public as recording artists. Even when signed to Chess as solo artists, some musicians would back up other performers. Little Walter, for instance, was appearing on Muddy Waters songs throughout the 1950s, long after he had made it on his own and stopped performing with Waters live. Drummer **Fred Below**, who appeared on many Chess sessions, was an unsung architect of rock 'n' roll, his jazzy, swinging backbeat laying part of the foundation for the steady, insistent rhythm that would take over popular music. Yet no one was more important to Chicago blues' classic era than **Willie Dixon**, the songwriter who devised stone-cold greats for many of the Chess artists and other performers in the Chicago area: *Hoochie Coochie Man, I Just Want to Make Love to You, Back Door Man, Wang Dang Doodle, My Babe, Spoonful, Little Red Rooster* and *Pretty Thing* were all from his pen – and Dixon also found time to play bass on many sessions.

1950s blues

Chess was at the vanguard of a mini-explosion of Chicago independent labels that recorded blues in the 1950s, such as J.O.B., Chance, United/States and Parrot. None of these achieved anything like the success of Chess and reissues of their material are far more sporadic, but they recorded fine blues records by solid Chicago bluesmen who weren't quite on the front line of the city's best, such as J.B. Lenoir, Johnny Shines, Sunnyland Slim, Walter Horton, Snooky Pryor and J.B. Hutto.

Aside from Chess, the most significant of the local labels recording blues was **Vee-Jay** (often abbreviated as **VJ**). Like Chess it wasn't limited to blues, also doing R&B and rock 'n' roll, but it did land two of the most prolific and popular blues singers of the era, **John Lee Hooker** (more properly part of the Detroit blues scene) and **Jimmy Reed**. Reed's success was based on his simplicity – he sang with an easygoing, unruffled charm over a steady, rockish beat decorated by simple but effective guitar figures and harmonica riffs. Another fine VJ performer was harmonica player and vocalist **Billy Boy Arnold**, a Bo Diddley sideman whose frugal but stellar VJ output had thumping beats and charged guitar-harp interplay that could stray close to rock.

Most of the early Chicago blues was played in the city's **South Side** but black neighbourhoods were also spreading to the West Side. In the 1950s a style of blues began to be identified with the West Side that was funkier and more modern in nature, in the mould of B.B. King, than the entrenched South Side approach, and sometimes using saxophones. **Cobra** was a notable short lived West Side blues label, employing Willie Dixon as its musical director when the great songwriter and arranger left Chess for a while in the late 1950s. Cobra's jewel was guitarist **Otis Rush**, the most skilled blues artist bar none when it came to working in minor keys, whose anguished vocals were complemented by devilish twisting riffs that both thrill the ears and give you goose pimples. *Double Trouble, I Can't Quit You, Baby,* and *All Your Love* were instant standards, yet Rush, only in his early twenties when he made his Cobra singles, has never been able to fully capitalize upon his genius. Throughout the 1960s and the first half of the 1970s, he was dogged by lousy record deals that curtailed his studio opportunities.

Elmore James flitted from label to label and did not confine his base of operations to Chicago, also recording in Mississippi, New York and New Orleans over the course of his nomadic discography. He nevertheless rates as an all-time Chicago blues great, as he was the most influential electric slide blues guitarist of all time. *Dust My Broom*, with its classic opening descending riff, had been around in the blues repertoire since Robert Johnson had cut it back in the 1930s. James was the guy who made it an instantly recognizable standard, however, giving the slide riff a gripping super-amped chill. Though he was to rely on this riff often, he did vary his slide style in interesting ways, creating a crying effect on slow burners like *The Sun is Shining* and its close cousin *The Sky is Crying*. He died in 1963, too soon to see his immense impact upon 1960s rock: Brian Jones of the Rolling Stones was so besotted with James that he called himself "Elmo Lewis" in the pre-Stones days, and Jeremy Spencer of the original Fleetwood Mac based almost his entire style around James's licks.

Chuck Berry and Bo Diddley

In 1955, two Chess guitarists recorded a new brand of blues-rooted music that had the ironic effect of mostly driving hardcore blues off the charts for good. **Chuck Berry**, although from St Louis, recorded at Chess in Chicago, often with stalwart Chess musicians such as Willie Dixon and Fred Below. Berry was not as grounded in country-blues as most of the city's leading players; he was born in St Louis, not a plantation, and had absorbed the innovations of jump-blues stars like Louis Jordan and country and western singers. Slow down the tempo of his first single, *Maybellene*, and you can imagine a hillbilly singer having a hit with it. In fact, it had started out as a demo called *Ida May* that bore some resemblance to a country tune called *Ida Red*, recorded by Bob Wills. But *Maybellene* was rock 'n' roll pure and simple, with its sped-up backbeat and furiously riffing guitar.

Berry has defined much of the basic vocabulary of rock 'n' roll, not only in guitar riffs but in lyrical content, venturing into almost journalistic observations on the nuances and frustrations of teenage and young adult life, and celebrating the joys of rock 'n' roll itself. For the rest of the 1950s, he knocked off one classic after another: *Roll Over Beethoven*, *Sweet Little Sixteen*, *Rock & Roll Music*, *School Day*, *Johnny B. Goode*, *Brown Eyed Handsome Man*, *Too Much Monkey Business* and *Carol* were some of the best. They were also inspirations for the best rockers of the 1960s – not just the Beatles and the Stones, but also Bob Dylan (whose *Subterranean Homesick Blues* is much like *Too Much Monkey Business*) – to write and sing their own material.

Lagging far behind Berry in sales, **Bo Diddley** over time proved to be almost as influential. A wild and wacky guitar innovator, he produced oceanic layers of reverb from his axe that sounded like outer-space shock waves by 1950s standards. Like Berry, he was a witty songwriter with acute powers of observation but, while Berry kept a detached ironic eye on things, Diddley yukked it up like life was just one big put-on. Diddley was a great performer too: Elvis Presley was said to have studied Bo's act closely and Diddley's featured oddly shaped guitars (most famously a square model) and acrobatic antics anticipated Jimi Hendrix's even bolder moves along those lines in the late 1960s.

Yet above and beyond his deeper skills, Bo Diddley's trademark is his beat. Described sometimes as a "hambone" or "shave-and-a-haircut", its bomp, ba–bomp-bomp, bomp–bomp pattern is one of the most irresistible rhythms known to humankind and although Diddley used it over and over it didn't get tiresome. Others adapted it for their own ends: Buddy Holly used it for *Not Fade Away*, which when covered by the Rolling Stones gave them their first big British hit. It was that beat, and that wild guitar playing, that made it impossible to call Diddley a bluesman, even though his music was soaked right through with R&B feeling. He built a catalogue of wonderful songs – *I'm A Man*, *Bo Diddley*, *You Can't Judge a book by Its Cover*, *Road Runner* and *Who Do You Love?* – that were ready-to-order for cover by bands all over the US and Britain. While Diddley passed away in the summer of 2008, Berry maintains an impressive touring schedule and still makes a regular gig once a month in a St. Louis club.

Blues in transition: the 1960s

In the early 1960s, blues had become a less significant part of the R&B singles market. Rock 'n' roll had eaten into its audience since the mid-1950s and soul music was beginning to gather steam. Both Chess and Vee-Jay were directing their resources toward their soul stars and, while there was still work for blues musicians in local clubs, there was less opportunity to record and innovate in the studio. However, a **blues and folk revival** was generating an interest among young, white Americans in blues music that had hitherto been confined to an almost exclusively black listenership; British rock bands were covering blues and R&B tunes and bringing the original artists to the attention of young white listeners in the US and UK who had never heard the sources. The Rolling Stones were the biggest of such acts; to their credit they didn't limit themselves to covering tunes in their effort to bring their heroes into the spotlight, recording in Chess Studio on their first visit to the US in 1964 (and naming an instrumental, *2120 South Michigan Avenue*, after the address of the Chess building), and having Howlin' Wolf guest on one of their television spots.

Other progress came in the form of how the music was recorded and packaged. **Junior Wells'** *Hoodoo Man Blues* (1965) was a departure in that it was hardcore modern Chicago blues recorded for the local Delmark label as an album, not a more or less random array of sessions. It was doubly significant for being the greatest Chicago blues recording of its time. Harmonica player Wells had been on the scene since the early 1950s, doing time in the Muddy Waters band and recording some fine sides as a leader on several labels. Like several of the younger veterans of the 1950s scene, he was not averse to adding some irreverent rock and soul flourishes to his sound. The result took the Chicago blues in new, exciting directions, Wells sometimes coming on like a blues James Brown on cuts like *Snatch It Back and Hold It*, bluesing up rock tunes like *Hound Dog* and even putting in a Latin influence on *Chitlin Con Carne*. The band on the album was tops, too, especially guitarist **Buddy Guy**, who would eventually make a stunning comeback in the 1990s, chalking up a bunch of Grammies with new recordings and establishing one of the city's best blues clubs, *Buddy Guy's Legends* (see p.198).

Harmonica player **James Cotton**, yet another alumnus of the Waters band, made some fine assertive soul-rock-blues in the late 1960s and was one of the most dependable fixtures of the live blues circuit through the 1990s, although he was always more impressive as an instrumentalist than as a singer. **Magic Sam** was the most mature exponent of the West Side sound, his finger-picked tremolo guitar and R&B-ish material marking him as one of the more versatile performers in the city. He had short hitches with several labels before finding a home on Delmark, where he made a couple of assured albums that found a satisfying midpoint between the soul-flavoured direction the blues was being pulled towards, and the loose-limbed spontaneity more characteristic of the 1950s. Unfortunately, he died unexpectedly of heart trouble in 1969, only 32 years of age.

At the same time as young whites were beginning to listen to the blues, they were also beginning to play the blues, not just in Britain but in Chicago too. The local white blues acts tended to be well-meaning but stiff interpretations of the form, the exception being the **Paul Butterfield Blues Band** (which was actually integrated, though its front line was white). Butterfield was only an adequate singer, but a fine harmonica player; his group was more noteworthy for two exceptional guitarists, **Mike Bloomfield** and **Elvin Bishop**. The Butterfield band played lean and mean, and were more open to rock and soul influences than most African-American bluesmen, as was especially evident in Bloomfield's and Bishop's fiery solos.

Although Chess's glory days as a blues powerhouse had passed, the label did record some quality blues in the 1960s. Howlin' Wolf and Muddy Waters made some good sides through 1965 or so, Buddy Guy spent his early career there, and Chicago's best female blues singer, **Koko Taylor**, got her start at Chess. A tough and swaggering belter in the mould of the most aggressive blueswomen, such as Big Mama Thornton, Taylor's became famous for her interpretation of Willie Dixon's *Wang Dang Doodle*. Originally recorded by Howlin' Wolf in 1960, Taylor made the hard-partying song her own and even got to #4 in the R&B charts with it in 1966, when top-selling blues singles had become a rarity. That didn't guarantee an easy ride for Taylor, who in the early 1970s was working as a maid to make ends meet. A long-running association with Alligator Records from the mid-1970s onwards, though, solidified her reign as the queen of the Chicago blues.

Modern Chicago blues

In the last generation, Chicago blues has adopted a brassier polish than its previous incarnations, both figuratively (in its good-time strutting) and literally (in the frequent deployment of **horns** in addition to guitars and a rhythm section). Soul, rock and funk shadings have become more prominent than they were in the 1960s, the tempo has generally become slower and funkier and the vocals more cocksure.

The label mostly responsible for giving both old-timers and newbloods a chance to record is **Alligator**, founded in the early 1970s. In addition to giving steady exposure to artists like Son Seals who had somehow missed out on studio opportunities, it also revitalized the careers of veterans like Koko Taylor, James Cotton and Billy Boy Arnold. Over the years it expanded its roster to include blues artists from all over the country, but Chicago performers remain central to its release schedule. Alligator's best records (aside from those by Koko Taylor) have been by guitarists. Its first release, by **Hound Dog Taylor**, was a throwback to the spontaneous, just-short-of-sloppy club and juke-joint blues of the 1950s, albeit with fuzzier tones, in a no-nonsense trio featuring Taylor's slide guitar. **Son Seals** was more a man for the times, speaking both through lengthy, feverish solos and gruff, unruffled vocals, using a funky bottom and beefy horn section. **Fenton Robinson**, whose *Somebody Loan Me a Dime* had already been exposed to rock listeners through Boz Scaggs' cover version, was a notable example of Alligator giving a proper chance to an artist who had only been able to record here and there. Other notable Chicago guitarists who took time-honoured yet updated styles to a fairly wide audience have been slide guitarist **Lil' Ed Williams** (of **Lil' Ed & the Blues Imperials**), **Jimmy Johnson** and **Eddy "The Chief" Clearwater**, who still does an uncanny approximation of vintage Chuck Berry.

Since the 1970s, Chicago blues has seen the best of times and the worst of times. On the positive side, general public awareness of the blues is higher than ever, particularly among whites, with clubs featuring blues mostly or occasionally springing up in Chicago and all over the US. Younger musicians like Melvin Taylor and Vance Kelly continue to wave the blues flag high, and their appearances at *Rosa's Lounge* and *Kingston Mines* (see p.199 for both) draw enthusiastic crowds. The spring of 2005 saw the opening of the **Chicago Blues Museum**, founded by guitarist and bluesman Gregg Parker, although currently the Museum is looking for new digs. On the negative side, the form has grown stale as fewer and fewer young African-Americans dedicate themselves to the style, either as listeners or musicians. Its original audience has changed too: blues is still played in some South Side joints, but the very popular clubs are on the affluent North Side, drawing white patrons almost exclusively. Rock, soul and then rap music siphoned off a lot of talent as trends changed and musicians in the blues field are now well aware that, with rare exceptions, they will be playing and selling to a specialist market that's a small slice of the industry pie. Chicago blues, like New Orleans jazz and R&B, is in something of a preservationist mode. There's lots of competent, energetic electric blues in classic styles for locals and tourists to enjoy, on stage and on record, but the time of greatest artistic innovation seems gone. Changing public tastes are only part of the reason, as the blues is a more rigidly defined style than most American popular styles and it's difficult to make an original statement when its boundaries and signature riffs have been so firmly laid down.

Discography

The following is a select list of essential blues recordings, which should all be available on CD.

Billy Boy Arnold *I Wish You Would* (Charly). Both sides of Arnold's six Vee-Jay singles from the mid-1950s, plus a couple of rare bonus items. An underrated source point for blues-rock with its propulsive beat and riffs, especially on *I Wish You Would* and *I Ain't Got You*.

Chuck Berry *His Best Vol. 1 & 2* (Chess). Almost every song on this pair of twenty-track anthologies is immediately familiar; if you haven't heard the original version, you've heard it covered by someone. Besides the big hits like *Sweet Little Sixteen, Maybellene, Johnny B. Goode* et al, there are relatively undiscovered secondary goodies like *Little Queenie, Oh Baby Doll*, and *I Want to Be Your Driver*.

Big Maceo *The King of the Chicago Blues Piano* (Arhoolie). Twenty-five sides from 1941 to 1945, sometimes with bass and drums and even some electric guitar.

Bo Diddley *The Chess Box* (Chess). Two-CD set that doesn't even get to all of his first-rate waxings but does have most of 'em: *Bo Diddley, I'm a Man, Pretty Thing, Diddy Wah Diddy, Who Do You Love?, Road Runner, You Can't Judge a Book by Its Cover, Mona* and hidden treasures like *Down Home Special* and *You Don't Love Me*. For less dough there's the single-disc *His Best*, which sticks to the most celebrated tunes.

Buddy Guy *The Very Best of* (Rhino). This serviceable eighteen-song best-of doesn't reach into his 1990s comeback phase, but covers highlights from the late 1950s to the early 1980s, including some Chess sides and supersession-ish tracks with guest spots by Junior Wells, Dr John, Bill Wyman and Eric Clapton.

Buddy Guy *Damn Right, I've Got the Blues* (Silvertone). Buddy Guy roared back onto the mainstream blues scene with this inspired album that featured guest spots by Eric Clapton and Jeff Beck. A solid set, whose standout cuts include the title track and *Too Broke to Spend the Night*.

Hound Dog Taylor *Hound Dog Taylor & The Houserockers* (Alligator). From the first dirty-amped run of notes, this is Chicago blues at its rawest, in a boogieing trio style that never gets too fussy or shambling. It's much more together and enjoyable than the somewhat similar minimalist Mississippi juke-joint blues that has received so much attention in the 1990s.

Howlin' Wolf *His Best* (Chess). Twenty tracks from the 1950s and 1960s, with a line-up including *Spoonful, Smokestack Lightnin', Wang*

Dang Doodle, Back Door Man, The Red Rooster, Killing Floor and *I Ain't Superstitious*. Great stuff that's simultaneously scarifying and exhilarating. Even if you're familiar with the above tunes, you'll also be blown away by more obscure items like *Shake for Me*, which has some of the snakiest blues guitar playing ever.

Elmore James *The Sky Is Crying: The History of Elmore James* (Rhino). Collecting James can be frustrating, as he recorded for numerous labels and did multiple versions of some of his best tunes. This smart 21-song compilation of 1951–61 material has the essentials, including the first *Dust My Broom, The Sun is Shining, The Sky is Crying, Shake Your Moneymaker* and *It Hurts Me Too*.

J.B. Lenoir *Vietnam Blues: The Complete L&R Recordings* (Evidence). Lenoir was a solid journeyman Chicago bluesman in the 1950s and grew remarkably as a songwriter in the 1960s, exploring Vietnam and racial discrimination with a directness rare in the blues. He also went to an acoustic format with minimal, almost African percussion. These mid-1960s recordings, still largely unknown even in blues circles (they were only available in Europe for a long time) are an intriguing glimpse into a road seldom taken.

Little Walter *The Essential Little Walter* (Chess). Two CDs of Little Walter is not too much, even if you're not a blues specialist. Besides ace standards like *Boom, Boom, Out Goes The Light, My Babe* and *Mellow Down Easy*, there's a bounty of hidden gems like the virtuoso bop-jazzy instrumental *Fast Large One*, the classic minor-key downer blues *Blue and Lonesome* and just plain-hot party blues like *Too Late* and *It Ain't Right*.

Magic Sam *West Side Soul* and *Live in Ann Arbor & In Chicago* (Delmark). The late great Magic Sam brought the electric guitar to a new level in the annals of Chicago blues and his staccato accented riffs are highlighted on these two albums. The first includes his own *That's All I Need* and a version of *Sweet Home Chicago* that makes it sound brand new. The second album documents a fierce outing at the long gone *Alex Club* on Chicago's West Side and a performance at the Ann Arbor Blues and Jazz Festival in 1969.

Jimmy Reed *Speak the Lyrics to Me, Mama Reed* (Vee-Jay). There have been, and will always be, a bunch of Jimmy Reed best-of compilations on the market that largely duplicate each other in track selection. This 25-song one is about the best, with the familiar hits and some less overexposed songs.

Otis Rush *His Cobra Recordings, 1956–1958* (Paula). All sixteen of the tracks Rush officially released on Cobra, plus four alternate takes. Most of this is also on the two-CD box *The Cobra Records Story* (Capricorn), which adds some interesting material from the same vintage by Magic Sam, Buddy Guy, Walter Horton, Sunnyland Slim and others.

Koko Taylor *What It Takes: The Chess Years* (Chess). Eighteen cuts from 1964 to 1971, including *Wang Dang Doodle* and other tracks reinforcing her persona as a woman not to be messed with.

Muddy Waters *His Best, 1947 to 1955* (Chess). This great twenty-song compilation is mostly killer – *I Can't Be Satisfied*, *I Feel Like Going Home*, *Rollin' Stone*, *Hoochie Coochie Man*, *I'm Ready* and *Trouble No More* – and also charts his progress from the sparse near-Delta blues of his first recordings to the full-bore electric sound of the mid-1950s. Also worthwhile is the next installment, *His Best, 1956 to 1964* (Chess), which has material not quite as well known, including *You Need Love* (the riff

of which was appropriated by Led Zeppelin for *Whole Lotta Love*).

Junior Wells *Hoodoo Man Blues* (Delmark). From the opening crash of *Snatch It Back and Hold It*, this varied set grabs your gut and doesn't let go, Wells blowing his harp feverishly and working the vocals like a soul showman while Guy drives things along with sharp and snazzy blues licks. Blues albums don't come any better than this.

Sonny Boy [John Lee] Williamson *Sugar Mama* (Indigo). Twenty-four songs from 1937 to 1942, including one, *Good Morning School Girl*, that became one of the all-time blues standards, covered by everyone from Junior Wells to the Grateful Dead.

Sonny Boy Williamson [aka Rice Miller] *His Best* (Chess). To-the-point twenty-song anthology that zeroes in on his most essential output: *Born Blind*, *Your Funeral and My Trial*, *Down Child*, *Help Me*, *One Way Out* and *Bye Bye Bird* just for starters.

Various Artists *The Alligator Records 20th Anniversary Collection* and *The Alligator Records 25th Anniversary Collection* (Alligator). Two double-CD retrospectives of Alligator's output. This doesn't stick solely to Chicago artists, but a lot are on these compilations, including Son Seals, Koko Taylor, James Cotton, Fenton Robinson, Hound Dog Taylor, Billy Boy Arnold, Carey Bell, Big Walter Horton and Jimmy Johnson.

Various Artists *Blues Masters, Vol. 2: Postwar Chicago* (Rhino). Decent introductory sampler of tracks from 1950 to 1961 within and without Chess, by legends like Howlin' Wolf, Muddy Waters, Little Walter, Jimmy Reed, Buddy Guy and Junior Wells, as well as significant artists such as J.B. Lenoir, Robert Jr Lockwood, Earl Hooker and Jody Williams.

Various Artists *The Chess Blues-Rock Songbook* (Chess). This is what you want to have handy if you're dead set on putting someone straight about all the Chess artists who cut original versions of songs that sold a lot more units after getting covered by white guys. Classics like *Spoonful*, *I Just Want to Make Love to You*, *Johnny B. Goode* and less obvious choices like John Brim's *Ice Cream Man* and Willie Mabon's *The Seventh Son*, let the music do the talking.

Various Artists *Chicago: The Blues Today!, Vols. 1–3* (Vanguard). Important series of compilations that documented the mid-1960s Chi-town blues scene with cuts by enjoyable second-line artists such as J.B. Hutto, Otis Spann, Homesick James, Big Walter Horton and Johnny Young, as well as tracks by Junior Wells and Otis Rush.

Adapted from *The Rough Guide to Music USA* (1999), by Richie Unterberger

C

CONTEXTS | Chicago blues

Books

Below we list a selection of recommended reading from the huge body of works relating to Chicago. Books tagged with the 🏃 symbol are particularly recommended.

History and society

Jane Addams *Twenty Years at Hull-House*. Reformer Addams tells the story of her upbringing and remarkable life working at the innovative settlement house she helped start in Chicago's industrial and impoverished West Side. A perceptive, extremely detailed account of the settlement's day-to-day struggles to improve the social conditions in the city's slums in the late nineteenth century.

🏃 **Nelson Algren** *Chicago: City on the Make*. Grittily lyrical time capsule, highlighting the state of mid-twentieth-century Chicago. Algren has deep affection for the city but he also has an unsentimental determination to point out its social carbuncles. A must-read for anyone keen to understand the history of blue-collar Chicago.

Eliot Asinof *Eight Men Out: The Black Sox and the 1919 World Series*. This 1919 scandal, when the heavily favoured White Sox threw the final game in the World Series in return for high bribes, rocked America after World War I. This brilliant book astutely examines the cause and effect of what the White Sox did and frames the story with lashings of anecdotes. A terrific, revealing read even for non-sports fans.

Nadine Cohodas *Spinning Blues into Gold*. A lively look at Chess Records, the blues label that began on the South Side of Chicago. Cohodas is strongest when examining the savvy marketing and business flair of the Chess brothers but much weaker when analyzing the music they packaged in its cultural or musical context.

🏃 **William Cronon** *Nature's Metropolis: Chicago and the Great West*. This important work looks at the ways in which a variety of industries (the stockyards, railroads and so on) came together in Chicago to transform the city and the region in the nineteenth century. It's a seminal work that takes a thoughtful look at how a range of commercial interests came to dominate the city's growth and development.

David Farber *Chicago '68*. Rip-roaring examination of the seminal event in Daley Sr's tenure as mayor – the (mis)handling of hippie protests at the Democratic Convention of 1968. Farber evokes the energy and excitement of the time, though he trips slightly when trying to draw wider conclusions from the highly localized events.

Peter Golenbock *Wrigleyville: A Magical History Tour of the Chicago Cubs*. Riveting account of the lame-duck team in sports-mad Chicago: the Cubs have hobbled from season to season for almost fifty years while headline-grabbers like the Bears and the Bulls have basked in glory. This affectionate, anecdote-packed account of the team provides terrific insight into why and how it kept stumbling.

Max Grinnell *Hyde Park, Illinois*. Through postcards, historic images and a host of other visual ephemera, the author takes readers on a rather jaunty tour of Hyde Park. There's plenty of information on the University of Chicago here, along with some good documentation of the area's history over the past 100 years.

William J. Helmer and Arthur J. Bilek *The St. Valentine's Day Massacre: The Untold Story of the Gangland Bloodbath that Brought Down Al Capone*. From the author of *The Gun that Made the Twenties Roar* and a former chief of the Cook County Police, this account of the events leading up to the infamous February 14, 1929 shooting on the Near North side reads like a Mickey Spillane potboiler and makes the argument that the incident was due more to bad timing than to Capone's desire for revenge. A very entertaining read.

🏃 **Blair Kamin** *Tribune Tower*. The *Chicago Tribune's* Pulitzer Prize-winning architecture critic has written a lovingly detailed, piercingly astute account of his paper's HQ. It's packed with sprightly stories and offers not only a glimpse at the story behind one of Chicago's best-loved buildings, but also an understanding of what happened to the city in the years between World Wars I and II.

Erik Larson *The Devil in the White City: Murder, Magic, and Madness at the Fair that Changed America*. It's hard to believe that this gruesome, outlandish tale of a serial murderer on the loose during Chicago's 1893 Columbian Exposition is actually a true story, so vivid and compelling is this work. Larson follows architect Daniel Burnham as he strives to pull off the fair, as well as the sinister doings of H.H. Holmes, who killed between 27 and 200 people (mostly young women) around the time of the fair.

Richard Lindberg *To Serve & Collect*. White Sox historian Lindberg has produced a heavily researched, controversial account of the corrupt cops who populated Chicago's police system for more than a hundred

years. His prose can tangle at times, and the text would have been shaped better by a sharper editor, but it's a worthwhile, if depressing, read.

Harold Mayer and Richard Wade *Chicago: Growth of a Metropolis*. Coffee-table classic, filled with glossy pictures and a correspondingly airbrushed account of the city's evolution. Not the pithiest of histories perhaps, but fun to flick through.

Donald Miller *City of the Century: The Epic of Chicago and the Making of America*. Chicago's apogee was the nineteenth century, and this account of the city from its founding through 1899 takes in every major historical figure from Marquette to Marshall Field. Miller's obsession with detail is admirable, but it also rather clogs his rollicking story; he's on surest footing when writing about later events, notably the World's Columbian Exposition of 1893 and the Great Fire.

Dick W. Simpson *Rogues, Rebels, and Rubberstamps: The Story of Chicago City Council from the Civil War to the Third Millennium*. A former local alderman, Simpson brings an insider's relish to the story of America's most battle-scarred, corruption-blighted local government. Simpson's use of Chicago's infamous city council as a touchstone for larger political themes is sometimes questionable and his prose can be clunky, but it's a fascinating story nonetheless.

🏃 **David Solzman** *The Chicago River – An Illustrated History and Guide to the River and its Waterways*. David Solzman, a professor of geography at the University of Illinois at Chicago, takes readers through the curves and bends of the Chicago River with an eye for pointing out the nuances of its physical character and natural history. The book also offers up a few thematic tours and suggestions for viewing different parts of the river.

Biography

Sanford D. Horwitt *Let Them Call Me Rebel: Saul Alinsky: His Life and Legacy*. Decades before another Chicago community organizer became President of the United States, Saul Alinsky was testing out his own theories of community organizing and direct action all over the South Side. His legacy resonates through the work of people like Cesar Chavez and others and Horwitt crafts an honest and thorough appraisal of Alinsky's highs and lows.

John Kobler *Capone: The Life and World of Al Capone*. Punchy, ambivalent account of the world's greatest gangster, pepped up by a vivid eye for period detail and a refusal to make simple judgements. Capone's the part of its past that Chicago is most determined to forget, but Kobler's juicy biography fills in many of the blanks that the city leaves undiscussed.

Mike Royko *Boss: Richard J. Daley of Chicago*. Local journalist Royko turns his take-no-prisoners sights on Chicago's mythical mayor. Given Royko's well-known antipathy towards his subject, he turns in a readable, surprisingly balanced account that documents the inner workings of the local Democratic party's Machine.

Robert Schoenberg *Mr. Capone*. A more scholarly, sober-minded take of Capone's myth than Kobler's thrill-ride, this biography adds much on Capone's pre- and post-Chicago lives – from his birth in Brooklyn to his syphilis-riddled final years in Miami. Schoenberg's prose is spritely enough to keep his story well-paced despite wads of detail. Arguably the definitive account of Capone and his times.

Travel, journalism and impressions

A.J. Liebling *Chicago: The Second City*. A.J. Liebling was a writer for *The New Yorker* magazine, who came to find out what made Chicago tick in the early 1950s. During his stay, he found time to explore the bawdy, frenetic activity of the city's nightlife and some of the city's notable personalities, like legendary *Chicago Tribune* publisher Colonel Robert McCormick. Liebling's portrait also gave rise to the "Second City" moniker, which raised the hackles of some in Chicago society.

Mike Royko *One More Time: The Best of Mike Royko*. The Pulitzer Prize-winning columnist chronicled the foibles and follies of the powerful for more than thirty years; this book brings together some of his pithiest, most enjoyable rants, and shows anyone unfamiliar with his work why his name is legend in Chicago. There is another collection of his columns called *For the Love of Mike: More of the Best of Mike Royko*.

Studs Terkel *Division Street: America*. Terkel's the undisputed chronicler of the voice of working-class Chicago and his reputation was founded on this absorbing, extraordinary book. His first-person interviews with men and women, black and white, as they tell the story of their lives in the city are impossible to put down. For a similarly absorbing collection of personal testimonies from working Chicagoans, read Terkel's *Working: People Talk About What They Do All Day and How They Feel About What They Do*.

Architecture, music and photography

Willie Dixon with Don Snowden *I Am the Blues*. The autobiography of the greatest behind-the-scenes architect of modern blues doesn't have as many absorbing stories as hoped. Still, producer, arranger, bassist and songwriter Dixon offers some fascinating insights into the gestation of numerous classic recordings.

David Lowe *Lost Chicago*. Splendid pictorial record – with more than 250 illustrations – of the city's vanished architecture. Spanning the early nineteenth century through the twentieth century, historian Lowe dwells on the grand mansions, stockyards, skyscrapers, movie houses and magnificent train stations that helped shape Chicago's architectural legacy.

Mike Rowe *Chicago Blues*. Originally titled *Chicago Breakdown*, though too detailed for the uncommitted blues fanatic, has a wealth of information on Chicago blues from the 1930s to the 1960s. It includes background on all Chicago blues labels and all the city's major classic blues artists, as well as lots of minor ones. Cool vintage photos.

Pauline A. Saliga (ed) *The Sky's the Limit – A Century of Chicago Skyscrapers*. Lushly illustrated, exhaustive survey of Chicago's significant buildings, emphasizing those that still stand over demolished masterpieces. Useful, detailed background for sightseeing, especially on modernist structures from the 1970s and 1980s.

Franz Schulze and Kevin Harrington (eds) *Chicago's Famous Buildings: A Photography Guide to the City's Architectural Landmarks and Other Notable Buildings*. Regularly updated pocket guide to Chicago. Each brief entry is accompanied by a black-and-white photo. Buildings have been organized by geographical location, including a number in the suburbs.

Alice Sinkevitch (ed) *AIA Guide to Chicago*. Pocket-sized encyclopedia on local buildings, useful mostly for its detailed maps and brief but detailed essays on the city's most important structures. A very thorough look at the architecture across the city, with particularly strong coverage of the Loop and Lincoln Park.

Susan Sirefman *Chicago: A Guide to Recent Architecture*. This palm-sized guide manages to squeeze in a diverse crop of notable buildings built in Chicago within the last fifteen years – from major office-towers to houses and restaurants, and even *McDonald's* hamburger university. Crisp b/w photographs accompany architect Sirefman's concise text.

Sandra B. Tooze *Muddy Waters: The Mojo Man*. Competent and lengthy bio of the pre-eminent Chicago blues musician, covering his life thoroughly, from his Delta days through his ascendancy to stardom on Chess Records and his final years as a revered elder statesman. It doesn't catch fire as often as you'd expect.

Fiction and poetry

Nelson Algren *The Neon Wilderness*. What Hemingway might have written about Chicago had he not fled the city as soon as he was able. Not the most uplifting collection, but the muscular, no-nonsense style and punchy stories are still a knockout.

Of Algren's other titles, the best is probably *The Man with the Golden Arm*.

Saul Bellow *The Adventures of Augie March*. Given what a grumpy curmudgeon Bellow became before his death in 2005, this novel with its relentlessly optimistic hero is a refreshing read. Other Chicago-based novels by the Nobel Prize-winner include *Herzog* and *Ravelstein*.

🏃 **Theodore Dreiser** *Sister Carrie*. Iconoclastic turn-of-the-nineteenth-century novel, with a resourceful, amoral heroine who sins but still succeeds in this ambiguous fable. Her story also spotlights the power department stores (and their seductive goods) had on working-class women – it's a quiet determination to acquire such finery that drives Carrie's every action.

Stuart Dybek *The Coast of Chicago*. Reminiscent of Sherwood Anderson's Midwestern masterpiece *Winesburg, Ohio*, Chicago native Dybek's collection of fourteen short stories offers quiet snapshots of life in the city's neighbourhoods.

James T. Farrell *Studs Lonigan* trilogy. Farrell's legendary novel follows an idealistic Irish-American boy as he's gradually ground down by the drudgery of life. Famed for its realism and unblinking depiction of early twentieth-century urban life, the novel hasn't aged well: its awkward prose can be wearing, especially given how little actually happens to Studs during this doorstopper of a book.

Andrew Greeley The Blackie Ryan mysteries. Outspoken Catholic priest and *Sun-Times* columnist Greeley moonlights as a writer of intriguing thrillers, whose hero, Bishop Blackie Ryan, is a Catholic priest on Chicago's North Side. Try *The Bishop and the Missing L Train*, which centres on a logic-defying kidnapping.

Eugene Izzi *The Criminalist*. Izzi's last novel (he hanged himself soon after the book was completed) is one of his best, filled with believably imperfect characters trawling through the grubbiest corners of Chicago. This time, homicide detective Dominick di Grazia investigates the brutal murder of a young, pregnant prostitute with the help of a feisty, fifty-something female colleague.

Frank Norris *The Pit: A Story of Chicago*. A strong companion novel to *Sister Carrie* (see opposite), Norris's story revolves around a greedy speculator and his complicit, compliant wife. Though less brutally amoral than Dreiser's take, it offers similar lessons about the lure of Chicago's wealth and power and is a good snapshot of the caffeinated early days of the Chicago Stock Exchange.

Sara Paretsky The V.I. Warshawski mysteries. Paretsky's ballsy, bittersweet female private eye V.I. Warshawski prowls the streets of Chicago solving crime. Try *Bitter Medicine*, where Warshawki investigates malpractice in an emergency room, or the first book, *Indemnity Only*, centring on the serpentine search for a missing co-ed.

Carl Sandburg *Chicago Poems*. The celebrated poet and Illinois native made his literary breakthrough with this earthy, evocative collection of free-verse poetry, a tribute to the beauty and violence of industrial Chicago. Highlights include such well-known poems as *Chicago* and *Fog*.

Upton Sinclair *The Jungle*. A hundred years before Eric Schlosser's megaseller, *Fast Food Nation*, Sinclair issued his disturbing portrait of the squalid meatpacking industry in Chicago. The muscular story of a stockyard worker who eventually finds salvation in socialism. The book is derailed by Sinclair's ideological rants toward the end, yet it's still a vivid story.

🏃 **Richard Wright** *Native Son*. Bleak but powerful, Wright's potent novel tells the story of an African-American in 1930s Chicago, who tries to cover up his accidental murder of a white woman with catastrophic results. A searing indictment of ghetto life, whose message about racial inequality still resonates today.

Small print and

Index

A Rough Guide to Rough Guides

Published in 1982, the first Rough Guide – to Greece – was a student scheme that became a publishing phenomenon. Mark Ellingham, a recent graduate in English from Bristol University, had been travelling in Greece the previous summer and couldn't find the right guidebook. With a small group of friends he wrote his own guide, combining a highly contemporary, journalistic style with a thoroughly practical approach to travellers' needs.

The immediate success of the book spawned a series that rapidly covered dozens of destinations. And, in addition to impecunious backpackers, Rough Guides soon acquired a much broader and older readership that relished the guides' wit and inquisitiveness as much as their enthusiastic, critical approach and value-for-money ethos.

These days, Rough Guides include recommendations from shoestring to luxury and cover more than 200 destinations around the globe, including almost every country in the Americas and Europe, more than half of Africa and most of Asia and Australasia. Our ever-growing team of authors and photographers is spread all over the world, particularly in Europe, the USA and Australia.

In the early 1990s, Rough Guides branched out of travel, with the publication of Rough Guides to World Music, Classical Music and the Internet. All three have become benchmark titles in their fields, spearheading the publication of a wide range of books under the Rough Guide name.

Including the travel series, Rough Guides now number more than 350 titles, covering: phrasebooks, waterproof maps, music guides from Opera to Heavy Metal, reference works as diverse as Conspiracy Theories and Shakespeare, and popular culture books from iPods to Poker. Rough Guides also produce a series of more than 120 World Music CDs in partnership with World Music Network.

Visit www.roughguides.com to see our latest publications.

Rough Guide travel images are available for commercial licensing at www.roughguidespictures.com

SMALL PRINT

Rough Guide credits

Text editor: Nick Edwards
Layout: Sachin Tanwar
Cartography: Karobi Gogoi
Picture editor: Sarah Cummins
Production: Rebecca Short
Proofreader: Samantha Cook & Janette McCann
Cover design: Chloë Roberts
Photographer: Greg Rodin & Enrique Vranga
Editorial: Ruth Blackmore, Andy Turner, Keith
Drew, Edward Aves, Alice Park, Lucy White,
Jo Kirby, James Smart, Natasha Foges, Róisín
Cameron, Emma Traynor, Emma Gibbs, Kathryn
Lane, Christina Valhouli, Monica Woods, Mani
Ramaswamy, Harry Wilson, Lucy Cowie, Helen
Ochyra, Alison Roberts, Joe Staines, Peter
Buckley, Matthew Milton, Tracy Hopkins, Ruth
Tidball; **Delhi** Madhavi Singh, Karen D'Souza,
Lubna Shaheen
Design & Pictures: **London** Scott Stickland,
Dan May, Diana Jarvis, Mark Thomas, Nicole
Newman, Emily Taylor; **Delhi** Umesh Aggarwal,
Ajay Verma, Jessica Subramanian, Ankur Guha,
Pradeep Thapliyal, Anita Singh, Nikhil Agarwal
Production: Vicky Baldwin

Cartography: **London** Maxine Repath, Ed
Wright, Katie Lloyd-Jones; **Delhi** Rajesh
Chhibber, Ashutosh Bharti, Rajesh Mishra,
Animesh Pathak, Jasbir Sandhu, Alakananda
Bhattacharya, Swati Handoo, Deshpal Dabas
Online: **London** George Atwell, Faye Hellon,
Jeanette Angell, Fergus Day, Justine Bright, Clare
Bryson, Aine Fearon, Adrian Low, Ezgi Celebi,
Amber Bloomfield; **Delhi** Amit Verma, Rahul Kumar,
Narender Kumar, Ravi Yadav, Debojit Borah,
Rakesh Kumar, Ganesh Sharma, Shisir Basumatari
Marketing & Publicity: **London** Liz Statham,
Niki Hanmer, Louise Maher, Jess Carter, Vanessa
Godden, Vivienne Watton, Anna Paynton, Rachel
Sprackett, Libby Jellie, Laura Vipond, Vanessa
McDonald; **New York** Katy Ball, Judi Powers,
Nancy Lambert; **Delhi** Ragini Govind
Manager India: Punita Singh
Reference Director: Andrew Lockett
Operations Manager: Helen Phillips
PA to Publishing Director: Nicola Henderson
Publishing Director: Martin Dunford
Commercial Manager: Gino Magnotta
Managing Director: John Duhigg

Publishing information

This third edition published July 2009 by
Rough Guides Ltd,
80 Strand, London WC2R 0RL
14 Local Shopping Centre, Panchsheel Park,
New Delhi 110017, India
Distributed by the Penguin Group
Penguin Books Ltd,
80 Strand, London WC2R 0RL
Penguin Group (USA)
375 Hudson Street, NY 10014, USA
Penguin Group (Australia)
250 Camberwell Road, Camberwell,
Victoria 3124, Australia
Penguin Group (Canada)
195 Harry Walker Parkway N, Newmarket, ON,
L3Y 7B3 Canada
Penguin Group (NZ)
67 Apollo Drive, Mairangi Bay, Auckland 1310,
New Zealand
Cover concept by Peter Dyer.

Typeset in Bembo and Helvetica to an original
design by Henry Iles.
Printed and bound in Singapore by SNP Security
Printing Pte Ltd
© Rough Guides 2009
No part of this book may be reproduced in any
form without permission from the publisher except
for the quotation of brief passages in reviews.
296pp includes index
A catalogue record for this book is available from
the British Library
ISBN: 978-1-84836-070-9
The publishers and authors have done their best
to ensure the accuracy and currency of all the
information in **The Rough Guide to Chicago**,
however, they can accept no responsibility for
any loss, injury, or inconvenience sustained by
any traveller as a result of information or advice
contained in the guide.

1   3   5   7   9   8   6   4   2

Help us update

We've gone to a lot of effort to ensure that the
third edition of **The Rough Guide to Chicago** is
accurate and up-to-date. However, things change
– places get "discovered", opening hours are
notoriously fickle, restaurants and rooms raise
prices or lower standards. If you feel we've got it
wrong or left something out, we'd like to know,
and if you can remember the address, the price,
the hours, the phone number, so much the better.

Please send your comments with the subject
line "**Rough Guide Chicago Update**" to ✉mail
@roughguides.com. We'll credit all contributions
and send a copy of the next edition (or any other
Rough Guide if you prefer) for the very best
emails.
  Have your questions answered and tell others
about your trip at
✉community.roughguides.com

Acknowledgements

Shea would like to thank her collaborator, Max Grinnell, for his wry and knowledgable insights; her editor, Nick Edwards, for his sharp eye and pen; Mani Ramaswamy of Rough Guides, for making the New York–London crossing so smooth; Kristin Unger of the Chicago Office of Tourism; Susan Ross of the Chicago Architecture Foundation; Chai Lee of the Art Institute of Chicago; and Marc, for his love and patience.

Max: Special thanks to Nick Edwards, Mani Ramaswamy, Shea Dean, Josh Schonwald, Heidi L. Olson, Terry Sullivan, and the City of Chicago Department of Cultural Affairs.

Photo credits

All photos © Rough Guides except the following:

Full page
View of Chicago and Lake Michigan from John Hancock Tower © Steve Craft/Masterfile

Introduction
Shopping on Magnificent Mile © PCL/Alamy
Lake Michigan © Jtb photo/Photolibrary

Food colour section
Hot dogs and French fries © Hendrik Holler/Photolibrary
Waiter serving summer lunchtime diners © Andrew Woodley/Alamy
Charlie Trotter looks on at his restaurant © Keith Philpott/Getty
Tru Restaurant © Hendrik Holler/Photolibrary

Things not to miss
12 Baseball game © i-stockphoto.com
14 Gas for less © courtesy of Chicago History Museum
18 Grant Wood, American Gothic, 1930 © courtesy of The Art Institute of Chicago: Friends of American Art Collection

Black and whites
p.266 Barack Obama © Anne Ryan/ISP Pool/Corbis

SMALL PRINT

Index

Map entries are in colour.

I

INDEX

Map symbols

maps are listed in the full index using coloured text

– – –	Chapter division boundary	⧫	General point of interest
	Interstate	ⓘ	Information centre
⑪	U.S. Highway	⊠	Post office
⑲	Highway	⊞	Hospital
	Main road	⧫	Museum
	Minor road	⊙	Statue
	Pedestrianized road	⊥	Fountain
	Railway		Golf course
	River		Church
✈	Airport		Building
Ⓜ	Subway station		Stadium
METRA	Commuter rail station		Cemetery
Ⓟ	Parking		Park

CHICAGO & AROUND

△ Evanston, Rogers Park, & north shore

CHICAGO NEIGHBOURHOODS

0   3 miles

N

PETERSON AVE.

14

North Shore Channel

FOSTER AVENUE

ANDERSONVILLE

LAWRENCE AVENUE

KEDZIE AVENUE

WESTERN AVENUE

LINCOLN AVENUE

ASHLAND AVENUE

BROADWAY

IRVING PARK ROAD

19

WRIGLEYVILLE

see 'Lincoln Park, Lakeview & Wrigleyville' map

ADDISON STREET

41

LAKEVIEW

Lake Michigan

DIVERSEY PARKWAY

HALSTED STREET

Chicago River

90
94

50

LINCOLN PARK

see 'Near North, The Gold Coast & Old Town' map

FULLERTON AVENUE

◁ Oak Park (5 miles)

KENNEDY EXPWY

BUCKTOWN

LINCOLN AVE.

NORTH AVENUE

64

OLD TOWN

WICKER PARK

GOLD COAST

DIVISION STREET

LASALLE STREET

CHICAGO AVENUE

UKRAINIAN VILLAGE

NEAR NORTH

Navy Pier

Garfield Park

WASHINGTON STREET

THE LOOP

see 'The Loop, South Loop & Grant Park' map

WARREN BLVD

Sears Tower

290

GREEKTOWN

EISENHOWER EXPWY

41

LITTLE ITALY

SOUTH LOOP/ NEAR SOUTH

ROOSEVELT ROAD

OGDEN AVENUE

STATE STREET

CERMAK ROAD

PILSEN

see 'The West Side' map

see 'South Side' map

Sanitary Ship Canal

55

31ST STREET

STEVENSON EXPWY

35TH STREET

DAN RYAN EXPRESSWAY

MICHIGAN AVENUE

DR. MARTIN LUTHER KING JR. DR.

41

SOUTH SIDE

KEDZIE AVENUE

ARCHER AVENUE

DAMEN AVENUE

ASHLAND AVENUE

WESTERN AVENUE

HALSTED STREET

PERSHING ROAD

OAKWOOD BLVD

DREXEL BLVD

LAKE SHORE DRIVE

90
94

47TH STREET

Washington Park

HYDE PARK

University of Chicago

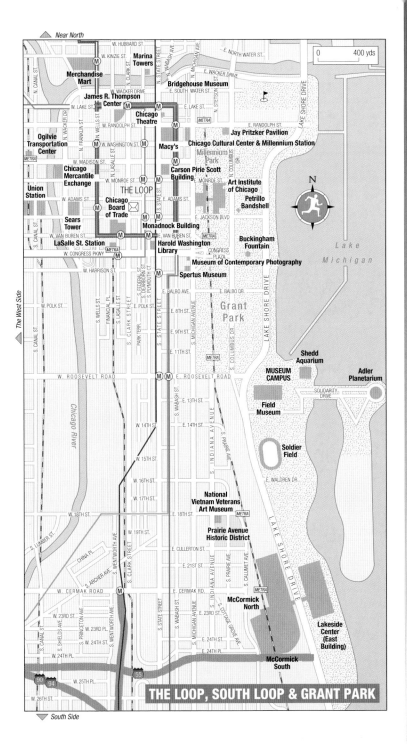

Lincoln Park

0   800 yds

N

ARLINGTON PL.

N. LAKE VIEW AVE.

FULLERTON PARKWAY

W. BELDEN AVE.

W. GRANT PL.

N. LINCOLN PARK W.

N. LINCOLN PARK W.

W. WEBSTER AVE.

N. HUDSON AVE.

N. SEDGWICK STREET

Lincoln Park

W. DICKENS AVE.

N. CLARK ST.

CANNON DRIVE

STOCKTON DRIVE

LAKE SHORE DRIVE

ARMITAGE AVENUE

N. LARRABEE ST.

N. MOHAWK ST.

N. CLEVELAND AVE.

W. WISCONSIN ST.

N. LINCOLN AVENUE

OLD TOWN TRIANGLE DISTRICT

W. MENOMONEE ST.

N. WELLS ST.

W. WILLOW ST.

N. FERN CT.

W. EUGENIE ST.

W. EUGENIE ST.

LA SALLE DRIVE

MEYER AVE.

St Michael's Church

Second City

Chicago History Museum

North Avenue Beach

Lincoln Park

SEDGWICK Ⓜ   W. NORTH AVENUE

OLD TOWN

W. BLACKHAWK ST.

W. BURTON ST.

International Museum of Surgical Science

N. LARRABEE ST.

N. MOHAWK ST.

N. HUDSON AVE.

N. SEDGWICK ST.

N. ORLEANS ST.

N. NORTH PARK AVE.

N. WIELAND ST.

W. BURTON ST.

W. SCHILLER ST.

N. LASALLE ST.

N. CLARK ST.

N. DEARBORN ST.

N. STATE STREET

N. ASTOR ST.

LAKE SHORE DRIVE

W. EVERGREEN ST.

E. BANKS ST.

Lake

W. GOETHE ST.

E. GOETHE ST.

N. CLYBOURN AVE.

GOLD COAST

Oak St Beach

Michigan

W. SCOTT ST.

E. SCOTT ST.

W. DIVISION STREET Ⓜ

CLARK/DIVISION Ⓜ

W. ELM ST.

W. ELM ST.

E. ELM ST.

CABRINI GREEN

W. HILL ST.

W. CEDAR ST.

W. MAPLE ST.

E. CEDAR ST.

E. BELLEVUE ST.

RUSH ST.

W. WENDELL ST.

W. OAK ST.

Newberry Library

E. OAK ST.

E. LAKE SHORE DR.

W. OAK ST.

W. LOCUST ST.

N. LARRABEE ST.

N. CAMBRIDGE AVE.

N. CLEVELAND AVE.

N. ORLEANS ST.

N. FRANKLIN ST.

E. DELAWARE PL.

Fourth Presbyterian Church

John Hancock Center

W. CHESTNUT ST.

E. CHESTNUT ST.

E. CHESTNUT ST.

W. INSTITUTE PL.

Washington Square Park

E. PEARSON ST.

Pumping Station

W. CHICAGO AVENUE Ⓜ

CHICAGO

CHICAGO Ⓜ

E. CHICAGO AVE.

Museum of Contemporary Art

N. KINGSBURY ST.

N. HUDSON AVE.

N. SEDGWICK ST.

W. SUPERIOR ST.

Water Tower

E. SUPERIOR ST.

STREETERVILLE

E. HURON ST.

W. HURON ST.

Holy Name Cathedral

N. ST. CLAIR AVE.

RIVER NORTH

W. ERIE ST.

E. ERIE ST.

N. LASALLE ST.

N. CLARK ST.

N. DEARBORN ST.

N. STATE ST.

N. WABASH ST.

N. MICHIGAN AVENUE

FAIRBANKS CT.

E. ONTARIO ST.

W. ONTARIO ST.

W. OHIO ST.

E. OHIO ST.

LAKE SHORE DRIVE

NEAR NORTH

N. RUSH ST.

W. GRAND AVENUE

GRAND Ⓜ

E. GRAND AVENUE

Navy Pier

W. ILLINOIS ST.

E. ILLINOIS ST.

STREETER DR.

Wrigley Building

Tribune Tower

Merchandise Mart Ⓜ

W. HUBBARD ST.

E. HUBBARD ST.

E. NORTH WATER ST.

MERCHANDISE MART

W. KINZIE ST.

E. KINZIE ST.

Chicago River

IBM Building

E. WACKER DRIVE

N. KINGSBURY ST.

W. WACKER DRIVE

N. JEFFERSON ST.

N. CLINTON ST.

N. CANAL ST.

W. SOUTH WATER ST.

E. SOUTH WATER ST.

N. STETSON AVE.

COLUMBUS DRIVE

LAKE SHORE DRIVE

W. LAKE STREET

W. LAKE STREET

E. LAKE ST.

N. WELLS ST.

N. FRANKLIN ST.

James R. Thompson Center

Ogilvie Transportation Center

W. RANDOLPH STREET

E. RANDOLPH STREET

THE LOOP

Marshall Field's

W. WASHINGTON STREET

N. ORLEANS ST.

N. WABASH ST.

W. MADISON ST.

W. ARCADE PL.

Chicago Mercantile Exchange

◁ Bucktown, Wicker Park & Ukrainian Village

◁ Lincoln Park

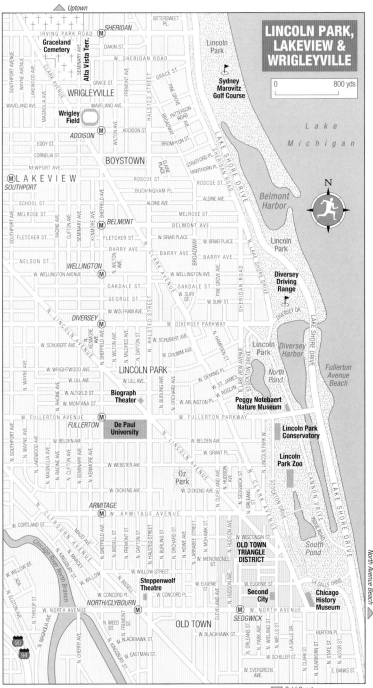

LINCOLN PARK, LAKEVIEW & WRIGLEYVILLE

0   800 yds

Lake

Michigan

N

Graceland Cemetery

SHERIDAN

IRVING PARK ROAD

DAKIN ST.

GRACE ST.

N. SHERIDAN ROAD

BITTERSWEET PL.

Lincoln Park

SOUTHPORT AVENUE

WAYNE AVENUE

LAKEWOOD AVENUE

SEMINARY AVENUE

MAGNOLIA AVE.

CLARK AVENUE

Alta Vista Terr.

WAVELAND AVE.

WRIGLEYVILLE

GRACE ST.

FREMONT AVE.

HALSTED STREET

PINE GROVE AVE.

Sydney Marovitz Golf Course

Wrigley Field

WAVELAND AVE.

WILTON AVE.

ADDISON

ADDISON ST.

BROADWAY

PATTERSON ROAD

BROMPTON ST.

EDDY ST.

CORNELIA ST.

NEWPORT AVE.

BOYSTOWN

STRATFORD PL.

HAWTHORN PL.

SHEFFIELD AVE.

SHERIDAN ROAD

ELAINE PLACE

ROSCOE ST.

LAKEVIEW

SOUTHPORT

BUCKINGHAM PL.

ROSCOE ST.

ALDINE AVE.

Belmont Harbor

SCHOOL ST.

SHEFFIELD AVE.

ALDINE AVE.

MELROSE ST.

MELROSE ST.

MELROSE AVE.

SOUTHPORT AVE.

RACINE AVE.

CLIFTON AVE.

SEMINARY AVE.

KENMORE AVE.

BELMONT

BELMONT AVE.

FLETCHER ST.

FLETCHER ST.

W. BRIAR PLACE

W. BRIAR PLACE

Lincoln Park

BARRY AVE.

BARRY AVE.

BARRY AVE.

Diversey Driving Range

NELSON ST.

WELLINGTON

WILTON AVE.

W. WELLINGTON AVENUE

CLARK AVENUE

BROADWAY

PINE GROVE AVE.

SHERIDAN ROAD

W. WELLINGTON AVENUE

OAKDALE ST.

OAKDALE ST.

GEORGE ST.

W. SURF ST.

W. SURF ST.

W. WOLFRAM AVE.

DIVERSEY

N. LINCOLN AVE.

KENMORE AVE.

SHEFFIELD AVE.

WILTON AVE.

N. DAYTON ST.

HALSTED STREET

W. DIVERSEY PARKWAY

DIVERSEY DR.

LAKE SHORE DRIVE

W. SCHUBERT AVE.

N. MILDRED AVE.

W. SCHUBERT AVE.

W. DRUMM AVE.

N. HAMPDEN CT.

Lincoln Park

Diversey Harbor

W. WRIGHTWOOD AVE.

N. WAYNE AVE.

N. RACINE AVE.

W. LILL AVE.

W. ALTGELD ST.

LINCOLN PARK

N. BURLING ST.

N. ORCHARD AVE.

W. DEMING PL.

W. ST. JAMES

N. ROSLYN

STOCKTON DRIVE

LAKEVIEW AVENUE

North Pond

Fullerton Avenue Beach

N. MAGNOLIA AVE.

W. LILL AVE.

Biograph Theater

W. MONTANA ST.

W. ARLINGTON PL.

Peggy Notebaert Nature Museum

W. FULLERTON AVENUE

FULLERTON

De Paul University

W. FULLERTON PARKWAY

N. LINCOLN PARK W.

Lincoln Park Conservatory

N. SOUTHPORT AVE.

N. WAYNE AVE.

N. LAKEWOOD AVE.

N. MAGNOLIA AVE.

N. RACINE AVE.

N. SEMINARY AVE.

N. KENMORE AVE.

W. BELDEN AVE.

W. BELDEN AVE.

W. GRANT PL.

Lincoln Park Zoo

W. WEBSTER AVE.

N. LINCOLN AVENUE

Oz Park

W. DICKENS AVE.

W. DICKENS AVE.

N. CLEVELAND AVE.

N. HUDSON AVE.

N. SEDGWICK ST.

N. ORLEANS ST.

N. CLARK AVENUE

STOCKTON DRIVE

CANNON DRIVE

LAKE SHORE DRIVE

South Pond

ARMITAGE

W. ARMITAGE AVENUE

N. CLYBOURN AVENUE

MAUD AVE.

N. BISSELL ST.

N. SHEFFIELD AVE.

N. FREMONT ST.

N. DAYTON ST.

N. HALSTED STREET

N. BURLING ST.

N. ORCHARD ST.

N. HOWE ST.

N. LARRABEE STREET

N. MOHAWK ST.

W. WISCONSIN ST.

OLD TOWN TRIANGLE DISTRICT

W. MENOMONEE ST.

RIDGE ROAD

W. CORTLAND ST.

N. KINGSBURY ST.

N. MARCEY ST.

W. WILLOW ST.

Chicago River North Branch

JODA

N. WILLOW

W. WILLOW STREET

Steppenwolf Theatre

W. CONCORD PL.

N. BISSELL

W. EUGENIE ST.

N. HUDSON AVE.

W. EUGENIE ST.

Second City

LA SALLE DRIVE

Chicago History Museum

W. ELSTON AVE.

W. THROOP ST.

N. NORTH BRANCH

NORTH/CLYBOURN

W. CONCORD PL.

W. NORTH AVENUE

SEDGWICK

BURTON PL.

90

94

W. NORTH AVENUE

OLD TOWN

W. WEED ST.

N. FREMONT ST.

W. BLACKHAWK ST.

N. MAGNOLIA AVE.

N. CHERRY AVE.

N. THROOP ST.

N. KINGSBURY ST.

W. BLACKHAWK ST.

N. ORLEANS ST.

N. PARK AVE.

N. WIELAND ST.

W. SCHILLER ST.

N. WELLS ST.

W. NORTH AVENUE

N. CLARK ST.

N. STATE ST.

N. DEARBORN ST.

N. ASTOR ST.

W. EASTMAN ST.

LA SALLE DR.

W. EVERGREEN AVE.

E. BANKS ST.

THE WEST SIDE

SEDGWICK

NORTH/CLYBOURN

CABRINI GREEN

CLARK/DIVISION

DIVISION

UKRAINIAN VILLAGE

CHICAGO

CHICAGO

CHICAGO

GRAND

MERCHANDISE MART

GRAND

GRAND AVENUE

ASHLAND

Harpo Studios

Ogilvie Transportation Center

THE LOOP

United Center

GREEKTOWN

Union Station

Sears Tower

DWIGHT D. EISENHOWER EXPWY

MEDICAL CENTER

RACINE

UIC-HALSTED

CLINTON

DWIGHT D. EISENHOWER EXPWY

University of Illinois

POLK

UIC

Jane Addams Hull-House Museum

Cook County

LITTLE ITALY

W. ROOSEVELT ROAD

UIC

National Museum of Mexican Art

18TH

PILSEN

CERMAK/CHINATOWN

N

0   800 yds

South Loop & Near South

Lakeside Center
(East Building)

SOUTH SIDE

McCormick
Place

0   1 mile

N

Lake Michigan

W. CERMAK RD.   E. CERMAK RD.
W. 23RD ST.   E. 23RD ST.
W. 23RD PL.
W. 24TH ST.   E. 24TH ST.
W. 24TH PL.
STEVENSON EXPWY
W. 25TH ST.
W. 26TH ST.   E. 26TH ST.
METRA
27TH ST.
W. 28TH ST.   E. 29TH ST.
W. 28TH PL.
W. 29TH ST.
W. 30TH ST.   E. 30TH ST.
W. 31ST ST.   E. 31ST ST.
W. 32ND ST.   E. 32ND ST.
W. 33RD ST.   E. 33RD ST.
E. 33RD PL.
SOX-35TH ST.   35TH ST.-   E. 35TH ST.
                  BRONZEVILLE-IIT
US Cellular   E. 36TH ST.   BROWNING AVE.
Field   E. 37TH ST.
W. 37TH ST.   E. 37TH ST.
W. 38TH ST.   E. 38TH ST.
W. PERSHING RD.   E. PERSHING RD.
E. OAKWOOD BLVD.
E. 40TH ST.
W. 40TH ST.   E. 40TH ST.
INDIANA AVE   E. 41ST ST.
W. ROOT ST.   E. 42ND ST.
W. 42ND ST.   E. 42ND PL.
W. 42ND PL.
43RD ST.   E. 43RD ST.
W. 43RD ST.
W. 43RD PL.   E. 44TH ST.
W. 44TH ST.   E. 45TH ST.
W. 44TH PL.   E. 46TH ST.
W. 45TH ST.
KENWOOD/47TH ST.
METRA
47TH ST.   E. 47TH ST.
47TH ST.   E. 48TH ST.
E. 49TH ST.
W. 47TH ST.   E. 50TH ST.
51ST ST.   E. 50TH PL.
W. 51ST ST.   E. 51ST ST.
E. 52ND ST.   HYDE PARK/53RD ST.
METRA
W. 53RD ST.   E. 53RD ST.
E. 54TH ST.
GARFIELD   Washington   GARFIELD   HYDE PARK
W. GARFIELD BLVD.   Park
E. 55TH ST.   55TH-56TH-57TH ST.
W. 57TH ST.   E. 56TH ST.
W. 58TH ST.   E. 57TH ST.   METRA
W. 59TH ST.   E. 58TH ST.
University of Chicago   UNIVERSITY OF CHICAGO
E. 59TH ST.   METRA 59TH ST.
MIDWAY PLAISANCE
W. 60TH ST.   E. 60TH ST.   Jackson
W. 60TH PL.   Park
W. 61ST ST.   E. 61ST ST.
W. 61ST PL.   E. 62ND ST.
63RD ST.   EAST 63RD-   E. 63RD ST.
W. 63RD ST.   COTTAGE GROVE   METRA
W. 64TH ST.   KING DR.   E. 64TH ST.   HAYES DR.
W. 65TH ST.   E. 65TH ST.   MARQUETTE DR.
W. 66TH ST.   E. 67TH ST.
W. MARQUETTE RD.
E. 67TH PL.
69TH ST.   Oakwoods   E. 68TH ST.   E. 68TH ST.
W. 68TH ST.   Cemetery   E. 69TH ST.
W. 69TH ST.   E. 70TH ST.   STONY   BRYN
W. 70TH ST.   E. 71ST ST.   ISLAND   MAWR
W. 71ST ST.   E. 72ND ST.   METRA   METRA
W. 72ND ST.   E. 72ND PL.   E. 72ND PL.

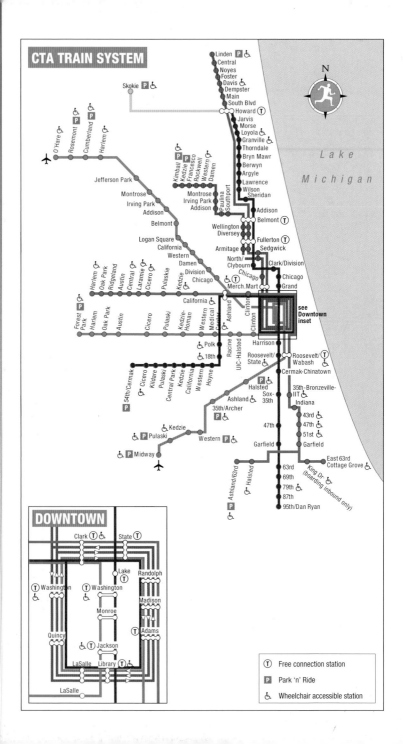